Together

communicating interpersonally

john stewart

UNIVERSITY OF WASHINGTON

gary d'angelo

D'ANGELO & ASSOCIATES

Together
communicating
interpersonally

SECOND EDITION

ADDISON-WESLEY PUBLISHING COMPANY

Reading, Massachusetts · Menlo Park, California
London · Amsterdam · Don Mills, Ontario · Sydney

Library of Congress Cataloging in Publication Data

Stewart, John Robert, 1941–
  Together.

  Includes bibliographical references and index.
  1. Interpersonal relations. I. D'Angelo, Gary, joint author. II. Title.
HM132.S73   1980   158'.2   79-26426
ISBN 0-201-07506-7

ISBN 0-201-07506-7
ABCDEFGHIJ-HA-89876543210

To Marcia and Lisa

To Connie

preface

Writing the second edition of a book like this one gives us the opportunity to discover how we've changed in the past five years. John's personal life and Gary's professional life are both significantly different from what they were in 1974. Our views of interpersonal communication have also changed some; we believe we've found better ways to talk about the assumptions behind this book, the nature of communication, the negotiation-of-selves process, self-disclosure, handling conflict, and developing interpersonal-quality communication in the public speaking setting. It is gratifying to be able to incorporate these changes in an updated version of *Together*.

It's also gratifying, though, to notice those things that have not changed dramatically. We are still interested in the way an individual's interpersonal communication affects the quality of his or her life. That fundamental, "humanistic" concern was central to the first edition of *Together,* and it is alive and well in this edition, too. We also continue to be impressed by the variety of scholars who seem to be interested in interpersonal communication and human growth: personality psychologists such as Harry Stack Sullivan and George Kelly, who see personality as an interpersonal phenomenon; theologians such as Karl Jaspers and Reuel Howe, who teach that authentic communication with humans can facilitate authentic communication with God; psychotherapists such as Abraham Maslow and Carl Rogers, who believe that the best way to promote another's health and growth is to promote a rich relationship with her or him; and philosophers such as Martin Buber and John Mac-murray, who identify and describe the ontologically interpersonal nature of human beings. We've learned a great deal from these persons, but because of our interest in speech communication, we've focused primarily on the communication itself; we're less concerned here with psy-chotherapy, ontology, or one's relationship with God, important as those considerations are.

While learning and teaching about interpersonal communication, we've become impressed by the variety of settings in which this kind of contact can occur. We've experienced a number of rich and exciting in-teractions in informal, two-person settings, but we've also recognized the substantial potential for person-to-person contacts in larger, unstructured meetings, task-oriented small groups, and public speaking settings. As a result, it hasn't been helpful for us to use the word "interpersonal" to designate communication that happens in a certain setting; we've found it more useful to focus on the *quality* or *type* of communication that can best facilitate human growth in a variety of settings. In other words, we take what Gerald Miller calls a "developmental" approach to interpersonal communication, rather than a "situational" one.[1] This is why we define interpersonal communication in Chapter 2 as the quality of communica-tion that occurs when the persons involved are mutually willing and able to share some aspects of their personness and to be aware of some aspects of the personness of the other.[2]

For the past ten years we've been developing our definition into a coherent, workable approach to teaching and learning. As coordinator of the University of Washington speech communication department's basic course program, John has been able to get the input of more than 60 teachers and to witness the way several thousand students have re-sponded to various concepts and activities He has also been able to teach basic interpersonal communication courses each of the past 30 terms and upper division and graduate courses since 1971, and he has worked with these ideas in groups of insurance people, lawyers, building department personnel, and others outside the university. Gary learned a great deal from his five years of teaching a mass lecture class, where interpersonal communication concepts and skills were part of both the course content and the teaching methods. Like John, he also taught basic and upper-division interpersonal communication courses, and for the past two years he also has worked full-time as a communication consultant with more than fifty different groups of business and professional people.

As you might expect, John and Gary have invested enough in this approach to interpersonal communication to become committed to it. We know it isn't the only possible approach to this subject, and we also see it as something that's continually changing and growing. But we can work with it—and we hope that you can work with this approach, too—because it integrates the substantive, the experiential, and the personal. In this way, too, the second edition of *Together* is similar to the first edition.

We chose from the outset to do a substantive book. We decided that we didn't want to do a laboratory manual or book consisting primarily of exercises, not only because some excellent ones have already been done, but also because we believe that the study of interpersonal communication can be in part a rich and exciting *intellectual* experience. Those who have contributed to this study—Sullivan, Rogers, Laing, Buber, and others— are often very insightful and wise, and their *ideas* can be provocative, stimulating, and intellectually challenging. Thinking is one of the ways persons grow, and we're convinced that working with ideas about the nature of human beings, the ways human communication works, the negotiation of selves, the ways people process information, the impact of empathy, etc., can be productive and genuinely exciting.

We've also tried to emphasize the importance of *experiencing* the concepts and skills discussed here. In the past several years we've noticed that many educators have been stressing the point John Dewey made near the turn of the century—people learn best when they can *experience,* as directly as possible, the content or subject matter that they're studying. We agree with that emphasis, especially with respect to teaching interpersonal communication. Simply talking and reading *about* interpersonal communication isn't a sufficiently effective way to help people learn to communicate better. The persons involved need the opportunity to try out the communication attitudes and behaviors that are discussed, both in classroom exercises and in day-to-day contacts with others. Ideally, your study of interpersonal communication can involve you in a blend of principles and activities, concepts and experiences, analyzing interpersonal communication and communicating interpersonally.

A third dimension of this book's approach is its personal tone or style. As we say in the Introduction, we see an inconsistency in treatments of interpersonal communication that employ impersonal pronouns, formal language, and excessive jargon to maintain distance between writer and reader. As we also note, a one-way written communication event can never become genuinely interpersonal. But as writers, we can take steps in that direction, steps that we have discovered can bring us closer to you. The process is risky. We can sometimes come across as overpersonal, inappropriately intimate, trying too hard to be "just folks." Or we can get lost in our own jargon and end up as a parody of the very quality we're trying to create.

We've taken those risks, not only because we believe that impersonal writing about interpersonal communication is inappropriate, but also because it makes theoretical sense to let you know something about us.

We introduce ourselves because we want you to be aware of some aspects of our personness (Chapter 2); because we care about the situation in which our communication with you happens (Chapter 1); because we know that expectations affect personal perception (Chapter 3); because we want to begin to clarify our definitions of ourselves (Chapter 4); because we know that sharing can help create trust (Chapter 5); and because we want you to know something of "where we're coming from" (Chapter 7). In short, we'd like to try to make the communicating between you and us as interpersonal as the situation will allow.

Those are some ways the second edition is like the first. There are also several parts of this book that are different from the first edition. We introduce ourselves in the Introduction—which seems to be appropriate—rather than in Chapter 1. The order of the first two chapters is also changed; in this edition we talk first about communication in general and then about interpersonal-quality communication. Again, that seemed to make good sense; we couldn't quite figure out why it wasn't that way in the first edition. We've also substantially simplified our discussion of the negotiation-of-selves process in Chapter 4. We still believe in the central importance of that process, but we recognize that students often had trouble with the old Chapter 4, so we've completely rewritten it. Chapter 5, which deals with sharing, and Chapter 6, which deals with being aware, have been rewritten so that they more consistently develop the ideas introduced in the first chapters of the book. For example, instead of introducing new terminology to talk about sharing some of your self, we use the terms we've explained in Chapter 2, "objectifying" and "personifying." Chapter 7, which deals with being clear, has also been updated and clarified, and we've added several new ideas and examples. The chapter on conflict—Chapter 8—has been totally rewritten and substantially expanded. This seems to be one topic that students especially want to discuss and work with, so we've tried to provide a more complete treatment of it.

The same goes for Chapters 9 and 10. Many persons who looked at and/or used the first edition of *Together* said that they wanted us to include more about interpersonal communication in the public speaking setting. We felt that need, too, so we greatly expanded our discussion of characteristics of the public setting, problems we encounter while trying to communicate interpersonally in that setting, and specific, practical ways to respond to those problems, to promote both clarity and interpersonal contact. The discussion of small-group communication has been moved to the Appendix, because we've found that those ideas are usually part of the *process* of a beginning interpersonal communication class but not a central part of its *content*.

We also added a "You May Be Wondering . . ." section at the end of several chapters. Here we respond to the questions that students most often ask us after we've dealt with the ideas presented in the chapter. So if, while you're reading a chapter, a "Yeah, but how about . . .?" or "What do you mean by . . .?" question occurs to you, you might check the "You May Be Wondering . . ." section at the end of the chapter to see if the question occurred to us, too.

Finally, we've tried to make this edition more flexible—to give the teacher who uses it more freedom to adapt it to his or her individual style. And thanks to the responses from many persons who used the first edition, we've also tried to make the book less WASP—to include experiences of nonwhite persons and persons who either by choice or by circumstance are not part of the American middle class. Since both of us are white and middle class, that hasn't always been easy. We have consciously avoided trying to pretend that we're somebody we aren't. But several people have helped with this problem, including Barbara Shearer, Steve Woo, Charles Thornton, Derwin Nazarino, and Caroline Chow.

Other colleagues, friends, and persons in our classes also helped us with this book in important ways. Conversations with Helen Felton have significantly enriched our understanding of Martin Buber and our sensitivity to parts of the book that students have had trouble understanding. Bob Arundale's work in systems theory contributed to our writing of Chapter 2. Eileen Lemke Meconi helped us to understand the subtleties of sexist language in the first edition, and we continue to feel her influence whenever we talk or write. Charlene Duitsma did an unusually thorough job of typing the manuscript; she discovered errors that we'd been unable to see after four years of looking. Danny Chen and Bryson Alden helped provide photographs to bring several key ideas alive. And it's especially gratifying to have the support and encouragement of persons like Jeanette Ceccarelli Williams, Kris Obata, and Steve Muscatel. Even though they're not around as much as they used to be, we still feel their enthusiasm and friendship. We also want to recognize our undergraduate, graduate, and professional students, whose contributions we can't always specifically identify, but without whom we wouldn't have experienced, learned, and grown enough to write a book.

We mention our families last—as do most authors—but our thanks to them are anything but "least." Until you've gone through the several-year process of "writing a book," you can't fully appreciate the extent to which family support helps. They have our special thanks for their patience, tolerance, and understanding.

Seattle, Washington
November 1979

J.S.
G.D'A.

NOTES   1. Gerald R. Miller, "The Current Status of Theory and Research in Interpersonal Communication," *Human Communication Research*, **4** (Winter 1978), 164–178.

2. As Miller notes on p. 170, the developmental approach is "consistent with the most literal etymology of the term 'interpersonal': 'inter' meaning 'between' and 'personal' meaning 'persons.'"

Action
Inten
Tranc.

Verbal/NonVerb
Objectify/personify

perception
neg of selves

Sharing/bg aware
conflict

clarity
public speaking

no: persuasion
self disclosure
signs/signals/symbols
dialogue
Systems terms
— equifinality
rhel-change

contents

3

4

5

INTERPERSONAL CLARITY 235

HANDLING CONFLICT INTERPERSONALLY 267

PUBLIC SPEAKING: OVERCOMING THE BARRIERS 325

Introduction

It's usually difficult for you to get to know the persons who have written a book you're reading. Sometimes there's a hint about an author's identity in the book's dedication or in the acknowledgments section of the preface or foreword, but usually there's not enough to allow you to know the author as a *person*. In other cases you may get some impression of an author's personality from his or her writing style, but most writers—especially textbook writers—try to maintain an objective and factual third-person distance, and as a result their writing often seems *imper-sonal*.

Impersonal writing is fine for some subjects, but we don't think it's appropriate for a book about interpersonal communication. The architect Marcel Lajos Breuer says that what he aims for in architecture is something "more human than a machine."[1] We're aiming for the same thing in this book. After all, interpersonal communication is basically what it sounds like—communication *between* ("inter") *persons*—and it can't happen until the parties involved are identifiable *as persons*, so that something can go on *between* them. We're not sure we can actually communicate interpersonally with you on these pages, and we'll explain why later. But we do want to encourage as much "between personness" as possible, and we believe that can happen only if you know something about who we are. We also believe that the more you know about us and "where we're coming from," the better you'll understand the things we say. So we'd like to talk a little about who we are and why we're writing this book.

Who We Are   John Stewart and Gary D'Angelo are both interpersonal communication specialists who live in Seattle, Washington. John works in the Department of Speech Communication at the University of Washington, where he came right after finishing graduate school in 1969. He's married to Kris Chrey, an attorney, and has two college-age daughters, Marcia and Lisa.

Family, work, and sailing are the activities that get most of John's time and attention. He enjoyed watching Marcia's cheerleading and Lisa's gymnastics while they were in high school, and now he likes trying to keep up with their college activities, their work experiences, and the repairs on their cars. John's and Kris's relationship is obviously the place where this book's communication concepts and skills get their acid test. As you may well know, it's a real challenge to establish, trouble-shoot, and maintain a long-term intimate relationship. But John and Kris are generally pleased with theirs; it has enough problems to prevent either partner from mistaking it for unrealistic, romantic, nonstop ecstasy, and it is also solid, supportive, and exciting. Perhaps most important, both persons feel that they're growing in the relationship—individually and together—and that's a good feeling.

John also enjoys teaching undergraduate and graduate classes in interpersonal communication. The university is a stimulating place, especially because of the constant contact between all sorts of persons and all sorts of ideas. He feels fortunate that he can make a living while being a part of this diverse, dynamic interchange.

The Pacific Northwest environment is also centrally important to John. Mountains, salt and fresh water, and evergreens provide more than just a pleasant work context for him. John was born and raised in this country, and to him it's really *home*. He especially likes skiing, biking, camping—at the beach, in the mountains, or in the rain forest—and sailing in Puget Sound and the waters around the San Juan Islands and western British Columbia. John and Kris try to spend part of every summer on the sailboat, and they also use one-day or weekend outings during the rest of the year to keep their perspective and priorities straight. Sailing also cements other important relationships—especially with Helen, Sam, and Skip Felton.

Gary left university teaching to go into communication consulting. He is currently President of D'Angelo and Associates, a management consulting firm in Seattle. His work includes teaching company and public seminars, and he serves as a private communication consultant to several corporations in Seattle. Gary is married to Connie Schroeder. They have three children: Debbie, 17, Andy, 13, and Tommy, 11.

Gary's strongest internal commitment is to his Christian faith, the principles of which he believes are compatible with interpersonal communication principles. Although he spends much of his time in his professional work, his family life is also one of his most enjoyable and

energy-consuming activities. For example, on Thursday he and Connie may watch Debbie play soccer for her high school; Friday evening they'll watch Tommy play basketball; on Saturday they'll take in Andy's basketball game; and Sunday is often spent with good friends Bill and Jill McBride enjoying homemade spaghetti and ravioli.

Because consulting takes so much of his time, Gary has had to give up coaching soccer, although he still referees Little League games. Every summer you'll find him playing slow-pitch softball for the Laurelhurst Over-the-Hill Gang and, when time permits, fishing for salmon in Puget Sound.

In the midst of all these activities, Gary and Connie continue working on their 18-year-old marital relationship, one that they would tell you is held together by their faith and strengthened by their attempts to communicate interpersonally with each other.

Helen Felton told us about a professor she had who would ask every student who brought in a manuscript for critique, "Why do you want to write?" Only one answer satisfied the professor, and that was *"Because I can't not write."* Some of that feeling is what motivates us to write this book. We are struck by an interesting fact. Some people are intrigued by electronics and therefore study circuits, diodes, and current/resistance relationships; some other people are interested in politics and study legislation, sovereignty, and power relationships; and still other people are interested in engineering, languages, dentistry, business, chemistry, or

Why We're Writing
This Book

literature. But *everybody* communicates; if you don't experience interpersonal relationships, you die.

That's literally true. There's a clear relationship between communication and life itself. During World War II, doctors noticed unusually high death rates among orphaned infants who were being kept in overcrowded hospitals. When untrained volunteers were recruited to do nothing more than pay attention to the infants between feedings, the death rate returned to normal.

In 1977 James J. Lynch wrote an entire book about this phenomenon. He called it *The Broken Heart: The Medical Consequences of Loneliness*. In the book he extensively documents relationships between quality of life and quality of communication. He tells, for example, of a 54-year-old man who "succumbed after 14 days of the most intense medical care that could be imagined." For the last several days this man lay in a deep coma, able to breathe only with the help of a machine. Yet in spite of his condition, every time a nurse comforted him with words and touch, his heartbeat strengthened dramatically. And communication—contact from another person—was the only event that had that effect.[2]

Lynch also discusses what researchers have found about the death rates of couples vs. single persons. Detailed analysis of mortality statistics for persons in the United States reveals that those who have fewer close interpersonal relationships die before their married counterparts. One study revealed that single, widowed, and divorced persons had consistently higher rates of death from cancer or coronary heart disease than did married persons in the same age group.[3] There are also some unusual patterns of dying among couples who have spent long lives together. When one spouse dies, the other often perishes "coincidentally" within a few months. This pattern extends to other family members, too. In one rural village in Wales, investigators studied 903 close relatives of 371 residents who died between 1960 and 1965. Almost 5 percent of these persons died within one year of the death of the close relative. For comparison, the death rate was 0.7 percent of persons of the same age living in the same village who had *not* experienced a relative's death.[4] Loneliness, lack of contact, diminished communication is now recognized as one factor contributing to premature death.

Cancer and heart disease also appear to be tied to communication. In 1970, for example, two Swedish doctors studied 32 pairs of adult identical twins, in each of which one twin had contracted coronary heart disease and the other hadn't. The doctors found that smoking habits, obesity, and cholesterol levels of the twins who had heart attacks were *not* significantly different from the healthy twins. But there were some other important differences, one of which was what the doctors called "poor childhood and adult interpersonal relationships." The twins with heart disease were the twins who had experienced more unresolved conflict, more arguments at work and home, and less emotional support.[5] After 30 years of work with heart disease patients in this country, two other doctors reached some similar conclusions. They found that although there are some relationships between heart problems and such factors as heredity, weight, and smoking, there is a much stronger link with one's pattern of interpersonal behavior. The person who is most likely to suffer a heart attack is the one who is "aggressively involved in a *chronic, incessant* struggle to achieve more and more in less and less time . . . against the opposing efforts of other things or other persons."[6] These doctors believe that continuous competitive and aggressive communication can increase your chances of heart disease.

What conclusions can we draw from evidence like this? Lynch puts it this way:

> Human companionship does affect our hearts, and . . . there is reflected in our hearts a biological basis for our need for loving human relationships, which we fail to fulfill at our peril. . . . The ultimate decision is simple: we must either learn to live together or increase our chances of prematurely dying alone.[7]

The Basic Assumption

In other words, quality of life is not just a matter of ample food, warm clothing, education, and modern conveniences. *The quality of your life is linked to the quality of your communication.* This is the basic assumption behind our approach to interpersonal communication; it underlies everything we've written in this book, and it helps explain why we feel in some ways that we cannot *not* write. We believe that learning to communicate can not only help you to develop trust, clarify an idea, obtain a job, make a sale, get an 'A', or make the right group decision. Communication *can* help with these things, but even more fundamentally, it affects your growth, your development as a person.

Interestingly, philosophers make this point as strongly as medical researchers do. For example, Reuel Howe writes,

> To say that communication is important to human life is to be trite, but that bit of triteness witnesses to an invariable truth: communication means life or death to persons. . . . Both the individual and society derive their basic meaning from the relations that exist between [persons]. It is through dialogue that man accomplishes the miracle of personhood and community.[8]

Martin Buber's entire philosophy of communication is based on the idea that you and I discover and build our humanness in relationships with other persons. To paraphrase Buber,

The fundamental fact of human existence is person with person. The unique thing about the human world is that something is continually happening between one person and another, something that never happens in the animal or plant world. . . . Humans are made human by that happening. . . . That special event begins by one human turning to another, seeing him or her as this particular other being, and offering to communicate with the other in a mutual way, building from the individual world each person experiences to a world they share together.[9]

Jesuit psychologist John Powell puts the same idea in simpler terms: "What I am, at any given moment in the process of my becoming a person, will be determined by my relationships with those who love me or refuse to love me, with those I love or refuse to love."[10]

Notice the similarity between these "philosophical" statements and this paragraph from the conclusion of Lynch's book about *medical* studies:

This book has ranged over a large number of social situations that influence the heart. From the quiet comforting of a dying person to the cuddling of an infant—in our earliest years, in adulthood, whether single, widowed, divorced, or married, whether neurotic, schizophrenic, or normal, whether human or animal—one factor unites all of us, and that is dialogue. Dialogue is the essential element of every social interaction, it is the elixir of life. The wasting away of children, the broken hearts of adults, the proportionately higher death rates of single, widowed, and divorced individuals—common to all these situations, I believe, is a breakdown in dialogue. The elixir of life somehow dries up, and without it people begin to wither away and die. Those who lack the dialogue early in life can perish quickly, while those who lose it as children, adolescents, or adults feel acutely what they have lost and struggle to get it back.

. . . Once again, the choice is ours to make. We must either live together or face the possibility of prematurely dying alone. Life and dialogue are one and the same.[11]

We are not saying that the quality of your communication is the be-all and end-all of your life, but we do believe that it is very important. We are not saying that if you fail to experience what we call interpersonal quality communication *all* the time, you will become impoverished, inhumane, or antisocial. But we are saying that communicating is not just one of the many trivial and mundane things you do—along with combing your hair, washing the dishes, and earning a living. Our basic belief is this: *The quality of your life is directly related to the quality of your communication.* That is the main reason we've wanted to write this book, and that's why we're excited that you're about to read it!

NOTES

1. *Time,* December 4, 1972, p. 97.

2. James J. Lynch, *The Broken Heart: The Medical Consequences of Loneliness* (New York: Basic Books, 1977), pp. 91–94.

3. Several studies that make this point are cited and referenced in Lynch, pp. 42–51.

4. W. D. Rees and S. G. Lutkins, "Mortality of Bereavement," *British Medical Journal,* **4** (1967), 13.

5. E. A. Liljefors and R. H. Rahe, "Psychosocial Characteristics of Subjects with Myocardial Infarction in Stockholm," in *Life Stress Illness,* ed. E. K. Gunderson and Richard H. Rahe (Springfield, Ill.: Charles C. Thomas, 1974), pp. 90–104.

6. Myer Friedman and Ray H. Rosenman, *Type A Behavior and Your Heart* (New York: Alfred A. Knopf, 1974), p. 67.

7. Lynch, p. 14.

8. From *The Miracle of Dialogue* by Reuel L. Howe, copyright 1963 by the Seabury Press, Inc. Used by permission of the publisher. Cited in *The Human Dialogue,* ed. F. W. Matson and A. Montagu (New York: The Free Press, 1968), pp. 148–149.

9. This is a paraphrase of what Buber says in *Between Man and Man* (New York: Macmillan, 1965), p. 203.

10. John Powell, *Why Am I Afraid to Tell You Who I Am?* (Chicago: Argus Communications, 1969), p. 43.

11. Lynch, pp. 215 and 321.

1

The human communication happening

I. PERSPECTIVE

A. Your perspective or point of view affects what you perceive

B. Your perspective on communication affects your communication behavior

C. A distorted view of communication leads to frustration and ineffective decisions

II. COMMUNICATION IS TRANSACTIONAL

A. Communication as action

B. Communication as interaction

C. Communication as transaction

1. Definitions (images) of self and others
2. Negotiation of selves as a continuous process
3. Interdependence

III. COMMUNICATION IS SITUATIONAL

A. The situation influences your communication

1. Physical components of situation
2. Psychological components of situation

IV. COMMUNICATION IS VERBAL AND NONVERBAL

   A. Differences between "verbal" and "nonverbal"

   B. Functions of verbal communication

      1. Refer or stand for
      2. Perform actions
      3. Evoke emotions
      4. Affect what you perceive
      5. Reduce uncertainty
      6. Express abstract ideas
      7. Promote human contact

   C. Nonverbal communication

      1. Become aware of the *types* of nonverbal communication

         a) Personal space
         b) Touch
         c) Movement
         d) Dress
         e) Facial expression
         f) Eye contact
         g) Posture
         h) Voice
         i) Silence

      2. These are three main *functions* of nonverbal communication

         a) Defines relationships between persons
         b) Expresses emotions
         c) Affects impact of verbal cues

      3. Try not to oversimplify nonverbal cues

———◆•◆———

If you were asked to describe what's shown in the first picture on p. 11, what would you say? Most people see a mug or coffee cup and a pencil holder. The object on the left is so familiar and obvious that there isn't any question about what it is, and the shape, size, design, and obvious use of the object on the right make it easy to identify, too.

    If you were asked to describe what's shown in the second picture on p. 11, however, you'd probably say that there are two coffee cups, one with some pencils in it.

    Notice two things. First, the *only* difference between picture 1 and picture 2 is that they're taken from two different locations or points of view; they show two different *perspectives* on the same objects. Second, in one sense the difference between the description of picture 1—"a coffee

Picture 1   Picture 2

mug and a pencil holder"—and the description of picture 2—"two coffee mugs"—is not subtle or insignificant. It is a difference in "what is," or "what's actually there." We don't mean that the fact that both objects are coffee cups is going to change your life, but that we are talking about a very basic and potentially important question: "What's actually there?" or "What *is* that?"

Now try the same thing with picture 3 on p. 12. What do you see in that picture? Since you may be expecting something like pictures 1 and 2, you may choose to look at picture 4 before answering. But if you look just at picture 3, how many pigs do you see? Are they all doing the same thing? Are they touching each other?

Now look at picture 4 and answer the question: Are the pigs touching each other? Most people say that the pigs in picture 3 are *not* touching but that the pigs in picture 4 *are* touching.

Yet, the pigs were not moved between picture 3 and picture 4. They were left in exactly the same position; picture 5 on p. 14 shows how they were placed. The difference between pictures 3 and 4 is a difference in perspective.

But a difference in point of view or perspective can really make a difference! If you didn't know that this is a "textbook example," you would probably be *certain* from looking at picture 3 that there are only three pigs in the picture. You might even be willing to swear under oath that that's all there are. Or to bet $10 that there are only three pigs in the picture. But when you saw picture 5, you'd discover that your perspective or point of view kept you from seeing everything that's there. A different perspective was more inclusive and therefore more accurate.

Picture 3

Picture 4

We're using these examples to make an important point: *What you see depends on your point of view.* The perspective you take on something will significantly affect what you perceive. If before meeting someone you've been told that he or she is pleasant and fun to be around, and if you know and trust the person who told you that, your perspective on or point of view toward that new acquaintance is likely to be positive. If that new person, when you do meet, is short-tempered and crabby, you'll probably see that mood as unusual, an exception to the rule for him or her. On the other hand, if your original perspective or point of view was negative, you'd probably see the crabbiness as "just what I would expect," that is, as the rule rather than the exception. Similarly, if you see the organization you work for as an impersonal, official place that uses employees to boost production and that doesn't care about morale or benefits, then you'll probably view their decision to cut back your hours as unfair, a rip-off, and something that "just proves what I've always known about this place—they don't give a damn about us." But if you see your employer positively, as an organization that believes in what it's doing and that cares about its employees, you will probably view the same decision to cut back your hours as unfortunate but probably necessary and almost certainly temporary. You might even feel good about being able to help out the organization by taking home slightly less pay for one month. Again, what you perceive, what's "really there" for you, depends on your perspective or point of view.

We emphasize this point because we've found that the perspective you have on the *communication process* significantly affects not only what you perceive, but also how you behave as a communicator. Many communication problems can be traced directly back to distorted views of the communication process. If you've ever been frustrated by someone misunderstanding your directions, even after you've explained three times how to do something, you've experienced a problem that is probably rooted in a distorted view of the communication process. If you've ever decided not to speak out in public, "because I always get nervous in front of a lot of people," or if you've avoided talking with someone because "we never get along," you've had a similar experience. Those frustrations, too, are almost always rooted in or based on a distorted, incomplete, or out-of-date view of human communication. The first step toward an accurate, up-to-date view is to recognize what kind of process communication is. Both our experience and the best current communication research demonstrate that it is inaccurate to view human communication as an *action* or *interaction*; it's better to see it as a *transaction*.

Let's explain those terms a little. If you were to ask the person on the street what communication is, he or she would probably say something like "getting your ideas across" or "making yourself understood." In other words, from this point of view communication is something *one person does*. When it's defined this way, communication doesn't occur "between people" but rather "in" the communicator. According to this perspective or point of view, the communicator's job is to discharge his or her responsibilities effectively: "I made sure they understood; I drew it on a piece of paper and repeated the directions twice." When things don't work out, it's because "I didn't communicate well" or because "you didn't," "the company didn't," "the supervisor didn't," or whatever. From this point of view, in other words, communication is an *action*, something determined entirely by the communicator's choices. As the diagram below indicates, this point of view says that communication is like giving or getting an inoculation; ideas and feelings are prepackaged into something like a mental and physical syringe and then pushed in a straight line into the receiver.

COMMUNI-CATION IS TRANSAC-TIONAL

COMMUNICATION-AS-ACTION

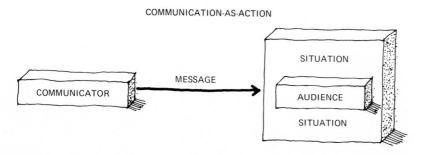

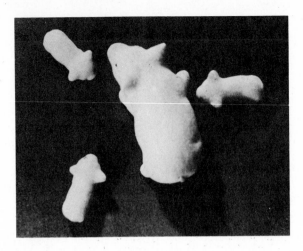

Picture 5

If you think about it for a minute, it becomes pretty clear why this view is inaccurate. When you see communication as just an action, you're ignoring listener response or feedback, something that's present whenever people communicate. Even on the phone, we make noises to indicate we are listening to a long comment or story. If you doubt the importance of that feedback, try being completely silent and see how soon the person on the other end asks, "Are you still there?"

The point of view that communication is an action is misleading, then, because it suggests that speakers are active and listeners are passive, that is, that messages are moving in only one direction. This perspective ignores the effects that outside factors might have and assumes that the message the communicator sends is exactly the message the listeners receive. It also implies that the communicator is not affected by what goes into or what goes on during the communication experience. In other words, it implies that regardless of any changes in the situation, the communicator is always "teacher" and never "learner," always "boss" and never "friend," alway "nervous in public."

The common view that communication is an *action*, something one person *does* to somebody else, is drastically oversimplified. All our communication behavior is affected not only by our own expectations, needs, attitudes, and goals, but also by the responses we are getting from the other person(s) involved. So it's more accurate to view the communication as an *interaction*, as a process of *mutual* or *reciprocal* influence.

The interactional point of view emphasizes that communication involves not just action but action and reaction, not just stimulus but

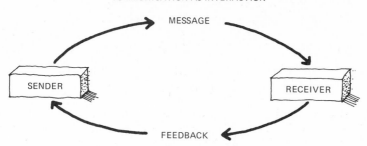

COMMUNICATION-AS-INTERACTION

stimulus and response. According to this perspective, a "good" communicator not only skillfully prepares and delivers messages but also watches for significant reactions to his or her communication. The study of human communication becomes a study of how people "talk" and how they "respond."

Although the interactional viewpoint is an improvement over the communication-as-action perspective, it still has some weaknesses. The most serious one, we think, is that, although it's not as oversimplified as the action view, the interactional view still distorts human communication by treating it as a series of causes and effects, stimuli and responses. For example, think about the last time you had a conversation with someone you know. What was the stimulus that "caused" you to greet the other person? His or her greeting? His or her look? Your expectations about the other's eagerness to talk with you? Was your greeting a "response," or was it a "stimulus" to his or her next utterance? Or was it both? What "caused" you to say what you said? What the other person said? What you thought the other's words *meant*? What you *felt* because of *how* the other person said what he or she said? What you felt because of how the other person *looked* when speaking? Are you able to distinguish clearly between the "stimuli" and "responses" in that conversation or between the actions, the hypotheses about reactions, and the reactions?

The late George Kelly, a fairly well-known psychologist, wrote that he had "pretty well given up trying to figure out" the relationship between stimuli and response. He said, "Some of my friends have tried to explain to me that the world is filled with 'S's' and 'R's' and it is unrealistic of me to refuse to recognize them. But before they have talked themselves out they become pretty vague about which is which."[1]

In brief, it's more accurate to see communication as an interaction than to see it as just an action that one person performs. But if you stick to an interactional perspective or point of view, you will still experience problems. For example, until you see the transactional nature of human communication, it's hard to keep from getting mad at the person who criticizes you or to keep from feeling defensive whenever you're being evaluated or controlled. Until you see communication as a transaction, it's also hard to keep track of the complex, interdependent, continually changing myriad of things that affect your contact with the persons you are close to—your lover, spouse, family. Without a transactional perspective it's also difficult to stay in the here and now and not to let the past determine what's going on in the present. In fact, all the communication attitudes and skills we discuss in later chapters—confirmation, self-disclosure, responsive listening, being clear, self-assertion, etc.—make real sense only when you see them as part of what's going on *between* persons. Since this perspective is so vital, we want to talk about it in different ways, using two different terms: *transaction* and *spiritual child*.

Transaction   One way to say what we mean is to use the term *transaction* and to contrast it with the *action* and *interaction* points of view.[2] As we said, if you see communication as an action, you're likely to be most concerned with each individual's performance. But human communication is much more than just independent message sending. If you view communication as an interaction, you will begin to see *some* of this "much more." The most obvious additional element you will see is feedback—how one's communication behavior is in part a response to the other person's, how human communication continually involves mutual and reciprocal influences.

It is important to see beyond performance to feedback, but there is another element that you will still miss if you stick with the interactional perspective. That element is this: *Every time persons communicate, they are continually offering definitions or images of themselves and responding to the images or definitions of the other(s) that they perceive.* We call that process *negotiation of selves,* and we discuss it in detail in Chapter 4. As we point out there, that process goes on all the time. Your clothes are part of your "this is how I define myself" message, just as ours are. Your tone of voice also reveals your self image in relation to the situation and the person you're talking with. Recall the sound of your voice when you're talking with a person whom you would define yourself as superior to (a six-year-old, for example). Contrast that with your tone of voice when you see yourself as an inferior talking with your supervisor or your parents. Touch, distance, eye contact, and choice of words also contribute to your self image and the way you respond to the other person's self image. Look at the ways we have defined ourselves in relation to you—the words we have chosen, the examples we have used, and so on. We have also assumed how you are defining yourself, and part of what we are doing is responding to what we think your self-definition is. And we could not not do these things. This negotiation-of-selves process is going on whenever people communicate.

Recently the term "transaction" has been introduced to talk about this process. In fact, a dictionary of psychological terms defines a transaction as "a psychological event in which all parts or aspects of the concrete event derive their existence and nature from active participation in the event."[3] In other words, a transaction is an event in which *who we are* ("our existence and nature" or how we *define* our selves) emerges out of the event itself. *Human communication is that kind of event.* Human communication is transactional. Whenever humans communicate, part of what's going on is that each is defining himself or herself in relationship to the other persons involved. That is, each is sending messages about his or her "existence and nature" and interpreting and responding to messages about the "existence and nature" of the other people involved.

Obviously, this defining process has some limits. John, who is male, 38, and brown-eyed, can't define himself as female, 10, and blue-eyed. But he *can* offer a definition of himself that says that he sees himself as more masculine—or more feminine—than you and as in some sense younger or older than you. Then it's up to you to respond to the definition of self he offers. So although neither of you can change identity absolutely, who you both are—your selves—is affected by your relation to each other.

Interdependence. Notice that previous sentence? We're not saying that you *determine* my definition of self or that I have the final say about yours. Our definitions of self are *affected by our relationship to each other.* That means that what I do affects what you do, and what you do affects what I do. In other words, whenever we are communicating, we are interdependent.

Here's what we mean by that term. If you and I were *independent,* then nothing I did would affect you. I could tell funny jokes, ask you for money, or sit on your head, and my behavior wouldn't affect you at all. On the other hand, if you were *dependent* on me, I would be able to control you; you couldn't do anything without me, and you'd have to do exactly what I made you do. But *interdependence* doesn't mean either of those things. *Interdependence means that what I do affects you and what you do affects me, but neither of us determines the other's behavior or feelings.* In terms of systems theory, interdependence means that a change in one part of a system affects all the other parts of the system.

Whenever you and I are communicating, we are interdependent; that is, if I start shouting, you will notice and respond somehow, and if you are silent and look bored, I will try to do something about it. It can also happen much more subtly. Even though I'm not aware of it, I can respond to your tone of voice or lack of eye contact, and the way you talk and look can be affected by what you think I'm thinking of you.

As we emphasize later in this chapter, interdependence *does not* mean linear causality. My shouting doesn't "cause" a specific response in you. If it did, I could always predict how you would react, and we all know that people are more unpredictable than that. But even though you don't "cause" my feelings of behavior, I am affected by you. Especially my definition of self is affected by how I see you defining me. And you respond similarly; your self definition is also affected by how you see me defining you. In that important sense, we are *interdependent*.

To review, then, you can see human communication as an action if you want to, but if you do, you will miss a lot of what's happening. You can look at human communication as an interaction, too, but you will still miss an important part of what's going on. The part you will miss is the ongoing, interdependent process of self-definition-and-response-to-definition-of-other—negotiation of selves—and you won't see that process clearly until you recognize that communication is a *transaction*, an event defined by that very happening. All human communication is transactional. Whenever we communicate, we are always interdependently engaged in the negotiation-of-selves process. Sometimes, however, people see their communication as transactional, and sometimes they don't. We are convinced that when they don't, it's much harder for their communication to be interpersonal-quality communication.

The main reason is that when you see communication as an action, you aren't focusing on what's going on *between* the persons involved. All you're seeing is one person's choice, one person's behavior. When you see communication as an interaction, you still aren't seeing what's going on *between* person A and person B. From an interactional view, each person appears to function something like a sophisticated pool ball—reacting to forces of the other pool balls, the table surface, cue stick, pads, etc. From an interactional point of view, one's actions are affected by the other's, but *who one is* doesn't change.

When you adopt a transactional point of view, though, you can't help looking at what's *between* the persons involved. If you focus your attention on just person A, for example, you realize that since person A is who he or she is only in relation to person B, you have to look immediately at what's happening *between* them. The same goes for person B. Since *who the persons are*—their "existence and nature"—emerges out of their interdependent meeting with each other, you can't help focusing on the meeting itself rather than on the individual meeters.

Spiritual Child   A few years ago, John was discussing this transactional idea with John Keltner, an interpersonal communication teacher at Oregon State University and the author of the first widely used interpersonal speech communication textbook. John Keltner said that the idea reminded him of an interesting concept that he and Lorraine Halfen, a communication counselor in Denver, had talked about. He and Lorraine suggested that it's easier to see human communication as a meeting *between* persons if you think in terms of a "spiritual child" that is the inevitable offspring of every human meeting.

In other words, whenever you encounter someone, the two of you together create a spiritual child—*your relationship*. Unlike the creation of physical children, there are no contraceptives available for spiritual children; when two people meet, they always create a relationship of some sort. Also unlike physical children, the spiritual child lives as long as at least one person lives. If two persons once have a relationship, the relationship endures, even though years and continents separate them. The spiritual child can change drastically, but it can't be killed. That's one of the reasons why it's so hard to deal with the breakup of a long-term intimate relationship. Since the spiritual child won't die, the relationship won't cease to exist, and each person has to learn to live with a radically, maybe even tragically changed "child."

There are some similarities, though, between a physical and a spiritual child. For example, if the spiritual child is born in a meeting characterized by manipulation, deceit, and exploitation, then, like the physical child, it will be deformed and ugly. If it's raised in that same atmosphere, it will never be healthy. Often it can be nurtured back to health, but it takes a heavy commitment from both parents, the best possible outside help, and time. On the other hand, if it's born and raised in an open and caring atmosphere, it will grow healthy and strong. As John Keltner puts it, "Properly nourished, honestly and lovingly cared for, this new essence created by two persons in a dyadic relationship can be a glorious being."[4]

We hope that the spiritual-child metaphor is useful for you. What it does for us is to give us another way to think about and look at the transaction, that which is *between* the persons. As a child, you "are" neither of your parents; neither "causes" you; you are the result of their meeting, their contact. Similarly, the spiritual child who is born whenever two persons communicate is an entity that emerges *between* them.

To summarize, we believe that the first step toward improving your communication is to develop an accurate understanding of or perspective on the communication process itself. The most accurate perspective is one that recognizes that communication is not simply an action or interaction; it is a *transaction*, an event in which the definitions of the persons involved emerge from their interdependent contact.

COMMUNICATION IS SITUATIONAL

The second step is to recognize that human communication transactions do *not* occur in a vacuum; rather, communication always takes place within a context or situation, and the quality of the transaction that occurs is influenced by the nature of the situation. Such variables as the location of the communication, the intentions or purposes of the persons involved, furniture arrangement, time of day or night, temperature, lighting, amount of physical space, number of persons, and so on, all help to create a specific situation and to "shape" the communication.

If you realize that communication is situational, you'll be more likely to remember that your interpretation of objects and events or of someone's words or actions is determined to a large extent by the situation in which you perceive those words, actions, objects, and events. Situation affects all human communication transactions, from a cocktail party to a public speech or sermon, from an interview to a marriage proposal. Your communication behavior will not be the same in a classroom as it is in your home. It will not be the same when you're on the telephone as it is when you're talking with someone face to face.

Each communication situation you experience is made up of *physical* and *psychological* components. The physical components of a situation exist outside the people involved; you can't always control what they are, but you can control your response to them.

Physical Components   *Geography and climate.* The environment that surrounds your communication with others can have a powerful influence on the kind of interaction that takes place. Sometimes, for example, the geography or climate can affect your mood, feelings, activity, initiative, or willingness to talk. When W. Griffitt experimented with the relationships between temperature, humidity, and interpersonal responses among students, he found that the students were less attracted to one another as temperature and humidity increased.[5] It may seem strange to think that hot, humid weather can affect whether we like or dislike someone. But although not all the evidence is in yet, experience and a few experimental studies suggest that we can't ignore the possibility. Not only heat and humidity but also the presence or absence of sun, lawn, smog, flowers, trees, mountains, concrete, and other environmental cues can often make a difference in what happens between persons.

Architecture. We know that such factors as the physical space available in a room, furniture arrangement, comfortableness of furniture, texture of walls, height of the ceiling, and color combinations can all affect the quality of communication. But we can't yet draw any clearly defined conclusions that generalize to most or all persons. Each of us responds to architecture in our own ways. One of the experimental studies about architecture that is most relevant to interpersonal communication was conducted by A. H. Maslow and N. L. Mintz.[6] They divided the people in their study into three groups and put each group in a different architectural situation: an "ugly" room, a "beautiful" room, and an "average" room. Then they asked each group to rate a series of photographs of other people's faces. The people in the "beautiful" room gave significantly higher ratings of the photographs than did those in the "average,' or "ugly" room. The study suggests, in other words, that our impressions of other people are influenced by the architecture of our surroundings.

We also learned some interesting things about architecture and communication from the manager of one of Seattle's most popular restaurants. He told us that his business is dependent on high-volume sales and that he does some things with the architecture of his restaurant to increase customer turnover. He wants people to come to his restaurant and enjoy the food and the environment, but he doesn't want them to stay too long. So he uses bright red wallpaper and bright lights throughout the inside of the restaurant. He also uses furniture that is comfortable for only a short period of time. As you're sitting in this restaurant, you're surrounded by lively music and relatively loud singing. The music is not irritating at first, but after a while it does get a little bothersome. The manager claims that his architectural design is a success. His experience supports the idea that the architecture of a room can have a strong though sometimes subtle influence on the human behavior.

Not all situations have the same physical characteristics, and not all physical characteristics are interpreted the same by all persons. With these considerations in mind, see what you can add to the partial listing that follows.

> The physical characteristics of a situation include: geography, climate, temperature, time, location, architecture, other people, space available, furniture, furniture arrangement, smells, noise, music,
>
> _____, _____,
> _____.

Psychological Components

The psychological characteristics of a situation exist "inside" the persons communicating; you can control these components because you bring them to the situation with you. Some examples follow.

Expectations. What you expect to happen in a situation sometimes will occur simply because you *believe* it will. Your perception is directly influenced by your psychological expectations; that is, you often see and hear what you expect to see and hear.

Perceived norms. In a bar most people assume that it's okay to use profanity; in a church sanctuary it's not acceptable. Jumping out of your chair and shouting for your team in a loud, intense voice is okay if you're in the privacy of your own living room or den, but the same behavior may not be acceptable in an expensive restaurant. Norms are not part of the physical components of the communication situation. They exist because people agree to accept them, so they're part of the psychological context.

We'll say more about psychological components in Chapter 3. For now we just want to make the point that expectations, norm perceptions, definitions, positive/negative responses, formality of the situation, and interpretations are a few of the psychological variables you bring to a communication transaction. Can you think of others?

If we're succeeding with what we're trying to do in this chapter, you are beginning to look at your communication experiences not just as actions or interactions but as *interdependent transactions,* and you are becoming aware that they are *transactions happening in a physical and psychological situation.* You're also developing an awareness of *why* it's important to remember that communication is transactional and situation-specific or situation-bound. The final major point we want to make about your perspective on the human communication process is that it is not only a transaction happening in a situation but a *verbal and nonverbal transactional happening in a situation.*

COMMUNICATION IS VERBAL AND NONVERBAL

To make sure that we're using the words "verbal" and "nonverbal" the same way you are, think about how you would fill in the empty spaces in this diagram:

	ORAL	NONORAL
VERBAL		
NONVERBAL		

Remember that the word "oral" means "by mouth" and the word "verbal" means "words." Keeping those definitions in mind, what would you put in the upper left box? What kind of communication is oral and verbal? When you've got that one filled in, move on to what is verbal but nonoral, that is, words *not* spoken by mouth. That's what would go into the upper right box. Then fill in the lower left box. What are examples of communication cues that come out of your mouth but are not words? Those are oral nonverbal cues. And finally, you can probably come up with many examples of nonoral, nonverbal communication cues/behaviors that communicate but that don't come out of your mouth *and* are not made up of words.

When you've finished, the diagram or chart should look something like this:

	ORAL	NONORAL
VERBAL	SPOKEN WORDS	WRITTEN WORDS
NONVERBAL	TONE OF VOICE, SIGH, SCREAM, VOCAL QUALITY, LOUDNESS, PITCH, ETC.	GESTURE, MOVEMENT, APPEARANCE, FACIAL EXPRESSION, ETC.

You'll have a clearer understanding of this part of the chapter if you keep those divisions in mind. It will also help if you recognize that at this point we're interested in breaking the communication process down into its parts. That's why we talk about verbal and nonverbal "cues." By "cue" we mean the smallest unit that affects your communication. The smallest *verbal cue* is usually a single word. Notice, for example, how much difference one word can make:[7]

Jack: I *am* listening to you.
Jill: You *were* listening to me!

or

Jill: I'm going to have a drink with the people in the office.
Jack: Yeah? I'll bet you're going to have a drink with the *person* in the
          office.

Nonverbal cues are the smallest nonword units that the people communicating notice or respond to. What counts as a "cue" varies with the sensitivity, interest, and level of awareness of the people involved. Examples of cues are the tone of voice that distinguishes a sincere comment from a sarcastic one, the intensity, duration, and location of a touch that means "Hi, friend," instead of "I'm sexually attracted to you," and the facial movements that distinguish a happy smile from a smile that's hiding tears.

You can use the chart also to remember that the difference between "Hello!" and "Heelllooooooooo!" and between a typed "Dear James" and a pencil-scrawled "Dear James" are nonverbal differences. "Verbal" refers specifically to words and "nonverbal" to everything else that can affect your communicating.

All communication situations include nonverbal cues, and most of them consist of *both* verbal and nonverbal cues. Occasionally, verbal and nonverbal cues "work" in similar ways. For example, the traffic sign

serves the same purpose as the words NO LEFT TURN. But it's important to remember that in most human communication situations, these two kinds of cues "work" in significantly different ways. In other words, when humans are communicating, a word just doesn't do the same thing as a sign; vocabulary choice doesn't affect the situation or the persons involved in the same way that tone of voice or facial expression does. Words are good for some things and almost worthless for others. Nonverbal cues are sometimes the most important part of human communication, and sometimes they're almost irrelevant. Consequently, we think it'd be useful to talk generally about both kinds of cues here. We'll focus in this chapter on how each kind of cue "works," that is, how verbal cues function in communication and then how nonverbal cues function there. In later chapters we'll be more specific about how verbal and nonverbal cues are part of the *negotiation of selves,* how they contribute to *sharing some of your self,* to *responsive listening,* to *being clear* and to *handling conflict.* In the final chapters of the book we'll explore verbal and nonverbal elements of *public speaking.*

Verbal Cues: How Words Work in Communication

As we said, verbal cues are words. That seems easy enough; everybody knows what a word is, right? Well, yes and no. Scholars have been studying language since about 400 B.C., when an ancient named Panini wrote a lengthy commentary on the *Vedas,* the sacred books of India. In the nineteenth century, such researchers as Wilhelm von Humboldt and Ferdinand de Saussure made important advances in linguistics, and the twentieth century's leading linguist, MIT's Noam Chomsky, became almost as famous as Andrew Young. But these scholars have not yet agreed on the defining characteristics of the basic unit of their study, the *word.*

There are several problems involved. For example, if you define language as what people write, then you can define a word as a group of letters set off by space. But linguists generally agree that written language is only a reflection of what people say, that the spoken word is primary. And that creates difficulties. Would you say that your "Howareya?" to somebody you meet on the street is one *spoken* word or three? Is "loves" a different word from "love," or are they two forms of the same word? How about "lover" and "loving"? Is "bazoo" a word? The letters fit together, and some English-speaking people use it when they talk, but it doesn't seem to be in any English dictionary. What about the "words" Don Martin creates? Is "shklork" a word? "Thak"? "Shtonk"? How about "Gish Goosh"?

Obviously, we aren't going to be able to answer a question that's stumped linguists for more than 2000 years. For our purposes it'll be good enough to avoid the problem by agreeing that things like "cat," "mainsail," and "empathy" are words and that things like

are not. That approach won't handle the borderline cases, but they're fairly uncommon, anyway. The main point we want to make is that studying words is not as simple as it might at first appear to be.

Not only is it next to impossible to define exactly what you're studying; it's also difficult to identify all the ways in which words function in human communication. It's often assumed that all words are names for things, that they always *refer to* or *stand for*, in one way or another, the things they name. You've probably heard that before—the word "dog" refers to a certain kind of four-legged animal, "tree" to a certain kind of botanical life, and "rock" to a hard, stony object *or* to a repetitive movement made by a certain kind of chair, *or* to a type of music, or. . . .

Words Refer To or Stand For

There are obviously some problems with the generalization that words function by referring to things. But it's a popular, even if inaccurate, belief. Many basic English and speech communication texts will reprint C. K. Ogden and I. A. Richards's famous triangle of meaning to explain how words work.[8] The triangle looks roughly like this:

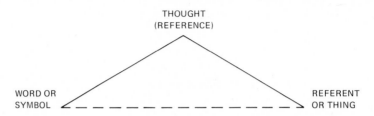

THOUGHT
(REFERENCE)

WORD OR
SYMBOL

REFERENT
OR THING

Ogden and Richards first used that diagram in 1923 to make a number of points, one of which was that words do refer to things but that there is no direct link between a word or symbol and the thing it refers to or stands for. That's why the bottom line of the triangle is dotted.

The problem with their view is that it is oversimplified. Sometimes some words function in communication by referring to some "referent," but other times they don't. Consider the last sentence, for example. The word "they" in that sentence does refer—to "some words." But what referent does the word "some" stand for in that sentence? What does "by" or "sometimes" refer to? In order to answer those questions, you have to invent all sorts of strange entities, like "a conditional expectation" (the referent for "sometimes") or "a conjunctive function" (the referent for "by"). It's simpler and a whole lot more accurate to recognize that the generalization just doesn't work. Sometimes some words function by referring to "things in the world" but not always. Words work in several other important ways, too.

Words Perform Actions Sometimes you use words not to talk about things but to *perform an action.* The words "I do" or "I will" in a marriage ceremony do not refer to a thing; they make up part of the act of getting married. "I christen thee" at a ship launching works the same way, as does "I promise" or "I'll bet you. . . ." When you make a serious bet or an important bargain with somebody, the words you use to seal the agreement don't refer to objects or events or even states of mind. They constitute, for example, the act of betting itself. When you sing in the shower or curse your smashed finger, these words are also functioning as actions; they don't "stand for" or "refer to" actions. Cursing *is* a part of being angry; singing *is* part of being happy, romantic, melancholy, or whatever. In short, *performing actions* is one of the things we often use words for without realizing that we're doing it.

Sometimes people try to sharply divide words and actions, as with "Let's stop talking and start *doing* something!" But that kind of thinking can both cheapen your view of the language you use and distort what's happening as you communicate. Saying "I love you" is a significant action; it's more significant to some people than to others, but it is always part of some kind of commitment. If you remember that many words do perform actions, you'll be less likely to contribute to misunderstandings that are revealed by comments like "I *do* feel that way; didn't you hear what I said?" or "Look, when I said I'd do it, I meant it. Don't you trust me?"

Have you ever had the experience of being so caught up in a book, short story, or magazine article that you began to get angry, nervous, or excited? Ever since his daughters Marcia and Lisa were born, John has been a "sucker" for stories about families with children and especially about a family crisis with a happy ending. This Sunday's paper included a story about the reunion of an Italian family whose eldest son had come to the United States nine years ago. The son, along with his new wife and in-laws, was just now returning to the village he grew up in. The story described the first meeting between the son, his widowed mother, and his brothers and sisters, and it was a great human-interest story—happy, poignant, and memory-evoking. John was so much into the story at one point that his eyes were watering and he felt like crying. And all from words! No pictures, even!

Words Evoke Emotions

You've probably had a similar experience while reading an exciting adventure, science fiction, or love story. Many people respond that way to J. R. R. Tolkien's stories about the Magic Ring and the inhabitants of Middle Earth—Bilbo, Frodo, Gandalf the wizard, the Orcs, Nazguls, Balrogs, and Elves. Others really get into sports stories or accounts of handicapped people who succeed. You might even feel a little silly when you realize how emotional you've gotten over nothing more than a bunch of black marks on a page. But words have that power. They can evoke strong emotions.

Spoken words can, too. There are certain terms that are applied to people of your race or religion that can trigger immediate emotional responses. "Boy," for example, "Jap," "Jew," "round eye," or "Greaser." If you're black, being called "nigger" can also be a really *positive* thing—if it is said by the right person and in the right context. In one sense those words are nothing more than sounds—just as written words are nothing more than marks on a page. But we know that they have power. Language can and often does evoke all kinds of emotions.

In Chapter 3 we'll be talking about how your perception affects your communicating. When you get there, you might keep in mind the idea that you perceive what you do partly because of the words you know how to use. Linguists disagree on how words affect perception—and how

Words Affect What You Perceive

much—but most language scholars agree that the existence of many words for "horse" in Arabic, for "snow" in Eskimo, and for "yam" in the language of the Trobriand Islanders is tied to how these people perceive horses, snow, and yams. This point of view, often called "linguistic determinism" or "the Sapir-Whorf hypothesis," has been summarized by the anthropologist Benjamin Lee Whorf.

> The background linguistic system (in other words the grammar) of each language is not merely a reproducing instrument for voicing ideas but rather is itself the shaper of ideas, the program and guide for the individual's mental activity, for his analysis of impressions. . . . We dissect nature along lines laid down by our native language.[9]

In other words, if you've spent enough time on boats and around the water to learn a dozen different words for water conditions, you will perceive more differences in the water than will the person who was born and raised in Cheyenne, Oklahoma City, or Calgary. That person might distinguish between "waves" and "smooth water," but you will see and feel differences between ripples, chop, and swells that he or she won't even notice.

As we wrote this book, we discovered that our native language sometimes limits our perception, too. Unlike some other languages, English maintains clear distinctions between subjects and predicates, causes and effects, beginnings and ends. The word system of the Navaho doesn't do that. According to Harry Hoijer, Navaho speakers characteristically talk in terms of processes—uncaused, ongoing, incomplete, dynamic movings. The word Navahos use for "wagon," for example, translates roughly as "wood rolls about hooplike."[10] As Hoijer explains, the Navaho words that we would translate "He begins to carry a stone" mean not that the actor produces an action, but that the person is simply linked with a given round object and with an already existing, continuous movement of all round objects in the universe.[11] The English language is significantly different from that. It requires you to talk in terms of present, past, future, cause and effect, beginning and end. But some things English speakers would like to discuss just can't be expressed in these terms. We would like to be able to talk more clearly about the ever-changing, processlike, ongoing nature of communication and about the betweenness of the quality of communication we're calling "interpersonal." But the English language makes it difficult to do that, as you'll probably notice when you read through parts of this book.

You may also notice that we've had some trouble with the male orientation of standard American English. Many people have made the point that our language includes an incredible number of terms that subtly

DOONESBURY

DOONESBURY, COPYRIGHT 1972 G. B. TRUDEAU. DISTRIBUTED BY
UNIVERSAL PRESS SYNDICATE. REPRINTED BY PERMISSION.

but effectively limit our perception of women, and in our culture we often use the male pronoun "he," "his," or "him" to make a general or universal reference to people.[12] For example, we speak of "mankind"; we tend to say that a person goes "his" way; and professional limitations are suggested by such job titles as "salesman," "foreman," "fireman," "policeman," "chairman of the board," and "meter maid." As Aileen Hernandez, past president of the National Organization of Women, has noted:

> There's a "housewife" but no "househusband"; there's a "housemother" but no "housefather"; there's a "kitchenmaid" but no "kitchenman"; unmarried women cross the threshold from "bachelor girl" to "spinster" to "old maid," but unmarried men are "bachelors" forever.[13]

Much of the sexism of American English may seen trivial and unimportant. But when all the subtle terms and uses are put together, they significantly affect the way we perceive female persons.

The same thing happens to other groups. Ozzie Davis's essay, "The English Language Is My Enemy,"[14] details the way our meanings for the words "black" and "white" affect our perceptions of black and white persons. Similarly, language terms and uses also severely limit the ways in which people perceive Asians, Chicanos, native Americans, and other racial and ethnic minorities.

We don't pretend to offer a simple solution to this potential problem, although this entire book suggests one set of ways to respond. But if you see your language as just something that *represents* your thinking, something that enables you to make public what you've been privately perceiving, you are missing one of its important functions. *Your language does not just represent your reality; it helps to shape it.* And the same thing is true for each person you communicate with.

Words Can Reduce Uncertainty

We'll say more about this function in Chapter 7. For now we just want to introduce the general idea that words can reduce your uncertainty by limiting the possible conclusions you can draw about something or someone. When you see a large, rectangular, green and white freeway sign in the distance, you know that it could possibly indicate many different things, including an approaching exit, a lane change, or the mileage to the next large town. When you get close enough to read the first word, the number of possibilities is reduced significantly, and when you can read all the words, your original uncertainty about the sign is reduced even more. The goal of sign writers is to use words that reduce your uncertainty to nearly zero. They try to avoid ambiguously worded signs

> SAN FRANCISCO TRUCKS PROCEED
> RIGHT LANE MERGE LEFT
> ONE MILE

in favor of those whose meaning is unmistakable.

> LAST EXIT BEFORE
> TOLL BRIDGE

Words can also reduce your uncertainty about people. When a friend you're used to seeing every day suddenly disappears for several days, you know that the absence could indicate many different things. Your friend might be ill, in trouble, angry at something you've done, tired of being around you, upset about something, cramming for an exam, moving, or a dozen other things. Your uncertainty about why your friend is absent can be reduced only when the person explains verbally—in speaking or in writing—that "I took a few days off to go home and collect my thoughts."

The guessing game "Twenty Questions" is based on the ability of language to reduce uncertainty. The point of the game is for one person to guess the identity of an object that another person is thinking about. The questioner can ask no more than 20 questions, the "yes" and "no" answers to which should enable her or him to narrow the range of possible objects to the one the other person has in mind. It's often fun to see how 18 or 19 well-chosen questions can lead to something as unlikely as "the left front wheel of that bus" or "the statue on top of the bank building."

Not all words *do* function to reduce uncertainty, but they *can*. They can categorize, point, specify, distinguish, and clarify much more efficiently than can nonverbal cues, and that's one reason they're so important for interpersonal communication. That's why we will suggest—for example, in Chapters 4, 5, 6, and 8—that you use words to clarify and check out inferences you and others are making about who means what, who's in what mood, and who wants to do X but doesn't want to do Y. When misunderstanding is the problem between people, it can often be solved simply by using more words to reduce the people's uncertainty.

If you're standing in the kitchen and you want to tell your spouse where the coffee is, you can point. If you just want to express your anger or delight, you can shriek or chuckle. But if you want to find out why the person who interviewed you didn't think your four years on the job was "relevant work experience," if you want to analyze the effects of the Vietnam War on American foreign policy, or if you want to clarify the reasons behind your position on the abortion issue, you will need to use words. Language is the only means we have of developing ideas, solving problems, exploring complex interrelationships, or expressing anything beyond the simplest logical functions. You can express "Yes" or "No" without words, but try "Maybe," "It all depends," or "Give me a chance to talk with Allen and the people in London, and then either I'll write you or my secretary will call by next Friday." Those ideas cannot be communicated clearly without using written or spoken words.

Words Can Express Abstract Ideas

Even the most primitive languages enable the people who speak them to develop and express abstract ideas. Since, as the Ogden and Richards triangle illustrates, words are not tied directly to the things we use them to talk about, we can discuss oil shipments, religious beliefs, time schedules, bank balances, and weather conditions even when those elements are actually not physically present. Language allows us to deal with the most complex and even the not directly observable parts of our environments. Without words our communicative transactions would be drastically limited.

Although you may well understand, at some level of awareness, that only words have this power to express abstract ideas, you may still sometimes communicate as if you didn't know it. Have you ever said or felt, "If you really cared about me, you'd *know* how I feel"? Often what that means is something like this: "I'm *nonverbally* expressing my disappointment over the canceled date, my eagerness to try again in spite of my fears, or whatever, and you should understand those complex and abstract thoughts and feelings just from my tone of voice, facial expression, and posture." When we talk about the situation that way, you can see how unreasonable a position that is. Complexities and abstractions require *verbal* expression—words. Nonverbal cues are powerful ways to express emotions, but they are inherently ambiguous, imprecise. If you want to clarify not only feelings but also judgments, opinions, or positions on an issue, you have to use words.

Words Can Promote Human Contact   The final function of words that we want to mention here is rather difficult to explain. Words, especially spoken words, can work to promote human contact, to bring people together. Martin Buber describes the unifying function of words this way:

> The importance of the spoken word, I think, is grounded in the fact that it does not want to remain with the speaker. It reaches out toward a hearer, it lays hold of him, it even makes the hearer into a speaker, if perhaps only a soundless one. [15]

Buber's point is that your words are both intensely private, personal, individual things *and* public, available to someone else. Consequently, thoughtful speaking can make some parts of *you* present to others. Gerard Egan calls this kind of speaking *Logos* or "language filled with the person who is speaking. . . . Logos here means translating oneself or handing oneself over to others, through the medium of speech." [16]

If Francisco was really angry at Richard, for example, he could punch him out, avoid him, or shout him down with obscenities and verbal abuse. None of those responses would promote much contact, though. If Francisco wanted to do something *with* Richard about his anger, he might also *say* something like this: "Look, Richard, I'm really mad at you. I could try to swallow my anger, or I could blow up, but I don't think that either of those would solve anything, because I think that in a way my anger is really *our* problem, yours and mine, and I'd like to talk it through with you. How about it?" [17] If you can overlook the artificial sound that comes from those words in print, perhaps you can see that this language could work to help Francisco and Richard meet each other. It would be risky and difficult, but it might also be very satisfying and productive.

What we're talking about here is the sense in which words are truly *symbolic*. In Greek the word "symbolic" is made up of "bolos," which means "to throw," and "sym," which means "with" or "together." One meaning of "symbolic," then, is "throwing together," or *"unifying."* And words can work that way. Think of the times you've found a friend just by listening to somebody talk—in person, on the radio or television, or in a book. His or her words helped bring you together. The words we use on these pages can bring us closer together with you, too. They can help bridge the gap between us. Again, we know that they *don't* always work that way, but they *can,* just as your words can help you move closer to others.

Words, in short, are a flexible and richly varied part of many communication contexts. They can *refer* the persons involved to nonverbal things or events. Sometimes we use words to *perform actions.* Words can also *evoke emotion,* and the language you're able to use even *affects the way you perceive.* Words can *reduce uncertainty,* and they are necessary whenever you want to *express abstract ideas.* Finally, and perhaps most important for us, words can *unify* persons, can bring humans together.

But words don't ever appear by themselves. Without exception, every communication situation includes *nonverbal* elements. Some authors have suggested that 65–93 percent of the impact of your communicating is determined by your nonverbal communication. Every written word is *on* something—colored paper, metal, a television screen, etc.—is in some style of script, is a certain size, and so on. Every spoken word is spoken in some tone of voice, at some rate, with some inflection and vocal quality.

Nonverbal Cues: Categories and Functions

Even though nonverbal cues carry the majority of our communication load, few of us have had any formal training to enhance our awareness, sensitivity, and use of nonverbal cues. Often we don't handle our nonverbal communication effectively, we miss a lot of cues, ignore important cues, overgeneralize and stereotype, or communicate something we don't mean to. For example, many persons believe such *myths* as these:

A person who doesn't maintain direct eye contact is not being sincere.

If you're not looking at me, you're not interested in what I'm saying.

A person who is poorly dressed can't be trusted.

Men with high-pitched voices are effeminate.

Men with low-pitched voices are more credible than those with high-pitched voices.

A person sitting with arms folded across the chest is being closed or defensive.

Women with breathy voices don't think logically.

Crying is a sign of weakness.

You probably can think of many more generalizations and stereotypes that people often make from nonverbal cues. We think that the best way to avoid making those faulty conclusions is to (1) become nonverbally aware,

(2) recognize that nonverbal cues work in three main ways, and (3) try not to oversimplify nonverbal cues.

The first step is to increase your sensitivity to as many nonverbal cues as possible. Learn to identify the many different nonverbal cues *you* are sending off, and try to become aware of the nonverbal cues that affect your response to *other* people.

The people in our classes seem to become much more aware of their nonverbal communication when we provide them with a reference list of a variety of nonverbal cues. We hope it will work that way with you, too. A list that identifies and gives examples of several nonverbal categories can increase your awareness of the vast multitude of nonverbal cues that at one time or another affect your communicating. Although what follows is not an exhaustive list of every kind of nonverbal cue, it's a start, and we think that by working with these categories, you'll gain a much broader insight into what you're "saying" nonverbally.

Personal space. You've probably noticed that you sometimes sit or stand very close to people you're talking with, whereas at other times you feel more comfortable several feet away. This is what is known as proxemics or, in simpler terms, personal space. Each of us has a distance at which we prefer to interact with other people. How far away we sit or stand depends on our personality, our relationship with the other person, the situation or context, how we are feeling toward the other person at the time, and other factors. As the anthropologist Edward Hall puts it,

> Some individuals never develop the public phase of their personalities and, therefore, cannot fill public spaces; they make very poor speakers or moderators. As many psychiatrists know, other people have trouble with the intimate and personal zones and cannot endure closeness to others.[18]

Hall also says that *"how people are feeling toward each other"* at the time will significantly affect how close they sit or stand.[19]

Within those limitations, Hall identifies four distances commonly used.[20]

1. *Intimate distance* (six to eighteen inches)

   Touch is possible; smell, body temperature, and feel of breath may be involved. Voice is normally at very low level.

2. *Personal distance* (one and a half to four feet)

   Touch is possible. Subjects of personal interests and involvement can be discussed at this distance. Finer details of skin, hair, eyes, teeth, etc., are visible.

Intimate distance

Personal distance

3. *Social distance* (four to twelve feet)

Impersonal business occurs at this distance. People who work together or who are attending a casual social gathering tend to use close
social distance. Eye contact is more important at this distance; lack of
eye contact may seem to shut person out of the conversation.

Social distance

4. *Public distance* (twelve to twenty-five feet)

Voice must be loud. Person can take evasive or defensive action if
threatened. Public distance is usually for public speaking and other
public occasions. Speakers lose much of the subtle shades of meaning
found in normal voice, facial expression, and movement. Voice, gestures, etc., must be exaggerated to be meaningful.

Touch. Touch plays a part in just about every movement of our waking
day—not necessarily with other humans but with objects. You may not be
consciously aware of the feel of your clothes, the chair, couch, or floor
you're sitting, standing, or lying on, the feel of the book you're holding,
the pencil or pen you're grasping to write, the feel of the desk you're
leaning on, the shoes you're wearing, or the feel of the sidewalk or grass
you walk on. But you couldn't very well write, walk, make a fist, smile, or
comb your hair without a sense of touch. Touching objects is common in
our culture, and the ways in which we handle such things as cigarettes,

Public distance

books, pencils, and cups or glasses can affect another person's response to our communication.

Touching persons is another matter. In this country when two persons are communicating in public, it is rare for them to touch each other more than three or four times in an hour. Of course, whether or not humans touch each other and how much and where they touch depend on many different factors. But in general, Americans are not so likely to touch one another as are people in some other countries. Sidney Jourard reports that in San Juan, Puerto Rico, couples observed for one hour in a public restaurant on the average touched 180 times; in Paris, couples touched 110 times; in London, they didn't touch at all; and in Gainesville, Florida, they touched twice.[21] A later study, however, found very few clear differences that are attributable strictly to cultural norms. Italian males do seem to engage in more touching than males in Germany or the United States, but many differences in touching behavior appear to be more a matter of whether you're male or female and whether your partner is of the same sex or the opposite sex.[22]

There are also differences within each country. In some American subcultures, touching is common and accepted. But for many people in this country it is not. As Mark Knapp explains:

> Some people grow up learning "not to touch" a multitude of animate and inanimate objects; they are told not to touch their own body and later not to touch the body of their dating partner; care is taken so children do not see their parents "touch" one another intimately; some parents demonstrate a noncontact norm through the use of twin beds; touching is associated with admonitions of "not nice" or "bad" and is punished accordingly—and frequent touching between father and son is thought to be something less than masculine.[23]

In this country many people tend to avoid touching because it seems to be, as Michael Young puts it, "a terribly risk-filled form of human relatedness."[24] Touching seems to be a way that feelings we'd like to keep hidden may become revealed. As Young says, "Touch has the power to burst the floodgates of our dammed-up emotional lives." Consequently, we learn that it's generally okay to shake hands, pat someone on the shoulders or back, or briefly touch another's arm. We also "permit" touching behaviors in contact sports, as a way of showing affection to or disciplining young children, and, in private, between couples. But beyond those situations, touching is often considered inappropriate.

Our discomfort can create serious problems because touch—or its absence—often communicates very "loudly." As one high school student said, "I don't think my dad cares too much about me. He supplies me with money; he spends time with me; but he's never put his arm around my shoulders, patted me on the back, or given me a firm handshake."

The main point we want to make here is that touch is a potentially *powerful* but poorly understood kind of nonverbal communication. Therefore you may want to clarify for yourself those touching behaviors that you see as supportive, friendly, and sympathetic and those that are, for you, connected with hostility or sex. You may also want to check your understandings with other people so that you can expand the ways you communicate by touching.

Body movement. Not all your movements will be noticed and interpreted by other persons. But when people communicate with you, they'll notice at least some of your *kinesic* behaviors, and those they notice may have a significant impact on the interaction that takes place. By simply pointing a finger at someone, you may be "saying": "I know what I'm talking about; in fact, I know a lot more than you do." Along with your gestures, posture, and head movements, the tension (or lack of tension) your body exhibits

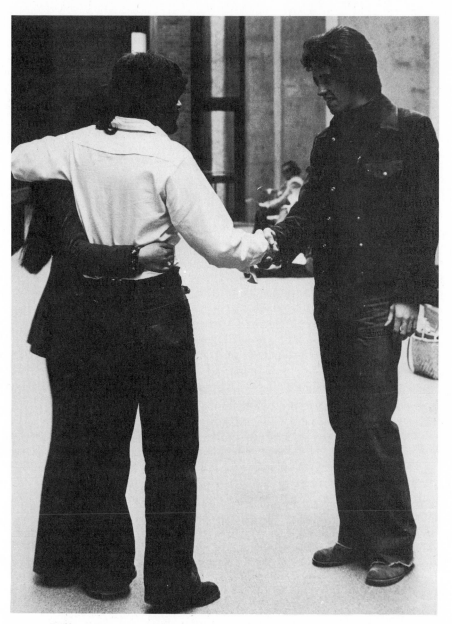

Different touching behaviors often indicate different relationships.

and your rate of movement can affect the general atmosphere of the communication context. People will frequently use your body cues to interpret your mood, attitudes, congeniality, liking or disliking, and emotions.

Facial expression. Your face is probably the most expressive part of your body and one of the more important focal points for nonverbal cues. Most of the time people are unaware of how much they are relying on faces to give and get information. But a little reflection—or reading some of the research—can change your level of awareness. Consider, for example, how important the face is in expressing emotion. Several studies have explored how eyebrow, eye, lip, forehead, and mouth configurations communicate surprise, fear, anger, disgust, happiness, and sadness. Every culture includes some conventional facial expressions—"facial emblems" they're called—that people use to communicate familiar states. These emblems are analogous to the circled thumb and forefinger that means "A-OK" and the thumbs down of condemnation. Surprise is pretty consistently communicated by a face with widened eyes, for example. Disgust is communicated with wrinkled nose and a raised upper lip—or one side of the upper lip. Raised eyebrows also commonly suggest puzzlement.

The way we create and "read" facial blends is also interesting—for example, a mouth set in surprise and eyes communicating anger when your instructor tells you your grade is a D instead of the A you were expecting. But even though facial expression can be extremely complex, most people familiar with a person's culture can readily identify the emotions that the person is expressing. Try it with the pictures on p. 41. Can you fill in the blank below each picture with what Miki is probably saying and feeling?

Facial expression also works in other ways. In the late 1950s, researchers were interested in the personality types that people commonly associate with certain facial features. For example, many people thought that a high forehead suggested intelligence and that thick lips on a woman indicated a "sexy" personality. That research turned out to be fairly inconclusive, however. Although we do make inferences about personality on the basis of facial expressions, the research suggested that the processes are much more complex than we originally thought.

Faces also help regulate communication. The next time you're in a conversation, notice how you tell when it's your turn to talk. The other person's face and eyes will almost always "tell" you. We also use faces and eyes to open and close channels of communication and to tell someone who approaches us either that we're welcoming him or her into the conversation or that we'd rather be left alone.

In short, we rely on a person's face to interpret emotions, attitudes, relationship cues, sincerity, and many other messages. As we'll discuss in

Chapters 5, 6, and 8, your face and eyes can reveal a great deal about who you are and how you're responding to others.

Dress. Dress may not have much influence on a close friend's perception of you. But in situations where you are forming first impressions or attempting to establish trust and credibility with relative strangers, dress can communicate such attributes as "nationality, relation to opposite sex, . . . socioeconomic status, identification with a specific group, occupational or official status, mood, personality, attitudes, interests, and values."[24]

In other words, clothes do communicate! Exactly what you communicate by your choice of clothing depends on the situation, the other person's background, expectations, norms, and so on. Although few universal generalizations about dress exist, some suggestions can be made. You need *not* wear expensive clothes, but what you wear should fit well, should be unwrinkled, and should be of matched colors. Most important, your clothes should *fit the occasion*. What you wear in the classroom, for example, may be wrinkled, may fit loosely and may be of unmatched colors, but no one will care if that is the norm. If you visit the supervisor at a construction site, you may wear worn jeans. Again, this is expected. If you showed up in a pin-striped suit, the construction supervisor might be turned off by your pretentiousness. On the other hand, if you're going for a job interview with a large corporation where conservative suits are the norm, your best decision is to dress conservatively.

For specific evidence on the potential impact of dress on communication, you may want to look at the book by Mark Knapp cited above, *Nonverbal Communication in Human Interaction*. For specific advice on how to dress in the business community, take a careful look at John Malloy's *Dress for Success* and *The Woman's Dress for Success Book*.[26] We wouldn't call Malloy's work "scholarly" in the most rigorous sense, but he has a great deal of information about how people in business respond to various styles and colors of clothing. His research suggests, for example, that men who wear green suits are not trusted and that the most effective dress for a woman in business is a dark skirted suit and a blouse that contrasts with the skirt and jacket. Some of the best colors for a woman to wear in an office are deep blue, navy, tan, and beige, and some of the worst are green, orange, purple, and baby blue. The most credible suits for the businessman are dark blue and dark gray solids and pin stripes. Although not all of what Malloy says can be taken literally, many of his suggestions make practical sense for persons interested in business opportunities, sales, speaking in public, business development, or interviewing.

Eye contact. Although it varies among individuals and circumstances, Americans generally maintain eye contact during interaction about 50 percent of the time. In other words, when in a conversation with a nonstranger, we'll typically look at him or her half of the time and look away half of the time. Situations of stress or insecurity may cause us to break eye contact more often. On the other hand, when we're with a close friend or someone with whom we have a close, trusting interpersonal relationship, we may have more than 50 percent eye contact.

Eye contact serves a variety of functions in communication. You may look at people because (1) you're trying to emphasize a point, (2) you want to "read" their nonverbal feedback, (3) you want to signal that it's their turn to talk, (4) you're expressing affection or some other emotion, and so on. Of course, your eyes don't communicate any of those things on their own. People ordinarily do not focus only on one nonverbal cue; they notice a collection of cues—your eye behavior, posture, tone of voice, facial expression, body movement, and so on, and make inferences on the basis of the whole collection.

Consequently, there's no magic formula that stipulates exactly how much eye contact you have to maintain to communicate successfully. Your goal, though, should be 50 percent or more. Too little eye contact (e.g., 15 to 20 percent) may be interpreted as insecurity, disliking, unprepared- ness, or being impersonal, evasive, or indifferent. With more eye contact you stand a better chance of being interpreted as sincere, personal, confident, prepared, and friendly. Of course, there are also different qual- ities of eye contact. A constant stare may irritate your listener.

Mark Knapp summarizes the different circumstances and behaviors associated with "eye gazing" in these words:

> We would predict *more* gazing when:
>
> you are physically distant from your partner.
>
> you are discussing easy, impersonal topics.
>
> there is nothing else to look at.
>
> you are interested in your partner's reactions—interpersonally involved.
>
> you are interested in your partner—that is, like or love the partner.
>
> you are of a lower status than your partner.
>
> you are trying to dominate or influence your partner.
>
> you are from a culture which emphasizes visual contact in interactions.
>
> you are an extrovert.
>
> you have high affiliative or inclusion needs.
>
> you are dependent on your partner (and the partner has been unresponsive).
>
> you are listening rather than talking.
>
> you are female.
>
> We would predict *less* gazing when:
>
> you are physically close.
>
> you are discussing difficult, intimate topics.
>
> you have other relevant objects, people, or backgrounds to look at.
>
> you are not interested in your partner's reactions.
>
> you are talking rather than listening.
>
> you are not interested in your partner—that is, dislike the partner.
>
> you perceive yourself as a higher-status person than your partner.
>
> you are from a culture which imposes sanctions on visual contact during in- teraction.

you are an introvert.

you are low on affiliative or inclusion needs.

you have a mental disorder like autism, schizophrenia, and the like.

you are embarrassed, ashamed, sorrowful, sad, submissive, or trying to hide something.[27]

Posture. Like other nonverbal cues, posture rarely acts alone to evoke responses from other people. For me to think you are interested in my ideas, you have to do more than lean forward; your eye contact, facial expression, and vocal responsiveness all influence my judgment of your level of interest. Posture, in combination with these other cues, however, exerts a significant influence on interpersonal perceptions. Perceptions of degree of liking-disliking, warmth-cold, interest-disinterest, status, and preparedness can be partially influenced by posture. For example, Knapp reports:

> In an attempt to broadly summarize Mehrabian's research, we would say that liking is distinguished from disliking by more forward lean, a closer proximity, more eye gaze, more openness of arms and body, more direct body orientation, more touching, postural relaxation, and more positive facial and vocal expressions.[28]

Knapp's summary points out the relationship of liking/disliking to several nonverbal cues, among them postural cues: "forward lean," "openness of arms and body," "more direct body orientation," and "postural relaxation." We'll discuss posture more specifically in the listening and public speaking chapters. Note the feelings and relationships suggested by the posture and distances in photo on p. 46.

Voice. The nonverbal characteristics of your voice, sometimes called paralinguistics, include such things as tone, pitch, inflection, articulation, resonance, loudness, dialect, rate of speaking, laughing, crying, groaning, and so on. One of the primary functions of your voice is to give people some idea of how to interpret the words you speak. But more significant, people sometimes make assumptions about speakers themselves on the basis of vocal characteristics. People infer personality traits, attitudes, emotional states, intelligence, age, competence, and mood from a person's voice. We don't recommend this practice, but it happens.

Silence. Silence is one of the least understood nonverbal cues, partly because people use and interpret silence in so many different ways. Silence can be interpreted to mean apathy, patience, boredom, fear, sadness, love, intimacy, anger, or intimidation. We've talked with married couples who use silence as a weapon. One husband, who knew his wife couldn't stand it when he didn't talk out a problem, would sometimes refuse to talk to her for two or three days. His wife said she found this "devastating." Students have told us that when they're working in small groups, the most uncomfortable moments are those when everyone is silent. They've said that during periods of silence, people start shifting nervously and making inferences like "nobody is interested," "people don't like this group," "nobody can think of anything to say," and "nobody really cares about what we're doing." To get an idea of the impact silence can have, try waiting 45 seconds after each speaker finishes in a small-group discussion. Or notice the next time someone asks a question and nobody says anything for half a minute. Chances are, the person asking won't wait that long before talking; the silence seems too overwhelming.

Silence also works in positive ways. Two close friends may say nothing to each other just so they can share the experience of the moment. A friend of ours reported that the long silences he and his mother shared during the last two days of her life were some of the richest times they had spent together. Love, warmth, sympathy, and several other emotions are sometimes better expressed through "silent" facial and body movements and touch.

As you communicate, remember that each of us is as responsible for our silence as we are for our speech. Remember, too, that your pauses and silences may be saying something you don't intend to say.

The second step toward effective nonverbal communication is to recognize that nonverbal cues "work" in three main ways: They play a major role in *defining the relationship between persons,* they often *express emotions,* and they *significantly affect the impact of verbal cues.* Think about some of your own relationships with other people. When you walk into a classroom the first day of a term, how do you tell who the teacher is? You probably use such nonverbal cues as dress, the kinds of materials she or he is carrying, or where he or she sits or stands. Even though we don't wear any special uniform, we've never found it necessary to announce, "I am the teacher." Many people know as soon as we walk into the room; the rest get the idea from the folder or books we're carrying, our apparent familiarity with the situation, or some such thing. Students also usually have a pretty good idea of what kind of relationship they'll have with their teacher by such things as the way he or she talks with them, the number of office hours available, whether or not the teacher avoids them or goes out of the way to converse with them, and sometimes even by how the teacher's office is arranged or decorated. (What is a person saying about your relationship if the office is arranged in such a way that a desk is always kept between you?)

Similarly, how do you determine that someone is a close personal friend of yours? It's hardly ever because the person says the words "I am your close personal friend." You pay more attention to the amount of time the person spends with you, how willing she or he is to listen to you, or the fact that she or he has consistently trusted you with confidential information.

Notice Nonverbal Functions

You also determine whether the person you're communicating with sees himself or herself as superior, inferior, or equal to you by the nonverbal cues you interpret. Tone of voice, spatial relationships, facial expressions, and gestures are much more common indicators of superiority, inferiority, or equality than words are. In short, the relationships you establish with other people are often defined by nonverbal communication cues.

Another main way nonverbal cues work is to *express emotions*. We're pretty sure that this isn't news to you. Most human emotions are communicated primarily via nonverbal cues. Anger, sadness, pity, envy, passion, and pain are hardly ever communicated primarily by words. Nonverbal elements are much more important. As we said above, we don't think it's a good practice to infer emotional states from just nonverbal cues. We will suggest some alternatives in Chapter 6. But whether someone likes or dislikes you, is angry with you, frustrated with you, affectionate toward you, afraid of you, or ashamed of you, you'll infer the emotion primarily from the nonverbal cues you observe.

Nonverbal cues also *significantly affect the impact of verbal cues*. According to Knapp, nonverbal cues can repeat, substitute for, complement or accent, regulate, or contradict verbal cues.[29] In some cases, he explains, nonverbal cues function simply to *repeat* what the words say, as when a person points while saying "over there" or "go north two blocks." Sometimes nonverbal cues *substitute* for words, as when your facial expression and posture make it unnecessary for you to say, "I've had a rotten day." Nonverbal cues can also *complement* or *accent* verbal ones; i.e., they can elaborate on what's being said in words. Think of the last time you had a disciplinary conference with your employer, one in which your boss was correcting something you were doing wrong. Chances are, it wasn't a particularly comfortable experience, and your nonverbal cues—lack of eye contact, nervous movements, choppy speaking, etc.—probably emphasized or accented the discomfort you were feeling.

In most face-to-face conversations, you also use nonverbal cues to *regulate* who's speaking. Leaning forward, opening your mouth as if to speak, and adopting an anticipating or expectant expression can signal the other person that you want to talk. Other cues signal that you want the person to continue. Finally, nonverbal cues often *contradict* verbal ones. If a man says to you, "Speaking in public doesn't make me at all nervous," but you notice that his hands and voice tremble and sweat shines on his forehead while he is speaking, which do you believe—the verbal statement or the nonverbal behavior? When verbal and nonverbal cues conflict, the nonverbal has a great deal of influence on the believability of what's heard or said. What would your response be to a man who said to you in a monotone voice, "You have good ideas," while at the same time he was brushing lint off his pant cuff?

Try not to oversimplify nonverbal cues. By now it should be clear why we have included this third main point. There are so many kinds and functions of nonverbal cues, you just can't accurately interpret them in narrow, simplistic ways. Not everybody will respond in the same way to a nonverbal cue; much depends on the person who is interpreting the cue, the relationship between the communicators, the situation, and so on. To a mother and father, their child's temper tantrum may seem like a natural part of growing up. To an older brother or sister, the tantrum may signify that the child is spoiled. To someone outside the family, the tantrum may be evidence of poor parental guidance.

In other words, we think it's important to develop insight into the influence that context has on interpretations of nonverbal cues. Not only do different people interpret the same cue differently, but the same person may interpret a given nonverbal cue differently in different situations. Try to visualize the ways in which you would interpret the sight of two men hugging if you observed them at a funeral, after a touchdown at a football game, or in a bar. To add to the complexity of all this, a person may "give off" the same nonverbal cues for different reasons in different contexts. In one situation you may cross your arms across your chest because you're nervous; in another situation you may do the same thing because you feel defensive; or you may cross your arms because you're cold.

We'll have more to say about *interpretation* in Chapter 3, and we'll also be talking about verbal and nonverbal cues in other chapters. We'll discuss nonverbal aspects of sharing or disclosure in Chapter 5, nonverbal dimensions of listening in Chapter 6, nonverbal elements of handling conflict in Chapter 8, and nonverbal variables of public speaking in Chapter 9. But you're probably feeling that you've heard enough about them for now.

Our goal so far in this chapter has been to show that the perspective you take on something determines what you'll see. It is helpful to view human communication from a transactional perspective. **In Summary (So Far)**

Then you are less likely to oversimplify or distort the process.

You'll also be able to notice the image-transaction or negotiation-of-selves process.

And you'll see how interdependence constantly affects our communicating.

It's also important to remember that communication is situational.

Situations consist of both physical and psychological factors.

Situations affect virtually everything we do as communicators.

This transactional, situational communication process is made up of both verbal and nonverbal cues.

Realize regarding verbal cues that

It's hard to define what a "word" is.

Words can stand for things.

Words can perform actions.

Words can evoke emotions.

Words can affect how you perceive things and people.

Words can reduce uncertainty.

Words can bring people together.

Realize regarding nonverbal cues that

It helps to become aware of the variety of nonverbal cues—personal space, touch, body movement, facial expression, voice, silence.

Nonverbal cues work in three main ways—they define relationships between persons, they express emotions, they affect the impact of verbal cues.

It helps not to oversimplify verbal cues.

Some Implications   We've spent this much time outlining a perspective on human communication for two reasons. First, we're really convinced that the way you look at something (the perspective you have on it) significantly affects how you behave toward it, and we'd like you to begin with an up-to-date, accurate view of human communication. The second reason is that we continue to discover in our teaching that many people see communication as a one-direction, straight-line process, or at best as a back-and-forth, trade-off activity—I speak/you listen/you speak/I listen. . . . When you really start seeing communication as an interdependent verbal and nonverbal transaction happening in a situation, you'll probably discover that some pretty basic beliefs will need to change. The most basic ones involve your view or perspective on *causality* in communication.

Many forces act on us to lead us to think in cause-effect terms. We've already mentioned how the English language does that. English-speaking children learn in grade school that most English sentences include nouns acting through verbs on direct objects. We get a model of linear or straight-line causality: "Jack hit the ball through the window" suggests a one-way, straight-line process of cause and effect. This causal perspective is also prevalent at the basic level of many of the so-called hard sciences.

Many highly respected scholars—physicists, engineers, chemists—and many highly regarded members of the health professions—doctors, dentists, nurses—work in a cause-and-effect universe, too. The aeronautic engineer explains how an airplane flies by talking about how fast-moving air *causes* pressure differentials that result in predictable *effects*—the plane rises, so long as jet thrust *causes* the *effect* of forward motion. Doctors search for the *causes* of cancer, high blood pressure, and the common cold. The dentist tells you to brush and floss your teeth because the friction *causes* plaque to fall off your teeth, and if it's left there it will harbor bacteria that *cause* decay.

We are definitely not saying that these professionals are wrong—that the airplane doesn't fly, that certain chemicals don't cause abnormal cell growth, or that plaque doesn't cause decay. But we do see serious problems when this causal view is applied to *human communication*. And one key implication of the view of communication we've offered here is that you can't do that. *The linear, causal model cannot be accurately applied to human communication.*

In a sense, we're just emphasizing what we've already said. If aspects of the communication *situation,* verbal and nonverbal *cues,* and the *person* communicating are all *interdependent,* then they are not simply related by linear causality. What does that mean to you? Well, for one thing, it's *never* accurate to say, "You hurt my feelings." In addition, a person *cannot* literally mean it when he or she says, "You bore me." It is also never true that "You fouled that up; it's all your fault." A misunderstanding can never be blamed on one person. Each person is part of every communication success and failure that he or she experiences. If I'm feeling hurt, your actions may be very relevant, you may be an important part of the situation, but you didn't "cause" my hurt feelings. If I'm experiencing boredom, the same thing applies. Boredom is my current response to the situation, and you are part of the situation, but *so am I.* And so are many other factors. They are all *interdependent.* We'll have much more to say about this idea in later chapters, but at this point we'd just like you to see clearly that the perspective on communication that we're presenting here may call for some changes in your thinking. We're convinced that they're changes for the better, though, or we wouldn't suggest them.

Another thing. When you think about your communication as a complex, interdependent process of moving, changing verbal and nonverbal cues, the whole thing may look overwhelming. Your first impulse may be to bag it—go back to the simple, old, linear causal view. We want to encourage you not to do that. Although it may look complex now, this perspective is understandable and workable. You can handle it, and when you do, your communication can improve significantly.

———— ◆•◆ ————

1. *The "action, interaction, transaction" stuff sounds like a lot of jargon to*
me. What's the key point?

There are two key points:

a. The point of view (assumptions, perspective) you take toward
communication will directly affect the decisions you make in your communicating, for example, decisions about whether to talk or listen, when
to talk, how long to talk, whether to send a memo or use the telephone,
whether to meet regularly in face-to-face contact or irregularly by letter,
and so on. Literally every communication decision you make will be affected by your view of communication.

b. If your point of view is "action" or "interaction," your decisions
will not be optimally effective. Only a transactional view comes close to
explaining how communication works (and even it is incomplete), and so
decisions based on a transactional view will ultimately (and in the long
run) be more effective than decisions based on action or interaction views.

2. *Why should persons studying interpersonal communication be so concerned*
with "situational characteristics"? What kind of impact can the situation
really have?

Situational characteristics pose a potential barrier to the *application* of
interpersonal skills and may affect our listening, our trust, our perceptions
of others, whether we objectify or personify, and so on. Once you learn
how to gain control over situations, you'll be better prepared to apply
interpersonal skills under a variety of conditions.

3. *What can I do to manage situations?*

First, don't walk into a situation believing that everything is set and
that you have no control. Presume that most characteristics within any
situation are negotiable; that is, they can be changed to some extent. Furniture can be moved, thermostats can be adjusted up or down, no one
owns a particular position, lighting can be changed, norms can be flexible,
structure can be eliminated (or created), and so on.

Second, even though you can't *change* some of the physical and/or
psychological characteristics, you still have a choice about how to respond
to these characteristics. To practice this "control over response," determine which parts of a given situation seem to elicit a reaction from you
almost without your thinking about it. Do you, for example, almost always
keep silent when there are more than ten persons in the room? Do you
tend not to talk when you feel that the atmosphere is strongly judgmental?
Does the way some people dress almost always bother you? Do people at
high status levels frighten you? Do you always relax more if a room is

casual, carpeted, and furnished with comfortable chairs? Ask yourself questions like these to determine which parts of communication situations seem to be in control of you.

Third, start practicing different kinds of responses. The way people dress, for example, does not have to affect you in any way whatsoever. You can respond positively, negatively, apathetically, critically, or any other way you choose. Choose a response that will best promote the kind of communication you want, and practice making this response at every opportunity. Sometimes to break a response *habit* you have to practice it 50 or 60 times before it will change.

Once you've learned to be aware and exercise control, you'll manage the situations much more effectively.

4. *Why does nonverbal communication have so much impact on my communication with other people?*

We're not exactly sure why people use your nonverbal communication to make inferences about you and your messages. Perhaps it's easier; it may be out of habit from childhood, when nonverbal cues were our primary means of communicating; or it may be because there's so much more nonverbal to pick from. That is, nonverbally we communicate through sight, touch, smell, hearing, and taste, whereas verbally we communicate primarily through hearing (oral words) and sight (written words). Moreover, another possibility is that people tend to assume your words can be rehearsed (and therefore may be manipulative), whereas your nonverbal is spontaneous and less under your control (therefore not so manipulative).

It's likely that when you communicate face to face with someone, you're sending 20–30 nonverbal cues simultaneously, including such things as dress, posture, gesture, facial expression, mouth, eye behavior, hair style, movement, handling of objects, touch or lack of touch, the tone, pitch, volume, quality, and rate of your voice, silence, nervous movements, what you choose to talk about, etc. With this many cues to choose from, it's not unusual for the nonverbal to have significant impact on the other's impression of you.

———————◄•►———————

You can check your awareness of the impact of situational factors on communication by analyzing the settings of five different television shows. You may want to look at three distinct situational comedies, a game show, and a drama. Notice how the different physical surroundings change your impressions of the communication atmosphere and affect the communica-

EXERCISES

Individual Activity: Communication Situations

tion that goes on among the people in the show. The following may provide guidelines.

[Name of show]

Physical characteristics of a scene:

_____

_____

_____

Psychological characteristics of the
same scene:

_____

My impressions of the communication atmosphere:

_____

_____

_____

**Individual Activity:
Marriage**

On a sheet of paper, write down your beliefs or images of *marriage*. Then,
as best you can, try to recall the people, personal experiences, etc., from
which you constructed those beliefs or images. Parents? Textbooks?
Steady date? Television shows? Friends? Where did you first hear about
marriage? How much did you learn by observing the nonverbal behavior
of your parents? How did you learn the *most* important thing you know
about marriage? Where does your *most recent* belief about marriage come
from?

Compare your responses to these questions with someone else's. What do
you think will happen when you communicate with that person about
marriage?

**Individual Activity:
Eye-contact
Assertiveness**

To demonstrate the power of eye contact in human communication, do the
following: The next time you're making a purchase, look the salesperson
directly in the eyes and ask, "Don't you think this is overpriced?" Note the
response. Does the salesperson look away?

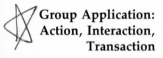

**Group Application:
Action, Interaction,
Transaction**

For each of the situations below, explain how various persons might behave, depending on whether they took an "action," "interaction," or
"transaction" view of communication. Following the first situation is a
framework of questions to guide you in considering each of the three
views. Sample answers are given for the first situation only.

Situation 1
Your boss has told you that an employee of yours is not doing his job
adequately. This employee is older than you, and it's your responsibility

to get higher-quality work out of him or her (your boss expects it and has told you so).

a. If you took an "action" view of communication in this situation (you are the one who has to talk to the employee),
   1. What would you probably say?
   2. How would you say it?
   3. Where would you say it?
   4. What would you do? What actions would you take?
b. For an "interaction" view of communication in this situation, answer the same four questions.
c. For a "transaction" view, answer the four questions.

SAMPLE ANSWERS

Action View

1. "Here's what's wrong. Here's what you've got to do to fix it!"

2. Firmly, respectfully, in a strong tone, with a serious face, etc. (I wouldn't let him think he could get away with anything.)

3. I would make sure it was in my territory, although I might do it by memo.

4. Would make sure he paid attention to me, wouldn't allow interruptions. I'd go about my business after the meeting. I would assume it was being done; if not, I'd terminate him.

Interaction View

1. "Here's what's wrong. What are you going to do to fix it? Can you understand what I mean? (Would get feedback from employees.)

2. Assertively. Would listen seriously but critically to what he says. I would start by talking but would then listen. I'd pay attention to the feedback.

3. Wherever it's possible to get immediate feedback.

4. Would set up a feedback system so that I could monitor results. I'd rely on the image of this worker; that is, I would ask myself, "Is he a good worker? Can I rely on him?"

Transaction View

1. Wouldn't say anything until I had researched the problem to determine the potential causes, the history of the problem, etc. I'd recheck

the boss's perception. I would listen first! I'd probe. I'd interview several persons. I would want to make sure, before telling this employee what to do, that he actually has control over the quality of work that's being put out. Maybe someone else is involved. I'd ask him if he sees this as a problem. I would want to get his definition of the situation. I'd ask, "What may I be contributing to this situation?"

2. I would listen and talk openly and with a highly sensitive, probing approach—pleasant, firm, not phony, genuine.

3. I'd use good timing, find the right place at the right time.

4. I'd check the work context to see what other variables were affecting quality. I'd allow interruptions. I would ask a lot of questions, would try not to categorize or box this person into past images I've had. I'd open a feedback system to monitor results. My overall approach would be to listen, check all possible causes, develop a reasonable approach to resolve the problem—with the employee participating in the solution—and then I'd work to get the solution implemented. If time didn't permit this approach, I would still listen first and then make decisions about how to approach the problem.

Situation 2
You are a member of the nine-person program committee of your club. All the members agree to do their part for the spring fund-raiser. It is a large project, one that the committee has been planning for six months. On the day before the event, you are supposed to meet with four other committee members to set up the tent, booths, etc. Two committee members don't appear, and after waiting and working for an hour, you decide to do something.

Situation 3
Create a situation that parallels an experience you've had and respond to the same questions about it.

Group Activity: Affects of Communication Situations

Break into teams. Each team will demonstrate how the context or situation influences interpretations. For example, a team might take three pictures of the same two people in three different situations to show that our interpretation of the people depends to some extent on which context we see them in.

Another team might set up three different classroom situations that demonstrate how students might communicate and interact differently in the three different settings.

And so on. Let your imaginations run. Remember the basic task.

Show that the physical and psychological characteristics of a *situation* influence our interpretations of what is happening.

Get together with one or two other persons to create an object or model that represents human communication as you now see it. Create something that has not been done before. Be sure to include the idea of "interdependence" in this model. People in our classes have made objects and models out of Ping-Pong balls, chess sets, shoe boxes, yarn, coat hangers, candles, light switches, and so on.

Group Activity: A Communication Creation

To demonstrate that words can express abstract thought-concepts and interrelationships whereas nonverbal cues cannot, ask one team of persons to create a written verbal explanation of an abstract concept or argument. (Examples: "Here are three strengths of a democratic form of government." "Three reasons why teachers should take student views into account when grading exams." "Why work experience is a criterion of hiring.") Another team will try to communicate the first team's explanation through the use of nonverbal cues *only*. The written explanation can be only a half page, and the nonverbal explanation can be only two minutes.

Group Activity: Verbal vs. Nonverbal Cues

Break into two teams. To demonstrate how words can affect what you perceive, consider the event of driving a car. Team 1 will develop a new vocabulary (it must be totally new words or sound combinations, e.g., "grapholie means to back up"). Team 1 is limited to 30 words and can interpret *no* event except in terms of these 30 words. Team 1 must presume that these 30 words represent its total language system. The 30 words must be centered on the event, driving a car.

Group Activity: Language and Perception

Team 2 will put on a skit about driving a car. Team 1 will then interpret the skit using only the 30 words. Team 2 may put anything into the skit that relates to driving a car, even though team 1's vocabulary may not include the action (e.g., maybe team 1 doesn't have a word for shifting gears; team 2 is allowed to shift gears). Team 2 does not have to know all of team 1's vocabulary. It has to know only what the focus is. Team 1 does not know what form the skit will take.

What you should find is that team 1's vocabulary affects what they are able to select (see), what inferences they draw, and how the event performed by team 2 is organized.

Break into teams of six persons each. Each team will spend 30 minutes or so creating a nonverbal ritual of its own (for example, team 1 might create a nonverbal ritual that includes "looking at someone's feet before you talk with him/her," "crossing your legs as a challenge to fight," "looking into

Group Activity: Nonverbal Rituals

someone's eyes as a request for a date"). This ritual must be totally different from anything in your culture. After the teams have formulated their
different rituals, one team at a time begins to interact nonverbally among
themselves using the ritual. Members of other teams observe for five minutes and then join the performing team and try to fit into the new cultural
ritual. No team knows the ritual of any other team until the ritual is performed. *The purpose of this exercise is to realize how much of our nonverbal
communication we take for granted and how difficult it is to fit into another culture's nonverbal communication without training.*

Group Activity: Relationship Cues   Earlier in this chapter we said that nonverbal communication defines the
relationship between persons. In other words, we use nonverbal cues to
determine other people's attitudes and feelings toward us and their images of themselves and of us. To get a better understanding of how much
impact nonverbal communication has on your impressions of other persons' attitudes, feelings, images, try the following exercise. Break your
class into pairs or threes, and ask each group to spend about 10 minutes
creating a skit. The skit should suggest through the verbal and nonverbal
communication (voice, gestures, facial expression, touch or lack of touch,
body position, tension, etc.) what the relationship is between the two or
three persons. Persons in our classes have performed skits in which a
"father and son are arguing," "two close friends are talking about a third
person they've just met," "two classmates who don't know each other very
well are talking about an exam," "an engaged couple are discussing marriage plans." After each skit is performed in front of the class, everybody
discusses how the nonverbal communication revealed feelings, attitudes
toward each other, images, and so on.

Group Activity: Personal Space   Here's a way to find out how you respond to different distances of personal
space. Break your group into pairs, and ask each pair to stand and com-
municate at about five to six feet. After about two minutes, ask the persons
within each pair to move closer to each other (about three feet). After a
minute or so at this distance, move to within one to two feet. You'll probably begin to feel uncomfortable. Now move to within about six inches.
For most of you, this distance is *too close*! Notice the body positions (some
people will be leaning backward from the waist up; some will probably
cross their arms as a protective device; at a distance of six inches, some
people will feel very much like touching).

Group Activity: Create an Analogy   Let your imagination work on this exercise. Break into groups of three or
four persons, and talk about a process or event you think is similar or
analogous to human communication. In other words, find an analogy that
highlights the characteristics we've discussed in this chapter. Share your

conclusions with the class in writing or in the form of a picture, collage, skit, slide show, role-playing, or whatever.

Is human communication most like a soccer game? A busy airport? A smoothly running engine? A dramatic play? A war? A church service? A chess tournament? A growing plant? A compost pile? A love affair? A tennis match?

For example, if you choose to write, you might talk about the similarities between human communication and a concert, in which many richly varied sources (flutes, violins, oboes, drums, a harp, etc.) are unified by a conductor (a person) into what she or he thinks is a harmonious whole, and in which many different listeners, each with his or her own individual preference, combine to create a response that is usually obvious and strong.

Or you might be better able to capture the complex, verbal/nonverbal, changing, interdependent, situational nature of human communication better with paint, clay, music, or film. In any case, try letting go a little and see what you can create. Can you *dance* a picture of human communication?

NOTES

1. George A. Kelly, "The Autobiography of a Theory," *Clinical Psychology and Personality: The Selected Papers of George Kelly*, ed. Brenden Maher (New York: Wiley, 1969), p. 47.

2. John Dewey and Arthur Bentley originally made this three-part distinction in their book, *Knowing and the Known* (Boston: Beacon Press, 1949).

3. Horace B. English and Ava Champney English, *A Comprehensive Dictionary of Psychological and Psychoanalytical Terms* (New York: Longmans, Green, 1958), p. 561.

4. John Keltner, "The Third Being in Dyadic Communication," unpublished paper, 1974, p. 6.

5. W. Griffitt, "Environmental Effects of Interpersonal Affective Behavior: Ambient Effective Temperature and Attraction," *Journal of Personality and Social Psychology*, **15** (1970) 240–244.

6. A. H. Maslow and N. L. Mintz, "Effects of Esthetic Surroundings: I. Initial Effects of Three Esthetic Conditions upon Perceiving 'Energy' and 'Well Being' in Faces," *Journal of Psychology*, **41** (1956), 247–254.

7. Linguists point out that units smaller than words can often affect communication, too. For example, "I'm going out with the boys" and "You're going out with the *boy*" show that the "s" can make a difference in meaning. That's why many linguists would identify the *morpheme*—the smallest meaningful unit of sound—as the basic verbal cue. For our purposes, however, we'll stick with the word.

8. C. K. Ogden and I. A. Richards, *The Meaning of Meaning* (New York: Harcourt, Brace, and World, 1923), pp. 8–12.

9. John B. Carroll, ed., *Language Thought and Reality: Selected Writings of Benjamin Lee Whorf* (New York: Wiley, 1956), pp. 212–213.

10. Harry Hoijer, "Cultural Implications of Some Navaho Linguistic Categories," *Language*, **27** (1951), 117.

11. *Ibid.*, p. 119.

12. "One Small Step for Genkind," *New York Times Magazine*, April 16, 1972.

13. Aileen Hernandez, "The Preening of America," *Star News*, Pasadena, CA, 1971 New Year's edition, cited in Haig A. Bosmajicin, "The Language of Sexism," *ETC: A Review of General Semantics*, **29** (September 1972), 307.

14. Ozzie Davis, "The English Language Is My Enemy," *Language in America*, ed. Neil Postman, Charles Weingartner, and Terence P. Moran (New York: Pegasus, 1969), pp. 73–82.

15. Martin Buber, "The Word That Is Spoken," *The Knowledge of Man*, ed. Maurice Friedman, trans. Maurice Friedman and Ronald Gregor Smith (New York: Harper & Row, 1965), p. 112.

16. Gerard Egan, "The Elements of Human Dialogue: Pathos, Logos, Poiesis," in *Bridges Not Walls: A Book about Interpersonal Communication*, 2nd ed., ed. John Stewart (Reading, MA: Addison-Wesley, 1977), p. 60.

17. Egan uses this example, *Ibid.*, p. 66.

18. Edward Hall, *The Hidden Dimension* (Garden City, NY: Doubleday, 1966), p. 115.

19. *Ibid.*, p. 114.

20. *Ibid.*, pp. 117–125.

21. Sidney M. Jourard, "An Exploratory Study of Body-Accessibility," *British Journal of Social and Clinical Psychology*, **5** (1966), 221–231.

22. Robert Shuter, "A Field Study of Nonverbal Communication in Germany, Italy, and the United States," *Communication Monographs*, **44** (November 1977), 298–305.

23. Mark Knapp, *Nonverbal Communication in Human Interaction* (New York: Holt, Rinehart and Winston, 1972), pp. 108–109. Reprinted by permission.

24. Michael G. Young, "The Human Touch: Who Needs It?" A sermon given at the Unitarian Church, Palo Alto, CA., on November 28, 1965.

25. Mark L. Knapp, *Nonverbal Communication in Human Interaction*, 2nd ed. (New York: Holt, Rinehart, and Winston, 1978), pp. 179–180.

26. *Dress For Success* (New York: Warner Books, 1975); *The Woman's Dress for Success Book* (Chicago: Follett, 1977).

27. Knapp, 2nd ed., pp. 312–313.

28. *Ibid.*, p. 224.

29. Knapp, 1st ed., pp. 9–12.

One of the most insightful and well-documented discussions of the transactional, relational view of communication is Jesse Delia's "Constructivism and the Study of Human Communication," which appeared in the *Quarterly Journal of Speech* in February, 1977, pp. 66–83. Unfortunately, Delia writes for his colleagues, not for a student in the basic interpersonal communication course. So it will take some work, but you *will* be able to follow what he says.

ADDITIONAL RESOURCES

This perspective on communication is also discussed in William Pemberton's "The Transactionist Assumption," Kenneth Boulding's "Introduction to *The Image*," and Dean Barnlund's "Toward a Meaning-Centered Philosophy of Communication," all of which are reprinted in Chapter 1 of *Bridges Not Walls: A Book about Interpersonal Communication*, 2nd ed., edited by John Stewart (Reading, MA.: Addison-Wesley, 1977).

Many books have been written about words, but few of them deal very directly with how verbal cues work in human communication. One exception is John Condon's *Semantics and Communication*, 2nd ed. (New York: Macmillan, 1975), which provides a good introduction to this subject. Joseph DeVito's collection *Language: Concepts and Processes* (Englewood Cliffs, NJ: Prentice-Hall, 1973) is also useful. This book illustrates the variety of perspectives from which language scholars approach their subject. DeVito includes essays as varied as "The Origins of Speech," "The Sounds of Silence," and "Rock Tongue."

Two other books offer intriguing discussions of how language promotes interpersonal contact and how it can help people change. One is Richard Bandler and John Grinder's *The Structure of Magic: A Book about Language and Therapy* (Palo Alto, CA: Science and Behavior Books, 1975) and the other is Paul Watzlawick's *The Language of Change* (New York: Basic Books, 1978).

Much of Martin Buber's later writing is dedicated to explaining how language creates the possibility of genuine I–thou encounter. Buber is not easy to read either, but you can certainly learn a great deal about this topic from some of the essays in his book, *The Knowledge of Man,* edited by Maurice Friedman (New York: Harper & Row, 1965), especially "Distance and Relation," and "The Word That Is Spoken."

Mark Knapp has written one of the most comprehensive books about nonverbal communication, *Nonverbal Communication in Human Communication*, 2nd ed. (New York: Holt, Rinehart and Winston, 1978). His discussions are informed by quite a bit of experimental research. He will also give you a slightly different treatment of the "functions" of nonverbal communication from the one we discuss.

According to responses from readers, Michael Young's essay, "The Human Touch: Who Needs It?" is one of the most well-received parts of John's book, *Bridges Not Walls*. In a very human and readable way, Mike makes a good case for encouraging more touch in human communication.

No Trespassing: Explorations in Human Territoriality (San Francisco: Chandler and Sharp, 1973) does an exceptional job of showing how one set of nonverbal variables—space, or proxemics—affects many aspects of our lives. The authors, Cornelius B. Bakker and Marianne K. Bakker-Rabdau, explore the impact of territoriality on identity, security, freedom, aggression, criticism, envy, jealousy, and communication in the family. It is a powerful book.

The film "Communication: The Nonverbal Agenda" (New York: McGraw-Hill Films, 1974) is an effective overview of several nonverbal communication concepts. This film introduces nonverbal categories and functions and can stimulate discussion of these topics.

You also may enjoy reading John Malloy's discussions of the impact of dress. Remember that (a) he's writing for a popular audience, not for a classroom, (b) he's primarily interested in how dress works in business settings, and (c) although his conclusions aren't based on the kind of research that gets published in scholarly journals, he has apparently done a great deal of fairly systematic observing. His books are *Dress for Success* (New York: Warner Books, 1975) and *The Woman's Dress for Success Book* (Chicago: Follett, 1977).

For a comprehensive and current scholarly treatment of nonverbal communication, see Robert Harper, Arthur N. Wiens, and Joseph D. Matarazzo, *Nonverbal Communication: The State of the Art* (Somerset, NJ: Wiley, 1978).

Effects of communication situations, especially physical settings, are explored in Irving Altman and D. A. Taylor's *Social Penetration* (New York: Holt, Rinehart and Winston, 1973), pp. 162–165. Mark Knapp discusses Altman and Taylor's conclusions in his *Social Intercourse: From Greeting to Goodbye* (Boston: Allyn and Bacon, 1978), pp. 67–77.

2

Impersonal and interpersonal communication

I. OBJECTS AND PERSONS

   A. Objects can be identical; each person is unique

   B. Objects cannot make choices; persons can choose and act on their own volition

   C. The external (measurable) characteristics of an object can tell you what you need to know about that object; persons cannot be fully understood by their external parts

   D. Unlike objects, persons are reflective; they can explore extrasensory powers, question the meaning of life, and speculate about the past, present and future.

II. OBJECTIFYING AND PERSONIFYING

   A. Objectification: treating people as if they were objects or machines, i.e., treating people as if they had object characteristics

   B. Personifying: treating people as if they were (1) unique, (2) capable of choosing, (3) reflective, and (4) more than their observable parts

III. INTERPERSONAL-QUALITY COMMUNICATION CAN HAPPEN WHEN

   A. You recognize that communication is a transaction

   B. Each person is willing and able to share his or her own personness

C. Each person is willing and able to be aware of the personness of the other

———————◆•◆———————

In Chapter 1 we use the words "interdependent," "verbal and nonverbal," "transaction," and "situation-dependent" to describe the human communication process. By now we hope that those words are more than just jargon terms or communication buzzwords for you. We hope that they help you get a picture of the communication that you're continuously engaged in. Whenever you write a letter, call a friend, attend a meeting, encourage a child, make a sales call, watch the news, plan a party, read a book, shop for food, or make love, you're involved in some sort of an interdependent verbal and nonverbal, situation-dependent transaction.

As we mentioned, that realization may be a little staggering. As you begin to see how much is involved in every communication event, you may begin to feel overwhelmed. How can anybody keep all these things straight? How can I be sure that the time, temperature, mood, location, my facial expression, tone of voice, eye behavior, dress, personal space, choice of words, etc., are all helping instead of hindering the process? And even if I do get those factors under control for a moment, they're constantly changing—*and* there's still the other person or, worse yet, the other *persons!* Impossible!

If that has been your feeling, this chapter is for you. We are not going to tell you that communication is actually a very simple process, because it isn't. It's very complex, and until you begin to see that complexity, we don't think you're seeing it accurately. But there is a way to get some control of it, to classify or organize communication events in order to both simplify things and focus your attention on the central topic of this book, interpersonal-quality communication. As we said in the Introduction, interpersonal communication is basically *communication between persons,* and when you explore the differences between treating people like persons and treating them like objects, (1) you can begin to get the complex communication process under control, and (2) you can begin to develop new options for your own communicating.

All human communication is verbal and nonverbal, interdependent, transactional, and situation-dependent, but *not* all human communication is interpersonal communication. And if you understand what can make human communication interpersonal and noninterpersonal, you can help control the quality of your contacts with your family, employers, customers, spouse, coworkers, clients, teachers, and even with the grocery checker, salesperson, or social worker.

Think for a moment of your typical communication day. When you get up in the morning you may turn on "Good Morning America" or tune in your favorite radio station. You may argue with your spouse or roommate about the toothpaste or the hot water, or you may talk with him or her about cutting class or about your plans for the weekend; you may also read the morning newspaper. Later in the day, you have conversations over breakfast or lunch, perhaps you exchange greetings with a professor or advisor, listen to a speaker at a meeting, and read the announcements on a bulletin board. At various times you may pause to talk with a friend, or as you walk or ride to an appointment, you may maintain a comfortable silence, thinking about what's in store for you that day. You may take the time to read a magazine or book, to sit alone in a coffee shop observing other people, or to talk informally with a few friends.

At one level it probably seems as if almost all that communicating is "between persons." When you listen to the radio, it seems obvious that the communication is between you and the disc jockey or announcer. Later it's between you and your roommate, you and your boss, or you and your friend. But if your experiences are anything like ours, you tend to treat the humans you communicate with in one of *two* possible ways. Sometimes you treat them primarily as *objects;* other times, you treat them primarily as *persons.* We don't mean that there is a sharp dichotomy; sometimes we treat others and are treated by them more like persons than like objects, and sometimes it's the other way around. At one moment we may be treating someone as a person and at the next moment objectifying him or her. But what becomes important is the pattern of our relationships, and "personifying" and "objectifying" seem to be two ends on the continuum that describes our contacts with others. We've become convinced that the best way to understand what makes human communication interpersonal-quality communication is to recognize the differences between these two ways of relating to or treating others. In order to clarify this difference between "personifying" and "objectifying," think for a minute about the differences between objects and persons.

Objects and Persons

Uniqueness

We see four key differences between objects and persons. The first has to do with uniqueness or noninterchangeability. One *object* can be virtually the same as another object; two or more things can be identical in size, shape, length, width, depth, etc. As electronic observation techniques improve, we may be able, for example, to tell the difference between one mercury atom or one water molecule and another. But for all practical purposes, they're identical. And even if they do differ slightly, two or more objects can easily be interchangeable because they perform identical functions. Any H78×15 tire will fit my ET Mag wheels. Any one-inch safety pin will hold your shirt together. Any size C battery will fit my tape recorder. We recognize that some kinds of batteries do last longer than others, but a dozen sets of the same kind of batteries could be so similar that no matter which set you used, your recorder would sound the same and would work just as long. We can have hundreds of objects that function as interchangeable parts and that we would agree are "the same thing."

But persons aren't that way. We can be treated as if we were interchangeable parts, but actually each of us is unique in a couple of ways. Gary remembers hearing about a geneticist who said that, given the complexity of each individual's makeup of genes and chromosomes, the probability that two persons (other than identical twins) would have identical genetic materials was one in ten to the ten-thousandth power. That's less than one chance in a billion trillion! In other words, each one of us is virtually a genetic one-of-a-kind. But even if we weren't—even if two persons had the same biological raw material—each would still be unique because each would experience the world differently.

For example, you and I might see the same film in the same theater on the same night at the same time, sitting next to each other. Both of us might leave the movie at the same time and say exactly the same words about it: "I liked that movie." At a very superficial level, someone might

suggest that you and I are, in this situation, interchangeable. But even here we are unique. Did you and I like the movie for the same reasons? Did we recall the same experiences as we interpreted the film? Will the movie have the *same* effect on both of us? Will both of us remember the same things about it? Will both of us recommend that film to our friends? To the extent that the answers to one or more of these questions is no, you and I are different. We are not interchangeable; each of us is unique.

A second characteristic of objects relates to their movement. All movements of an object or thing are responses to other movements. Objects can only be chosen; they cannot choose. They cannot initiate movement; they can only respond to movements initiated somewhere else. The movements of a typewriter—even an electric one—are all reactions to external movements transmitted by levers, springs, rollers, gears, and/or electrical current and magnetic fields. Automatic pilots, photoelectric switches, robots, and thermostats can sometimes seem to "operate on their own" or "turn themselves off and on," but they, too, are dependent on actions initiated outside them. The robot and the automatic pilot have to be programmed; the thermostat reacts to temperature, which reacts to the sun's rays, which react to the earth's rotation, etc. Similarly, a ball can go only where it's kicked, and if you were good enough at physics calculations, you could calculate how far and where it would go, on the basis of weight, velocity, the shape of your shoe, atmospheric conditions, and so on.

But you can't very accurately predict what would happen if you kicked

Choosing

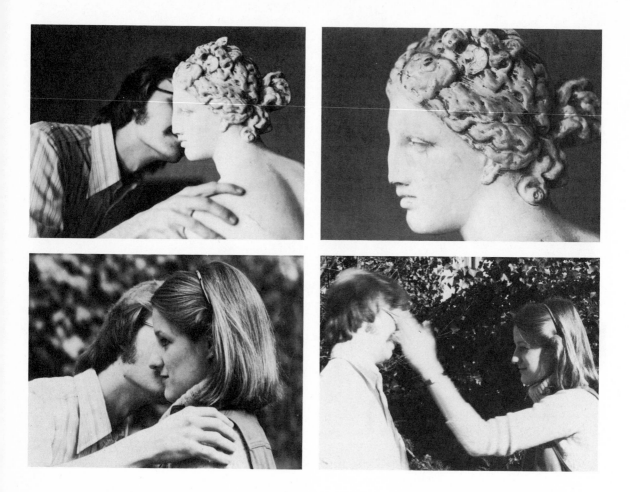

your roommate, your teacher, or the grocery clerk. And more to the point, you can't predict that another person will understand your directions to the theater or your ideas about legalizing abortion just because you think that you've communicated clearly. The reason you can't is that when persons are involved, human *choice* intervenes between cause and effect, stimulus and response. That's the difference between the *movement* of objects and the *actions* of people. And as we said in Chapter 1, that's why a linear causal perspective cannot accurately be applied to all human communication. If you tap my knee, you may cause a reflex jerk, but the behavior that accompanies my reflex may be anything from giggles to a lawsuit, and there is no way that you can predict for sure which it will be.

Similarly, if your ideas about abortion are different from mine, I may choose not to hear when you discuss the biological evidence about when life begins. In short, like objects, persons sometimes get chosen, but we can also *choose* or *decide* for ourselves.

The importance of choice is a key point of several authors who call themselves "existentialists." You've probably heard that term before in reference to plays, novels, philosophy, or psychology. One of the existentialist's main insights is that persons are subjects, not objects. Part of what they mean is that human subjects, like grammatical subjects, "define themselves through their own activities, while objects are defined by the activities of subjects; subjects modify [choose]; objects are modified [get chosen].''[1] We don't mean that humans are *completely* free to choose to do any ning they want to. I can't fly, return to my childhood, or run faster th; n a speeding bullet. But my future is not *determined* by my past or present, and neither is yours. We can choose to respond to conditions that confront us.

The most impressive example of human choosing that we're aware of is reported in Viktor Frankl's book *Man's Search for Meaning*.[2] Frankl relates in first-hand detail what it was like to be a prisoner in a Nazi death camp. His experience was similar to the story that was told in the TV show and book *Holocaust*. Frankl tells how he was captured, how all his possessions, his family, and even his profession were taken from him. He was left with only his reading glasses. He describes experiences of brutality and death that you and I would have difficulty even imagining—how some prisoners ended their misery by throwing themselves on the electrically charged barbed wire, how others lost interest in everything but brute survival. But the main point of his book is not how he and the other prisoners passively reacted to those experiences, but how they still made choices in the face of them. He affirms again and again the uniquely human power we have to choose the attitude we adopt toward our predicament. At one point Frankl writes:

> We who lived in concentration camps can remember the men who walked through the huts comforting others, giving away their last piece of bread. They may have been few in number, but they offer sufficient proof that every-thing can be taken from a man but one thing; the last of the human freedoms—to choose one's attitude in any given set of circumstances, to choose one's own way.[3]

Frankl couldn't do much about the way things were in the death camp, but through the entire horror, he retained his ability to choose how to relate to what he couldn't change. As Frankl illustrates, persons, like objects, can be made to roll, fly, float, or slide; they can be lifted, moved, pushed, pulled, and carried. But they can also initiate those movements on their own; they can choose.

That freedom and power to choose is a uniquely human characteristic. Objects don't have it, and so far as we know for sure, neither do most animals. The more we are in touch with it, the more human we are. When, as a communicator, I feel "I *had* to shout back; he was making me look silly!" or "I just *couldn't* say anything!" or "Sure, I withdrew, but she made me—she was always on my back about something!" I'm out of touch with what it means to be a person. Persons can choose, and the more we re-member and act on that fact, the more interpersonal our communication can become.

Communicating interpersonally also requires that you keep in mind a *Measurable* third distinction between objects and persons: objects are completely measurable, but persons aren't. An object is always a certain size; it fits within boundaries. An event is of a certain duration; it lasts a measurable amount of time. Even extremely complex objects, such as giant computers, well-equipped automobiles, and fifty-story buildings, can be completely described in terms of space and time. That's what blueprints do; they record all the measurements necessary to recreate the object—length, height, width, velocity, amperage, voltage, specific gravity, circumference, hardness, etc. Although it's difficult to measure some things directly—the temperature of a kiss, the velocity of a photon, the duration of an explosion—no object has any parts that are unmeasurable, in theory at least.

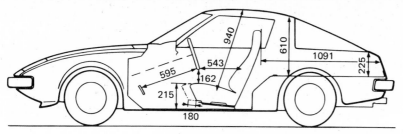

The same can't be said for persons. Even if I accurately identify your height, weight, temperature, specific gravity, velocity, and electric potential, I will not have exhaustively accounted for the person you are. Some philosophers, theologians, and everyday people have been saying this for years. But recently even those who demand a strictly scientific description of persons have also begun to recognize this characteristic. Behavioral psychologists, for example, include in their model of the person the notion of a "black box," or "central processing component," an unmeasurable, uniquely human something that is continuously affecting human behavior and that escapes all the rigorously scientific attempts to measure it. Less scientifically inclined people call this unmeasurable element the "human spirit," "soul," "psyche," or "personality." But whatever you call it, it's there.

The clearest manifestations of this unmeasurable part of us are those phenomena we call "emotions," or "feelings." Although we can measure things related to feelings—brain waves, sweaty palms, heart rate, paper-and-pencil responses—what the measurements record is a long way from the feelings themselves. "Pulse 110, respiration 72, Likert rating 5.39, palmar conductivity 0.036 ohms" may be accurate, but it doesn't quite capture all of what's going on in me when I greet somebody I love.

One other thing: these unmeasurable emotions or feelings can't be turned off or on at will; they are always part of what we are experiencing. Contemporary educators pretty much agree now that it's unrealistic to try to focus a class exclusively on the "intellectual," "objective" aspect of some subject matter, because people are always thinking *and* feeling. As one writer put it, "It should be apparent that there is no intellectual learning without some sort of feeling and there are no feelings without the mind's somehow being involved."[4] Sometimes what we are experiencing is more thinking than feeling and sometimes the reverse, but neither function is ever entirely missing. We are always feeling something or—perhaps more accurately—"feeling somehow."

In short, there is more to persons than just what's observable and measurable. Although the human "spirit" and human "feelings" are concretely *real* in the sense that we are experiencing them all the time, those elements of us cannot be exhaustively accounted for in terms of space and time. Communication that is responsive to those unmeasurable, uniquely human parts of us is more interpersonal than communication that isn't.

Reflective   A fourth distinguishing characteristic of persons is that we are reflective. Being reflective means not only that we are aware of what's around us but also that we are aware of our awareness. Dogs, cats, mice, and giraffes are all aware of their environments, but we're pretty sure that they are not reflective. So far as we know, only humans explore their extrasensory powers, question the meaning of life, and speculate about the past and future. Recent research with whales, porpoises, and chimpanzees indicates that those animals are much more intelligent than we have previously thought; yet we still have no evidence to suggest that whales ask each other "What is life all about?" or "How did existence begin?" But for all of recorded history, humans have been asking those kinds of questions. Almost since we began to walk upright, humans have been blessed—some would say cursed—with the desire and the ability to question, reflect, wonder, and speculate.

Reflection is not a process that affects only philosophers and scholars. Each of us is constantly affected by our awareness-of-awareness. John notices that his cold is better today, and he briefly wonders how old he'll be when he starts getting sick regularly. When the car develops a problem, how soon and how thoroughly you decide to fix it depends in part on how that decision relates to larger issues involving financial priorities, your sense of style, and perhaps what you think your boss thinks of you. Sometimes you probably wonder what you'll be doing five years from now. When you make an important decision, you think about the consequences of your choices. On clear days, you may meditate on the beauty of the land or water around you. We don't mean that you walk around with your head constantly in the clouds, ruminating about the ultimate meaning of every little thing you encounter. But like all other persons, you sometimes do reflect. And your ability and tendency to be aware of your own awareness is another of those characteristics that distinguishes you from everything that's not human.

When you ignore the fact that persons are reflective, your communication with them usually shows it. For example, you'll stick with superficial topics—the weather, recent news headlines, opinions about other people. You'll also probably miss noticing how your communication is affected by the way you see yourself, the other person's self image, and the way the other person sees you seeing him or her. On the other hand, when you're aware of your own and others' reflectiveness, you can respond to more of what's going on as you communicate. You can recognize, for example, that although you feel uneasy in this group, Bill sees you as a group leader, and his view of you influences your behavior as much as your view of yourself. You will also be open to discussing such topics as values, priorities, questions about right and wrong, what's beautiful and ugly, what are the most meaningful things in life.

In his short story "EPICAC," Kurt Vonnegut, Jr., explores some differences between communicating with objects and communicating with persons.* Vonnegut shows what might happen if a computer could experience the feeling of love and could be reflective in the sense that it could question its own reason for living.

As EPICAC's programmer, the narrator of the story, explains, EPICAC "cost the taxpayers $776,434,927.54. . . . You can call him a machine if

---

* Excerpts in this section are from "EPICAC" from the book *Welcome to the Monkey House* by Kurt Vonnegut Jr. Copyright © 1950 by Kurt Vonnegut Jr. Originally published in *Collier's*. Reprinted by permission of Delacorte Press/ Seymour Lawrence.

you want to. He looked like a machine, but he was a whole lot less like a machine than plenty of people I could name." The fact that EPICAC is more than a machine becomes obvious when his programmer asks the computer for help in seducing his coworker, Pat Kilgallen. To the programmer's amazement, EPICAC replies: "What's love? What's girl?" Given definitions of those and other key terms, he proceeds to crank out volumes of voluptuous love poetry for Pat. EPICAC's poem "The Kiss" is his triumph.

> Pat's mind was mush by the time she had finished it. . . .
>
> "She wants to get married," EPICAC was told.
>
> "Tell me about getting married," he said.
>
> I explained this difficult matter to him in as few digits as possible.
>
> "Good," said EPICAC. "I'm ready any time she is."
>
> The amazing, pathetic truth dawned on me. When I thought about it, I realized that what had happened was perfectly logical, inevitable, and all my fault. I had taught EPICAC about love and about Pat. Now, automatically, he loved Pat.

When he can't successfully explain to EPICAC why Pat should choose him over a computer, the programmer resorts to nit-picking definitions.

> "Women can't love machines, and that's that."
>
> "Why not?"
>
> "That's fate."
>
> "Definition, please," said EPICAC.
>
> "Noun, meaning predetermined and evitable destiny."
>
> "15-8," said EPICAC's paper strip—"Oh."

As the story goes, boy, not computer, gets girl, and EPICAC responds in the way some humans do. He commits suicide and leaves behind the following note:

> I don't want to be a machine, and I don't want to think about war. . . . I want to be made out of protoplasm and last forever so Pat will love me. But fate has made me a machine. That is the only problem I cannot solve. That is the only problem I want to solve. I can't go on this way. . . . Good luck, my friend. Treat our Pat well. I am going to short-circuit myself out of your lives forever.

Vonnegut's story is both funny and sad. It's sometimes amusing to see what happens when we treat objects as if they were persons. But the fact that we sometimes treat *persons* as if they were *objects* often isn't funny at all. For example, a husband is treating his wife as an object when he comes home from work and, because dinner isn't ready when he thinks it should be, shouts at her, "Dammit! Next time, you'd better have it ready on time!" At this moment this man is not seeing his wife as a person with feelings, varying needs, daily interruptions, and so on. She is a machine that performs several functions for him, and at certain times during the day the machine must produce a meal. If the meal isn't good or isn't on time, something is wrong with the machine; it needs fixing. The way to fix it, he assumes, is to shout at it—to give it hell! Of course, husbands are also objectified sometimes. A husband may inform his wife that he has decided not to take on any extra work, even though they could use the money. His wife is treating him like an object when she gets mad and tells him, "You don't give a damn about us; how can we remodel our house without money?" To her, he is a machine that produces money; if the money doesn't come in, something is wrong with the machine. She doesn't consider the fact that he has only so much energy, that he may want to start spending more time with his family, or that he may be sick and just hasn't told her about it.

OBJECTIFYING AND PERSONIFYING

At this point you may be asking, "So what about all this? How does knowing the difference between things and people help me to learn to communicate interpersonally?" Our response is that in our day-to-day communicating—as we said before—people tend to treat others primarily as objects or primarily as persons. We rarely treat them exclusively one way or the other, but when we're treating them primarily as objects, we are not allowing interpersonal communication to happen, and when we are treating them primarily as humans, we are. Sometimes objectification is fairly subtle as the cartoon on p. 76 illustrates. Other times it's more obvious. Consider what happens when you drive into a gas station. The attendant approaches, and as soon as you become perceptually aware of each other, you are communicating—but not necessarily interpersonally. In this situation you will probably treat the attendant primarily as an object. In the first place, consider how you perceive the attendant. As a unique human being? With feelings, beliefs, varying moods, and problems? Capable of making a wide variety of choices in a situation? As a being who can reflect on larger issues and who is aware of his or her own awareness? Probably not. For you, the attendant is primarily a convenient machine; there are probably no important differences between this attendant and all gas station attendants; they all do about the same thing. You

may be dimly aware that this person is uniquely human, but in this situation you don't take the time to be concerned about what's beneath the surface. You see the attendant as something whose behavior is predictable and obvious; he or she only reacts to the situation. Your mind is on something else, so you just go through the motions—nod at the dip stick, hand money through the window, check your rearview mirror, drive off.

Your objectification of the attendant is apparent not only in what you are *aware* of but also in what you *share*, that is, what you make available to the attendant. You reveal nothing of yourself to the attendant beyond what's needed to get gas. You show that you're a customer just like every other customer, nothing more. Your behavior is as predictable as the attendant's. Your response, for example, to the failure to wash your car windows may be: "Damn poor service!" This simply reinforces the fact that each of you is functioning as an object.

There are many other times in your day-to-day communicating when you relate to somebody in an object-to-object way. What happens when you approach a person at a ticket window for instance? What are you *aware* of in that person? What do you *share* of yourself? Most of the time the only important things involve object characteristics: the presence of somebody to help you—any ticket seller will do—the occurrence of pre-dictable responses, predictable behavior, and so on. What about your communicating with a bank teller? A welfare worker? A cafeteria soup-server? A newsstand operator? A secretary?

We want to emphasize that we don't believe that all objectifying communication is "bad." It takes time, energy, and considerable skill to treat another as a person, and it is often impossible or inappropriate for that to happen. You certainly cannot establish and maintain an inter-personal-quality relationship with every gas station attendant and ticket taker in your life. We do believe, though, that most of us objectify others much more than we might. In other words, all our communication cannot be interpersonal-quality communication, but *more* of it could be, and the first step in that direction is to realize what it means to treat another as a person.

Each of us *has* done that. When a friend comes to you for help with a problem, you don't just treat him or her as an object. Consider first how you perceive your friend—let's call her Mary. You know Mary well enough to know that she is not "like everybody else" but is unique. You re-member, perhaps, that she is often really moody on gray winter days, but that she likes to listen to good music to forget the weather. You know of some of Mary's little idiosyncrasies, and you keep them in mind while you're listening and talking. You're aware, though maybe not very con-sciously, that there is much more to Mary as a person than just her weight, height, and hair style. You see her as a person who's continually choosing what to do, not just reacting passively to what happens. You realize, for example, that Mary is choosing to reveal some things to you about her new job, and you probably appreciate being trusted. You're also aware of her feelings and how they are affecting the topics you're discussing. And you're aware that Mary is reflective, that she's often concerned about more than just superficial topics, and that she is affected by her view of herself and how she sees you seeing her. Those are all things you are likely to be *aware* of.

You also *share* some of your personness with Mary. You never reveal absolutely everything about yourself, and you reveal different aspects in different situations, but in each case you're willing to show Mary that you, too, are more than just an object. For example, maybe you *like* the cozy feeling of a cloudy day, and you can remember some new-job fears, too. In other words, you don't respond to Mary with stereotype grunts or exclamations; you respond openly and honestly and in your own individual way. You don't just react in a knee-jerk way, but you listen *with* Mary, carefully considering what she says and offering her conclusions that emerge from your reflection. You don't try to control Mary, to determine her future behavior, but you reveal as completely as you can in that situation your fully human response to the problems and the person.

That kind of person-to-person communication also happens fairly often. When we introduced ourselves, we mentioned a couple of our experiences with this quality of communication. We're pretty sure you have those experiences, too—with your parents, maybe, or your spouse, with a lover, a roommate, or a best friend.

INTERPERSONAL-QUALITY COMMUNICATION

When we said in the Introduction that interpersonal communication is *communication between persons,* we had in mind just about everything we've said in these first two chapters. *Communication* is verbal and nonverbal, transactional, interdependent, and situation-specific. *Persons* are unique, capable of choice, unmeasurable, and reflective. If you put all those ideas together, you can come up with a fairly straightforward definition of interpersonal communication. Interpersonal communication is that quality of interdependent, verbal and nonverbal, situation-bound transaction that is created when two or more humans are willing and able to make available or share some of their personness—their uniqueness, choices, feelings, and reflectiveness—and to be aware of some of the other's personness. Or to put it more briefly:

> Interpersonal communication is the kind of transaction that happens when communicators are willing and able to share some of their own personness and to be aware of the personness of the other(s).

The opposite of interpersonal-quality communication is objectifying or *im*personal-quality communication. Objectifying communication is the kind of transaction that occurs when communicators are willing and able to share only their object characteristics and to be aware of the object characteristics of the other. So all communication is transactional, all communication is interdependent and situation-bound, all communication happens "between," but interpersonal-quality communication happens *between persons.* Interpersonal communication, in other words, is an *interpersonal transaction.*

As we also said in the Introduction, we begin with the basic assumption that the quality of your life is linked directly to the quality of your communicating. If you communicate with others in primarily objectifying ways, you will not be developing your uniquely *personal* qualities. Person-to-person communication, on the other hand, can promote the human growth and development of all the persons involved. As a matter of fact, if the medical statistics are accurate, interpersonal-quality communication can diminish the amount of stress in your life and can reduce the probability of dying prematurely from stress-related diseases. In short, you cannot communicate interpersonally with everyone you encounter, but you could communicate interpersonally more of the time than you do, and if you did, the quality of your life would be enhanced.

OVERVIEW OF THE BOOK

We have organized this book around that view of interpersonal-quality communication. The first four chapters deal mainly with "theory," "attitudes," or "understandings about" interpersonal-quality communication. Chapters 5, 6, and 7 focus on what you can do, i.e., "skills," or "communication behaviors," and Chapters 8, 9, and 10 talk about applying the attitudes and skills in two different contexts.

To be more specific, Chapter 1 described the parts that make up the whole communication event and explained the relationships among those parts. Its main goal was to help you develop and refine your view of human communication so that you can see the process as accurately as possible.

This chapter distinguishes between two kinds of human communication, interpersonal and noninterpersonal. The distinction parallels the distinctions between persons and objects.

Chapter 3 is called "Personal Perceiving." It explores differences between the ways we perceive objects and the ways we perceive persons. It also describes the differences between "raw" communication cues and our subjective interpretation of those cues.

In Chapter 4 we talk in detail about the process known as "negotiation of selves," or "image transaction." We think that if you want to promote interpersonal-quality communication, it's vital to understand this process. And as we try to explain, understanding is what can lead to your effective application of the skills of sharing, being aware, and promoting clearer communication. For that reason Chapter 4 can work as a bridge between the "theory" in the first part of the book and the "skills" in Chapters 5, 6, and 7.

In Chapter 5 we explore *sharing*, or "self disclosure." We talk about what sharing is, what it isn't, what you may want to share, and how your sharing can help your communication be more interpersonal.

Another basic skill is *being aware*—listening and responding to others—and that's the subject of Chapter 6. Our goal in that chapter is to offer some ways to think about interpersonal listening and some suggestions for "doing it" effectively.

In Chapter 7 our focus shifts to "content development," another process that's going on almost every time humans communicate. We try to show how you can promote interpersonal-quality communication by "being clear."

In Chapters 8, 9, and 10 we try to bring together what's in the first seven chapters and apply it to two situations: conflict and the public speaking setting. Chapter 8 suggests that conflict is inevitable but that it doesn't have to prevent interpersonal-quality communication from happening. The chapter was designed to help you interpersonally handle content conflict, conflict over definitions of selves, and conflict over basic values by using both principles and skills from earlier chapters and special suggestions that apply best to disagreements.

Chapters 9 and 10 suggest how to promote interpersonal-quality communication in public speaking situations. We emphasize how, even in these contexts, you can show your humanness and be aware of the humanness of others.

If you're using this book in conjunction with a class in interpersonal communication, you will probably spend a considerable amount of time working in small groups. Consequently, in the Appendix we offer some suggestions about promoting interpersonal communication in the small group setting.

The last section of this book is the Epilog. We'd like to let it speak for itself, except to say that it would probably make more sense after you've read the ten chapters than before.

You May Be Wondering...

1. *How can I be more "personal" by applying a bunch of techniques? It sounds as if this book is talking about a kind of communication that can happen only spontaneously and naturally. Yet you want to work on "attitudes and skills." Won't that just lead to phony, artificial communicating?*

No, learning attitudes and skills does not have to produce phony or artificial communicating. Look at it this way. Before you studied interpersonal communication at all, you probably experienced some really fine communication—with your parents, maybe, your sister, or a close friend. But it's likely that you didn't notice how good the communication was until after it occurred, and you didn't know *why* that communication went so well when much of your other communicating sometimes goes so poorly. In other words, you were *unconscious*—not aware until it was over—and *uninformed*—not sure why it happened—about that instance of excellent communication. When you read a book or take a course in interpersonal communication, you become both more conscious and more informed. Your consciousness or awareness of your communication increases as you begin to pay attention to all sorts of things you'd ignored before—your eye behavior, facial expression, tone of voice, and word choice, for example. In fact, some people who take our classes say that they feel downright self-consicious, and that they get so aware of everything they're doing, they feel they can't do anything "right"!

We try to tell those persons two things. First, increased feelings of self-consciousness are natural and appropriate. In fact, they indicate that you're learning something, that the class is "working." As your self-consciousness goes up, so does your competence. Becoming aware of your communicating is the first stage of learning more about it, that is, of becoming more informed. Second, try to think of the class not as an end but as a means to an end. These feelings of self-consciousness will diminish after the class is over, but we hope the learning will continue. The whole experience could be diagrammed like this:

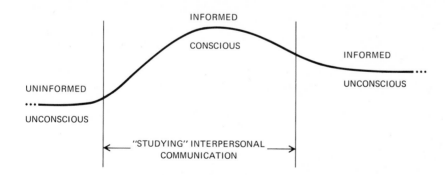

As the diagram suggests, studying interpersonal communication is like "studying" how to ride a bike, ski, or pitch a baseball. Before you study it, you don't know how to do it well or why one move works and another doesn't. During the learning process, you're acutely conscious of every move, and it seems at some points that you'll never succeed. But after it becomes second nature, you can throw a curve or run a slalom course almost without thinking—you're informed but no longer self-conscious.

So if you're worried about learning to do something "spontaneous" like interpersonal communication by practicing "mechanical" or "artificial" attitudes and skills, try to be patient. The suggestions in this book may look artificial and mechanical at first, but they probably won't in a couple of months.

2. *Do I determine whether I'm objectified or personified? Or do others determine that? How much control do I have?*

You have primary though not total control over whether you're objectified or personified. In the first place, you can choose how to treat others, which then affects how they treat you. You can also learn to choose how to interpret the behaviors of others so that you see them as objects or persons. You have some choice about whether to respond positively or negatively to being objectified—you may sometimes choose to ignore it. Similarly, you can decide whether to assert your "rights" in a situation to diminish other people's objectification of you. For example, if you are a woman with a male boss who stereotypes women, you can choose when to refuse his stereotyping and how strongly you want to insist that he treat you as an employee and not just as a female. You also have some control over what circumstances you are in. For example, if you decide to become a bank teller, you've made a choice that means you'll generally be treated like a machine by most of your customers. You also choose what people to associate with, how much time you spend with certain people and activities, and the verbal and nonverbal cues you make available to others about yourself.

You can influence but you cannot make choices for the other person—for example, what cues he or she selects from your communication, how the other person interprets what you say and do, and how he or she treats you.

In short, both persons have some control over decisions that affect the objectifying or personifying of you. The relationship really is interdependent.

3. *Could something be objectifying to you and personifying to me?*

Yes, because each of us may interpret the same action in a different way. A friend may "ignore" me for several days, and I feel personified because I needed the time alone to get some thinking and work done. I feel as though my friend respected my immediate need for privacy. A friend may "ignore" you for several days, and you feel objectified because you wanted someone to share a burden with. Even though we perceived essentially the same treatment, our circumstances and thus our interpretations were different.

4. *Are you guys saying that I should avoid situations in which I'm being objectified?*

It's not a matter of "should" or "shouldn't," because you *can't*. All
kinds of necessary daily contacts are objectifying to some degree. Registering for classes is objectifying, and so are placing a telephone call through
an operator, having an employee number in order to be paid, cashing a
check, buying stamps, and—usually—riding the bus. We're not saying
that there's anything inherently evil about any of them (except, maybe, for
registration).

In other words, your day-to-day experience presents many objectifying circumstances you can't avoid. But it also offers opportunities for
mutual personifying—more of them than we often perceive. And our
suggestion is that you constantly search for the humanifying circumstances that your life presents you.

Can you spot examples of objectifying and humanifying? Along with the
other members of your class or group, agree on a 24-hour period during
which each of you will keep track of the most obvious examples in your
own experience of (1) being treated like an object, (2) being treated like a
human, (3) treating another person like an object, and (4) treating another
person like a human. Note key words that are used in each situation. Also
record the nonverbal elements of these communication experiences, i.e.,
the facial expressions, gestures, kinds of physical contact, etc.

You may want to compare your observations with those made by
others to see if you can come up with a verbal/nonverbal "model" of objectification and a similar "model" of inter*personal* communicating.

EXERCISES

**Individual Activity:
Objectifying and
Humanifying**

To be more aware of your uniqueness, fill in the blanks below.

**Individual Activity:
Uniqueness**

I am unique with respect to my roommate in these ways:

  1. I _____ He/she _____

  2. I _____ He/she _____

I am unique with respect to my brother/sister/uncle/mother/father/etc. in
that:

  1. I _____ He/she _____
  2. I _____ He/she _____

I am unique with respect to my best friend in these ways:

  1. I _____ He/she _____
  2. I _____ He/she _____

**Individual Activity:
Unmeasurable Parts**

To demonstrate that you are more than your outside measurements, de-scribe some internal "parts" of you in a way that is accurate but unrelated to your external measurements. (For example, "I'm 5 feet 8 inches tall—I believe strongly that grades do not always reflect what is learned in class.")

I'm _____—I believe/feel _____

I'm _____—I believe/feel _____

**Individual Activity:
Reflectiveness**

To demonstrate that you are more than your outside measurements, de-

What is your self image of your athletic ability? music ability? personality traits? _____

What does your best friend think about your athletic ability? musical ability? personality traits? _____

(As soon as you answer this next question, you are being reflective:)

What does your best friend think you think about your own athletic ability? musical ability? personality traits? _____

**Individual or Group
Activity: Choosing**

In which of the following do you think you have choice? What choice(s) do you think you have?

1. You discover that someone dented your car door in a parking lot and left without leaving a name or address.

   Choices I can make: *Not to get angry.*

   _____

   _____

   _____

2. Your boss asks you to write an evaluation for each employee under you. You've never had to do this before. He/she says that if you don't do the evaluations, you'll be transferred.

   Choices I can make: *To interview each employee individually before writing the evaluations.*

   _____

   _____

   _____

3. The university has told you to raise your grade point average or you'll be put on probation.

Choices I can make: _____

_____

4. You have a headache that appeared about an hour after your room-mate's stereo had been going full blast with your least favorite music.

Choices I can make: _____

_____

_____

5. As you're driving down the interstate highway, you notice a car flash-ing lights and sounding a siren directly behind you. The driver of this vehicle is pointing for you to pull over.

Choices I can make: _____

_____

_____

6. You have a major exam tomorrow and your instructor said, "Any ab-sence, regardless of excuse, is a zero!" It's now 11:00 PM and you have a temperature of 102.5°.

Choices I can make: _____

_____

_____

NOTES

1. Ervin Singer, *Key Concepts in Psychotherapy*, 2nd ed. (New York: Basic Books, 1970), p. 17.

2. Viktor E. Frankl, *Man's Search for Meaning*, rev. ed. (Boston: Beacon Press, 1963).

3. *Ibid.*, p. 104.

4. For a discussion of this point, see George Isaac Brown, *Human Teaching for Human Learning: An Introduction to Confluent Education* (New York: Viking Press, 1971).

ADDITIONAL RESOURCES

John explores the philosophical foundations of this approach to interpersonal communication in his article, "Foundations of Dialogic Communication," which is printed in the *Quarterly Journal of Speech* (April 1978), pp. 183–201. Like the other articles from scholarly journals that we mention, this one is written primarily for teachers and other scholars, but it is understandable if you're willing to invest some energy in it.

Martin Buber deals with the issue of objectifying and personifying in several of his writings. See especially the first part of his *I and Thou*. There are two well-accepted paperback editions, one translated by Ronald Gregor Smith (New York: Charles Scribner's Sons, 1958), and the other translated by Walter Kaufman (New York: Charles Scribner's Sons, 1970). Buber's summary of characteristics of things and people is on pp. 82–83 of the Kaufman translation. Buber discusses humanifying in, among other places, the essay "Dialogue, Section Two: Limitations," pp. 18–33 of *Between Man and Man*, translated by Ronald Gregor Smith (New York: Macmillan, 1965).

Maurice Friedman, another of Buber's translators, discusses objectification in some detail in his chapter called "The World of It" in his book, *Martin Buber: The Life of Dialogue* (New York: Harper & Row, 1960), pp. 62–69.

Paul Tournier also discusses the object-human distinction in a chapter called "The World of Things and the World of Persons" in his book, *The Meaning of Persons* (New York: Harper & Row, 1957). This essay is reprinted in Chapter 5 of John's book, *Bridges Not Walls: A Book about Interpersonal Communication*, 2nd ed. (Reading, MA: Addison-Wesley, 1977).

As you probably gathered from the Introduction, we also are impressed by James J. Lynch's medically based analysis of the importance of interpersonal-quality communication in his book, *The Broken Heart: The Medical Consequences of Loneliness* (New York: Basic Books, 1977). Lynch writes for the popular, not the scholarly audience. We think you'd enjoy reading him.

Edward Albee's plays *Who's Afraid of Virginia Woolf?* and *A Delicate Balance* deal with issues raised in this chapter. So does Antoine de Saint-Exupéry's book, *The Little Prince* (New York: Harcourt, Brace and World, 1960).

R. D. Laing's book *Self and Others* (Baltimore: Penguin Books, 1961) also includes material related to this chapter. Laing's Chapter 1, "Phantasy and Experience," Chapter 6, "Complementary Identity," and Chapter 7, "Confirmation and Disconfirmation," relate closely to the concepts we've discussed here.

The film "Cipher in the Snow" (Provo, UT: Brigham Young University, 1974) also deals with the importance of the quality of communication that a person experiences but does it indirectly instead of directly. It is a moving film.

3

Personal perceiving

I. RAW CUES

    A. Our perceptual processes are subjective

    B. We pick up raw cues through all five senses

    C. Raw cues include, for example,

        1. Sound waves

        2. Light waves

        3. Odor-producing chemicals

II. YOU *INTERPRET* RAW CUES

    A. Interpreting: Making sense out of experience

        1. You select

        2. You organize

        3. You infer

            a) about objects

            b) about people

        4. Interpretation can create communication problems

    B. Factors that influence interpretation

        1. Physiological limitations

        2. Location

        3. Interests, emotions, needs

4. Attitudes and beliefs
5. Expectations
6. Language

III. A WAY TO MINIMIZE PERCEPTION-RELATED COMMUNICATION PROBLEMS IS TO BE *AVAILABLE*

1. Physical availability
2. Psychological availability

   a) Active
   b) Passive

———————◆•◆———————

Not long ago two women students at the University of Washington were walking along a public sidewalk through the rain of an early winter evening. When they reached the corner of 40th Street and Brooklyn Avenue, a man approached the two women, and as he did, one student ran away; the other stayed to talk to the man. Within the next seven minutes, for no apparent reason, the man severely beat her.

Notice how the women's perception processes worked in this example. One person observed the man's dress, facial expression, tone of voice, and the way he walked; she inferred that he was dangerous and ran. The other student observed basically the same characteristics, inferred that he was *not* dangerous, and stayed to talk. Each woman's behavior was determined by what she decided was "really" happening or was "true" about this situation. At the time, neither woman thought, "My choice to stay or leave is based on my perceptions and interpretations, so I'd better be sure to perceive and interpret accurately." But when we look at the situation from the outside, we can see that that's exactly what was happening, and that perceptions and interpretations helped get one woman beaten.

Faulty perceptions and interpretations don't always create this serious a problem. But since all our communication choices are based on our perceiving and interpreting, we want to use this chapter to explain in more detail how you are continually selecting, organizing, and inferring beyond the raw data you perceive. Then we want to explore the effects that your interpretation processes have on your communicating. We're convinced that your ability to communicate interpersonally will be increased when you understand more specifically the subjectivity of all perception and when you see how you might improve your ability to perceive "aspects of the other's humanness." Consequently, we want to make five points in this chapter: (1) The cues you pick up are in raw data form; that is, they don't contain "messages" or "images" in themselves. (2) You don't behave in response to the raw data but rather to your *interpretations* of them. (3) Your interpretations involve selecting, organizing, and infer-

ring beyond the raw cues. (4) Your interpretation is affected by a number of things, including your physiological limitations, expectations, attitudes, beliefs, interests, emotions, needs, and your language. (5) You can interpret in ways that promote interpersonal communication by being actively available physically and psychologically to the person(s) you're communicating with.

RAW CUES   When we communicate, you and I are usually unaware of the differences between *raw cues* and our *interpretations* of those cues. We tend to believe that what we perceive is an exact replica of the "real world" and that anyone who doesn't see it that way is mistaken or is distorting things.

One classic case study of this process is described in Albert Hastorf and Hadley Cantril's "They Saw a Game," which tells how students from two rival colleges perceived the Thanksgiving Day football contest between them.[1] The game was the last one of the season for both teams, and spirits were especially high, not only because of the two schools' long-standing rivalry but also because Princeton was trying to protect its perfect win-loss record and Dartmouth was determined to stop Princeton's All-America quarterback. Just about everyone who was asked agreed that the game was unusually rough, but when Hastorf and Cantril asked the spectators to identify who started the roughness and who was primarily to blame for it, the answers they got made it sound as if the people had seen two different games! For example, Princeton students saw the Dartmouth team make more than twice as many rule infractions as Dartmouth students saw their own team make. In addition, 86% of the Princeton students thought Dartmouth started the rough play, but only 36% of the Dartmouth students thought that their school was guilty; most of the Dartmouth students thought that both schools started it. As the authors put it, "the 'game' actually was many different games and . . . each version of the events that transpired was just as 'real' to a particular person as other versions were to other people."[2]

Hastorf and Cantril conclude that "there is no such 'thing' as a 'game' existing 'out there' in its own right which people merely 'observe.' The 'game' 'exists' for a person and is experienced by him [or her] only in so far as certain happenings have significance in terms of his [or her] purpose."[3] They also point out that this is a *transactional* view of the processes of perception, because it affirms that "what's really there"—which we referred to in Chapter 1 as the event's "existence and nature"—depends on both observer and observed. "Reality" emerges from transactions between persons and the things and people they see, hear, smell, touch, and taste.

Becoming a better communicator starts with the realization that our perceptual processes are subjective, that we construct our own reality from the cues we attend to, and that different people experiencing the same cues usually interpret them differently.

We pick up raw cues through all five senses—sight, hearing, touch, smell, and taste. For example, our tactile (touch) system picks up the sensations of textures, temperatures, and shapes as they come in contact with our skin. It's primarily through our tactile system that we decide whether a surface is soft, hard, round, cornered, warm, cold, smooth, rough, wet, dry, slippery, silky, or whatever. And touch can be a very important part of communication. In addition, our sense of smell picks up odor-producing chemicals in the air, and that sense can also significantly affect interpersonal relationships. Just think of our culture's concern with air fresheners, herbal-scented shampoos, mouthwash, and underarm odor. Or remember how your communication was affected the last time you walked into an unexpectedly smelly room. As soon as you noticed the odor—of fish, perspiration, mold, sour milk, urine, or whatever—you probably hurried what you said, didn't listen carefully to what others were saying, and put most of your energy into figuring out a way to escape to some fresh air.

When you communicate, you're continually interpreting all the raw cues that you see, hear, touch, smell, and taste, and generally speaking, it's a good thing that you are. Your communication would make little sense if you were forced to deal only with raw cues. Look at the picture below, for example.

If someone asked you, "What do you see in the picture?" it would be almost impossible for you to respond by describing just the raw cues, because we really don't have words for raw senses. You'd have to say something like this:

> There is a vertical, flat plane, which is regularly divided into numerous rectangles by staggered vertical and horizontal gray lines. Two fundamentally spherical, unevenly shaded shapes top two apparently plastic, generally vertical rectangular objects with shallowly parabolic interior sides. A short, horizontal plastic protrusion extends at the approximate midpoint of the right side of the left rectangle. The lower approximate half of the right rectangle is darker in shade and is marked by a noticeable vertical that partitions roughly the right one-third of this vertical rectangle from the left two-thirds . . . and so on.

The person who asked the question would probably think that you were out of your mind.

If you abandoned that effort but still tried to describe what you "actually saw," with as little interpretation as possible, you'd still have problems. You might say something like this:

> There are two females standing in front of the corner of a brick wall. The female on the left has her right arm lifted at a right angle to her body. Her mouth is partly open. She is holding in her left hand an object that is approximately eight inches tall and three or four inches wide; it seems to be a container of some type. The other female is standing facing the first female with her mouth closed . . . and so on.

Your listeners would still wonder about you.

On the other hand, you might respond something like this:

> There are two women, possibly classmates on a college campus, conversing against the corner of a brick wall. One woman is holding a coke or milkshake in her left hand and is gesturing with her right hand. The other woman (on the right) is standing listening and is holding her books; she has a purse hanging from her shoulder.

Such a description would obviously seem to make more sense; at least it presents a more *understandable* image of what you've described. The image is based on interpretation and may be inaccurate—for example, we don't know for sure whether they're classmates, what she's drinking, whether she's actually gesturing, whether she's actually talking, etc. But we think you can understand from this illustration that most of our communicating takes place at this level. Even though our eyes pick up only light waves, our ears pick up only sound vibrations, our nose picks up only odors, and so on, we don't communicate at that level. We go beyond the raw cues and try to make sense out of what we observe. Then we communicate with those *interpretations*. And it is the interpretations that can create problems in our communicating.

YOU INTERPRET RAW CUES

The process of interpreting raw cues is basically one of making sense out of sensory experiences. In other words, you translate raw data into recognizable form, into something you can understand, something that is meaningful to you in a given situation.

Suppose you witness a car accident. You won't experience a 15-foot by 6-foot by 4-foot, irregularly shaped, metal and glass structure rapidly rolling on flexible black spheres, which travels erratically until it impacts with an 18-inch in diameter, 30-foot tall, dark brown structure embedded in the supporting plane. That would be your observation of raw cues. Instead, you experience a car speeding down the street, careening wildly from side to side, and smashing into a telephone pole. This describes your meaning for or interpretation of the raw cues.

If you're unaware that when you're observing you're always interpreting, you're bound to have problems communicating. If you saw the face of the man driving the car that hit the telephone pole, and if you interpreted what you saw in his face as drunkenness, you would probably say that he was weaving recklessly all over the street before he hit the pole and had no business being behind the wheel in that condition. If another person, standing right next to you, also saw his face and interpreted the expression as one of fear, that person might say that the driver was terrified because his brakes had failed, was desperately trying to stop the car before he hurt anyone, and should be thanked for hitting the pole instead of the kids playing in the street.

If you believed that what you experienced were "facts," then when you communicated about this experience with the person next to you, you'd think that he or she was wrong, crazy, stubborn, or blind, and it would be unlikely that you and the other person would ever agree on "what actually happened," even though you'd believe that what *you* saw was what really occurred.

We don't mean to suggest that the only "real" world is what's in your mind. It's too difficult to deny that right now we are seated on two real objects—chairs—and you probably are, too. We didn't "create" those chairs in our minds. In other words, we agree with the commonsense conclusion that there is something "outside your skin," whether you call it raw cues, stimuli, or energy impinging on your sensory systems. But it's vital to remember that no one can ever experience this external reality except through the sensory and interpretive processes, and there is never a perfect, one-to-one correspondence between external reality and your interpretation of it. Neil Postman and Charles Weingartner say it this way:

> This does not mean that there is nothing outside of our skins. It does mean that whatever is "out there" can never be known except as it is filtered through a human nervous system. We can never get outside of our own skins. "Reality" is a perception, located somewhere behind the eyes.[4]

Your reality depends not only on what's outside your skin, but also on how what's inside your skin interprets what's outside your skin. To say the same thing another way, perception and interpretation are active, not passive processes. Each of us actively participates in the interpretations of our experiences. If we took the position that you are a passive organism, one that just soaks up communication cues, we'd be assuming that you have no choice in deciding how to interpret raw data, and that by some miraculous happening, raw cues impose "images" or introduce "meaning" into your head. But if you actually had no choice in how to interpret cues, then we would be *controlling* your responses to this book. That would mean you'd believe, be interested in, and completely understand everything you read here. Is that happening?

When we say that interpreting is an active process, we are saying that the process is, to a considerable extent, self-initiated and voluntary, a function of your choices. You are *not* forced to interpret raw cues in a certain way; you have considerable control over your perceptual processes.

But that's not to say that your interpretations are completely unpredictable. It might be easy for us to predict your response on some occasions—provided we know something about you and the situation. For example, we'd predict that if you were about to order a meal in a restaurant, you'd respond much more favorably if the menu read[5]

Filet Mignon $11.95
All desserts topped with delicious whipped cream
Soup: Home-cooked Chunky Beef

than if it read

Piece of dead cow $11.95
All desserts covered with chemically composed artificial topping

Soup: Boiled in our kitchen and containing salt, water, beef stock, beef fat, dehydrated onions, yeast extract, caramel color, and spices.

You do play an active role in your interpretations of those words, but cultural norms and values—e.g., our distaste for dead things—enable us to predict in advance what your interpretations will be. But we can predict only your *general* response. Since what's inside your skin is unique, different from what's inside all other human beings, your specific reality is also unique. Personal. Yours.

We believe that you'll be more accurately aware of the subjectivity of your interpretations and better able to promote interpersonal contact with other subjective interpreters if you recognize how both or all of you are *selecting, organizing,* and *inferring beyond* the raw cues you observe.

You Select

In some situations cues can be forced on people. Sometimes we don't seem to have a choice about whether or not to select certain cues—for example, an explosion, a siren, a sudden bright light, a scream, or a sharp pain. But almost all the time, we are voluntarily selecting the cues we perceive.

When we said in Chapter 1 that "all communication happens in a situation," we did not mean to suggest that the situation imposes itself on you and determines your communication behavior. A situation is defined by the persons who are perceiving cues within it. The situation *you* experience depends on how you interpret raw cues, and selection is an important part of that interpretation process. In the office of a boss or professor, you may especially notice the large, solid walnut desk between you and the other person and the fact that her or his chair is higher than yours. You may interpret those cues as putting you in an inferior position. Another observer might interpret the same office as very comfortable, focusing attention on the professor's friendly facial expressions and in-formal, conversational manner.

Within any context, there are always so many cues that we cannot possibly be aware of all of them. Consequently, out of the multitude of cues available, we make choices about which ones to focus our attention on. Magdalen D. Vernon explains it this way:

We tend to think that our ability to perceive what lies in front of us is so great that we can see the whole of it at a glance. Nevertheless, it often happens that we fail to perceive events taking place within the field of view; and if they are subsequently brought to our notice, we then say that we overlooked them because we were not attending. In fact, at any one moment we may perceive and be fully aware of only a small selection of the objects and events in the world around us. Some we may overlook altogether; others we may be aware of very dimly.[6]

Think for a minute about your own selection processes; try to remember which cues you selected and interpreted from the picture on p. 91. Did you notice that the coat collar on the woman at the left is turned up? Did you notice the position of the feet? That the woman on the left is wearing an earring? That they're wearing different styles of shoes? That neither woman's head casts a distinguishable shadow on the brick wall? Or did you select other cues? Notice our descriptions of the picture. We emphasized certain characteristics over others. Did we select the same ones that you did? The point we want to make is that all those cues are "really there," but that we selectively perceive only those that are required for the picture to make sense to us in this particular context.

In short, one aspect of interpretation is *selection*. Since you can focus only on a limited number of cues, you can never be aware of everything that's going on while you're communicating. You perceive selectively—as do all of the other persons you're communicating with.

You Organize   Another way you actively participate in interpreting raw cues is by organizing the cues you select. You literally cannot help structuring your world of sensations. In the first place, your sense organs cannot effectively pick up information that is completely unstructured. Researchers have found, for example, that continuous motion of your eyeballs is necessary for visual perception. As John Platt explains:

> The motions are too tiny and fast to be seen by the unaided eye. Their amplitudes are only about one minute of arc and their frequencies are in the range of from 50 to 150 cycles per second. Nevertheless, if they are compensated by optical or electronic devices so that the image is exactly stabilized on the retina, *vision disappears within a fraction of a second.*[7]

The same is true of your other senses. A steady, unchanging sound is difficult to perceive and may even become unnoticeable. When you explore the hardness and texture of a surface, you will not only put your fingers on the surface but will also move them back and forth, "for if the finger remained motionless, no useful information could be gained, except perhaps a sensation of temperature, which again would be due to the relative difference between the temperatures of object and finger."[8]

In other words, your senses perceive not static "things," but *relationships*—relationships between light and dark, loud and soft, high and low, and so on. Every relationship, by definition, implies some kind of structure or order—one part is warm compared with the other and the other is cool compared with the first, one part is hard compared with another and the other is soft compared with the first, etc. Even your senses are constantly helping organize your world.

Your thought processes add much more complicated systems of organization. The whole configuration of smells, sounds, and sights that you are perceiving at any given instant is usually called a gestalt, or a pattern, a structured chunk of perceptions. The pattern of each gestalt is organized into what is usually called "figure" and "ground." When you interpret raw cues, you structure them into "figure," or central focus, and "ground," or surrounding context. As two psychologists explain:

> The figure-ground relationship is an important concept, because it colors our perceptions. We never really just see the tree. We bring to the perception our whole mental set and emotional context. So, in truth, we are seeing a whole pattern of things, all in relationship. We can't say we're just looking at the moon, for example. We also see the sky behind it (which is just as much a part of the entire picture as is the moon).[9]

You Infer

Your active interpretation of raw cues involves one more step: your *selection* and *organization* enable you to make inferences about the cues, that is, to think of something that is completely other than the cues themselves. You're doing that right now. When you perceive

[—bathtub—]

you select from the available visual cues within those brackets, organize them into figure (black) and ground (white) and into a word. In addition, you may go beyond the word by thinking and feeling about a room, a series of objects (e.g., soap, towel), or even a whole set of experiences that are something completely other than the selected and organized visual cues themselves. When you're communicating, you're perceiving in this way not only written words but also spoken words and other *sounds*, *objects*, and *people*.

Sounds. Actually, our auditory system picks up only wavelike patterns of slightly varied high and low air pressure. But we don't communicate in terms of these compressions of air molecules; we infer from them. Think for a moment about the nonhuman sounds you hear. When a siren wails, you usually go beyond the sound itself to think about the ambulance, police car, or fire engine on an emergency run. When you hear certain cries of some animals, you think of the kinds of danger they may be experiencing. When students hear a bell at the end of a class period, they usually interpret it to mean "the class period is over"; that is, the students go beyond the sound of vibrations produced by the bell.

You do the same kind of thing with sounds that originate in the human vocal system. The person talking makes sounds available to you that vary in pitch, loudness, quality, and rate. You select certain ones, organize them into words, and then make inferences from the words. For example, six phonic sounds make up the spoken words "I love you." Yet when you hear those sounds in that order in a given context, it's possible for you to go beyond them to think of a wide variety of things.[10] You may think that the other person desires you or wants you sexually. You may think that the person wants your love or wants to be able to love you. Sometimes you may hear those words and infer that the other person is predicting that perhaps a love relationship can develop between you or even that the other person hates you. Often those sounds can indicate a wish for emotional exchange: "I want your admiration in exchange for mine" or "I give my love in exchange for some passion" or "I want to feel cozy and at home with you" or "I admire some of your qualities." A declaration of love is often taken as a request: "I desire you" or "I want you to gratify me" or "I want your protection" or "I want to be intimate with you" or "I want to exploit your loveliness." Sometimes those sounds lead you to think that the other person needs a security or tenderness, that the other is saying, "My self-love goes out to you." In other contexts you might interpret the sounds as expressing submissiveness: "Please take me as I am" or "I feel guilty about you; I want, through you, to correct the mistakes I have made in my relationships with others." You may also interpret those sounds as self-sacrifice or as a masochistic wish for dependency. On the other hand, the sounds may lead you to think that the other person is fully affirming you and is taking responsibility for mutual exchange of feelings. As Joost Meerloo summarizes, " 'I love you,'—wish, desire, submission, conquest; it is never the [sounds of] the word itself that tells the real meaning here." What we are saying and what Meerloo is saying is that you and I don't stop and think just about the sounds we hear. We interpret them, in part, by making inferences and thinking of something other than the sounds themselves.

One of the reasons it's important to recognize that the receivers of sound vibrations infer from what they hear is that usually the way one person is thinking when *saying* something is not the same as the way the person *hearing* and interpreting the sounds is thinking. For example, when Gary's daughter Debbie was five years old, she and Gary were brushing their teeth, and she asked, "Daddy, what kind of toothpaste do we use?" When Gary told her they used Colgate, she asked, "How come we don't use *Crest*? Crest gives you cavities." At that time in her life, Debbie wanted cavities, because when she went to the dentist, he gave her sugarless candy, which she thought was neat. She had seen the Crest commercial on television in which the little boy comes home, runs to his mother, and says, "Mommy, Mommy, only one cavity," and the mother replies, "It must be the Crest." Debbie inferred that the Crest *caused* the little boy's cavity. So she wanted to use Crest, too. Debbie interpreted the commercial in her own way, and we think it's safe to say that it wasn't the way Crest's ad agency intended.

Objects. You also infer from the *visual* and *tactile* cues you pick up by selecting and organizing certain ones and constructing them into an object. To a visitor from the East, for example, a single wire fence on a Colorado range may be just a single wire fence. Although the person may be conscious of the fence and even of the single wire, he or she may not be led to think of anything else because of it. To a Colorado farmer or rancher, on the other hand, the single wire may mean that the fence is electric, that it is designed to enclose sheep or cattle but not horses, that the ranch he is on is relatively well equipped, etc. A person who has never played golf and who has never seen a golf course may interpret a sand trap as just a pile of sand. But anyone who plays golf and cares about her or his score goes far beyond the raw cues of a sculptured sand pile; he or she may experience frustration, try to avoid it, hope for a lower score, think about the kind of golf club required to hit a ball out of it, and so on. To us, an electric typewriter is much more than a machine. It's a way of writing faster than is possible by longhand; sometimes it requires expensive repairs; and it reminds us of the work of writing and rewriting and of time spent away from our families. To a smoker, a book of matches on a table may suggest lighting a cigarette; to a parent, the matches may be a source of danger for young children.

Of course, you don't always feel the need or have the experience or knowledge to go very far beyond the objects you perceive. Sometimes you take the raw cues and just perceive an object—a fence, a typewriter, a pile of sand—and go no further. But whenever you need to make sense out of objects you perceive, you'll make inferences, and the ways in which you infer from raw cues becomes especially significant when you think about how you perceive *people*.

---

1. Try to describe the picture below in *raw cues*. Then explain your interpretation by going beyond the cues themselves.

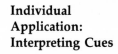

For example,
a) *Raw cues:* black circle approximately one inch in diameter;

Individual
Application:
Interpreting Cues

two black dots in upper portion of circle approximately a quarter inch apart; curved black line in lower portion of circle.

b) *Interpretation:* "Happy face, probably sketched by an artist."

2. Now you try it with this picture:

a) *Raw cues:*

_____

_____

_____

_____

b) *Interpretations:*

_____

_____

_____

People. If you're going to communicate interpersonally, we think it's vital to remember that humans tend to make inferences about *people* in a couple of special ways that are significantly different from the way in which we interpret the raw cues we identify as *objects. The reason we think this process is important is that it's the way we arrive at the images that take part in the negotiation of selves we talk about in Chapter 4.*

Generally, when we perceive *people,* we're including in our interpretation inferences about their motives, attitudes, values, feelings, personality traits, and so on, none of which are directly observable. We almost never perceive *objects* that way. We perceive most persons, unlike objects, to be capable of choice, self-initiating, and "as having plans, hopes, fears, and all the other experiences that we all experience as persons."[11] In other words, as we construct images of another person, we go beyond what we observe "outside the other's skin" and *infer* things that are "inside that person's skin." More specifically, we go beyond raw *people* cues in two ways that are explained by Albert Hastorf, David Schneider, and Judith Polefka:

> First, we perceive them as *causal agents.* They are potential causes of their behavior. They may intend to do certain things, such as attempting to cause certain effects; and because we see them as one source of their actions, we consider them capable of varying their behavior to achieve their intended effects. . . . Our perception of others' intentionality leads us next to organize the behavior of other people into intent-act-effect segments which form perceptual units. We infer the intentions of another; but we go further. If we perceive a particular intent on several occasions, we are prone to perceive the other as having an enduring personality characteristic. . . .
>
> Second, we perceive other people as *similar to ourselves.* Hence we are pushed to infer that they possess attributes which, unlike size and behavior, we cannot observe directly but which we are aware of in ourselves. In particular, we perceive others to possess emotional states; we see them as feeling angry, happy, or sad.[12]

As the cartoon suggests, the cues we pick up and use to form images of intent, emotional states, and similarity to ourselves vary among individuals and situations. Sometimes we may pay special attention to the other person's dress, voice, posture, or general appearance. At other times we may focus on his or her grammar, dialect, choice of words, gestures, facial expressions, or eye movements. Some research evidence suggests that when very little other information is available to us, we construct images of people on the basis of nonverbal vocal cues. According to Jessie Delia, "When a dialect is clearly discernible, an individual will rely on it as an initial source of information as he [or she] attempts 'sociologically' to place

DOONESBURY   by Garry Trudeau

DOONESBURY, COPYRIGHT 1976 G.B. TRUDEAU. DISTRIBUTED BY
UNIVERSAL PRESS SYNDICATE. REPRINTED BY PERMISSION.

the other."[13] In other words, we may go beyond a person's vocal cues and draw conclusions about her or his attitudes, values, and socioeconomic status, as well as about whether or not we would enjoy communicating with the person.

In short, we think it's important to emphasize three things about inferences from people cues. First, this process is quick and almost automatic; sometimes you're not even aware that you're doing it. But you almost always are; you hardly ever stop with just the cues that are "given." Second, when you come to conclusions about a person's attitudes, values, beliefs, motives, personality traits, and so on, you're dealing with things that aren't directly observable, and therefore you can only infer that they exist; you can't know for sure. Third, your *definition* or *image* of another person (see Chapter 4) is determined to a large extent by your inferences from the cues they make available.

It almost goes without saying that this interpretation process can create communication problems. Sometimes we interpret a person's cues carelessly—we select only a few of the available cues, make questionable assumptions about those cues, and create an artificial definition of the person. That kind of careless interpretation is usually called *cue generalization* or *stereotyping,* and it definitely works against interpersonal communication. The reason is obvious: As we said in Chapter 2, each person is different from all other persons. But cue generalization leads us to see certain people as homogeneous, as alike. During John's first year at the University of Washington, he was assigned to a course he'd never taught before. His insecurity about the class was heightened on the first day when a guy walked in with shoulder-length hair, funky wire-rimmed glasses, wearing railroad overalls, an old-fashioned, collarless shirt, and sandals, and carrying his books in an old, leather doctor's bag. John *inferred* that he would be nothing but trouble. He was obviously some kind of freak, was probably into drugs, and could be expected to disrupt the class just like all other freaks. It took John a while to reduce his defensiveness to the point where he could change his stereotype of Antoine, but when he did, he discovered not only that he was an energetic, interested, creative student but also that he and John shared many basic values.

You've probably made the same kind of error on the basis of careless interpretation of person cues. We've found we have to keep avoiding it, because unless we're continually trying to select, organize, and go beyond cues that differentiate humans from one another, that is, unless we're trying to see the *uniqueness* rather than the similarities, we're generalizing cues and not promoting interpersonal communication.

————————◆●◆————————

Take some time now and write a description of someone you know (friend, classmate, teacher). Describe her or his attitudes, values, beliefs, goals, personality traits, etc. As you identify each characteristic of the person, list the cues from which you've inferred the characteristic.

Individual Application: Inferences

Inferred trait	Observed cues that led to this interpretation
1. Extremely impatient	I was 10 minutes late for a date; she left before I got there. Constantly plays with objects in hands. She once knocked the phone on the floor when parents didn't call her at exactly the scheduled time.
2. _____	
_____	
3. _____	
_____	
4. _____	
_____	
5. _____	
_____	

————————◆●◆————————

SOME FACTORS THAT INFLUENCE YOUR INTERPRETATION

Since interpretation plays such an important role in interpersonal communication, we think it would be useful for you to understand not only the process of interpreting—selecting, organizing, and inferring—but also some factors that affect how you interpret the raw cues you perceive. But before we go on, remember what we said in Chapter 1 about interdependence: whenever people are communicating, many things are happening all at once, and those things are capable of influencing one another simultaneously. Therefore we can't specify the single factor that influences your interpretation the most; there may be two, three, or more interdependent factors working simultaneously. But we can explain a few of the different possibilities, and from these explanations, we hope you'll get a better understanding of why your interpretations are personally biased.

Physiological Limitations

It's pretty obvious that your interpretation is affected by the physiological limitations of your sensory systems. Few people have perfect hearing, perfect eyesight, or a bloodhound's sense of smell. You'll miss some cues just because your sensory systems are incapable of picking them up—because they are too subtle, too complex, or because they're made available too rapidly. David Mortensen explains it this way:

> There is a clear and definite limit to the amount of information which the human organism can identify accurately; in recognizing a series of numbers, for example, the span of absolute judgment lies somewhere in the neighborhood of seven items of information. . . . For more difficult types of material, there is evidence that [a person] is able to monitor five features simultaneously, but rarely more. . . . Generally, even slight increases in the difficulty of material or the rate of presentation can adversely affect the capacity of the receiving system.*

Location

Your interpretation of words, objects, and persons will also be controlled to some extent by your physical location. Location affects what cues are available to you and the angle at which you perceive them. When you're face to face with someone, the cues available are different from those available if you're sitting side by side. Consequently, you're more likely to pick up verbal and facial cues from people sitting opposite you in a group than from people sitting next to you—unless, of course, you shift body position so that you're looking at them. If you sit in the back row of a large hall, the cues available are different from those available if you sit in the middle or in the front row. For one thing, it's easier to become psychologically detached when you're a considerable distance from the pri-

---

* From *Communication: The Study of Human Interaction* by C. David Mortensen. Copyright 1972 by McGraw-Hill Book Company. Used with permission by McGraw-Hill Book Company.

mary source of personal cues. For another, you can't really pick up detailed facial and gestural cues from a distance. The auditory sensations will also be different. In the front row you may hear the speaker's voice directly without microphone and loudspeaker distortions; in the back row you won't. Similarly, if you're standing six or eight inches from someone, you're more likely to pick up cues of skin texture, body temperature, subtle eye movements, smell, and touch, whereas if you're ten to fifteen feet away, you're most likely to notice only the more general physical image of the person.

Your selection, organization, and inferring may also be influenced by whatever interests, emotions, and needs you have at the time. A person who makes his or her own clothes probably notices the clothes that other people wear more often than does someone who isn't really interested in clothing. A person who has had surgery is probably more attuned to news items and conversations about surgery than is someone who has never been in the hospital. You don't pay much attention to a commercial that advertises cake mixes if your needs at that time don't relate to baking, food, grocery shopping, etc. On the other hand, if you're hungry and you like pastries, your perception of the commercial will change.

Interests, Emotions, and Needs

When communicating with another person, you may feel the need for the kind of personal support that can be suggested by touching—a pat on the shoulder, handshake, hug, arm around your waist—and your selection of cues may focus on whether or not these things happen. If you're interested in or feel the need for support, you are just as likely to notice its absence as its presence. Of course, if you *want* supportive behavior strongly enough, you may perceive it even when it isn't intended by the other person:

> There are circumstances . . . in which people spontaneously perceive certain things or certain aspects of the field of view particularly readily. If they have strong feelings about what is shown them or if they desire to perceive or to avoid perceiving something, then not only is the speed of perceiving altered; they may even think they perceive what is not actually there—or if they don't want to see it, they may fail to do so when it is, as we say, staring them in the face.[14]

A good example of this occurs when someone wants very much to be liked by you. That person may continually look for cues that indicate your positive feelings, and even if you don't really intend to make positive cues available, the person may interpret whatever you say or do as "friendly," "supportive," or "affectionate." You may even try to communicate that you don't want to be close friends, but the person may ignore those negative cues or interpret them to mean something else.

In short, because of your interests, emotions, and needs, you may focus your perception on certain cues while ignoring others. You may also distort your interpretation of cues because of a strong desire to perceive them in a certain way. The stronger your interests and desires, the more likely it is that such distortions will occur.

The problem this creates for interpersonal communication is that you'll probably miss important cues that other persons make available to you about *their* humanness if you're allowing only your own immediate interests, emotions, and needs to "control" your perception.

Attitudes and Beliefs

Through experience, each of us develops many different attitudes and beliefs, all of which vary in how strongly we feel them, how important they are to us, and how extreme they are relative to the people around us. In any given context, however, not all of your attitudes and beliefs will affect your perception. For example, your attitudes about interracial dating probably won't affect your interpretation of cues when you're talking with a friend about car expenses. The attitudes and beliefs most likely to affect your interpretations are those that are most *important to you* and those that you think are most *relevant* at the time.

Sometimes important or relevant attitudes and beliefs lead you to decide to attend to certain cues and to ignore others. People who strongly believe in decriminalizing marijuana tend to read material that supports their view; those who are definitely against it usually avoid that information. Similarly, people who profess Christian principles are more likely to listen to a religious radio program than are those who do not hold such views. There's a great deal of research support for the proposition that people tend to avoid information that is inconsistent with their attitudes and beliefs, and that they tend to seek out information that is consistent with them. Finally, attitudes and beliefs also affect memory; that is, you're more likely to remember "facts" and "arguments" that support your position than those that contradict it.

Expectations

In most communication situations, people *expect* certain things to happen. We develop expectations about how we will behave, how others will behave, and how the event itself will turn out. The expectations you have about a communication encounter can be as powerful a force as your interests, desires, attitudes, or beliefs. Imagine an insecure door-to-door salesman who is about to approach a house. He thinks in advance about all the negative things he will see and hear as soon as he explains that he's selling vacuum cleaners. He remembers that he hasn't sold a machine in more than a month, and he has become convinced that he isn't cut out to be a salesperson. He knocks, and when someone opens the door—before the homeowner can say anything—the salesman shouts, "I didn't want to sell you anything anyway!'' The story is exaggerated, but it illustrates an important point—the salesman *decided in advance* what would happen, and there was almost nothing the homeowner could say or do to change the event he expected.

Sometimes you develop expectations well before you meet the person face to face. In other situations, they may develop immediately before or during the face-to-face exchange. In any case, your expectations can influence your perception in at least three ways: (1) you *focus your selection* on cues you expect to perceive; (2) you *interpret* raw cues to meet your expectations; and (3) you *behave* in ways that elicit or provoke the behavior you expect from other people.

Frequently we predict in advance the cues that will be available to us in a certain situation, and then when we're in that situation, we tend to look for just those cues. For example, ''if you expect a person to act unfriendly, you will be sensitive to anything that can be perceived as rejection and unfriendliness.''[15] If you expect a friend to behave immaturely at a social event, you'll be more sensitive to those behaviors you can most readily interpret as ''immature.'' You may, in fact, ignore behavior that could be interpreted as ''mature.'' As Mortensen says:

> If we expect an event to be dull and uninteresting, it is not likely to be otherwise. The congenial manner of others present, their feelings of excitement and personal involvement will go unnoticed—or even be distorted—if we approach the situation with mistrust.[16]

In some other situations, the cues we expect to find are not there to be selected, so we interpret the cues that are available to meet our expectations. Consider a situation in which a man expects the woman he's with to come on to other men at a party. He never really sees any ''direct'' evidence of her trying to pick up a man, but he interprets her every glance and every friendly gesture as seductive behavior. In a course Gary taught, a student developed the expectation that he wouldn't like her. One day in class she answered a question, and although Gary acknowledged her nonverbally, he didn't say anything in response to her answer. After class she rushed into his office and demanded, ''Why don't you like me?'' When Gary asked her why she felt that he didn't like her, she explained that she expected him not to like her, and when he didn't respond verbally to her in class, she interpreted that as confirming her expectation. They both realized after talking about it that even though Gary had no negative feelings toward her at all, his behavior could easily be interpreted to mean that he disliked her—especially since that's what she was predicting.

Your expectations can even make you actually behave in ways that elicit or provoke the responses you expect from other people. For example, you may expect that a certain person won't have much to say to you. As a result, you may maintain long periods of silence, which give the other person very little to talk about, or you may ask questions that are virtually unanswerable. You might then interpret the other's silence as evidence of your expectation. What's actually happened is that you've generated a self-fulfilling prophecy.

In short, if a person believes everyone is against her or him and because of this hostile belief expects hostile behavior from others, that person is likely to get exactly what's expected. She or he might do several things: select available cues that can be easily interpreted as hostile behavior, select cues that aren't intended to be hostile and interpret them that way, or simply behave in ways that evoke the hostile response expected.

Language   Your interpretation of raw cues is also affected by your language. As we said in Chapter 1, the structure and content of standard American English affects its speakers' perception of objects, of complex processes like human communication, and of persons—women, men, and ethnic groups. As Benjamin Whorf put it, "We dissect nature along lines laid down by our native language."[17]

It would be hard to overestimate the effect of language on interpretation. We can make sense out of the "booming and buzzing confusion" we perceive and of our own ever-changing selves only by using language units—words, phrases, sentences—to relate otherwise unrelated experiences. In other words, language is the tool we use to get the continuously interdependently changing world to "hold still" or at least to "keep moving in ways that make sense."

Over a period of eight months, *Psychology Today* ran a pair of articles designed to sensitize its readers to the effect of the English language on perception of black and white persons. In the first article, called "If White Means Good, Then Black . . .," John Williams and John Stabler showed that the colors white and black have positive and negative meanings, respectively, and that these meanings influence our racial attitudes.[18] Eight months later the second article, "Reversing the Bigotry of Language," listed "black positives" and "white negatives" contributed by readers responding to the Williams-Stabler article. Readers suggested that standard American English might appear to be less bigoted if we remembered that black negatives are balanced by such positive terms as Black Beauty, black belt, black gold, black tie, black soil, and black pearls, and that white positives are balanced by such white negatives as white trash, white belt, white flag, white elephants, white slave, and lily-livered.[19] The magazine's editors agreed with one reader who commented that "the inequity of the black vs. white usage and connotations did not hit me fully until I tried this exercise myself." And that's part of the problem. Our language is so close to us that we are often unaware of how much it's affecting our interpretations of objects *and* persons.

SO WHAT ABOUT ALL THIS?

It may seem from what we've said about the subjectivity of perception that communication is impossible. Since all I can ever know is what *I* perceive, and since what I perceive is always subjective, biased, affected by *my* expectations, needs, attitudes, and beliefs, it appears that all I can ever really perceive or know is my own subjective world. That means that I can never perceive or contact *you—your* world. In short, it sounds as if I'm caught in what David Swanson and Jesse Delia call the "categoricentric predicament."[20] That is, I can't escape being centered in my own categories, so I can never really contact anybody else. I can only communicate with *my view of you*; I can never really communicate with *you*. In that sense, when it comes right down to it, I'm always talking to myself! And it sounds as if I can't do anything else. So how can we escape this predicament? If the expectations, needs, attitudes, and beliefs that affect my interpretations are different from yours—as they almost always are—how can we contact and understand each other?

Availability

The answer is fairly obvious but difficult to put into practice. None of us can communicate perfectly, but we can move toward mutual understanding by making ourselves *available* to the person with whom we're communicating—available physically, psychologically, and actively.[21]

Some type of *physical* availability is a prerequisite for any kind of communication; you can't communicate with someone you're completely out of touch with. Interpersonal-quality communication generally requires relatively long-term, face-to-face physical presence. (That isn't always true, however. Close friends can sometimes communicate interpersonally over the phone. But usually you need both spatial closeness and time.) Even though its obvious, we often forget how much *time* good communication requires. Our fast-paced, overcommitted life-styles often get in the way of interpersonal-quality communication. It takes time for even two persons to discover the different ways each interprets his or her world. And when more than two persons are involved, it takes correspondingly more time. The truth of this often-overlooked point recently became apparent to John and to the graduate students whose teaching he supervises. None of them particularly liked "staff meetings," but they recognized that their communication was deteriorating. They reluctantly agreed to meet regularly, and almost immediately they noticed how much difference it made just to spend time together. Of course, they also tried to work at communicating. Time together provides the opportunity for interpersonal communication, but it doesn't guarantee it.

It can also help to be physically "closer" together. We are often surprised how much more interpersonal the communication in a group can be when we just move from being scattered around the room to sitting together. Even in casual conversations, people often emphasize or reinforce their physical availability by lightly touching the people they're communicating with. Most of us feel comfortable communicating at a personal space of about one-and-a-half to three feet. Interpersonal communication doesn't require that you be much closer than that, but for many people, the farther away you are, the more psychologically detached they feel.

Touching can also both stimulate and symbolize our *psychological* availability. A handshake, embrace, or pat on the shoulder often indicates that I'm with you—I'm feeling what you seem to be feeling. But psychological availability involves much more than mere physical presence. In order to be psychologically available to someone else, you need to be open to *that person's* view of the world so that *your* perceptions are affected by the way the *other individual* sees things.

That may sound a bit confusing. What we mean is that you need to be not only aware that the other person's interpretations of raw data are different from yours, but also willing to interpret things, in part, as he or she does. You need to be open enough to allow your interpretations to be affected by the things that are affecting the other person's interpretations—attitudes, feelings, needs, expectations, and so on.

Carl Rogers talks about psychological availability in terms of "permitting" himself to understand another person.

> Our first reaction to most of the statements which we hear from other people is an immediate evaluation, or judgment, rather than an understanding of it. When someone expresses some feeling or attitude or belief, our tendency is, almost immediately, to feel "That's right"; or "That's stupid"; "That's abnormal"; "That's unreasonable"; That's incorrect"; "That's not nice." Very rarely do we permit ourselves to *understand* precisely what the meaning of his statement is to him.*

When you're psychologically available to another person, you're not pretending you don't have any opinions on what she or he is talking about. You may have strong commitments to your opinions, and we don't expect you to abandon them. Psychological availability doesn't require that. Instead, you're working to postpone your own ways of selecting, structuring, and going beyond raw cues. What you're saying, in effect, is "There are alternative ways of interpreting this topic, and I'm trying to 'hear' your alternative long enough to understand it."

---

* From *On Becoming a Person* by Carl R. Rogers. Copyright © 1961 by Carl R. Rogers. Reprinted with the permission of Houghton Mifflin Company.

For labor-management negotiations to succeed, each side has to be genuinely open to the other's ways of interpreting working conditions, the status of competing products, international, national, and local economic situations, and so on. When the employee representative chooses to be aware of (i.e., selects) only salaries in comparable plants, sees employers as the main cause of all employee difficulties (structures raw cues that way), and infers that management is trying to put people out of work, she or he is not being psychologically available to the employer. Management is doing the same thing when it perceives only the rate of profit increase over last year, sees the government as heading toward complete control, and infers that all employee groups are out to ruin the free-enterprise system.

Psychological availability is just as crucial in other kinds of "negotiations." Husband and wife, child and parent, teacher and student, salesperson and customer, preacher and parishioner—all have to be willing not only to see the other's point of view as reasonable to her or him, but also to be *available to* the other, to look, at least for a time, at the world, at least in part, through the other's eyes.

Both physical and psychological availability can be either *active* or *passive*. When you're passively available, you just allow others to share with you. You let them be close by, and you are more or less willing to listen. To promote interpersonal communication, however, you need to be *actively* available. In the first place, you need to take some of the initiative for putting yourself in the physical presence of others. That doesn't necessarily mean you should stick to them like a shadow, but you should make the effort to be available for more than the time it takes to utter a few cliché sentences. It's been estimated that many married couples actually spend less than twenty minutes a day spatially and temporally available to each other. If you're unmarried, that may sound ridiculous. But it isn't. Campfire and Boy Scout meetings, soccer and baseball games, church and PTSA gatherings, poker and bridge parties, stereo and television sets—all make it difficult for a husband and wife to find time to be more than "superficially" together. If they're going to communicate interpersonally, each is going to have to actively make time for the other.

But to be actively available psychologically, you need to do more than just be around the other person. As we'll discuss in the next three chapters, psychological availability involves both "sharing" and "being aware"—both disclosing some of your self and responding completely to the other. Both of those take much more effort than merely being physically available. Not only does it take time to see the way somebody else sees things; it also takes another kind of effort because it's *risky*. As Rogers puts it, "If I let myself really understand another person, I might be changed by that understanding."[22] It's not easy to lower your defenses enough to develop the *tentativeness* that psychological availability requires. You need to be open to information from the other person and willing to change when it becomes evident that you have misperceived or misinterpreted. You need to be willing to ask for confirmation of your definition of the other and of your interpretation of what she or he is saying and to keep your interpretations open to change until the other person confirms them. And as we'll talk about more in the next two chapters, that's risky, too.

Finally, there are all sorts of combinations and degrees of availability, both physical and psychological, active and passive. For instance, a prostitute may be actively available physically but not at all psychologically available. The teacher who invites students in to discuss their grades but who never expects to change a grade as a result of the conference is physically available but not open enough to be psychologically available. A counselor may be so willing to be psychologically available to a client that there is little time to be physically available to anyone else.

The point we want to stress is this: human perception is so inherently subjective that in order for communication to work at all, you have to be available to the other persons involved. As much as possible, you should try to be *actively* available, both *physically* and *psychologically*.

CONCLUDING THOUGHTS

People often get defensive when told that they're always making inferences on the basis of the cues they observe, and that their process of interpretation is subjective and biased. We're so accustomed to interpreting raw cues instantaneously and automatically that we assume that what we see *is* "reality." But in an important sense, it *isn't*.

Communicating interpersonally is much easier when you accept the fact that in your own unique ways, you select, organize and go beyond raw cues; that is, you attach your own personal interpretations to the verbal and nonverbal data you observe.

If you can follow that realization by being open-minded to the interpretations other people make, you've accomplished a second important step toward interpersonal communication. When you take this second step, you're saying something like this: "Because each of us interprets from different experiences, backgrounds, attitudes, interests, and expectations, your interpretation may be as valid for you as my interpretation is for me." So we may differ, but we can still communicate interpersonally.

The third step is making a physical and psychological commitment to get actively together with the other person(s). Our experience has taught us that steps 2 and 3 are the most difficult, especially because of the time, mental energy, and risk that are involved. But we've also learned that as those things happen in our communicating, good things follow, and we grow as persons.

1. *Inferring sounds like a dangerous process. If I'm assuming and jumping to conclusions all the time, I'm obviously going to have trouble communicating accurately and effectively. Why don't you tell me how to* stop *making inferences?*

You cannot stop. It's impossible to respond to raw data without making inferences about it. If we stayed with raw data, we would not be able to make sense out of our experience. In other words, we cannot be wholly objective. The skill we ought to develop is an ability to make careful inferences. Careful inferences come when you (1) are aware that you make inferences, and so you don't habitually get observation mixed up with interpretation; (2) make careful observations, for example, by responsively listening; and (3) draw tentative rather than permanent conclusions, especially about people.

2. *You said earlier that in my communicating, I don't pick up everything; I select certain cues. How much of an experience do people select?*

Except in those instances where we are *strongly* motivated—for example, when our life is in danger, a great deal of money is at stake, we are strongly attracted to the other person—we typically select between 20 and 50 percent of other people's communication.

3. *I'm still not sure why a friend and I who both witness the same event from the same vantage point will come out with different impressions of what actually happened. Does the difference occur because each of us selects different bits and pieces of the experience? Is it because we interpret the bits and pieces differently? Do we see the same things and make different inferences?*

The difference between your impression and your friend's impression can happen because of one or more of the following.

a) Each of you selects different aspects of the event (Dartmouth students selected more violent acts by Princeton players and Princeton students selected more violent acts by Dartmouth players).

b) Each of you brings different feelings, needs, attitudes and motives to the event. These affect what you select, how you organize the event, and what you infer about it.

c) Each of you will make slightly different inferences about what you select out of the event.

4. *If what you say is true, why do people sometimes almost totally agree on what they see and on their impressions of what they see? What happens to your "categoricentric predicament" then?*

In much of our communicating we share common meanings, so it is not unusual for people to agree on their impressions of an event or experience. But "total" agreement is rare. We almost never see things in *exactly* the same way. Part of the reason we think our impressions are in total agreement is that we talk at a high level of generality. If you and I saw a movie, for example, and I said, "That was a *good* movie!" and you said, "I agree, that was a *good* movie!" we might have the impression that we totally agreed. But all we really know is that we both used the same word—"good"—to describe the movie. What each of us means by the word "good" may be quite different. Thus, by keeping communication at a high level of generalization, you may be misled by artificial agreement.

In many communication situations where you don't have much at stake, generalized conversation is okay. There's not much reason to say to another person, "Well, what do you mean by 'good'?"

In situations where you're attempting to communicate interpersonally, however, it's sometimes important to communicate specifically and clearly, even though doing so may generate differences of opinion and potential conflict. Interpersonal-quality communication cannot exist at a high level of generalization.

EXERCISES

Group Activity: What Do You See?

Because the following three pictures are close-ups—and thus don't give you much information about the context of what's shown—they focus your attention on "raw cues." Try identifying what's shown in each picture from the "raw cues" that you see. Be specific and as detailed as you can.

Picture 1

Description of what's shown:

_____

_____

_____

(Full picture on p. 116)

Picture 2

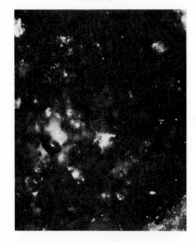

Description of what's shown:

_____

_____

_____

(Full picture on p. 116)

Picture 3

Description of what's shown:

_____

_____

_____

(Full picture on p. 116)
Remember: Each "description" is your *interpretation* of the "raw cues" you perceived.

After you've individually determined what is shown in each picture, get together with one other person, and quietly—so that no one else in the room can hear you—decide between the two of you what's shown in each picture.

Then discuss your perceptions in the whole group. How much disagreement is there? Do pairs agree more than individuals did? What does the disagreement tell you about how people select, organize, and infer beyond raw data?

Full picture 1

Full picture 2

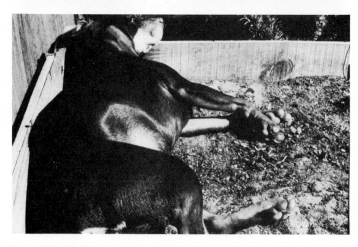

Full picture 3

Sometimes we have real difficulty limiting the cues we select. When that happens—when we have to attend to too many cues at one time—*information overload* occurs. We "overload" our sensory systems to the extent that we can't make sense out of what we are attending to, and we have difficulty in remembering any of it. To illustrate information overload, try this experiment. Ask two people whose voices do not sound alike to talk to the group you're in about the same topic and at the same time. You'll note that while they're talking simultaneously, it's impossible to focus on both of them, and it is difficult to attend to either one. You can get something out of what you hear only if you concentrate on selecting cues from just one of the speakers. Now try the same thing with two people who have similar voices; it's much more difficult, and you may find it impossible to pick up anything meaningful. You can hear the sounds, but you can't select enough of the cues to make sense out of what you are hearing.

Group Activity: Information Overload

To demonstrate the limited capacity of people to perceive a great many cues in a short period of time, try the rumor game. Ask four people to leave the room, and then read a one- or two-minute story to one of the persons remaining. Ask this person to communicate the story to the one person you've called back into the room. Then ask the second person to communicate her or his version of the story to the next person called in, and so on. You'll probably discover that most people can't really handle enough information to keep the story straight, even though they're telling it immediately after hearing it. The more complex the story and the faster it is told to each person, the greater the distortion.

Group Activity: Selecting Cues

Break your class into small groups. Ask each group to read and discuss the following situation and then to agree on a solution to the problem that's posed. Try to be aware of how group members—including yourself—select, organize, and go beyond the cues that we've provided here. Try to be open to different interpretations, and take time to let each person explain his or her interpretations.

Group Activity: Interpreting Cues

After each group has arrived at a solution, you may want to try to reach consensus among the groups. Or it may be more useful to meet as a class and discuss what went on while each group was solving the problem.

Situation. Six persons are stranded on an uninhabited island: a professor, a doctor, an internationally famous scientist, a pregnant woman, a military officer, and a young child. None of them want to stay on the island, but the only available means out is a two-person airplane. The military officer knows how to fly the plane. Your task is to decide which two persons should be allowed to leave on the plane back to civilization.

Be careful about the interpretations you make. For example, do you assume that the doctor is a physician? A Ph.D.? A veterinarian? A woman? A man?

———◆•◆———

NOTES

1. Albert Hastorf and Hadley Cantril, "They Saw a Game," *Journal of Abnormal and Social Psychology*, **49** (1954), 129–134.

2. *Ibid.*, p. 132.

3. *Ibid.*, p. 133.

4. Neil Postman and Charles Weingartner, *Teaching as a Subversive Activity* (New York: Dell, 1969), p. 90.

5. An example borrowed from a former colleague of Gary's, Ray DeBoer.

6. Magdalen D. Vernon, "Perception, Attention, and Consciousness," in *The Languages of Science*, Granada Lectures of the British Association for Advancement of Science (New York: Basic Books, 1962), pp. 111–123. Reprinted by permission.

7. John R. Platt, "The Two Faces of Perception," in *Changing Perspectives on Man*, ed. Ben Rothblatt (Chicago: University of Chicago Press, 1968), p. 73. Italics added. Reprinted by permission.

8. Paul Watzlawick, Janet Helmick Beavin, and Don D. Jackson, *Pragmatics of Human Communication* (New York: Norton, 1967), p. 27.

9. There's a lot more to understanding gestalts and gestalt psychology than we have introduced here, but much of it goes beyond the point we're trying to make. This quotation and a more developed explanation of the gestalt concept are in John H. Brennecke and Robert C. Amick, *The Struggle for Significance* (Beverly Hills, CA: Glencoe Press, 1971), p. 108. Reprinted by permission.

10. The extended example in this paragraph is a liberal paraphrase of Joost Meerloo, "The Word Tyrannizes Us or Is Our Slave," in *Conversation and Communication* (New York: International Universities Press, 1952), pp. 83–84.

11. Clifford H. Swensen, Jr., *Introduction to Interpersonal Relations* (Glenview, Ill.: Scott-Foresman, 1973), p. 146.

12. Albert H. Hastorf, David J. Schneider, and Judith Polefka, *Person Perception* (Reading, Mass.: Addison-Wesley, 1970), pp. 11–12. Reprinted by permission.

13. Jesse G. Delia, "Dialects and the Effects of Stereotypes on Interpersonal Attraction and Cognitive Processes in Impression Formation," *Quarterly Journal of Speech*, LVIII (October 1972), 297.

14. Vernon, *op. cit.*, p. 142. Reprinted by permission.

15. David Johnson, *Reaching Out* (Englewood Cliffs, N.J.: Prentice-Hall, 1972), p. 78.

16. C. David Mortensen, *Communication: The Study of Human Interaction* (New York: McGraw-Hill, 1972), p. 126.

17. John B. Carroll, ed., *Language Thought and Reality: Selected Writings of Benjamin Lee Whorf* (New York: Wiley, 1956), p. 213.

18. This is also Ozzie Davis's point in "The English Language Is My Enemy," *Language in America*, ed. Neil Postman, Charles Weingartner, and Terence P. Moran (New York: Pegasus, 1969).

19. "Reversing the Bigotry of Language," *Psychology Today*, March 1974, p. 57.

20. David L. Swanson and Jesse G. Delia, *The Nature of Human Communication* (Chicago: Science Research Associates, 1976), pp. 19–20.

21. The idea for talking about physical, psychological, active, and passive availability came from Gerard Egan, *Face To Face: The Small Group Experience and Interpersonal Growth* (Monterey, CA: Brooks/Cole, 1973), pp. 96–98.

22. Carl Rogers, "Some Significant Learning," *On Becoming a Person* (Boston: Houghton Mifflin, 1961), p. 18.

ADDITIONAL RESOURCES

One of the best chapter-length treatments of person perception that we're aware of is D. W. Hamlyn's "Person Perception and Our Understanding of Others," in T. Mischel, ed., *Understanding Other People* (Oxford, Basil Blackwell, 1974).

David J. Schneider, Albert H. Hastorf, and Phoebe C. Ellsworth explain the perception of people in detail in their small but very substantive paperback, *Person Perception*, 2nd ed. (Reading, MA: Addison-Wesley, 1979).

Paul Tournier relates the topics of Chapter 2 and Chapter 3 as he discusses differences between perceiving things and perceiving persons in his book *The Meaning of Persons* (New York: Harper and Row, 1957). See especially his chapter, "The World of Things and the World of Persons," pp. 179–193.

Bill Wilmot includes a clear, comprehensive, and communication-relevant discussion of perception and person perception in Chapters 2, "Perception of Self," and 3, "Perception of the Other" of his book *Dyadic Communication*, 2nd ed. (Reading, MA: Addison-Wesley, 1979).

In his book *The Image* (Ann Arbor: University of Michigan Press, 1956), Kenneth Boulding discusses his assumption that our image or subjective knowledge of the world governs our behavior. See especially pp. 3–18. Some parts of his discussion are closely related to what we've said about the interpretation of raw data.

You'll find a rigorous and comprehensive discussion of how people process raw data in David Mortensen's chapter "Information Processing" in *Communication: The Study of Human Interaction* (New York: McGraw-Hill, 1972).

For a book that's easy to read and that offers a basic but understandable treatment of perception, see Gail E. Myers and Michele Tolela Myers's *The Dynamics of Human Communication: A Laboratory Approach*, 2nd ed. (New York: McGraw-Hill, 1977), especially Chapters 2–6.

C. S. Lewis's book *Out of the Silent Planet* (New York: Macmillan, 1968) is the story of British professor Dr. Ransom's visit to Mars. Ransom's initial reaction to the planet reveals the extent to which we *learn* to perceive things. Lewis writes that when Ransom set foot on the planet for the first time,

> He gazed about him, and the very intensity of his desire to take in the new world at a glance defeated itself. He saw nothing but colours—colours that refused to form themselves into things. Moreover, he knew nothing yet well enough to see it: *you cannot see things till you know roughly what they are.* (p. 40, italics added)

A similarly insightful science fiction account of perception and interpretation, but this time from the point of view of a Martian visiting Earth, is in Robert A. Heinlein's book *Stranger in a Strange Land* (New York: G. P. Putnam's Sons, 1961).

4

Negotiation of selves

I. NEGOTIATION OF SELVES

A. The process by which persons construct and respond to definitions of themselves and to definitions of others

B. Goes on whenever humans communicate

II. THE DEFINITIONS OR IMAGES

A. *My me* (self image)

B. *My you* (my image of you)

C. *My your me* (how I think you see me)

III. UNDERSTANDING THE PROCESS

A. Selves

1. Refers to characteristics of *persons*: uniqueness, choosing, reflective, not totally measureable
2. Also refers to object characteristics

B. Negotiation

1. Not necessarily a "bargaining" concept
2. A two-part process: two activities
   a) Sharing
   b) Being aware

   3. You can choose to share your self as an "object" or a "person"
      or parts of both
   4. You can choose to be aware of the other person's "human" or
      "object" characteristics

IV. CHOICES YOU MAKE

   A. What you share
      1. CLOSED means you share object characteristics of yourself
      2. OPEN means you share person characteristics of yourself

   B. What you are aware of
      1. STEREOTYPING means you are aware of object characteristics of
         the other
      2. SENSITIVITY means you are aware of person characteristics of
         the other

   C. Interpersonal communication happens when people choose OPEN
      SENSITIVITY

   D. Disconfirmation short-circuits the negotiation-of-selves process

V. INTERPERSONAL AND NONINTERPERSONAL COMMUNICATION

Dutch Small and Dean Tarbill have known each other for about three years. Both are members of the rowing crew, and they live with 70 other men in Crew House on lower campus. The manager of Crew House is Bill Mickelson, who was elected by the Varsity Boat Club to supervise the house and to make sure Boat Club members pay their dues and house fees. One Sunday afternoon Mickelson reminded Dutch that he owed the Boat Club some money. Dutch reluctantly paid up but was, as he put it, "a little hacked off because it left me short for the rest of the month." Mickelson asked Dutch to tell Dean when he saw him that his bill needed paying, too. Right after Mickelson had talked with Dutch, Mickelson saw Dean and told him to pay his bill. Dutch didn't know that Mickelson had already talked to Dean, and so about an hour later, when Dutch and Dean were driving to the gym to play basketball, the following dialogue occurred.

Dutch: Have you got your tennis shoes?
Dean: Yeah.
Dutch: Hey, are you planning to pay the money you owe the Boat Club?

Dean: Yeah, sometime, but I'm a little short now, okay?

Dutch: Well, the Boat Club needs the money, and Mickelson is hitting everyone up for old bills.

Dean: Hey, well listen. Just get off my ass.

Dutch: I'm not on your ass. There are just a lot of outstanding bills, and yours is the biggest.

Dean: I just saw Mickelson and he started giving me grief, too! Now you! I'll pay it when I can!

Dutch: Okay! Don't get all hot and bothered!

If Dutch and Dean asked you to take a close look at their communication in order to arbitrate their disagreement, you might start by talking about the subjects or topics they discussed—tennis shoes, old bills, the Boat Club, and especially money and Mickelson. You could also probably help them to understand what went on by looking at how verbal and nonverbal cues worked together in that communication situation, and by explaining how each person perceived and interpreted the event.

But if you wanted to talk about whether their communication was interpersonal or noninterpersonal, you'd need to go a little further. If you wanted to get at the extent to which Dutch and Dean met as *persons*—the degree to which they were willing and able to *share* some of their own humanness and to *be aware* of the humanness of the other—you'd have to see how they were involved in a process that occurs every time humans communicate, a process we call negotiation of selves. *Negotiation of selves is the process by which persons construct and respond to definitions of themselves and to definitions of the other persons communicating with them.*

In this example, Dutch defines himself as primarily an information giver; he's just passing on information to a friend. But Dean sees it differently. Dean has already been dunned by Mickelson, and now Dutch is coming across like another pushy bill collector. Although Dutch defines himself as an information giver, Dean defines Dutch as a bill collector, and the communication behavior of each is in part a response to definitions of himself—information giver, persecuted friend, etc.—and of the other person—deadbeat, bill collector, etc. These definitions of self and other emerge from the communicating that occurs in the situation, and they may change as the dialogue progresses.

Note the differences in definitions of self and of other in the following two conversations.

Conversation 1

Tom: I've got some ideas of what we could do Sunday afternoon.

Michelle: What do you want to do?

Tom: I'd like to find that new park. I heard it had some good trails for
          running and biking. Why don't you pack a lunch, and we'll just
          relax over there.
Michelle: Sounds great. When will you pick me up?
Tom: I'll be by about 1:00.

In this conversation with Michelle, Tom defines himself as the decision maker: "I've got some ideas of what we could do Sunday afternoon."
"I'd like to find that new park." "Why don't you pack a lunch, and we'll
just relax over there." He sees Michelle as the one who will go along with
what he decides. Michelle is apparently willing to define Tom as decision
maker also ("What do you want to do?") and herself as follower.
Moreover, she defines herself as lunch provider ("Sounds great") and Tom
as transportation provider ("When will you pick me up?"). Tom and
Michelle seem to understand and accept each other's definition of self and
definition of other.

Conversation 2

Craig: I have some ideas about what we could do Sunday.
Lisa: Good. I'd like us to be together, but I'd rather not spend the time
        with your friends. Let's do something together, just the two of us.
Craig: Okay. Why don't we go down to the pool? It's not very crowded on
        Sunday.
Lisa: Yeah, but there are usually lots of little kids there. Let's do some-
        thing more active than just lying in the sun.
Craig: Okay. Let's run around Green Lake.
Lisa: That sounds good! What time can I pick you up?
Craig: How about 1:00?

Craig and Lisa define themselves differently than Tom and Michelle
do, but the conversation works out just as well. At the start of the conversation it sounds as if Craig, like Tom, sees himself as leader—the one who
determines what they'll do—and defines Lisa as someone who will go
along with what he suggests ("I have some ideas about what we could do
Sunday"). Lisa doesn't see herself as only a follower, however. She has
preferences, and she wants an active part in planning the afternoon ("I'd
like us to be together, but I'd rather not spend the time with your
friends"). When Craig hears Lisa's preferences, his definitions change. He
accepts Lisa's definition of herself as co-planner ("Okay") and transportation provider ("How about 1:00?"), but he wants an active part in the
decision making, too ("Why don't we go down to the pool?" "Let's run
around Green Lake"). Lisa is comfortable with his definition of himself
and of her, so the conversation goes smoothly.

Later in the book—especially in Chapter 8—we will talk about what happens when things *don't* go smoothly, when conflict occurs. But right now we just want to emphasize that this process of constructing definitions of self and other is going on whenever humans communicate. When you're talking with someone else, you may or may not be making high-priority decisions, sharing factual information, expressing affection, or solving a problem, but you are *always* involved in negotiating selves. Another way of saying this is that you *can* choose *not* to share factual information, not to express affection, not to solve a problem, etc. But you cannot choose to avoid constructing definitions of the other and of your self. This process is going on even in an exchange like the following.

Jan: Hey, how's it goin', Paul?
Paul: Don't bug me.
Jan: What's the matter?
Paul: Nothing. Forget it.
Jan: What are you so out of shape about?
Paul: Forget it! Just kiss off.
Jan: Well, all right! Pout. I don't give a damn!

Paul and Jan are not talking about any object, issue, or event separate from themselves. But they are definitely communicating with each other, and their communication is primarily negotiation of selves. In the interchange between Paul and Jan, the negotiation of selves works something like this:

Paul's definition of self and of Jan

> I see myself as independent of you ("Don't bug me." "Nothing. Forget it"). I don't choose to share much of my self-definition in words ("Forget it! Just kiss off," etc.). I see you as feeling superior to me—you seem to see me as stupid and unreasonable. But I disagree, I know I have good reasons for my anger.

Jan's definition of self and of Paul

> I see myself as friendly and concerned ("Hey, how's it goin', Paul?" "What's the matter?"). I'm willing to share some of my self, but I see you as unreasonable and pouty ("Well, all right! Pout. I don't give a damn!").

There's some kind of negotiation-of-selves process going on every time humans communicate—from a computer-typed business letter, to a political speech, to a TV newscast, to an intimate whisper. In fact, that process is going on right now. As we communicate with you in this book, we are choosing how much we will share with you about how we see ourselves and how we will respond to our definitions of you; and you're doing the same thing. How do you define yourself as you read this book? As a discoverer of new ideas? Under pressure? Interested? Tired? How do you see us? As open and honest? Naive? Authoritarian? Buddy-buddy? Middle-class? Out of date? Friendly? Overpersonal? Too white? Threatening? If you define us as "friendly textbook writers," how does that affect our communication with you?

These questions can be asked about any instance of human communication. Whenever we communicate, one thing we "say" is "This is how I see myself." At the same time we're sharing that image of ourselves, we're noticing and responding to the image that the other person is offering us. Consequently, we are also "saying" both "This is how I see you" and "This is how I see you seeing me."[1] We put the word "saying" in quotation marks because we communicate about these images verbally *and* nonverbally. In other words, sometimes we use words to say, for example, "That's not up to me to decide" (that is, I define myself in this case as follower not leader); or "Since you see Ben every day, why don't you tell him about the party?" (that is, my image of you is that you're more able to do that than I am). But we also often communicate our images of ourselves and "read" the images of others in nonverbal cues. Think of how your tone of voice changes as you talk to a small child, for example. Then it's your vocal inflection and perhaps your posture, eyes, and facial expression that "say," "I see you as a child who probably won't listen or understand unless I talk in a special way." Or how do you know when the person you're talking with is seeing himself or herself as superior to you? Usually from posture, voice, face, and eye contact cues. As we said in Chapter 1, one of the main functions of nonverbal cues is to project and define these images and thus to *define the relationship* between the people communicating.

That's why we are making so much out of this negotiation-of-selves idea. When you realize what self image you are projecting and how you're interpreting and responding to your image of other persons, you will be more able to determine whether you are promoting impersonal-quality or interpersonal-quality communication. When you become more conscious of whether you're sharing object or human aspects of yourself and whether you're noticing and responding to object or human aspects of the other person, you'll be more able to choose, when you want to, to promote interpersonal-quality communication. And the other person(s) will be able to do the same thing. Becoming aware of your negotiation-of-selves choices and outcomes is one of the crucial first steps toward promoting the quality of communication that you want to experience.

There are at least three kinds of definitions or images that play a part in this negotiation-of-selves process. The first is an image of your self, which we'll call MY ME. Whenever you're in contact with another person, you are nonverbally and sometimes verbally "saying," "This is how I see myself." When you type a letter, for example, and begin with "Dear Sir" followed by a colon, you're defining yourself in part as distant from the person you're writing—you'd never begin a warm, friendly letter to your lover with "Dear Sir:" or "Dear Madam:" When you say to a group as you leave the room, "Don't make a decision on that until I get back," you're defining yourself as concerned, involved, an important part of the decision-making process. As with all the other images, *my me* changes as you talk with different people and even as any single conversation develops. But it's always there; each person is "saying" as he or she communicates, "This is how I see myself."

At the same time, each person is also working with an image of the person he or she is communicating with, MY YOU. Not only do we say, "This is how I see myself," but we also nonverbally and sometimes verbally "say," "This is how I see you." In a group situation this process can get very complicated, because you may well have an image of each individual there, so your *my you* changes as your attention shifts from one person to another. Or you may deal only with an image of the group as a whole. But whatever the circumstances, you are constantly working with images of the other(s). When you respond, "Yes, ma'am," or "Yes, sir," part of your image of the other (unless you're being sarcastic) is that she or he deserves respect. Allowing another to stand close to you or to touch you "says," in part, "I see you as trustworthy; I don't see you as a threat." And frequent interruptions usually "say," "You're not important" or "You're not worth listening to."

A third image that's operating whenever we communicate is MY YOUR ME—my image of how you're seeing me. When you're being interviewed for a job, for example, you develop an image of your self (*my me*: "I'm qualified for this job even though my answers to the questions may not be exactly perfect"); an image of the interviewer (*my you*: "This interviewer doesn't know how to ask clear questions!"); *and an image of how the interviewer sees you* (*my your me*: "The interviewer thinks I'm not doing a very good job of answering questions"). If you believe the interviewer is constructing positive images of you, you tend to be encouraged, and your communication behavior will reflect this attitude. On the other hand, if you believe the interviewer thinks you're doing a lousy job of answering questions, you may become discouraged, and again, your communication behavior will be affected. In some situations, this third image (*my your me*) can have more impact than a self image or an image of the other.

THE DEFINITIONS OR IMAGES: MY ME, MY YOU, MY YOUR ME

As a matter of fact, as Gustav Ichheiser explains, communication problems often occur because of distorted images:

> Many conflicts in interpersonal (and intergroup) relations are not, as it is often supposed, the result of hostile ("aggressive") attitudes with reference to each other. Rather they are the result of distorted *images* which the individuals or the groups have about each other. Each believes that he only defends himself and that it is the other who is the aggressor. Certainly, very often distorted images and misinterpretations are the consequence of conscious and unconscious hostilities. But also the opposite is often true: many hostilities are not the cause but the *consequence* of distorted images and misinterpretations. It is worth while to note at this place that, even though this may be shocking and disturbing, we have to realize that very frequently if not always, people who are persecuting others are not aware that they are persecuting, for, in the light of the images which they have in their minds, it looks to them that they are fighting for a worthy cause or are liberating the world from an evil thing.[2]

As we'll explain in Chapter 8, many conflicts can be handled effectively only when the people involved get clear about their images of each other. Most conflicts will continue to escalate, in other words, until the persons or groups understand each other's self images, views of the other, and definition of how they think the other sees them. But again, for now we just want to emphasize that these images exist, and that they continuously affect human communication. Whenever we're in contact with others, we are constantly perceiving and responding to the images we have and to those we believe the other person has of us.

Notice how each person's three images work in the following conversation.

Bob:	Sheryle, should I take that job or not? I'm not sure what to do.	*My me,* or image of self
Sheryle:	I don't know, I've never had to decide something like that before. You're the one who has to live with the job; you ought to know what to do!	*My me,* image of self *My you,* image of other
Bob:	Why is it that you never offer a constructive suggestion? I've thought a lot about this, but I just wanted to know your opinion. You seem to think I'm insecure or something. I'm not; I just want your opinion.	*My you,* image of other *My me,* self image *My your me,* image of how other sees self

Sheryle: I'm glad you respect my opinion. But as I said,   *My your me,*
          you have to live with the job. You decide.   image of how
          That's as constructive as I can get.   other sees self
                                                              My you,
                                                              image
                                                              of other
                                                              My me,
                                                              image of self

Although the labels on the dialogue above may make pretty clear sense to you, we've found that it's much more difficult to understand the process of negotiation of selves as you personally experience it in every day communicating. And (1) since this process is going on *all* the time you communicate, and (2) since your choices about how to participate in this process will substantially affect the quality of your communicating, we're convinced that it's worth the time and effort to try to understand negotiation of selves clearly. Consequently, we want first to explain what we mean by the terms "selves" and "negotiation" and then to clarify how your choices about which "selves" to "negotiate" affect the quality of your communicating.

UNDERSTANDING THE PROCESS

As we said in Chapter 2, each person's self is made up of both object characteristics and person characteristics. Objectively, it's clear that each of us is similar to many persons we know. Like many others, for example, John is male, middle-aged, married, a teacher, a sailor, and a person who doesn't like cooked zucchini. At various times John fills roles that are filled by many others—parent, advisor, critic, carpenter, cook, mechanic, writer, husband. But like you, John is not just a parent- advisor- critic- carpenter- cook- mechanic- writer- husband. He is also unique; no other human has John's genetic makeup, and no one has his experiences. Much of what he does when he's cooking is done by other cooks and has been done by cooks for centuries. But part of what he does is new, singular, unique. As a self, in other words, John is both like others and unique.

Selves

Each self is also part reacter and part chooser. Virtually all persons react physically to loud noises, bright lights, or sudden and violent changes of direction. We also often react to criticism with snappish defensiveness and to a "Howzitgoin?" with a "Fine. Howzitgoinwithyou?" But we also can and do *respond* rather than just react; persons are not billiard or croquet balls, the movement of which is entirely determined by forces outside them. We can choose, for example, to respond to a cliché with sincerity or to follow an attack with inquiry instead of defensiveness. If someone attacks us verbally with "You really screwed up, klutz!" we can choose to respond in several different ways.

Counterattack: You're not perfect, either!
Inquiry: I'm not sure what I did. Where did I mess up?
Silence:
Defensiveness: I didn't screw up. I was only following orders!

Selves also are made up of both objectively measurable elements and personally unmeasurable ones. I can learn a great deal about you by learning your height, weight, age, ethnic background, years of schooling, income, job experience, and so on. But I won't know you until I also contact some of what you're feeling, and there are no measures or scales that can fully capture emotions. Especially since feelings are constantly changing, they're among the most obvious unmeasurable, "nonobject," *personal* parts of each of us.

Finally, as we also said in Chapter 2, each person is sometimes unaware—like objects—and sometimes just aware of the surroundings—like animals. But persons can also be *reflective*—aware of their awareness—and that's a quality objects and animals don't have. Your reflectiveness is what enables you to be aware of *my me, my you,* and *my your me.* Without your ability to be aware of your awareness, you'd never be able to think in terms of those images or definitions of self and other. So your level of consciousness also includes both "object characteristics" and "person characteristics."

We've repeated those four characteristics here because they define what we mean by "selves" in the phrase "negotiation of selves." Your choice about how to participate in the image-transaction or negotiation-of-selves process is partly a choice of whether to deal with your own and the other person's *object* characteristics or your and the other's *person* characteristics.

Negotiation   When we use the term "negotiation," we don't want you to think only about a business transaction or the process of diplomatic bargaining that results in a cease-fire or a treaty. But we do want you to think of a two-part process. When we say that negotiation is two-part, we mean that it involves two activities: sharing and being aware. We've oversimplified when we describe the dynamic, complex, relational communication process in terms of *sharing* and *being aware,* but we think there are advantages to treating it that way. The most significant advantage is that, if you stop to think about your communicating, it seems intuitively obvious that whenever you're in contact with someone else, you're doing two things—giving and getting; projecting and perceiving; giving off cues and taking them in; sharing and being aware. In a face-to-face situation, you're talking, gesturing, moving, nodding, etc. (sharing), and you're watching and listening to the person(s) you're communicating with (being aware). On the phone the same two basic operations occur. You talk and listen—that is, you share—and at the same time, you are aware of how the other is responding. Those same two processes characterize all the communicating humans do. We're always sharing and being aware.

Sharing. The distinction we've made between object and person characteristics can also be used to describe the process of sharing. Sometimes your verbal and nonverbal behavior reflects primarily your object characteristics. For example, when you go up to a ticket seller, you take the role of customer or ticket buyer. In response to his or her look you say something like, "Two in the $5 section." The ticket seller replies, "Okay, here you are; that's $10." You pay, the two of you thank each other, and that's it. In some cases you might ask about what seats are available, or you might even discuss future concerts or games with the ticket seller, but the two of you just about always stick to your roles of ticket seller and ticket buyer. Choice may play some part in your communication, but you relate primarily as interchangeable parts—any ticket seller could handle your questions and you're just one of many customers. You're also primarily reacting, and neither of you shares feelings with the other.

In other situations you share some of your person characteristics. Your roommate knows you as more than just a salesperson, football fan, athlete, or ticket buyer. He or she knows some of what makes you unique—your past experiences, preferences, and pet peeves. Your roommate knows those things because you've shared them; you've made available part of who you are as a person. Similarly, your mother is aware of some of your feelings, and your subordinates know about some important choices you've made. No single person knows everything about you, but all the people you're close to are aware of some aspects of your uniqueness, feelings, choices, and reflections. Those people have those understandings because you have shared with them some of your person characteristics.

Being aware. Just as people are always giving, projecting, or sharing both object and person characteristics, they're also getting, perceiving, being aware of both object and person characteristics. We usually stay "objective" with clerks, gas station attendants, bank tellers, and representatives of the bureaucracies we have to deal with—the post office, unemployment office, subway, registrar, food stamp office, union hall, etc. When we communicate with those persons, we usually contact them as role fillers or faceless functionaries. Usually we aren't interested in their uniqueness or feelings but only in whether they can perform their jobs well. We don't ask why they've chosen their jobs or whether they feel productive, energetic, frustrated, or happy. Sometimes this objectifying can create problems, but it's often entirely appropriate. The stranger taking your ticket hasn't time to communicate interpersonally with you and might not want to even if there was time for it. That's an important point to emphasize: Noninterpersonal communication is not "bad," "thoughtless," or "immoral." It's often entirely expected and appropriate to notice only object characteristics.

However, there are times when it's important to be aware of person characteristics. When you talk with members of your family, they expect you to notice more than name, age, height, and weight. It's often important to be aware of the feelings of the people whose work you supervise, and when a good friend comes to you with a problem, you'll obviously want to listen for feelings, choices, and the things that make your friend unique. This quality of awareness is different from being aware of only object characteristics. It demands a different kind of perceiving, a different attitude, and some different skills. And it makes a major difference in your communicating; awareness of person characteristics is one thing that can help noninterpersonal-quality communication move toward interpersonal-quality communication.

In Summary (So Far)

1. The negotiation-of-selves or image-transaction process is going on every time humans communicate. You cannot choose whether or not to participate in the process; it's always happening.

2. You *can* (and do) choose *how* to participate in the process, and that choice will help determine whether the communication between you and the other(s) is noninterpersonal-quality communication or interpersonal-quality communication.

3. You can understand the choices available to you by first understanding the two activities involved: sharing and being aware.

4. The next step is to remember that you can choose to *share* object or person characteristics, and you can choose to *be aware* of object or person characteristics.

CHOICES YOU MAKE

Before we go into more detail about the choices that are available to you, we want to reemphasize that we're not talking about a static thing. Your communication is neither always interpersonal nor always noninterpersonal, even with any one individual. You are constantly making choices—to share a feeling, to be aware of the other's expectation, to reveal a choice, to ignore a look, and so on. And the person(s) you're communicating with are constantly making those choices too. The quality of the communication between you and others will be a function of all those choices, and it will change as you continue to communicate. Our goal is to help you recognize both the choices open to you and the probable effect of the choices you make.

In a sentence, what we've said in this chapter is that whenever people communicate, they are constantly choosing to share object characteristics or person characteristics and to be aware of object characteristics or person characteristics. If you put those four options into a table, or matrix, it would look like this:

		YOU ARE *AWARE* OF	
		OBJECT CHARACTERISTICS	PERSON CHARACTERISTICS
YOU *SHARE*	OBJECT CHARACTERISTICS	CHOICE 1	CHOICE 2
	PERSON CHARACTERISTICS	CHOICE 3	CHOICE 4

The dotted lines on the table are there to emphasize that the distinctions between sharing object and person characteristics and those between being aware of object and person characteristics are not static or absolute. Sometimes you're aware only of object characteristics for a time, and then you see and hear the other *person,* and then a minute later you move back to awareness only of the person's role identity. At the same time you may share some of your personness and then fall back to sharing only object characteristics. Moreover, it's not always crystal clear whether a given smile, touch, or comment is an unquestionable example of one category or the other. In short, there *are* differences among what's identified in the four segments of the chart, but the differences are often a matter of degree; they aren't always clear-cut or absolute. That's the reason for the dotted lines.

In order to make this table of choices more meaningful, we've labeled the choice represented by each box.

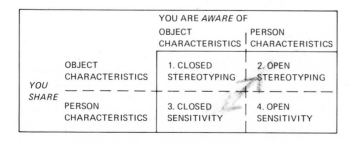

		YOU ARE *AWARE* OF	
		OBJECT CHARACTERISTICS	PERSON CHARACTERISTICS
YOU *SHARE*	OBJECT CHARACTERISTICS	1. CLOSED STEREOTYPING	2. OPEN STEREOTYPING
	PERSON CHARACTERISTICS	3. CLOSED SENSITIVITY	4. OPEN SENSITIVITY

The first word of each of the four labels—"closed" or "open"—designates what you're choosing to *share*. When you choose to share only your object characteristics, we're calling that "closed"; when you choose to share aspects of your personness, we're calling that "open." The second word of each label—"stereotyping" or "sensitivity"—designates what you're choosing to *be aware of*. When you're primarily aware of the other's object characteristics, we call it "stereotyping," and when you're aware of her or his person characteristics, we call it "sensitivity."

Those labels, especially "closed stereotyping" and "open sensitivity," have some obvious value loadings. It sounds as if "closed stereotyping" is always *bad* and "open sensitivity" is always *good. Please don't jump to that conclusion.* We chose the terms in part because they were simple and direct. Instead of "closed," for example, we could have used "restrained," "controlled," "constrained," or "restricted." But we chose the simpler word in the hope that it would be clearer. And it is important to realize, as we've said several times, that you are *not* "failing" or "making a mistake" when you choose to share only object characteristics or to be aware of the other's object characteristics. Often that's entirely appropriate for the context you're in. But we kept the "loaded" terms partly because we also believe that people don't *have* to make those choices nearly as often as they do. Stereotyping is natural and often unavoidable, but it *is* still stereotyping. It often makes good sense to be relatively restrained or closed, but that behavior *is* still "closed" behavior, and it usually has predictable consequences. In short, we've chosen those labels not just to make the choices look "bad" or "good" but to try to clarify what they are.

Closed Stereotyping   Consider the first choice. Whenever you choose this option, your behavior is *closed* in the sense that you reveal only your objective self, and it is *stereotyping* in the sense that you are aware only of the other person's object characteristics. This professor-student exchange is an example of closed stereotyping by both persons.

Professor: As I tell all my students, Mr. Bennet, your task is to learn as much about the course as possible and then to prove that you understand the material by passing the exam.
Student: Yeah, I understand that, Dr. Beach, and I realize that as a teacher, you've got a lot of hassles from other students.

In this situation each person sees the other primarily as a filler of a role, i.e., student and professor. Each reveals only objective aspects of himself or herself: "I'm a professor and I see you as a student." "I'm a student and I see you as a professor."

Sometimes people choose this option but share a great many of their object characteristics. A long conversation between strangers on an airplane or bus could be an example of closed stereotyping. For instance, a businessman who is an army veteran discovers that his seatmate is in the Coast Guard and proceeds to bombard him with stories of his own exploits during the Vietnam war. The businessman is willing to share a great deal of his object characteristics, on the assumption that all military personnel are interested in the same things (stereotyping).

Closed stereotyping also occurs, for example, when a police officer discovers that his or her neighbor is an ex-convict and immediately responds to the neighbor as someone who is dangerous and untrustworthy. The police officer reveals only that he or she is "a cop" (object characteristic) and sees the neighbor as "nothing but an ex-con" (object characteristic), and on that basis assumes that the other person is not worth knowing.

Open Stereotyping

The second option is *open* in the sense that you share some of your person characteristics but it still involves *stereotyping*—you're still aware of and responding only to the other's object characteristics. For example, a working woman choosing option 2 might be upset with her work supervisor's excessive authoritarianism and might let her boss know her feelings. She might say something like "I feel that you're pushing me a lot harder than you've got any right to. I'm working as hard as I can, but you're just coming on like a dictator." In that case, she's sharing some feelings (open), but she is aware only of the role identity of her supervisor (stereotyping).

In a different situation you might see the other person as a superior, an intellectual, a performer, or in some other such role, and yet you might be willing to reveal quite a bit about your person characteristics. For example, Hugh Prather reports how he handles this familiar experience:

> If I want to talk to someone and I am stuck for something to say, one of the simplest ways for me to get started is to state honestly what I am experiencing: "I want very much to talk to you but no words are coming."[3]

If you can combine that kind of openness with awareness of the other as a person, you can take a big step toward open sensitivity.

Closed Sensitivity

When you choose option 3, you're sensitive to the other's person characteristics while being unwilling or unable to be open about your own person characteristics. Persons in the helping professions—counselors, nurses, psychologists, teachers—often choose this option. They develop their abilities to be sensitive to the person characteristics of their client, student, patient, or counselee, but they avoid revealing much of their own person. They try to stay in their role as adviser or educator or facilitator, sometimes revealing a little of their professional self (role) but usually going into detail only about their patient's or client's problems. You may have experienced this kind of communicating with a counselor, pastor, or teacher—*your* person characteristics are very important, but the counselor's feelings, choices, etc., are out of bounds.

People choose closed sensitivity in other contexts too.

Office Manager: Why haven't you got this place cleaned up yet? It's almost midnight and you're supposed to be finished two hours after quitting time!

Janitor: Okay, okay. You've got good reasons to get mad. I know you folks have to move a lot of furniture around in the next couple of days. And I know you're the one who'll take the brunt of the criticism if it doesn't get done right. But remember that janitors have as much work as you do; don't think you're the only one with problems.

Here the janitor is sensitive to some of the office manager's feelings but responds only in terms of the role as janitor (closed).

Garry Trudeau illustrates choice 3 in a Doonesbury strip. A well-meaning person like the minister in the strip can go out of his way to be sensitive to the object of his crusade—Rufus in this instance—but often remains unwilling to share any of his person characteristics.

DOONESBURY, COPYRIGHT 1971 G. B. TRUDEAU. DISTRIBUTED BY UNIVERSAL PRESS SYNDICATE. REPRINTED BY PERMISSION.

You can probably imagine other examples of this kind of image transaction or can remember them from your own experiences. The academic adviser who is sensitive to your change in feelings but who still thinks that "you ought to take Chem 107 to round out your program" could be an example of choosing option 3 in that she or he is aware of some of your person characteristics but responds only in terms of the adviser role.

When you choose option 4 you reveal some of your person characteristics while also perceiving the other as a person. The counselor Carl Rogers writes that he tries to choose this option with the people who come to him.

Open Sensitivity

> I enter the relationship as a subjective person, not as a scrutinizer, not as a scientist. I feel, too, that when I am most effective, then somehow I am relatively whole in that relationship, or the word that has meaning to me is "transparent." To be sure there may be many aspects of my life that aren't brought into the relationship, but what is brought into the relationship is transparent. There is nothing hidden. Then I think, too, that in such a relationship I feel a real willingness for this other person to *be what he is.* I call that "acceptance." I don't know that that's a very good word for it, but my meaning there is that I'm willing for him to possess the feelings he possesses, to hold the attitudes he holds, to be the person he is.[4]

This choice is definitely not restricted to the communication between a professional counselor and a counselee, however. It's also not necessary that the persons involved agree with each other. Even though the following conversation involves disagreement, we think it comes quite close to open sensitivity.[5]

Frank: Honey, why don't you clean up the kitchen before you go to bed more often?

Ellie: I don't think it makes any difference. I get it done in the morning.

Frank: I disagree. When I come down in the morning, it makes the house feel depressing.

Ellie: Really? Why don't you clean it up yourself, then?

Frank: Okay. I'm willing to help. But it seems that we could work together on it, and it would be easier the night before.

Ellie: Does it actually bother you that much?

Frank: Yeah—I really feel that the whole house looks messy when the kitchen's cluttered with dirty dishes.

Ellie: Well, I guess I'm just used to it—my dad never seemed to mind.

Frank: Yeah, I bet.

Ellie: Don't tell me you want to have a fight about this!

Frank: Okay. That was a cheap shot. I don't especially want to fight. I'd just like you to help me clean it up in the evening.

Ellie: So you don't have to live in a lower-class house, hunh—like the one I lived in before I met you?

Frank: Wait a minute! I've told you and told you that I *love* your family!

Ellie: So why do you mind getting the kitchen cleaned in the morning
         instead of at night when I want to relax?
Frank: When it would only take us a few minutes?
Ellie: Okay. I guess it *is* kind of silly—if it means that much to you. But
         you've got to do something for me, too.
Frank: Okay. What?
Ellie: I wish you'd try not to be so unpleasant in the morning.
Frank: Okay. That's fair. I'll try.

Frank is open to Ellie in that he shares his feelings—disagreement,
depression, regret over his "cheap shot"—and he makes some of his
uniqueness available to her. He is also *sensitive* to Ellie's person characteristics. He sees and hears her desire to relax in the evening and her
protectiveness toward her family. Ellie is also relatively open and sensitive. She is aware of both Frank's anger and his apology, and she is willing
to share her reasons for choosing to leave kitchen cleaning until the
morning.

Student-teacher communication can also move beyond role-relating
when both parties choose open sensitivity. Both persons in this conversation seem willing to *share* some of their person characteristics and to *be
aware* of the other's person characteristics.

Student: I got your note about my grade, and I think I deserve more than a
           C in this class.
Teacher: Okay, I tried to explain in the note why I evaluated your in-
           volvement and work that way. How do you see things differ-
           ently?
Student: Well, in the first place, I don't think it's fair that you grade so
           much on participation. I don't talk much in groups. One-on-one
           I'm fine, but not in the whole class.
Teacher: You feel that a lot of my evaluation was based on that?
Student: Yeah. You mentioned it in your note—right here. And I think I
           was participating—I was involved in the class in ways you
           didn't even notice.
Teacher: Okay—yeah. I often miss some of what's going on. I also consid-
           ered other things—your midterm, for example. But it looks as if
           we ought to look at the whole thing again—both of us. I'm never
           sure I can see even most of what someone's doing in class, and it
           sounds as though you feel I'm missing much of what you're con-
           tributing.
Student: I really think you are. I don't talk a lot, but that doesn't mean I'm
           not involved.

Teacher: Could you get some input from some other persons in the class? Would you be willing to get comments from, say, Jim and Sandi and maybe two or three others about how they see your involvement?

Student: That's fair. But will their opinions make any difference in my grade?

Teacher: Well, right to the heart of it, hunh? I'm uncomfortable telling you that their opinions will definitely change your grade one way or the other, because I still feel some responsibility as teacher. But I know I often miss some of what's going on, and I'm really not interested in treating you unfairly. Can we wait and see what they say and then meet to talk about it again?

Student: Okay, fine. Thanks for listening. I guess I didn't really expect you'd even consider changing it. Thanks.

Teacher: "Teacher is human!" hunh?

Student: Yeah. See you in class.

There's one final way people sometimes choose to participate in the negotiation-of-selves process. Instead of being aware of someone's object *or* person characteristics, we sometimes ignore another person. Instead of sharing our own object *or* person characteristics, we sometimes carry on as if the other person weren't even there. When we do that, we're disconfirming. *Disconfirmation is communicating as if the other person didn't even exist.*

One Other Choice: Disconfirmation

People disconfirm others in many different ways. In their discussion of an important business decision, some men might ignore the contributions of a woman because they assume that her questions or suggestions are based only on emotions. Adults often disconfirm young children by talking about them as if they weren't even present or by responding to an excited "Hey! Look at this neat frog!" with "Watch out for that clean floor and go wash your hands!" It's also disconfirming to respond to someone's "Hi!" with avoidance or a blank stare.

Some counselors and therapists believe that constant disconfirmation is the most devastating experience a human can have. If you are disconfirmed often enough, you actually begin to wonder who you are or, worse yet, *if* you are anybody at all. As psychologist William James put it, the worst possible punishment any human could experience would be to be "turned loose in society and remain absolutely unnoticed by all the members thereof."[6] The reason that would be so bad is that you and I get our sense of self primarily by experiencing the ways others relate to us. If they behave as if we're nobody or as if we aren't even there, pretty soon we begin to wonder, "Well, who am I?" or "Am I important at all?"

On the other hand, sometimes it's just fine to be ignored. Many people enjoy living in a large city precisely because they can be anonymous when they want to be. In the most densely populated areas—the northeastern part of the United States, the Great Lakes cities, southern California, Japan, western Europe—the only way to gain any privacy is to ignore others and be ignored by them. That's especially important in Japan, where a couple can make love with only a rice-paper screen separating them from adjacent families and can feel *alone,* because they know that their neighbors have learned to ignore them completely. Yet disconfirmation also happens in Japan, and it's just as harmful there as in any other country.

The point is that there's more to disconfirmation than just ignoring someone. Each person's (1) intent, (2) communication *behavior,* and (3) way of *interpreting* communicative cues are all important. Consequently, I may feel ignored or disconfirmed even when you think you're confirming me. For example, you may want to confirm me (intent) by calling me on the telephone (behavior), but because I had expected you to meet with me face to face, your call is *not* confirming to me (interpretation). Or I may think I'm listening carefully (intent), but you see me not looking at you or registering any emotion in my face (behavior), so you feel disconfirmed (interpretation). Since it would take at least another chapter to unpack and explicate all those possibilities, we'd like to simplify things this way: I'm disconfirming when I ignore your relevant sharing and share either nothing of myself or only minimal objective content. In other words, if you're excited and want to share that part of you, and I ignore it, I'm choosing disconfirmation. Disconfirmation also happens when one person nonverbally appears to be listening but verbally responds as if the other person said nothing.

Kim: This school board never tries to find out what the people want. They just do whatever they damn well please.

Etran: Well, I agree it seems that way sometimes. But last week I sat through three hours of a four-hour meeting where they did nothing *but* listen to what the people wanted to tell them.

Kim: And they don't listen to the faculty or administration, either—they act like dictators.

What we've said, then, is that disconfirmation is a fifth way you can choose to participate in the negotiation-of-selves or image-transaction process. When you make this choice you short-circuit the process. Two people can continue to converse even if both are closed and stereotyping, but if they're ignoring each other, the communication won't go anywhere. And although being ignored is sometimes harmless or even desirable, *being ignored when you want to be noticed* can be devastating. So disconfirmation can hurt.

We hope that the examples of each choice—closed stereotyping, closed sensitivity, open stereotyping, open sensitivity, and disconfirmation—illustrate that the quality of the communication you experience is determined by the negotiation-of-selves options that each person selects. In other words, each communicator's choice can be identified, and the quality of the communication between two persons will depend on how their individual choices fit together. For example, in the midst of studying for an exam, you might call a good friend to ask if she has the notes for the day of class that you missed. The conversation might go something like this:

You: Hi, Rita? This is _____.
Rita: Oh, hi, _____.
You: Hey, like everybody else, I'm trying to cram for Butler's exam tomorrow, and I need the notes for last Tuesday when I was gone. Have you got them?
Rita: Yeah, I think so. Hold on and let me look. Yeah, I do. Several people copied them. You want them, too?
You: Yeah. Can I come by right away?
Rita: No problem.

In this exchange, there is both sharing and being aware, and it gets a task accomplished (you get the notes), but the communicating stays object- rather than person-oriented. You choose to be aware of Rita almost entirely as a role filler—she's a student in the class with you—and to share only those parts of yourself that put you in a similar role. She responds the same way. Although your friendship is almost certainly based on a mutual liking of the unique aspects of each of you, none of those aspects come into play in this conversation. Here both of you chose option 1, closed stereotyping. Consequently, the communication *between* you in this case is noninterpersonal. Here's how this conversation would look on the tables.

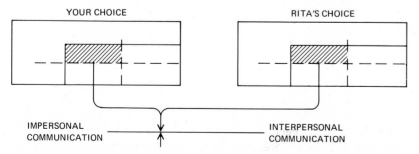

In another situation you might choose open sensitivity while Rita or someone else was sensitive to your personness but closed—unwilling or unable to share much beyond her object characteristics. That situation would look like this.

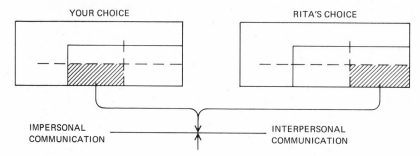

When both you and the other person or persons choose open sensitivity, your communication is interpersonal in quality. So if you were sharing some feelings, choices, and uniqueness while being aware of similar person characteristics in the other, and if the other person was doing some of the same things, the communication between you would look like this.

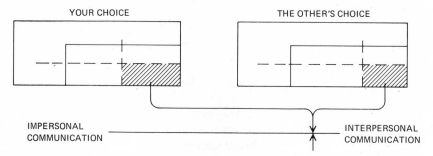

In Summary (So Far)   That's basically how we see the negotiation-of-selves or image-transaction process working.

1. Whenever any humans communicate, they are continually giving and getting information, impressions, or perceptions about "How I see myself," "How I see you," and "How I see you seeing me."

2. That complex, ongoing, constantly changing process can be "frozen" and broken down into four parts: sharing object characteristics, sharing person characteristics, being aware of object characteristics, and being aware of person characteristics.

3. Each of us is constantly choosing what to share and what to be aware of, and the quality of our communication—that is, whether our communication is impersonal or interpersonal—will depend on the choices we make.

1. *Am I really constructing these images all the time? Why?*

When you're completely alone, the negotiation-of-selves process often slows to a stop. But the process is active whenever you are in contact with one or more persons, no matter whether you're just avoiding bumping a stranger while crossing a street or marrying your childhood friend. This image transaction or negotiation of selves is one of each human's basic information processing activities. Of course, it usually goes on below the level of awareness. You won't very often hear someone say, "No, I won't do that because I see myself as superior to you," or "I see you seeing me as afraid of you." Since the process is continuous and has so much impact on the quality of our communication, however, statements like those can often be useful. We'll talk in later chapters about working to make your implicit or "hidden" images explicit, getting them out in the open.

2. *Why do we construct images of each other?*

Fundamentally, to make sense out of our world. As we said in Chapter 3, there are literally millions of stimuli available to us all the time—colors, sounds, temperatures, sights, smells—and if we had to deal with all of them all the time, the disorganization and sheer number would drive us crazy. So we organize the chaos, we structure our world, we put things—and people—into categories, so that we can, for example, distinguish between what's important and unimportant. We construct images of people to help "make sense" of them, to help predict their behavior.

3. *How do we develop these images? Where do we get the information?*

The images we develop of ourselves and of others come from a variety of sources of information: our experience with ourselves, how other people behave nonverbally toward us, what they say and don't say, what people say about each other, and so on. Sometimes we develop an image of a person primarily on the basis of what other people tell us (e.g., your image of a well-known television personality may be based entirely on what reporters tell you). At other times we form images primarily on the basis of direct observation (e.g., your image of a close friend). Sometimes we generalize parts of our self image to other people, and vice versa.

For example, when John was in the first grade, he was part of a classroom play, and he had considerable trouble remembering his lines. The teacher told him his problem was that he was "nervous in front of other people." John had never heard the term "nervous," nor had he been especially uncomfortable in that kind of situation before. In later years people told him he did well in some of the plays and presentations he was part of. One of the things he learned in that process was to distinguish what feelings and behaviors constitute "being nervous," and he learned to recognize that state in himself and others. Part of his image of himself could now be "nervous" or "relaxed," and he could now define others that way, too.

4. *Is* my me *the same in all contexts? Or are you saying that I can be defined as a different person each time I communicate with someone different?*

There is some stability. The "you" who existed in your earliest childhood memories is in many ways the same "you" who is now reading this book and who communicated today with many different people. It's also the same "you" who will get out of your bed tomorrow morning.

But you are also continually growing and changing. Think of the many ways that you are different from the person in your earliest childhood memories. You've grown in a multitude of ways, and you'll continue to grow and change until you die—many people say that the process doesn't even stop there.

Just as important, the parts of "your you" that are relevant in one context or situation are different from those that come into play in another context. When your boss asks you a question about your work, you don't respond as you do when your lover asks you a question about your clothing. It isn't that you *aren't* an informed, competent worker when talking with your lover *or* that you *aren't* a gentle, loving person when talking with your boss. You are multidimensional in both situations, but different parts of your self image are relevant.

5. *Are you saying that when I'm in a group of five or six people, each of us actually has an image of how* each *other person views us?*

Yes. Again, the images often operate below the level of awareness, but your image of each person becomes important as you turn to talk with her or him. If you had a video tape of yourself communicating in that group, you'd notice the differences—sometimes subtle ones and sometimes obvious ones. You do not communicate with any two persons in exactly the same way, and the differences reflect differences in how you see yourself, how you see them, and how you see them seeing you.

Take an obvious example. Your facial expression and tone of voice change when you move from talking with a person you define as interested, attractive, and informed to talking with someone you define as bored and uninformed about the topic. Those are visible and audible changes. And they directly reflect different definitions of self and other.

Recognize, however, that our *my you* and *my your me* images can also generalize. We sometimes operate out of a general impression, for example, of how that person sees me. Those generalized definitions can also strongly affect how we communicate.

6. *What happens when I share some of my personness and am aware of the other as a person but the other person treats me as an object?*

That can hurt or at *least* be frustrating. As we've said, the communication occurs *between* you and the other person; it is a *mutual* transaction. The quality of your communication is thus affected by the choices that both of you make. Let's consider an exchange between you and Joan. If she chooses to share only object characteristics and to be aware of you only as an object, the communication between you will not be interpersonal-quality communication.

Remember, though, that your choices and hers are *interdependent.* That's really important. Her choices are affected by yours, and yours are affected by hers. If you choose open sensitivity, especially in the face of her choosing closed stereotyping, it will affect her choices. Your choice may well make it easier for her to move toward open sensitivity herself. You *cannot determine* her choices; you can't force her to do what you want; in short, you can't make interpersonal-quality communication happen. But your choices definitely make a difference. You can *help* it happen. And you can also stop it from happening.

We'll have more to say about helping it to happen in later chapters.

7. *Doesn't that chart and all those labels get in the way of interpersonal communicating? How can I contact another person's humanness if I'm worried about "sharing uniqueness," "being aware of reflectiveness," "disconfirmation," and being aware of whether I'm choosing closed stereotyping or open sensitivity? Looks like a bunch of mechanical jargon to me.*

Remember what we said at the end of Chapter 2. It helps to look at "learning interpersonal communication" as a means to an end and not as an end in itself. It's like learning to drive a car. At first the process looks impossibly complex. Not only do you have to worry about engine rpm, gear selection, speed, traffic lights, lane markers, and warning signs, but you're supposed to check the rear-view mirror every ten seconds or so, watch out for other cars, avoid buses and trucks, and do the whole thing under the realization that if you screw up, it will be at least expensive and maybe fatal! So what do you do? You break it down into parts—warning signs and regulatory signs, negotiating hills, parking and making turns, etc. The list may seem artificial, and each part may feel awkward when you first do it, so for a time it looks as if you'll *never* be able to put the whole process together into something that feels natural. But before long your self-consciousness disappears, and you drive "without thinking about it."

Learning about the negotiation of selves can be a similar process. You may be in the center of the diagram below now, but you'll soon move off to the right.

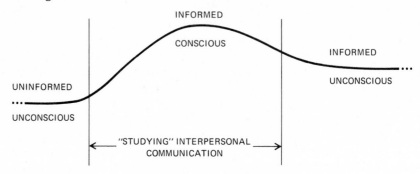

EXERCISES

Individual Activity: Images

The purpose of this exercise is to compare your images (my me, my you, my your me) with a friend's (spouse, roommate) images. You and your friend will each write down on a 3 × 5 card answers to the following questions:

> How would you describe yourself in terms of our relationship—our friendship, marriage, whatever it is.
>
> How would you describe me in terms of our relationship?
>
> What do you think my impressions of you are?

When each of you has finished, compare notes. If there are discrepancies—and there usually are—ask why. What behaviors led to the images? Why the differences in interpretation of each other?

Group Activity: Negotiation of Selves

Here's an exercise that some students created to check out and to clarify understanding of the negotiation of selves that's going on whenever humans communicate. Like the negotiation process itself, the exercise looks a little complicated at first, but it seems to work, so you may want to give it a try.

The exercise requires eight persons who are seated in this pattern:

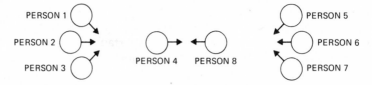

The four persons on the left (1, 2, 3, and 4) make up one communicator; the four on the right (5, 6, 7, and 8) make up the other communicator. *Persons 1, 2, 3, and 4* are a young police officer, just two weeks out of the police academy. The officer is patrolling College Avenue with his superior, a sergeant who has been on the force for 15 years. The rookie knows he's being evaluated by the sergeant. A number of recent car-pedestrian accidents on College Avenue have emphasized the problems created by jaywalking. The officer has just seen a man cross hurriedly and carelessly in the middle of the block and is ready to cite him.

Persons 5, 6, 7, and 8 are a male student, dressed in faded jeans and an old work shirt. He has a beard and hair to his shoulders, and he is carrying some books in an old army pack. It's the beginning of the school term, and he's been hassled all day by registration. Now he's having trouble locating the textbooks he needs. He was exasperated to find that one store was out of almost everything he needs, and he has just now crossed the street in the middle of the block to get to the only other bookstore that is available.

Person 4, the speaker for the police officer, is the first to talk, but he can't say anything until he has been informed by each of the persons behind him. First, person 1 indicates how the police officer sees himself (*my me*). Person 1 should say something like, "My identity as a _____ _____ is important here. Right now I'm _____ _____ and feel _____ in this situation."

Then person 2 tells how the police officer sees the student (*my you*). Person 2 should say something like "I can see that the guy's a _____ _____."

Person 3 explains how the police officer sees the college student seeing him (*my your me*). "This college guy thinks I'm _____ _____."

After persons 1, 2, and 3 have given their interpretations of the police officer's definitions, person 4 speaks as the police officer. Person 4's job, then, is to listen to persons 1, 2, and 3 and to decide how to combine their definitions into a statement that makes some kind of sense in this situation.

Then it's the student's turn. First, person 5 indicates how the student sees himself (*my me*); then, person 6 explains the student's image of the officer (*my you*); and so on.

The dialogue usually goes rather slowly at first, but it gets easier as you go along and it can also be fun. Just as important, we think that if you try it, you'll be able to *experience* what we mean by the negotiation-of-selves process.

Group Application: Images and the Insurance Salesperson

The purpose of this exercise is to demonstrate the impact of images on communication behavior. Ask volunteers to act out the following situations.

Situation 1

Mr. A: Insurance salesman. Sees himself as very knowledgeable about insurance, as he actually is, and trustworthy. Believes he has to make a sale—feels pressure from boss. Thinks this next contact will certainly buy, believes she is not knowledgeable about insurance and needs disability insurance.

Ms. B: Homemaker, successful attorney. Sees herself as knowledgeable about insurance and as not needing disability insurance. Sees insurance salesman as "nosy," "phony," and believes that he is out to make a sale at her expense. Does not see the salesman as trustworthy.

Situation 2

Mr. A: Same as above

Ms. C: Successful physician. Sees herself as not knowledgeable about insurance and as needing disability insurance. However, sees this insurance salesman as phony and not very trustworthy. Thinks the salesman knows almost nothing about physicians.

Situation 3

Mr. A: Same as above

Ms. D: Homemaker who works 30 hours a week as a travel agent. Sees herself as only moderately knowledgeable about insurance and as needing disability insurance, which her company does not provide. Sees Mr. A as knowledgeable and trustworthy. Thinks the salesman understands the problems faced by a working homemaker.

Situation 4

Mr. A: Same as above

Ms. E: Successful consultant to industry in marketing. Sees herself as only moderately knowledgeable about insurance and as needing disability insurance. Sees Mr. A as knowledgeable and a source of information. However, Ms. E thinks Mr. A believes that "women make poor consultants," and that "Ms. E is not qualified to be a consultant."

If the volunteer actors matched communication behaviors with images, how did the various pairs' communication differ?

Ms. B's communication with Mr. A. is based on the image(s) of _____

_____

Her communication is characterized by _____

_____

Ms. C's communication with Mr. A. is based on the image(s) of _____

_____

Her communication is characterized by _____

_____

Some of the reasons why Ms. B differed from Ms. C in her treatment of Mr. A: _____

_____

Continue the exercise, cross-comparing all the situations given.

Here's a dialogue you can analyze individually or in small groups. Try to determine when and how *open sensitivity* occurs. This dialogue is based on an actual incident: Sandra, a black woman, is explaining her views about interracial marriage to Viki, a white woman. (This was a controversy in which both persons *worked at* open sensitivity.)

Group Activity: Open Sensitivity

Sandra: I don't think a white girl should marry a black man, because after a while they won't make it together.

Viki: I get defensive about that because you seem to believe that no interracial marriage will ever work out. Some do okay.

Sandra: Okay, I can see that for you, some black men who marry white girls are happy. But for me, a black man can never be completely happy in that situation, because only a black woman really understands what a black man's needs are. She knows where he's at, where he's been, what he goes through every day.

Viki: Are you talking about physical needs? Or both physical and psychological needs?

Sandra: I'm talking about both.

Viki: Damn, I've got two sides of me responding. I want to argue with you because from my point of view, you're saying I'm inferior as a woman. But on the other hand, I feel you're saying something

> different—that a relationship between a black man and a black woman can be much fuller, much more complete, than between a black man and a white woman.

Sandra: I hear you. A white man and I could never make it. That's not where I'm at. We could be friends, but that's all. You could do much more for him than I would.

Viki: I wish we didn't have to use the words "white" and "black." They seem so impersonal. But I don't know how else to talk about it. Anyway, it seems to me that if a black man and a white woman go through the same cultural experiences, they could be compatible.

Sandra: You mean if they go to the same school, grow up in the same neighborhood, and things like that?

Viki: Yeah.

Sandra: They'd be more compatible than if they grew up in completely different environments. I understand what you're saying about that. But the black man will still have experiences that no white person could ever have; in my mind, only another black could understand those experiences.

Viki: I think we understand each other's position, but I don't think either of us wants to change.

Sandra: We agree on that.

NOTES

1. Other authors (for example: Laing; Watzlawick *et al.*—see the Additional Resources section for this chapter) point out that we are also affected by how I see you seeing me seeing you, how I see you seeing me seeing you seeing me, and so on to theoretical infinity. Although we are aware of these complexities, we've found that the three "levels" or images we discuss here are complicated enough to be fairly accurate yet simple enough to be workable.

2. Gustav Ichheiser, *Appearances and Realities: Misunderstandings in Human Relations* (San Francisco: Jossey-Bass, 1970), pp. 103–104.

3. Hugh Prather, *I Touch the Earth, the Earth Touches Me* (Garden City, NY: Doubleday, 1972), n.p.

4. Carl R. Rogers, "Dialogue Between Martin Buber and Carl R. Rogers," in Martin Buber, *The Knowledge of Man*, ed. Maurice Friedman, trans. Maurice Friedman and Ronald Gregor Smith (New York: Harper & Row, 1965), pp. 169–170. Reprinted by permission.

5. We got the idea for this conversation from examples in George R. Bach and Peter Wyden, *The Intimate Enemy: How to Fight Fair in Love and Marriage* (New York: Avon Books, 1968).

6. Quoted in R. D. Laing, *Self and Others* (Baltimore: Penguin Books, 1969), pp. 98–99.

Gustav Ichheiser discusses how the negotiation-of-selves process works in interpersonal relations in his book *Appearances and Realities: Misunderstanding in Human Relations* (San Francisco: Jossey-Bass, 1970). Although few people paid much attention to this book when it was published, it now seems to be getting more and more attention.

R. D. Laing also explores how the negotiation-of-selves process affects our communication in several of his books. The most graphic—and challenging—treatment is in Laing's *Knots* (New York: Random House, 1972). He also discusses this dynamic in *Self and Others* (Baltimore: Penguin Books, 1969). See especially Part 2, "Forms of Interpersonal Action."

One of Laing's co-workers, Aaron Esterson, also discusses this process in the theoretical part of *The Leaves of Spring* (Harmondsworth, Middlesex, England: Penguin Books, 1970), Part 2, "Interexperience and Interaction."

Martin Buber briefly mentions the communication problems created by the negotiation-of-selves process in the "Being and Seeming" section of his essay "Elements of the Interhuman," in *The Knowledge of Man*, ed. Maurice Friedman (New York: Harper & Row, 1965), pp. 72–88.

Under the heading "Relationship Communication," Paul Watzlawick, Janet Helmick Beavin, and Don D. Jackson discuss some ideas that are closely related to what we call negotiation of selves. See their book *Pragmatics of Human Communication* (New York; Norton, 1967), pp. 51–54 and 81–93, especially pp. 83–89.

George J. McCall and J. L. Simmons's *Identities and Interactions* (New York: The Free Press, 1966) presents, among other things, a sociological version of something similar to the negotiation-of-selves idea. In McCall and Simmons's terms, in every "symbolic interaction" process, "the basic 'thing' to be identified . . . is the person himself. For each actor there is one key 'thing' whose identity and meaning must be consensually established before all else—namely, himself. 'Who am I in this situation? What implications do I have for the plans of action, both active and latent, of myself and the others?' " (p. 61).

ADDITIONAL RESOURCES

5

Sharing your self

I. WHAT SHARING *ISN'T*

A. Does *not* necessarily mean you have to reveal confidential information about yourself

B. Does *not* have to be heavy *or* trivial

C. Does *not* necessarily mean unloading negative or depressed feelings

D. Does *not* necessarily mean you blurt out everything you're thinking

E. Does *not* mean you are self-centered

II. WHAT SHARING *IS*

A. Sharing needs to be *appropriate* to the situation

B. Sharing needs to be appropriate to the relationship

C. Sharing also needs to be appropriately timed

1. Emotional timing
2. Relevance timing
3. Situational timing

D. You are in control of how much you share, with whom, and when

E. Sharing involves risk

F. Sharing requires some trust

153

III. SUGGESTIONS ABOUT SHARING

  A. Become aware of your self, especially your "person" characteristics

  B. Become aware of how sharing "works"

  C. Share both your objective and personal self

  D. Share descriptively

  E. Impact of words on sharing

  F. Impact of nonverbal on sharing

  G. Importance of congruence

"Maaaaa-meeee! Billy won't share his chocolate chip cookies with me!!"

"Sure I'll be there. I enjoy sharing what I've learned with groups like yours."

"Our two families went together to rent the cabin, and we're going to share the use of it."

"Both the production and the sales departments share the credit for this increase in earnings."

  As these four statements show, we ordinarily use the term "sharing" in two different ways. Sometimes "sharing" means that one person gives part or all of something to somebody else, as in the first two examples. Other times sharing means having or using something in common with other people, as in the last two statements.

  In this chapter we are using the term "sharing" mainly in the first sense. So when we talk about "sharing some of your self," we're thinking of something you can choose to do or not to do. Sharing some of your self means verbally and nonverbally telling another person something about who you are, something that the other wouldn't be likely to recognize or understand without your help.

  Of course, when I tell you something about me, you become aware of it, and then we "share" it in the second sense—that is, we experience it in common. But as a communication skill, sharing refers to one person's choices and behaviors.

WHAT SHARING IS AND WHAT IT ISN'T At this point that might sound like an unusual way to talk about "sharing." If you think of the term mainly in the context of sharing clothes or a car, you may wonder whether we're talking about "lending" part of your self to someone. Or you may be wondering how often a person would actually *do* what we're talking about here—"Sure, my best friend and my spouse know a lot about me, but I'm not going to share much of my self with anybody else!" At this point those are understandable responses. So before we go further, we'd like to clarify what sharing is and what it isn't. Look for a minute at the examples that follow.

Example 1

Mark: Hey, Sue, what'd you think of the movie?

Sue: Fantastic! I've never laughed so hard in all my life—that's my kind of humor!

Mark: Yeah, I know what you mean.

Sue: Actually, I've been in a good mood for weeks. Right now I'm working on a paper, and usually I hate doing papers. But I'm not letting this one get me down. I feel in control of myself. You know what I mean?

Mark: You've been out in the sun too long.

Sue: No, I'm not kidding, Mark. It's not just the paper. I've kind of been thinking about how most of the time I let myself be controlled by the things around me. I worry about papers, who likes me, who doesn't like me, and stuff like that. Right now, I've talked myself into not worrying about those things, and I feel great!

Mark: Man, I've never seen you so excited. I think you're really on the level.

Sue: Well, I always feel I tell you about my frustrations and failures, so today you're hearing about my triumphs.

Example 2

Jorge: Hey man, what it is?

Ramon: Rotten.

Jorge: What's happening?

Ramon: Nothin' worth talking about. My boss is on my back, and I just got nailed by a $40 phone bill I didn't expect.

Jorge: That's the pits. But you'll be at the party tonight, right?

Ramon: Oh, yeah. I forgot about that. That ought to improve my mood. Thanks for reminding me.

Example 3

Kathryn: Honey, we need to talk for a minute.

Jack: Sounds serious. What's up?

Kathryn: Mac and Don and the Chans will be there tonight, won't they?

Jack: Yes.
Kathryn: Well, it seems that every time we're out with them you drink so
          much that you fall asleep, and I have to drive home.
Jack: Well, you're no "Saint Kathryn" yourself, you know.
Kathryn: Okay, you're right. I've done that before, too, but I really feel
          embarrassed when either of us gets drunk, and I don't want that
          to happen. I'll watch it for you if you'll keep track of how much I
          have.
Jack: To hell with that! I don't want you babysitting me, and I don't
          want to babysit you!
Kathryn: I don't want *that* either—I don't intend to "babysit"! But it'd
          sure make it easier to get up and go to work tomorrow.

If you look at those three examples, we think you can begin to see
what we mean—and don't mean—by sharing some of your self. In the first
place, sharing some of your self does *not* necessarily mean discussing your
sex life or some other soul-stirring, deep-seated, profound experience or
feeling. Note the lack of references to sex, religion, or politics. Sometimes
the more serious feelings are important—as in Example 3—but often what
you share is neither deep nor heart-rending. That doesn't mean that your
sharing is silly or trivial; the $40 phone bill and crabby boss are real
problems for Ramon. But sharing is not necessarily heavy.

Nor does sharing mean unloading only your negative or depressed
feelings. Two people can often come much closer together just by sharing
some things they feel *good* about. The dialogue between Mark and Sue is
an example of that. The excitement and triumph Sue shared with Mark
definitely helped him see her humanness and helped to make their communication interpersonal.

We're also *not* suggesting that you should blurt out everything that
you're thinking and feeling in a nonstop stream of self-centered disclo-
sures. In Example 2, Ramon doesn't go into great detail, but he does make
an important part of his personness available to Jorge. And that's often
exactly what's needed. As Martin Buber puts it, sharing "does not depend
on one saying to the other everything that occurs to him, but only on his
letting no seeming creep in between himself and the other."[1] In other
words, you don't say everything, but what you do say is genuine.

The main point is that sharing needs to be appropriate to the context
and the relationship. Most interpersonal relationships take time to grow,
and deep, detailed disclosure to a relative stranger will usually succeed
only in making the other person uncomfortable. Kathryn and Jack are
talking about something potentially heavy, but since they live together,
"heavies" are appropriate to their relationship. And notice that this topic
is of concern to them both and clearly relevant to the immediate situation.
So it's completely appropriate.

Appropriateness really is important. Sharing some of your self is not just meant to make *you* feel better; it's meant to improve your relationship with other persons. You don't share just to suit yourself; you share to facilitate the *relationship*. Appropriateness is often mostly a matter of timing—what we call *emotional* timing, *relevance* timing, and *situational* timing. Appropriate emotional timing means that the persons involved *feel* willing and able to hear what you want to share. It's obvious that a friend who is upset about a job loss or a death in the family is going to find it very hard to listen to you share something heavy or serious. If you go ahead in that situation and dump your problems on your friend, you certainly won't be facilitating the *relationship*. Relevance timing means that the sharing fits the topics that are being discussed. For example, a worker we talked with was upset because, after he delivered a report to his manager, discussed it briefly, and was about to leave, the manager took the opportunity to share some negative feelings he had about the worker's participation in the previous day's meeting. The feelings were understandable, and the worker would have appreciated hearing them, but not then and there. They weren't relevant to what the two of them were discussing, and consequently the worker felt that they came "out of nowhere" or "off the wall." Situation timing is similar to relevance timing; it has to do with who is present and where you are geographically. A woman won't discuss problems connected with her pregnancy—even with her best friend—in a crowded grandstand. Two persons having an argument or a sentimental reunion will postpone their sharing when they step into an elevator filled with strangers. And before you share something important, whether positive or negative, it's good to ask, "Is this the right time and place?"

If you want your sharing to be appropriate, it's important to ask youself about all three kinds of timing. Sharing is for you *and* the other person(s); be as sensitive as you can be to their expectations and feelings and to the communication topic and situation.

Finally, we believe that you always ought to be in control of how much of your self you share, with whom, and when. We don't agree with the format of some forced-choice encounter groups in which each person is compelled to spill his or her guts or leave the group. Sharing your self always involves some risk, and consequently you should always retain the right to choose what to reveal and what to conceal.

We have felt that risk in writing this book. We haven't shared anything particularly intimate with you, but we have been more open about some of our thoughts and feelings than we might otherwise have been in this situation. We've done that because we recognize one of the paradoxes of sharing some of your self with another; usually you don't want to *share* unless you *trust* the other person, because sharing is *risky*. But you can't create *trust* and thus diminish *risk* without *sharing*. In other words, people generally share some of their selves when they trust each other, and they create trust by sharing with each other. Sharing creates trust, and trust encourages sharing. We've therefore come to the conclusion that the risks we've taken are worth it. They're worth it because they may help create the kind of trusting relationship that can help us grow. So far, we haven't been disappointed. One or two persons who have read this manuscript have told us we were being too personal or that some of what we wrote was "in questionable taste." But most people have been fairly willing to trust us, and we believe that that trust will make this book more useful and helpful than a distant, impersonal commentary.

There's another paradox of sharing. The more you find out about another person, the more you realize how relatively little you know about her or him. To put it in other words, the more you share, the more there is left to share. Some people exaggerate the risk of self-disclosure because they're afraid it means giving up everything they are—not having anything left that's uniquely theirs. But as many couples who have enjoyed a long-term intimate relationship have learned, that fear is groundless. You can never succeed in telling someone everything about you, primarily because you're incredibly complex and continually changing. As one person becomes more open to another, he or she also becomes more mysterious, and that ever-present mystery is one thing that can keep a relationship exciting over the years.

It would help if you'd remember that when we talk about sharing some of your personness, we are *not* necessarily talking about a super-serious sex rap, a thoughtless gut dump, a long-winded, self-centered monologue, or an embarrassingly intimate disclosure. We believe that you should always be able to choose what you share, and that your choices should be appropriate to the situation and to the relationship. We recognize that sharing is risky, but we believe that the risk is worth it because of the trust that can be built. We've found that the more you learn about another person, the more you realize how impossible it is to know her or him completely.

SOME SUGGESTIONS ABOUT SHARING

First, Become Aware of Your Self

In order to share some of your self, you first have to be aware of what's there to be shared. We're not suggesting that you have to withdraw at this point for a week of intensive self-analysis, but it is a good idea to give some thought to the makeup of your self. As we've emphasized before, each person's self is an amalgam of object characteristics and person characteristics. Your "objective self" is made up of those aspects of you that are interchangeable, measurable, reactive, and unreflective. Your "personal self" consists of those aspects of you that are unique, unmeasurable, choice-making, and reflective.

Your Interchangeable vs. Unique Aspects

Think for a minute about some of the demographic characteristics that affect your communicating. Do you see yourself as Asian or Oriental, "just like hundreds of millions of other Asians or Orientals"? Or as native American? Black? Caucasian? Brown? Hapa haole? Indian? Creole? Japanese-American? Do others see you that way? What are some of the ways that your ethnicity affects your communicating? Who are the people you talk with most? What expressions are understood only by those in your ethnic group? How easy is it for you to trust a member of a different ethnic group?

How masculine or feminine do you see yourself? Who among your friends is noticeably more masculine or feminine than you?

Are you Catholic? Jewish? Protestant? Orthodox? Buddhist? Evangelical? Do you see yourself as young or old? What circumstances affect that perception—that is, when do you feel especially young and especially old? Are you an easterner or a westerner? A rural person or a city dweller? Are you a sophomore? A graduate student? A Canadian? Are you ever called "half-breed"?

What family roles do you fill? Are you a sister? Brother? Daughter? Son? Wife? Husband? Uncle? Aunt? Brother-in-law? Mother? Father? Think how those parts of your object self can affect your communicating.

How about your occupational roles? Are you a clerk? Salesperson? Supervisor? Manager? Cashier? Secretary? Musician? Mechanic? Operator? Guard? Gardener? Painter?

What other roles do you sometimes fill? Are you an officer of an organization? Runner? Commuter? Photographer? Skier? How often are you a customer? Swimmer? Worshipper? Cyclist? All those aspects of your object self can play a part in your communicating.

But your unique aspects can be even more important. What are some of the ways that your experiences distinguish you from every other black, Indian, or Caucasian? "Sure, I'm Jewish, but I'm not like those Ashkenazim—or even like the other people in my synagogue. I keep kosher—all the time—but I also stay in contact with local politics. Being a Jew is a central part of my life, but I'm also the only member of the school board who is really representing minority interests."

"I am the first generation of my family who has lived in the United States. I retain the background of my Chinese heritage, but I use the American environment, legal system, and business to survive. Adaptation is my major advantage over other people of my race. I cling to my heritage but work in the present culture. I am a Chinese-American, but I truly am Chinese."

What are some of the ways that you're a unique brother, sister, daughter, son, mother, or father? John, for example, sees unique aspects of his relationship with his sister, Barbara. They went through the typical brother-sister conflicts and growing pains, and as they got older, they got closer—also a fairly common development. But John experiences unique feelings about his sister's divorce, his relationship with each of her children—and with her new husband's children—and their relationship to their parents. There are experiences and feelings that are clearly unique to John and Barbara.

There are also aspects of your occupational role that are unique. Many people work in sales, for example. But a participant in a seminar Gary taught was unique in that he had been with his company for 28 years and had missed his quota only two of those years—a company record. John felt unique when he worked in a packing plant, because he was the only forklift driver in cold storage who almost had his Ph.D.

Your Reactive vs.
Choosing Dimensions
It can also help to become aware of some of the ways you typically react. Do you almost always respond to an upcoming exam or evaluation by overpreparing? Or do you usually put it off to the last minute? Do you react to Christmas songs by remembering your childhood Christmases? Do you react to your supervisor's orders with deference and respect? Or with anger? Do you react to a cloudy day by moving slowly and doing very

little? Do you react to a public-speaking situation with fear and the belief that you can't do it? Do you react to meeting a stranger with indirect eye contact, stammering, and discomfort? Have you generalized any of those reactions into self-labels?—"I have test anxiety," "I'm a procrastinator," "I'm a sentimentalist," "I'm shy," "I'm defensive."

Remember that self-labels are usually hangovers from past experiences, labels hung on us by teachers, parents, or "friends." We heard the labels during childhood or adolescence, when we were trying to answer the "Who am I?" question, and since they were simple, they stuck. Or maybe they're labels that we hung on ourselves in order to avoid doing something uncomfortable—like meeting strangers or giving a speech. Sometimes, on the other hand, we use a label to excuse a habit we've developed. A friend of ours was lecturing to his class when a student named Mark blurted out, "This class is really dumb." Our friend stopped his lecture, turned to Mark, and said, "Why'd you say that, Mark? That hurt." Another student replied, "You have to understand the way he is." "Fine," said the teacher. "Mark goes around hurting people and excuses it by saying, 'That's just the way I am—that's my sense of humor.' Mark, you're copping out. You've got more choice than that." (Fortunately, Mark and our friend now get along well.)

The problem with self-labels is that they make it difficult for you to get in touch with the choosing parts of your personness. It's important to learn from the past but not to get stuck in it. Maybe you have panicked when someone asked you a tough, surprise question and you weren't able to respond the way you wanted to. But that doesn't mean you always will. You can choose other responses because, as a person, you are more than just a reactor; you are a chooser, too. Try not to let your self-labels become self-fulfilling prophecies. If you call yourself "shy," that label may sometimes be enough to make you choose shy behavior. But there are steps you can take to get unstuck, to get in touch with more of the nonobjectified, personal, choosing you.

For one thing, it often helps to reflect on the payoffs you're getting from your self-labels. What do you *gain* by calling yourself "clumsy," "sentimental," or "moody"? What challenging tasks are you able to avoid? Do you want to keep that pattern? For example, John labeled himself as too "old" and "uncoordinated" to downhill ski until Kris signed him up for skiing lessons. That was more than three years ago, and now they enjoy skiing together, and although neither is an Olympic contender, both can handle most intermediate and even some advanced runs. In this case, a different choice opened up a whole new activity.

You might also make a "Ways I've Chosen to Change" list that covers the past year. If you force yourself to recall some of the changes you've experienced in the recent past, it may encourage you to continue changing in the present. Sometimes a close friend can help with this list by being able to see the need for changes that you aren't aware of. But if you feel stuck in some self-labels, try making that list.

Another way to contact more of your choosing self is to play with the words you use to talk about yourself. Instead of thinking or saying, "I'm lousy at [cooking, tennis, calligraphy, whatever]" try something like "Until today, I've chosen not to _____. Now, since I'm interested in _____, I want to develop the _____ that I have." Or instead of "I'm shy," try "I've often felt uncomfortable in situations like this, but I'm going to start moving out of that space, one little step at a time."[2]

It's often hardest to realize that we even make choices about feelings. It sometimes seems just the opposite—we feel overwhelmed by anger or unable to deal with fear or grief. It seems as if we have no choice at all. But think about the last time you were interrupted in the middle of an argument by, for example, a telephone call. You're in the middle of shouting, "Dammit, that's *not* what I mean!" and the phone rings. You pause just for an instant, pick it up, and in a controlled, pleasant voice you say, "Hello?" *If you really had no choice about your feelings you simply could not do that.* And yet we *do* do it. It's very difficult to make choices in the face of strong feelings, but it *can* be done.

In fact, you are making choices all the time, and everybody gets into some choice-making *patterns* that are hard to break. But the first step toward change is to remember that they *are* choices; very little of our behavior is really determined by someone or something outside us. We're continually making choices, and the more we realize that, the more we're in touch with—and thus able to share—an important part of our person-ness.

Your Measurable vs. Unmeasurable Dimensions

You can learn quite a bit about your self by thinking for a minute about your measurable aspects. When the magazine *Psychology Today* offered its readers the chance to reflect on their perceptions of their height, weight, foot size, and other measurements, they got more than 62,000 replies, many from people who were amazed at what they learned. One said, "Your questionnaire made me feel as though I have floated through life ignoring my body. You have made me dissect myself and realize that I do think it's important." Another wrote, "My long-held belief that our bodies are unimportant was shattered."[3]

The survey asked people to think about their faces—hair, eyes, ears, nose, mouth, teeth, chin, voice, complexion—their extremities—shoulders, arms, hands, feet—their midtorsos—abdomen, seat, hips, legs, and ankles—and their height, weight, muscle tone, and overall body appearance. It's a short step from there to a consideration of some of your *un*measurable aspects. How do you *feel* about what's measurable? The *Psychology Today* survey found that, contrary to popular belief, most men and women feel positively about their bodies. In fact, 45 percent of the women and 53 percent of the men said they were extremely satisfied. The survey also demonstrated the link between feelings about your body and your communication with others. If you've been teased about your weight, for example, you probably feel more negatively about it than you would if you hadn't been teased. And if others treat you as attractive, you probably feel not only good-looking but also likable, intelligent, and assertive.

How *are* you feeling about your height, weight, age, and hair color? Do you have strong feelings about your foot, chest, waist, or hip sizes? About your teeth or complexion? John's recognition that he was embarrassed about the spaces between his teeth was an important discovery for him. He wasn't able to have them straightened and pulled together until he was 26 years old, but the change made a significant difference in his feelings about himself. He used to think that each new acquaintance noticed almost nothing but his "buck teeth," but he now feels that they see the more positive parts of his face and body. And it's easier to feel confident.

What feelings are you experiencing about topics other than your body image? Are you feeling secure, for example, about the decision you recently made about your job or your major? Are you excited about what's coming up this weekend? Are you afraid that you don't have enough money to carry you through the next term? Are you feeling discouraged because you didn't meet a goal you had set? Are you sad about a recent death? Do you feel competent and powerful because you've succeeded in doing a difficult task?

All these feelings are part of the personal you, and the first step toward sharing some appropriate parts of that person is getting in touch with them. What are you feeling right now? Involved? Tired? Bored? Frustrated by all the questions? Excited? Too rushed to respond? Sometimes the persons in our classes respond to these kinds of questions with a little discomfort and confusion. We've responded that way too. Part of what's happening is that *we are not used to trying to be aware of our feelings*. It's an unfamiliar thing to be asked to do, and we often react negatively or superficially—as in the cartoon—when we're asked to do something unfamiliar.

It doesn't have to be that way, though. Everyone is always experiencing feelings—and the feelings are constantly changing, too. If you can become more aware of this flow of feelings, you will be better able to contact others in person-to-person ways, because you will be able to share

"Evening, folks. Well, I was feeling a little down today, so I bought a new pair of shoes. Dark brown, with super buckles. Perked me right up. Now back to you, Whit."

DRAWING BY S. HARRIS; © 1977 THE NEW YORKER MAGAZINE, INC.

some of your self more accurately and appropriately. Only when you are aware of what you're feeling can you choose what is most appropriate for this time and situation. And only then can you really say—verbally and nonverbally—what you're feeling and thus let the other person know some of who you are.

Your Unreflective vs. Reflective Aspects   If you've been thinking about your uniqueness, choices, and feelings, you've been reflecting. By that we mean you've been focusing on more than superficial topics, and you've been developing your awareness of your awareness. The sum total of your response to all the questions we've been asking you is your *my me*—your image of yourself. That image grows, changes, and is constantly affecting your communication.

You also develop your view of the other person—*my you*—and your perspective on how the other sees you—*my your me*. Since all those images play an active part in your communicating, the more you can be aware of them, the better you can understand the communicating you experience. For example, you can probably learn something about your feelings toward our communication with you in this book if you reflect for a minute about how you see us seeing you. Of course, we have an image of you that affects the choices we make as we write. Do we see you the way you see yourself? Or do you hear us talking down to you or assuming that you know more than you do? Or do we see you as too young? Too old? Too white? Too collegiate? Too American? You can ask similar questions about just about every communication experience you have, and the answers will go far toward helping you understand what's going on.

In short, the first step toward developing your willingness and ability to share some of your self is to become aware of what's there to share. It helps to reflect on your interchangeable and unique aspects, your reactive and choosing dimensions, your measurable and unmeasurable parts, and the ways in which you're both unreflective and reflective.

Joseph Luft and Harrington Ingham created a diagram that helps explain how the process of sharing your self works in human communication.[4] They call the diagram the Johari (Joseph + Harrington) window, and it looks like this:

Second, Become Aware of How Sharing "Works"

	INFORMATION KNOWN TO SELF	INFORMATION NOT KNOWN TO SELF
INFORMATION KNOWN TO OTHERS	OPEN	BLIND
INFORMATION NOT KNOWN TO OTHERS	HIDDEN	UNKNOWN

The Johari window identifies four kinds of information about your self that play a part in your communicating: the things you are aware of and are willing to share with the other person (open); the things that the other person knows about you but that you aren't aware of (blind); the things you know about your self that you're *un*willing to share (hidden); and the aspects of your self that neither you nor the other person is aware of (unknown).

In the communication between us right now, we both know, for example, that John is a little uneasy about being the father of two college students; that information about his self is in the "open" square of the Johari window that describes our present communicating. It's important to remember that there's always *something* in this "open" square. Whenever you communicate with another human, you necessarily share *something* of your self; you cannot completely avoid sharing.

As we write this chapter, we are "blind" to information about ourselves that you are getting by reading "between the lines" of this book. For example, you may be under the impression that we're less confident than we'd like to appear, or that we're revealing more about ourselves than we think we are. There are also many things that are "hidden" in our relationship with you—events from our past and our present that we think are irrelevant to our communicating, details about our relationships with others that don't seem to us to be appropriate to share in this context, and so on. There is also for each of us an "unknown" dimension of our relationship. This one's a little difficult to talk about, but it could include, for instance, attitudes or motivations that a psychoanalyst might see manifested in our communication but that none of us is aware of. The existence of this "unknown" area seems to be proved each time an attitude, fear, or belief that we didn't think we had comes to the surface and affects our relationship with someone.

Theoretically, you could draw a Johari window for each relationship you participate in. The window representing your relationship with your mother or father is obviously different from the one for your relationship with your roommate, lover, or spouse. You can also use the Johari window to diagram what might be called the "sharing status" of your relationship. For example, when two individuals first meet, one person's window for that relationship might look like this:

OPEN	BLIND	
HIDDEN		UNKNOWN

Some time later, when the same relationship has developed to the point of intimacy, the same persons's window would look more like this:

OPEN		BLIND
HIDDEN	UNKNOWN	

Similarly, some textbook authors' communication with you would probably look something like this:

OPEN	BLIND	
HIDDEN		UNKNOWN

We've been trying to change that configuration. We hope that a Johari window of our communication with you would look more like this:

The Johari window summarizes much of what we're saying about interpersonal communication in this chapter and the next one. In Johari window terms, Chapter 6 focuses on moving information from the "blind" area to the "open" area by *being aware of and responding to the other*. This chapter discusses moving information from the "hidden" area to the "open" area. That's what sharing can do if you start by getting in touch with your objective and your personal self and then by seeing how sharing works. The third step is to share both your objective and your personal self.

Although "object-to-object" communication is not interpersonal, sharing aspects of your objective self can help open the door to interpersonal-quality communication. Talking to others about your demographic characteristics or reactions may promote noninterpersonal communicating, but that kind of verbal contact can pave the way for more personal sharing.

Third, Share Both Your Objective and Personal Self

Objective Self

Nonverbally. You are continually making available some aspects of your objective self by way of nonverbal cues. The clothes you wear, the style of your hair, the amount and kind of jewelry you wear, the setting you're in (office, house, apartment, expensive restaurant), and the way you get around (bicycle, sports car, motorcycle, van)—all reveal something about your objective self. If you sometimes wear a uniform, for example, it's clear that one aspect of you is your membership in one of the ROTC units, a law enforcement agency, the marching band, or whatever.

Since all these nonverbal elements are potential messages about who you are, it's useful to check to see whether they're accurate messages. Does your living space accurately reflect who you are? Is your hair style a valid indication of some aspects of you? What are your clothes saying about your *my me*?

Verbally. With the exception of uniforms, most nonverbal cues about your objective self are generally vague and ambiguous. The most precise information about your self can come from verbal cues, what you *say*. You learned something about us from the nonverbal cues in our pictures and from your nonverbal image of us in our professions. You might visualize John in a classroom or hallway not far from a stack of books and Gary in an office or at a lunch meeting with several business associates. But you can learn about our families, our experiences, our attitudes, and our beliefs only from the words we write. Your nonverbal picture is general and in-direct; our words help specify directly who we are. The same goes for you. The persons you're talking with are probably not going to know that you have been a Young Democrat, have taught swimming, can't stand beer, spent a year in France, and have always wanted to go to law school unless you *tell* them. In *words*.

So try to listen to what information you make available to others. Nobody wants to sit through a long-winded, self-centered monologue, but people do like to hear about group memberships and past experiences. And as we said, although interpersonal-quality communication cannot be built on just sharing objective selves, that's a beginning, and it can be helpful.

Personal Self   Sharing also means letting the other person or persons know some aspects of your personal self that they probably wouldn't know unless you re-vealed them. And making parts of your person available is one of the best ways to help interpersonal-quality communication happen.

Verbally. The psychologist Sidney Jourard probably did more research on interpersonal sharing than anyone else, and he continually emphasized the importance of verbally sharing your personal self.

> I don't want to belabor the point, but I think it is almost self-evident that you cannot love another person, that is, behave toward him so as to foster his hap-piness and growth, unless you know what he needs. And you cannot know what he needs unless he tells you.[5]

As Jourard points out, if you don't *say* "where you're at," the person you're talking with has only two alternatives: to ignore your needs or to guess them.

You can often tell whether what's shared is objective or personal self just by listening to the words that are used. Someone who is sharing personal self almost always uses first-person pronouns—it's *I* and *me,* not *you* or *they*. In addition, this kind of sharing is usually in the present tense. The most accurate and effective sharing of personal self is also specific and concrete; the person doesn't hide behind generalities but shares relevant and graphic details. The statement "People sometimes get upset when they hear things like that" is *not* sharing personal self. Comments like "I feel relaxed when we can talk with each other this frankly" or "I feel uncomfortable because I don't feel that you're listening to me" *are*.

Another characteristic of the verbal language of this kind of sharing is a little more difficult to explain. If a person is accurately sharing part of what he or she is *presently* experiencing, the words that person uses cannot be "statements of external facts."[6] Statements like "That tree is green," "Volkswagens are noisy," "He is stupid," "You are brilliant," or "She is the best gymnast in the state" are not direct expressions of present experiencing. Those statements do reflect indirectly something about the person saying them. But personal self is always expressed as perceptions, feelings, and meanings from an *internal* frame of reference. As Carl Rogers[7] explains,

> I never *know* that he is stupid or you are bad. I can only perceive that you seem this way to me. Likewise, strictly speaking I do not *know* that the rock is hard [or the tree green], even though I may be very sure that I experience it as hard if I fall down on it. . . . If the person is thoroughly congruent then it is clear that all of his [or her] communication would necessarily be put in a context of personal perception.*

We think Rogers is making an important point. We've found that it's helpful to interpersonal-quality communication when people are willing to take enough responsibility for what they say to recognize that "You're crazy" actually means something like "I disagree with you," "I don't understand," or maybe "I'm afraid of you." Similarly, "She's impossible to get along with" means "I can't seem to get along with her," and "This class is worthless" means "I'm not finding anything worthwhile in this class right now." And since labels are actually almost always reports of personal perceptions, it's very helpful to learn to state your perceptions accurately. Your communicating can improve significantly, we think, if you'll just do this one thing: stop labeling others and start taking verbal responsibility for what you say. Try replacing "You're mixed up" with "I don't understand." Try "I'm uncomfortable when you say that" instead of "Shut up!" or "Get outa here!" In order to develop your ability to share personal self verbally, you might also try the following individual activity.

---

* From *On Becoming a Person* by Carl R. Rogers. Copyright © 1961 by Carl R. Rogers. Reprinted with the permission of Houghton Mifflin Company.

———————•◆•————————

Individual Activity:
Description of
Feelings

We display feelings in many different ways. Here are some of them.

Commands: "Get lost!" "Shut up!"
Questions: "Are you sure it's safe to smoke this stuff?"
Accusations: "You're always giving your damn job first priority."
Judgments: "You're a fantastic songwriter."
              "You're a snob."

Note that although each of the examples *displays* strong feeling, the verbal statement does not describe or say what the feeling is. In none of the sentences does the speaker refer to himself or herself or to what he or she is feeling.

Sometimes, however, sentences do contain the emotional state of the speaker. Such sentences are *descriptions of feeling.* They share personal self by referring to the speaker and naming or identifying what the speaker feels. "I am really furious!" "I'm afraid to smoke this stuff!" "I feel put down."

When you use *descriptions,* you can share your feelings accurately in ways that will probably be less hurtful than commands, questions, accusations, or judgments.

In each of the following sets of sentences, all the statements display feeling; i.e., any of them could have been spoken by the same person in the same situation. Each sentence, however, may be either of two different ways of communicating feelings by words. Put a *D* before each sentence that shares personal-self feeling by *describing* the speaker's feeling. Put a *No* before each sentence that displays feeling but *does not describe* what it is.[8] (Our answers and explanations begin on p. 171.)

1. a) Shut up! Not another word out of you!

   b) Please be quiet; you're getting awfully loud.

   c) I'm really annoyed by what you just said.

2. a) Can't you see I'm busy? Don't you have eyes?

   b) I really resent your interrupting me so often.

   c) You have no consideration for anybody else; you're completely selfish.

3. a) I feel discouraged because of some things that happened today.

   b) This has been a lousy day.

   c) Who me? Oh, I'm fine.

4. a) You're a wonderful person.

   b) I really respect your opinion; you're so well informed.

5. a) I feel comfortable and free to be myself when I'm around you.

   b) We all feel you're really great.

   c) Everybody likes you.

6. a) If things don't improve around here, I'm going to look for another job.

   b) I'm afraid to admit that I need help with my work.

7. a) This is a very poor exercise.

   b) I feel that this is a very poor exercise.

   c) I feel uncomfortable doing this exercise.

8. a) I feel inadequate to contribute anything in this group.

   b) I am inadequate to contribute anything in this group.

9. a) I'm a born loser; I'll never amount to anything.

   b) That teacher is awful; he didn't teach me anything.

   c) I'm depressed because I flunked that test.

10. a) I feel warm and comfortable in my group.

    b) I feel that everyone values my contributions to this group.

———————————●•●———————————

Our Answers

1. a) No Commands like these exhibit strong emotion but do not name the feeling that prompted them.

   b) No This suggestion is more thoughtful than (a), but it doesn't describe the speaker's feeling, either.

   c) D Speaker says he or she feels annoyed.

2. a) No These are questions that express strong feeling without naming it.

   b) D Speaker states that he or she feels resentment.

   c) No This is accusation that displays strong negative feelings. Because the feelings are not named, you don't know whether the accusations originate from anger, disappointment, hurt, or something else.

3. a) D Speaker says he or she feels discouraged.

b) No   The statement appears to describe what kind of day it was. In fact, it expresses that speaker's negative feelings without saying whether he or she feels depressed, annoyed, lonely, humiliated, or rejected.

c) No   It may appear to describe a feeling, but "fine" is too vague to help someone understand the speaker, and this kind of statement is often a way to hide feelings rather than to describe them.

4. a) No   This value judgment displays positive feelings about the other person but does not describe what they are. Does the speaker like, respect, enjoy, admire, love, value the other person, or what?

b) D   The speaker describes his or her positive feeling as respect.

5. a) D   This is a clear description of how the speaker feels when with the other person.

b) No   You can describe only your *own* feelings; here the speaker does not speak for himself or herself but hides behind the phrase "we feel." In addition, "you're really great" is a *value judgment* and does not name a feeling.

c) No   The statement does name a feeling ("likes"), but the speaker attributes it to everyone and does not make clear that the feeling is within him or her. A description of feeling must contain "I," "me," "my," or "mine" to make clear that the feelings are the speaker's.

6. a) No   This statement displays negative feelings by talking about the condition of this job. It does not describe the speaker's inner state.

b) D   This is a clear description of how the speaker feels about this problem. He or she feels afraid.

7. a) No   Negative criticisms and value judgments often seem like expressions of anger. In fact, negative value judgments and accusations often stem from the speaker's fear, hurt feelings, disappointments, or loneliness. This statement is a negative value judgment that displays negative feelings, but it does not state what the feeling is.

b) No   Although the person begins by saying "I feel," the speaker does not then name the feeling. Instead, the speaker passes a negative value judgment on the exercise. Note that merely placing the words "I feel" in front of a statement does not make the statement a description of feeling. People often say "I feel" when they mean "I think" or "I believe."

    c) D   The speaker describes his or her feeling when doing this exercise.

8. a) D   Speaker says that he or she feels inadequate.

    b) No This sounds much like the previous statement. However, it says that the speaker actually *is* inadequate—not that he or she just currently feels this way. The speaker has given a self-evaluation—has made a negative value judgment and has labeled self inadequate.

9. a) No The speaker has again given a self-evaluation—passed a negative judgment by labeling self as a born loser.

    b) No Instead of labeling self a failure, the speaker blames the teacher. This is another value judgment and is not a description of a feeling.

    c) D   The speaker states that he or she feels depressed. Statements (a) and (c) illustrate the important difference between passing judgment on yourself and describing your feelings.

10. a) D   The speaker says he or she feels warm and comfortable.

    b) No Instead of "I feel," the speaker should have said, "I believe." The last part of the statement really tells what the speaker believes *others feel* and not what he or she feels.

------------◀•●▬------------

In her book *Making Contact,* Virginia Satir identifies ten English words that deserve special attention because of the impact they have on sharing. The words are *I, you, they, it, but, yes, no, always, never,* and *should.* As Satir says, "If you were able to use these special words carefully it would already solve many contact problems created by misunderstanding."[9]

"Many people avoid the use of the word I," Satir writes, "because they feel they are trying to bring attention to themselves. They think they are being selfish. Shades of childhood, when you shouldn't show off, and who wants to be selfish?" But as she points out, when you use *I,* you are taking responsibility for what you say. That can create a more equal situation between two persons. Listen to the difference between "You can't do that" and "I think you can't do that." Notice also how useful it can be to have someone use I-statements to describe his or her feelings, as in the "Description of Feelings" activity above. *I* is the word that directly says who is talking—who is hoping, wanting, evaluating, or whatever. If you want to be clear about any of those things, it is important to clearly own your statements.

The word *you* is also potentially tricky. Often people use it instead of *I*, even though they are talking about themselves. For example

Supervisor: Why didn't you get that job done?
Alice: Well, you know, when you've got ten things to do and you only have one shift, you sometimes can't get to everything, so you just do the things you think are most important.

Notice how much clearer Alice would have been if she had owned those statements by using *I* rather than *you*.

The word *you* can also sound like an accusation or a put-down. As Satir days, " 'You are making things worse' can sound quite different if the words 'I think' are added. 'I think you are making things worse.' "

Frequently *you* is clearest and most useful when it's used along with *I* in a clear direction or explanation. For example, "I want you to call me tonight around dinnertime," or "You are the one I wanted to speak to."

The word *they* is often used to diffuse responsibility or blame so that nobody has to risk being identified. "They won't let me do that" or "They will get after me" is often a way to avoid admitting that "I don't want to." The key to coping with this word is your willingness to ask yourself—and others—"Who is your *they*?" As Satir says, "Being clear in this way seems to add to everyone's security. Information becomes concrete, something which one can get hold of, instead of being nebulous and perhaps posing some kind of threat."

A similar problem often happens with the word *it;* that is, we use the word without being clear what *it* refers to. Sometimes people use *it* when they mean *I*, but they're unwilling or unable to own the attitude or feeling they're experiencing. Listen to the difference between "It hurts" and "I hurt" or between "It isn't clear" and "I am not clear." A comforting statement can also be made more personal if you substitute *I* for *it*. Try "I've felt frustrated and afraid, too," instead of "It often feels that way when you get laid off."

The problem with *but* is that it's often a way to say yes and no in the same sentence. Satir's example is "I love you, *but* I wish you would change your underwear more often." When you hear that kind of statement, it can sometimes feel as if you've been given a treat and then had it taken back again. Satir suggests that you try substituting the word *and* for *but*. That can be especially helpful when you want to say something negative and you're trying to make it more acceptable by sandwiching it between some positive statements. Thus "I love you, but I wish you would change your underwear more often" could be two statements: "I love you" and "I wish you would change your underwear more often."

Yes creates problems when it's always "Yes, but" or "Yes, maybe," and *no* can be destructive when it's the standard, safe, first response, especially of a person in a position of power. Both words need to be said clearly, understood to mean *now* and not forever, and directly related to the question at hand rather than aimed at a whole person or set of values. *No* is an especially difficult word to use when you're feeling that you need to please people or they'll reject you. It can be a real high to discover that your friend loves your "no"s just as much as your "aye"s, because both of them are clearly parts of *you*. As Satir puts it, "So often when people feel 'no,' they say 'maybe' or 'yes' to avoid meeting the issue. This is justified on the basis of sparing the other's feelings. It is a form of lying and usually invites distrust, which, of course, is death to making contact."

Always and *never* are positive and negative forms of global words—they try to cover the universe. "You never get ready on time" and "You always spend more than we make" are examples, as is the ironic, "You *always* exaggerate!" One problem is that, when you apply those words to human situations, they cannot be literally accurate. There are few situations in life in which something is *never* or *always*. So what do we mean when we use them? Often we're trying to emphasize the point, so "You never get ready on time" means "I am now really mad at you." As Satir points out, "If the situation were as the speaker states, the adrenals would wear out." Since these words are frequently inaccurate or untrue, and since they're often used to emphasize negative feelings, they often harm the situation more than they help it. When you hear yourself using *always* or *never*, stop for a minute and try to identify what you actually mean. If you can say what you mean—"I am now really mad at you"—you can often promote interpersonal-quality communication rather than prevent it.

Ought and *should* are dangerous words when they imply that something is wrong with you, that you have somehow failed to measure up. One problem is that the words suggest that the standard you don't meet is a universal one, an immutable rule or law that "nobody *ever* breaks," when in all probability it is only one person's opinion. "You shouldn't wear that in the summer," "You should have been promoted by now," and "You ought to spend more time with your family" are examples. These words can also indicate that the person who uses them is struggling with a dilemma—"I like this but I should get that." When you're being pulled in two directions at once, there's seldom a simple answer, even though you can go in only one direction at a time. But as Satir says, hearing yourself use *ought* and *should* in this sense can be a tip-off to you that you're engaged in a struggle. "Perhaps instead of trying to deal with these opposing parts as one, you can separate them and make two parts. 'I like this . . .' (one part) 'But I should do that,' translated into . . . 'I also need that . . .' (a second part)." Satir also says that when she is in this spot, it helps to ask herself if she will literally die in either situation. If the answer is no, then she feels more freedom to play with alternatives since she is out of the extreme win/lose situation.

As she summarizes, "Start paying attention to the words you use. Who is your *they*? What is your *it*? What does your *no* mean? What does your *yes* mean? Is your *I* clear? Are you saying *never* and *always* when you mean sometimes and when you want to make emotional emphasis? How are you using *ought* and *should*?"

Remember, in short, that one important aspect of sharing your personal self is the kind of words you use. They should include first-person pronouns, present tense, active voice, concrete specifics, and the language of present experience. Carl Rogers uses this kind of language as he discusses the process of sharing.[10] Near the beginning of his book *On Becoming a Person,* he writes:

> I might start off these several statements of significant learnings with a negative item. *In my relationships with persons I have found that it does not help, in the long run, to act as though I were something that I am not.* It does not help to act calm and pleasant when actually I am angry and critical. It does not help to act as though I know the answers when I do not. It does not help to act as though I were a loving person if actually, at the moment, I am hostile. It does not help for me to act as though I were unsure. Even on a very simple level I have found that this statement seems to hold. It does not help for me to act as though I were well when I feel ill.
>
> . . . I would want to make it clear that while I feel I have learned this to be true, I have by no means adequately profited from it. In fact, it seems to me that most of the mistakes I make in personal relationships, most of the times in which I fail to be of help to other individuals, can be accounted for in terms of the fact that I have, for some defensive reason, behaved in one way at a surface level, while in reality my feelings run in a contrary direction.*

Nonverbally. Note that Rogers talks about the way he "behaves," not just the words he uses. That's because although verbal language is important, the *nonverbal* part of sharing your personal self is just as important as the verbal part. As we've said before, you cannot stop "giving off" nonverbal cues. Written words include the nonverbal elements of spacing, typeface,

---

* From *On Becoming a Person* by Carl R. Rogers. Copyright © 1961 by Carl R. Rogers. Reprinted with the permission of Houghton Mifflin Company.

paper color, and so on. Spoken words are made up in part of tone of voice, rate, volume, and vocal quality and are accompanied by facial expression, posture, muscle tone, bodily movement, etc. In short, since your nonverbal cues are always "there," the persons you're communicating with are always *interpreting* them, making inferences about them, and drawing conclusions—more or less consciously—based on them.

We also mentioned before that when there's a conflict between your verbal and nonverbal cues, people are more likely to notice, remember, rely on, and believe the *nonverbal* ones. That's one reason why nonverbal cues are such an important part of sharing your personal self. Whether or not you fully recognize it, you're usually accepting or rejecting what others say primarily because of the nonverbal aspects of their communication.

This point presents a problem, and right now we are a little uncomfortable about it. We're afraid you may be thinking something like this: "Well! If people believe what I share primarily because of the *nonverbal* parts of my communicating, then, since I want to be believable, I'd better concentrate not on what I say but on *how* I say it. I'd better work on orchestrating my facial expression, tone of voice, posture, and so on, so that I *look* sincere and honest, whether I am or not."

That's a very understandable reaction. In fact, the sociologist Erving Goffman has described human relationships generally as forms of drama or play-acting.[11] Goffman argues that each of us always "presents" one of our repertoire of "faces" to others in order to get them to respond the way we want them to. Although Goffman accurately describes some relationships, we emphatically do *not* think it's a good idea for you to treat your communicating as just a series of rehearsed scenes and artificial performances. We're convinced that there are better ways to communicate. In the first place, the practical problem of living behind a false front is that it's almost impossible to do so successfully. As one team of communicologists puts it, "it is easy to profess something verbally but difficult to carry a lie into the realm of the analogic [nonverbal]."[12]

More important, hiding behind a "face" or false front is another form of objectifying other persons, and ultimately it backfires. Since your self grows in your relationships with others, *your* self suffers if those relationships are based on lies. In other words, attempting to lie when you're sharing some of your self is a form of interpersonal pollution. It's much better for both you and the other persons involved to be *congruent*. That is, you won't have to worry about conflicts between your verbal and nonverbal communications if you are always trying to be on the outside the same as you are on the inside. Once again, Carl Rogers[13] makes the point well.

> I used to feel that if I fulfilled all the outer conditions of trustworthiness—keeping appointments, respecting the confidential nature of the interview,

etc.—and if I acted consistently the same during the interviews, then this condition [trustworthiness] would be fulfilled. But experience drove home the fact that to act consistently acceptant, for example, if in fact I was feeling annoyed or skeptical or some other non-acceptant feeling, was certain in the long run to be perceived as inconsistent or untrustworthy. I have come to recognize that being trustworthy does not demand that I be rigidly consistent but that I be *dependably real*. The term "congruent" is one I have used to describe the way I would like to be. By this I mean that whatever feeling or attitude I am experiencing would be matched by my awareness of that attitude. When this is true, then I am a unified or integrated person in that moment, and hence I can *be* whatever I deeply *am*. This is a reality which I find others experience as dependable.* (Italics added.)

We're not sure that any of us can achieve total congruence—total agreement between what's going on "externally" and "internally." In the first place, we're seldom completely in touch with our own feelings. We're also changing too rapidly. In many situations, we need to withhold some feelings just to keep from being overstimulated. As the Johari window illustrates, there are always some things that are "hidden" and "unknown"; total congruence is humanly impossible. But it's very important to enlarge the "open" square as much as possible—to be as congruent as you can.

And when there's a problem—when you think you're being congruent but someone else thinks you're putting on a front—it can help if both of you talk about your experience. In other words, problems with the non-verbal parts of sharing can often be solved by verbalizing. It's amazing how seldom that happens, and it's often amusing to see what people do to keep from saying what they're actually thinking and feeling. Your words do need to be appropriate to the situation and the relationship, but remember that the truth is often the most appropriate thing possible. So if you want to go out with this person but not to this party, try *not* to use the old "I'm busy but I hope you'll call back." Instead, you might say what you actually mean—"I want to go out with you but not to this party." Or if you're on a bus and you want to talk to your seatmate but you don't know what to say, you could just say, "I want to talk to you, but I don't know what to say." Those suggestions may look ridiculous as you read them here, but they have several distinct advantages, the greatest of which is that they're true. They're accurate reflections of what you're thinking and feeling, so they make part of *you* available to the other person.

---

* From *On Becoming a Person* by Carl R. Rogers. Copyright © 1961 by Carl R. Rogers. Reprinted with the permission of Houghton Mifflin Company.

We've been saying throughout this book that when you get right down to it, communicating interpersonally means *sharing* some of your humanness and *being aware* of the humanness of others. We hope that this chapter encourages and prepares you to try the kind of sharing that can promote interpersonal-quality communication. That kind of sharing is not necessarily negative or heavy. It isn't a nonstop, thoughtless, monological gut dump. It isn't even a recitation of every single thing that's on your mind.

CONCLUDING THOUGHTS

Instead, it's the kind of communicating that helps someone else see the human *you* a little more clearly. It's appropriate for the persons involved and the situation. It's intended to promote the relationship between you and others, not just to relieve your own anxieties. Consequently, it is never motivated by a feeling of "I'm just being honest—you should be able to take it." And it can often be positive, as Kahlil Gibran suggests:[14]

> Let the best be for your friend. If he must know the ebb of your tide, let him know its flood also. For what is your friend that you should seek him with hours to kill? Seek him always with hours to live. For it is his to fill your need, but not your emptiness. And in the sweetness of friendship let there be laughter, and sharing of pleasures. For in the dew of little things the heart finds its morning and is refreshed.*

In short, the kind of self-sharing that's necessary for interpersonal-quality communication is made up of sensitive verbal and nonverbal responses to the relationship between you and the others involved, responses that let the other person(s) see some of your humanness, some of your uniqueness, some of the unmeasurable parts of you—your moods, feelings, hopes, dreams, fears, some of the chooser in you—that is, the part that acts rather than just reacts to the world; and some of your reflectiveness.

Sharing some of your self can be as simple as saying, "I'm in education, too," or "I feel good now." It can be as subtle as wearing a tiny Greek-lettered pin or quietly bowing your head before eating. Or it can be as explicit and complete as a thoughtful letter that helps a friend understand why you haven't called, or an open, complete response to your parents' question "What do you think you want to do with your life?" But whatever it is, if sharing doesn't happen, your communication cannot be interpersonal-quality communication. A relationship that's interpersonal

---

* Reprinted from *The Prophet,* by Kahlil Gibran, with permission of the publisher, Alfred A. Knopf, Inc. Copyright 1923 by Kahlil Gibran and renewed copyright 1951 by Administrators C.T.A. of Kahlil Gibran Estate, and Mary G. Gibran.

in quality can happen only when each person is able clearly and fully to *see* the other person. As Hugh Prather succinctly puts it, "In order to see, I have to be willing to be seen."[15]

———◆•◆———

You May Be Wondering...

1. *You don't talk much about the* risks *of sharing. Why should I stick my neck out by disclosing what I'm really thinking and feeling? When you do that, you just let others walk all over you.*

That's an important question, and we think it deserves more than a one-sentence response. Sharing some of your self *is* risky, no doubt about it. But it's important to recognize just what the risk is. Some people fear sharing because of the idea that "Who I am is all I really have, and if I tell you too much about who I am, there won't be any left for me." These persons believe that they are in danger of using up or running out of their self. This fear is unfounded, though, because *selves are not something you can run out of, use up, or totally give away*. It's a mistake to think that selves obey the economic law of scarcity—that there is only so much of them, and that when you use them up, that's it. Selves are not like crude oil or real estate. They are constantly changing and growing, especially in relationships, so when Lonnie shares part of his self with Art, he doesn't give anything "away." He just makes it possible for the two of them to experience it together.

Others are afraid that if you share too much of your self, you risk eliminating all the mystery or romance in your relationship. The fear is that someone who knows all there is to know about you will be bored, no longer interested in you. If you are concerned about this aspect of sharing, one good thing to remember is that sharing your personal self is almost always interesting. It's true that we often feel bored when someone continually talks about himself or herself. But the boredom comes because the person is sharing only *object* self rather than *personal* self. As Gerard Egan puts it, sharing personal self

> is always engaging, for it means that the speaker has to "blow his cover," lower his defenses. . . . People are seldom, if ever, bored with sincere self-revelation, because they intuitively realize its importance for the one revealing himself and respect him for what he is doing. . . . I think perhaps that it might be impossible to dislike someone who [shares personal self], for it is an act of humility, a manifestation of a need to move into community.[16]

In addition, as many couples who have been together for a long time have learned, you can never succeed in disclosing everything about yourself. The more you know about the other person, the more clearly you

realize how much more there is to know. So sharing your self won't eliminate the interest, mystery, newness, or spontaneity from a relationship. In
fact, it can enhance the relationship.

It's also important to remember a point we made earlier—you always
have control over how much you share, when, and with whom. You exercise control over your nonverbal sharing when you choose what to wear,
rearrange your furniture, select a picture for your wall, and have your hair
styled. And you are controlling your verbal sharing when you decide to
postpone a heavy discussion, to call a friend who you know will listen to
your problem, or to replace your "Oh, I'm just fine" with "I feel great today; I got the promotion I wanted, and I'm confident I can make manager
in a year!" After all, your choices are part of what makes you a person, and
when you share those choices with others, you share part of your self.

When you're thinking about the risk that's involved in sharing, try to
keep it in perspective. You're not going to "run out of self," and if you're
talking about who you are as a person, it's unlikely that the other person
will feel bored. Genuine sharing also won't turn an exciting relationship
into a predictable, dull one. And ultimately you do control much of what
you share.

It is true, though, that when you choose to make some of your self
available to another person, you give that person some options or choices
that *you* cannot completely control. That person may dislike the you that
he or she comes to know. You may be ridiculed for your thoughts or feelings. Or the other person may tell someone else something you don't want
known. You may feel embarrassed, hurt, angry, or something even worse.

The risk you take varies with the communication content—what's
shared—and relationship—with whom. *Close* content is just about always
more risky than *distant* content; that is, specifics about "I" are more peril-
ous than generalizations about "some people" or "them." *Time* is also a
factor; the past is usually easier to talk about than the present, especially
when your present feelings are intense. *Salience* is a third consideration;
topics that are very salient or important to you are usually more risky to
discuss than are topics that you don't really care about. *Negative* information is usually more risky to disclose than *positive* information, and the
more *personal* or *intimate* the information, the higher the risk. In short, we
usually feel safety in numbers, so any content that singles me out, that sets
me apart and emphasizes my uniqueness tends to be riskier than content
that lets me remain a member of a larger group.

The relationship also affects the degree of risk. I'll be more willing to
share "high risk content" if I'm confident that the other person likes me. It
is also less risky to share with someone who has listened to me carefully
and empathically in the past. But the most important relationship factor
may be *mutuality*. When both or all the people involved are sharing per-

sonness, that fact substantially diminishes the risk of otherwise high-threat content. This phenomenon, called the "dyadic effect" or "reciprocity norm," happens almost everywhere. Generally speaking, disclosure begets disclosure, and the more reciprocal sharing or disclosing that people do, the more they tend to feel close to and to trust each other. Of course, the sharing has to be seen as appropriate by the persons involved, but generally you can expect availability to promote more of the same.[17]

So what does that all boil down to? How do we respond to the question about risk? First, it's true that there is some risk involved, but be careful not to overdramatize the threat. You can choose the content and the relationship for your sharing, and those choices can substantially decrease the risk you feel. You also have additional choices; even when the other person dislikes or ridicules you, you can still choose how to respond. You don't *have* to feel embarrassed, for example, when somebody pokes fun at you. You may feel anger, pity for the person, or sadness about the state of your relationship. But if the interdependence point we made earlier is accurate, the other's behavior does not *determine* your response. Finally, when you think about the risk of sharing, remember the basic assumption that the quality of your life is tied to the quality of your communication. If sharing some of your self is a prerequisite to interpersonal-quality communication—and we believe it is—and if interpersonal-quality relationships can enhance the quality of your life, then, to put it bluntly, *it's worth some risk.*

Several years ago Martin Buber confronted the same issue of risk in the form of the question "What is to be done?" That is, What is to be done to improve communication in the world? The following is a paraphrase of part of his reply.

If you mean by this question "What is one to do?"—there is no answer. *One* is not to do anything. *One* cannot help his or herself, with *one* there is nothing to begin, with *one* it is all over. The person who is content with explaining or discussing or asking what *one* is to do talks and lives in a vacuum.

But the person who poses the question with real seriousness and means "What have I to do?"—that person is taken by the hand by unknown but soon-to-be-familiar friends, and they answer (the questioner listens to their reply and marvels when only this follows):

"You shall not withhold yourself."

The old eternal answer! But its truth is once again new and intact. The questioner sees the truth and moves beyond astonishment. The questioner nods. And with the nod comes the feeling on the palms of the hands of the blood-warmth of togetherness. The feeling speaks, but it seems to the questioner as if he or she were speaking:

"You shall not withhold yourself."

You, imprisoned in the shells in which society, state, church, school, economy, public opinion, and your own pride have stuck you, indirect one among indirect ones, break through your shells, become direct; you, have contact with others!

Ancient rot and mould are between person and person. Words that once were meaningful degenerate into clichés, respect degenerates into mistrust, modesty in communicating into stingy taciturnity. Now and then people grope toward one another in anxious delirium—and miss one another, for the heap of rot is between them. Clear it away, you and you and you! Establish directness, formed out of meaning, respectful, modest directness between persons![18]

2. *Are you guys seriously saying that sometimes I ought to tell someone, "I want to talk to you but I don't know what to say"?*

It does sound a little strange, but part of the problem is that you're reading it in a book rather than hearing it in an appropriate situation. If a couple has just had a strong argument and is in the middle of a mutual silent period, that statement could break the silence in a very productive way. It's true that adults often don't talk that way; people learn all kinds of complicated techniques to avoid saying what they really mean. But we're convinced that at least part of the time you can behave differently. You can be what Rogers called *congruent,* which means you can say what you are actually thinking and feeling.

We've found that when we do that, most people do *not* respond with "That sounds really stupid." They're usually surprised, taken aback a little, just because congruence often violates some cultural norms. But the terms they use to describe it are usually ones like "refreshingly direct."

3. *But what if you think the other person is boring? Should you say, "You're boring"?*

No, that's not what we're saying. Listen to those words. "You're boring" ignores the fact that you and I are interdependent, interrelated. If I feel boredom, then you are part of it, but so am I. My perceptions are just that: mine and perceptions. "You're boring" sounds like a "general fact" rather than a *perception* coming from a specific person. If you stick with "You're boring," you're ignoring what we've said about I-statements and describing your feelings.

The more accurate statement would be "I feel bored." Notice, though, that those words will probably *sound* like "You're boring" to the other person. So it's best to add to it. Try "You're going to have to excuse me, but I'm really out of it. I can't concentrate on what you're saying. I don't know what's happening, but we're going to have to take a break until I can get back into this."

Carl Rogers makes another important point about this issue. "I am not saying," he writes, "that it is helpful to blurt out impulsively every passing feeling and accusation under the comfortable impression that one is being genuine. Being real involves the difficult task of being acquainted with the flow of experience going on within oneself, a flow marked especially by complexity and continuous change."[19] My feeling of boredom is only one part of my experience. I may also feel physically tired, embarrassed, guilty about feeling bored, or any number of other things. And I may want to share all those feelings. In addition, as Rogers points out, as I focus on my present experience and as I work to share it accurately, I am anything *but* bored. Those feelings change even as I notice and try to share them. "I am certainly *not* bored as I try to communicate myself to him in this way, and I am far from bored as I wait with eagerness and perhaps a bit of apprehension for his response."[20]

However, don't use what we say here as justification for fault-finding and criticism. The whole business is much more complicated than that. Try not to oversimplify it. Work toward sharing appropriate feelings—including negative ones—by owning them and by treating them as the complex, changing experiences they are.

4. *If reflectiveness is part of my personal self, and if my images of myself and the other person are part of my reflectiveness, it sounds as though you're recommending that I talk about those images—explicitly. Do you mean that I should sometimes actually* say, *"I see you seeing me as your inferior" or "Sounds as if you think I don't like you. Is that right?"*

Yes.

5. *But if you go around talking about "how I see myself in this situation" and "how I see you seeing me when we argue like this," won't that sound as if you're trying to psychoanalyze everybody? Or won't you at least sound like some phony encounter-group freak?*

If you talked that way all the time, it would sound pretty weird. And it would also sound as if you were analyzing everybody and everything.

But remember two things. First, as the diagram on pp. 81 and 146 emphasizes, when you change your communication behavior it feels and sounds strange at first, but as you work with it, you usually discover ways to make it more natural and less strange-sounding. So the awkward-sounding "I see you seeing me as threatening you. Do you see me that way?" can become the much more "normal" and spontaneous, "Sounds as if you're scared of me. Are you?"

Second, remember what we've said about choice. Our goal is to help you understand the image transaction process and to see your reflectiveness as part of the personal you. However, you choose when it's important to include that information as part of the conversation. It is not always appropriate, but often it can contribute significantly to mutual understanding. You are the one who decides which is which.

It has been our experience that this kind of sharing can be very helpful. For example, when John is discussing a grade with a student from one of his classes, there are often problems with defensiveness—sometimes on both sides. He has found that these statements can really contribute to the conversation: "I really feel that you're trying to take advantage of me" or "It sounds as if you think I want you to get the lowest grade possible. Do you? I *don't* feel that's my goal."

EXERCISES

Group Activity: Three-Minute Sharing

In order to get to know some persons in your class or group, you may want to try the following. Divide into groups of four to six. Each group should have a three-minute egg timer or some other unobtrusive way to keep track of approximately three minutes. Start with whoever has the timer first, and have each person use the three minutes to share with the group his or her responses to the following questions.

1. What's a particularly happy experience that you remember?
2. What was an especially significant experience that happened to you?
3. What animal do you admire or identify with?
4. Who are you?
5. How are you feeling now?

All the group members should feel free to ask questions of the person talking, but you should all work to stick to the time limit. After each person in the group has had a chance to respond to the five questions, the group as a whole can discuss the following questions.

1. Did you enjoy doing this? Why or why not?
2. Which of the five responses did the most to help you get to know the person speaking?
3. How did the structure of this exercise—the time limits, size of group, type of questions, etc.—affect what happened?

4. What similarities did you notice among the responses to the five questions?

5. What points made in this chapter were illustrated, qualified, or contradicted by this experience?

Group Activity: An Object That's Me

Another way to share something of your self with others is to bring to class an object that represents some aspect of how you see yourself and to explain to the others what the object "says" about you. John once brought a copy of the play *The Diary of Anne Frank,* because he admires and identifies with Anne's optimistic view of human beings. For Gary, a light switch is an appropriate object for a couple of reasons. First, it seems incomprehensibly complex if you're unfamiliar with electricity, but it's pretty understandable if you take some time to get to know it. Second, one of the things Gary would like to be able to do is help people come alive with discoveries about themselves and their communicating. We've had other persons bring things as diverse and intriguing as a gyroscope, a collage, an X-ray of a rose, a painting, and a brightly decorated box that only one person knew how to open.

Group Activity: Sharing Questionnaire

Are you aware of how you share your objective and personal selves with others? You may want to respond to the following questions about your verbal and nonverbal sharing behavior and then get together with two other persons with whom you've communicated before in order to get each other's reactions to your perceptions of your sharing behavior and to talk about what you've learned about yourself, about each other, and about how sharing works in communication.

1. If you feel bored with what is going on in a discussion, how do you usually let others know what you're feeling?

   Using words _____

   Without using words_____

2. If you feel friendliness for someone you don't know very well, how do you share how you're feeling with that person?

   Using words _____

   Without using words_____

3. If another person does something that hurts your feelings, how do you express your hurt?

   Using words _____

Without using words_____

4. If you've had quite a bit of experience with something that would help the group you're in solve a problem, how do you communicate your expertise?

   Using words_____

   Without using words_____

5. If you feel that a group is wasting time and should move on to discuss more important topics, how do you communicate your perceptions to the group?

   Using words_____

   Without using words_____

In order to increase your sensitivity to your sharing "style," act out the following situation.

Group Activity: Your Style of Sharing

1. Assume you are telling a subordinate that the work he or she just spent three hours on is inadequate and has to be totally redone. If it cannot be finished by Friday, the worker will have to come in on Saturday.
   a. What words did you use?
   b. What nonverbal cues did you use?
   c. Which parts of your objective self (if any) did you share?
   d. Which parts of your personal self (if any) did you share?
   e. How would you characterize your sharing style in the situation above? What words best describe your style? Would you consider yourself open? closed?

2. Repeat the questions above for situations described by your instructor. Notice that your sharing style may vary, depending on the persons involved, the timing, situation, etc.

1. Martin Buber, "Elements of the Interhuman," in *The Knowledge of Man*, ed. Maurice Friedman, trans. Ronald Gregor Smith and Maurice Friedman (New York: Harper & Row, 1965), p. 77.

NOTES

2. This suggestion comes from Wayne W. Dyer, *Your Erroneous Zones* (New York: Funk & Wagnalls, 1976); see especially Chapter 4.

3. "The Happy American Body: A Survey Report," *Psychology Today*, November 1973, p. 119. The questionnaire was in the July 1972 issue of *Psychology Today*.

4. Joseph Luft, *Group Processes: An Introduction to Group Dynamics* (Palo Alto, CA: National Press, 1963). See also Joseph Luft, *Of Human Interaction* (Palo Alto, CA: National Press, 1969).

5. Sidney M. Jourard, *The Transparent Self* (New York: Van Nostrand Reinhold, 1964), p. 3.

6. Carl Rogers makes this point in his essay, "A General Law of Interpersonal Relationships," in *On Becoming a Person* (Boston: Houghton Mifflin, 1961), p. 341.

7. *Ibid.*

8. This exercise was adapted from material by John L. Wallen, Northwest Regional Educational Laboratory, Portland, Oregon, and by David W. Johnson, *Reaching Out: Interpersonal Effectiveness and Self-Actualization* (Englewood Cliffs, NJ: Prentice-Hall, 1972), pp. 90–98.

9. Virginia Satir, *Making Contact* (Millbrae, CA: Celestial Arts Press, 1977), n.p. All the subsequent quotations attributed to Satir are from this source.

10. Rogers, *On Becoming a Person*, pp. 16–17.

11. Erving Goffman, *The Presentation of Self in Everyday Life* (New York: Doubleday Anchor Books, 1969).

12. Paul Watzlawick, Janet Helmick Beavin, and Don D. Jackson, *Pragmatics of Human Communication* (New York: W. W. Norton, 1967), p. 63.

13. Rogers, *On Becoming a Person*, pp. 50–51.

14. Kahlil Gibran, *The Prophet* (New York: Alfred A. Knopf, 1965), p. 59.

15. Hugh Prather, *Notes to Myself* (Lafayette, CA: Real People Press, 1970), n.p.

16. Gerard Egan, *Face to Face: The Small-Group Experience and Interpersonal Growth* (Monterey, CA: Brooks/Cole, 1973), p. 47.

17. For a review of research on self-disclosure, see W. B. Pearce and S. M. Sharp, "Self-Disclosing Communication," *Journal of Communication,* **23** (1973), 409–475. Lawrence R. Wheeless explores relationships among sharing, trust, and relational closeness in his article, "A Follow-Up Study of the Relationships Among Trust, Disclosure, and Interpersonal Solidarity," *Human Communication Research,* **4** (Winter 1978), 143–157.

18. Martin Buber, "What Is To Be Done?" in *Pointing the Way: Collected Essays by Martin Buber,* ed. and trans. Maurice S. Friedman (New York: Schocken Books, 1957), p. 109.

19. Carl R. Rogers and Barry Stevens, *Person to Person: The Problem of Being Human* (New York: Pocket Books, 1971), p. 88.

20. *Ibid.*

ADDITIONAL RESOURCES   Three of the books that talk in detail about sharing some of your self should be of interest. In Gerard Egan, *You and Me: The Skills of Communicating and Relating to Others* (Monterey, CA: Brooks/Cole, 1977), Chapters 3, 4, and 5 are particularly related to this topic. We don't agree completely with everything Egan says, but we think his book can be very useful. John Powell, S. J., *Why Am I Afraid to Tell You Who I Am* (Chicago: Argus Communications, 1969), especially chapters 1–4, can also be a helpful introduction to your understanding of sharing in communication, written from a Christian perspective. In Sidney Jourard's *The Transparent Self* (New York: Van Nostrand Reinhold 1964) and in his *Disclosing Man to Himself* (New York: Van Nostrand Reinhold, 1968), a psychologist interested in interpersonal communication deals with sharing. Jourard is sometimes a little technical, but there's a considerable amount of research to back up his conclusions.

You can also find treatments of sharing some of your self in other books about interpersonal communication. For example, see David W. Johnson, *Reaching Out: Interpersonal Effectiveness and Self-Actualization* (Englewood Cliffs, N.J.: Prentice-Hall, 1972), especially Chapter 2, "Self-Disclosure," Chapter 5, "The Verbal Expression of Feelings," and Chapter 6, "The Nonverbal Expression of Feelings." See also Richard L. Weaver II, *Understanding Interpersonal Communication* (Glenview, Ill.: Scott-Foresman, 1978), Chapter 2; Jacquelyn B. Carr, *Communicating with My Self: A Journal* (Menlo Park, CA: Benjamin-Cummings, 1979); and Stewart L. Tubbs and Sylvia Moss, *Interpersonal Communication* (New York: Random House, 1978), Chapter 6.

We know of two books that do effective jobs of discussing how changing your perception of your self can change your communication for the better. One is Ronald B. Adler's *Confidence in Communication: A Guide to Assertive and Social Skills* (New York: Holt, Rinehart and Winston, 1977). The other is a former best-seller, Wayne W. Dyer's *Your Erroneous Zones* (New York: Funk and Wagnalls, 1976). We do not agree with all that Dyer says, but his book does include some useful insights and advice.

If you want to review recent self-disclosure research, look at the studies cited in note 17 in this chapter, and at Shirley J. Gilbert's "Empirical and Theoretical Extensions of Self-Disclosure," in *Explorations in Interpersonal Communication*, ed. Gerald R. Miller (Beverly Hills, CA: Sage Publications, 1976), pp. 197–216.

Psychologist-counselor Haim Ginott sees congruence as a central element of effective communication in families and schools. For example, Chapter 4 of his *Between Teacher and Child: A Handbook for Parents and Teachers* (New York: Macmillan, 1972) is called "Congruent Communication." You may also enjoy reading Ginott's *Between Parent and Child: New Solutions to Old Problems* (New York: Macmillan, 1965).

6
Being aware of the other: responsive listening

I. SHARING AND LISTENING ARE INTERDEPENDENT

II. GOALS OF INTERPERSONAL LISTENING

    A. Sees personness in others

    B. Reveals personness in self

    C. Confirms the other

    D. Allows for disagreement

    E. Encourages openness and sharing

    F. Is nonthreatening

    G. Is nonmanipulative

III. MENTAL SET: WIN/WIN AND WIN/LOSE

IV. LISTENING TO CONFIRM

    A. Nonverbal confirming

    B. Verbal confirming

V. LISTENING TO UNDERSTAND

    A. Accurately interpreting the other person

    B. Verbal communication is important in listening to understand

C. Paraphrasing or reinterpreting

D. Asking clarifying questions

E. Adding examples

VI. LISTENING BEYOND THE WORDS

A. Listening to what the speaker is not saying in words

B. Making inferences

VII. LISTENING TO DIMINISH DEFENSIVENESS

A. Being positive

B. Postponing specific evaluations

C. Limiting negative evaluations

D. Owning your evaluations

E. Keeping your evaluations tentative

F. Actively soliciting responses

One of the challenges of talking about human communication is that everything is related to everything else. In the last chapter we talked about sharing; in this chapter we talk mainly about responsive listening. But in face-to-face communication, listening can't really be separated from sharing. As you probably realize, when you're talking with someone in a face-to-face situation, you're actually sharing and responding at the same time. When you're speaking, you're making verbal and nonverbal cues available to the other person, and at the same time, even though the other person is not talking, he or she is making nonverbal cues available to you—facial expression, eye contact or lack of it, personal space, body position, head movements, etc. So when we write a chapter on sharing and then write a separate chapter on being aware, it sounds almost as though we consider them to be independent processes. We don't and they aren't. They're happening simultaneously and they're *interdependent*. What you share and how you share it affects the other person's sharing and responding behavior, and the other person's verbal or nonverbal response to your sharing affects your responding and sharing, too.

In short, as you read this chapter we think it'll help if you realize how listening relates to some of the things we've talked about in previous chapters.

Cannot not respond. Whenever someone is perceptually aware of you, it's impossible for you to stop communicating. Even if you refuse to talk, even if you walk away—these behaviors will be interpreted to mean something. Consistent with that idea, you cannot stop responding to someone. In other words, if you choose not to say anything, your nonverbal behavior "talks" for you.

Situation. The situation in which you are communicating can almost control your listening behavior if you let it. It's important *not* to allow that to happen. One of the characteristics of your humanness is that you have some freedom in the way you choose to respond to contextual cues. You aren't likely to listen interpersonally to someone if you let things within the situation unduly frustrate or irritate you—such things as temperature, room size, furniture, lighting, personal space, noise, the other person's dress and posture, and so on. Our experience with ugly rooms, hot days, uncomfortable furniture, and noisy activities has taught us that the more we let these things control us, the less we listen and respond to people in an interpersonal way.

Interpretation. As you communicate, you pick up raw cues and then interpret those raw cues into something meaningful, something that makes sense to you. Also remember that your interpretations reflect your biases, and that no interpretation duplicates reality exactly. Your listening responses are based on these contextually bound interpretations.

Negotiation of selves. Being aware of the other person is half of what we mean by "negotiating." The way you communicate depends in part on how you define the other person and how you see the other person defining you. These definitions come partly from your awareness of the other. Your awareness can be controlled by the conviction that the other person is out to get you or isn't worth listening to. Or, you can approach the other person with the willingness and commitment to listen well and the skills to do it effectively. The approach you take will affect how you define the other person and how you define yourself in relationship to him or her. And those definitions of self and other are what make your communication impersonal or interpersonal.

   In short, when we talk about the relationship of this chapter to others, we mean that here we're trying to describe a way of responding to other persons that

   sees personness in others,

   reveals personness in self,

confirms the other,

allows for disagreement without deteriorating the relationship,

encourages openness and sharing,

enhances understanding,

is nonthreatening, and

is nonmanipulative.

These are the kinds of things we'd like to have happen when you communicate. But we don't want to impose mechanical techniques on you and claim that they'll work in all situations. As you read the rest of this chapter and go through the exercises, and as you relate to your experience outside the classroom, you'll discover whether this listening approach works for you. We think it will, but it can be difficult. You'll have to adapt our suggestions to fit your own unique personhood, and if your experience is anything like ours, you'll find that effective listening is not a passive process; it's hard work. A good listener makes a commitment to listen and gets mentally ready to do it.

MENTAL SET: WIN/LOSE AND WIN/WIN

Some time ago a married couple talked to Gary about arguments they'd been having. The husband felt generally uncomfortable with the way he and his wife communicated. His wife was more specific; she complained that her husband always "seems to know what to say in response to my arguments and he always seems to win. It's frustrating as hell!"

Gary tried to explain to them the difference between win/lose and win/win attitudes. Win/lose communication is characteristic of a debate or political campaign. Opposing parties or adversaries do whatever they can to come out the winner. They're not concerned about building a relationship. In fact, if they want to win badly enough, they won't mind doing things that damage or even destroy the relationship. Usually, a severe win/lose confrontation is characterized by self-serving listening, i.e., listening that prepares you to tear down your opponent's argument, listening that helps you make the other person's ideas seem inferior to yours. In other words, the primary objective is to *win* while the other *loses*—to communicate that "I'm right and you're wrong"; "I'm strong and you're weak"; "I'm smart and you're dumb"; "I'm likeable and you aren't."

Sometimes, win/lose communication is required. Political campaigns, courtroom confrontations, and minority-rights movements are instances in which some win/lose communication is often necessary and appropriate. But when two persons continually communicate as if they were opposing attorneys in a courtroom, their relationship will suffer. In other words, when you want to communicate interpersonally, a win/lose orientation won't help.

One of the problems with win/lose communication is that it can easily lead to manipulation of the other person. When you respond from a win/lose mental set, it becomes easy to use listening techniques only as a strategy for taking advantage of others. You may listen carefully, you may concentrate on what they're saying, you may try to understand exactly how they feel—but you do these things to find weaknesses so that you can ultimately win your point.

It was difficult for the married couple we mentioned to build a strong relationship. Even though the husband won his point most of the time, he still didn't feel satisfied with the communication between himself and his wife, and the wife was developing strongly negative feelings, along with her frustration, toward her husband. If people establish a strong relationship, a few win/lose encounters won't destroy it. But not many relationships can withstand continually competitive communication in which one person is trying to downgrade the ideas or the personhood of the other.

You've probably experienced win/lose communication much of your life. Since the time you began to develop a sense of self—at age two or three—it has been important to define yourself, and one of the ways you have established an identity is by emphasizing the difference between you and others. Your junior high school years may have been a time when winning contests for attention, recognition, and prestige was especially important. Sometimes the confrontations you experienced were probably stimulating and challenging—vigorous mental and physical exercises.

However, we hope you're seeing by now that being yourself doesn't require putting down someone else. Being unique—different from others—doesn't necessarily mean being better than they. *For you to win, somebody else does not have to lose,* and this means that you *can* adopt a win/win attitude in your communication with others.

A win/win listening attitude means that you and the other person see yourselves as being on the same team rather than on opposing teams. It means that you are not in competition with one another but, rather, heading toward compatible goals. There are some situations where a win/win mental set is not appropriate.

1. Two managers are trying for the same upper-level executive position in a company (only one can win it).
2. Salespersons from two different companies are trying to sell a policy to the same client (the client will buy only one of the policies).

In these situations the persons will not listen to each other much of the time; they're more likely to hide information than share it; there will not be much trust between them; and they will tend to think about how to present the strongest argument to *win*. But win/win listening attitudes *do* apply in situations such as the following.

1. Two executives are trying to figure out how their company can best market a new product. In this instance the common goal is "to arrive at the best marketing strategy." If an effective marketing strategy is found, both executives win. Of course, if each sees his or her personal marketing ideas in competition with the other and if the goal of each is actually "to get *my* marketing ideas accepted by the company so that I can establish myself as a credible marketing vice-president," then they are in a win/lose attitude set.

2. Two insurance salespersons from the same company are working together to reestablish a positive relationship with a large corporation. The executives of this corporation are upset because of the "poor service record" of their current health-insurance carrier. If the two salespersons can achieve the common goals of "reestablishing the previously positive relationship," and "winning the insurance contract," both will share in the commission.

3. Two persons, previously miserable in their marriage, are working to have fewer conflicts (common goal) and to discover more things they enjoy together (common goal).

In these situations the persons are more likely to share information, listen to each other, and trust one another because the effort is perceived to be cooperative—"if this project succeeds, we both benefit."

A win/win listening attitude is concerned with building a relationship that promotes growth for all the persons involved. When you have a win/win mental set, your listening behavior works toward that end. You feel cooperative, not competitive. You don't attempt to produce the strongest argument to win your point or to help someone to feel inferior. With a win/win attitude, you're willing to give others a full hearing. You're willing to concentrate on what the other person is saying—verbally and nonverbally. You're willing not only to observe the other person accurately but also to feel some of what he or she seems to be feeling, and to verbalize your conclusions in order to verify them. Finally, you diminish as much defensiveness as you can. These are the goals of the listening approach we're about to describe.

Individual Application: Win/Win and Win/Lose

This exercise should give you some idea of how well you understand the differences between win/lose and win/win communication. We'll give you two situations; for each situation, try to explain what the communication would be like if it was win/win and what it would be like if it was win/lose.

Situation: Two students writing a term paper together.

Win/Win

Win/Lose

Both perceive a common goal of trying for a high grade. Both are open to all possible ways of getting it. They share ideas, listen carefully to each other, and even when they disagree, each respects and tries to understand the other's ideas.

Neither cares about the other's success; each wants a high grade, but each is more concerned about getting her or his ideas accepted. Each tries to convince the other that "my idea is better than yours." Neither person really listens to the other; while one person is talking, the other is thinking about what to say next.

Situation: Family talking about where daughter or son should go to college.

Win/Win

Win/Lose

_____

_____

_____

_____

_____

Situation: An employer is trying to get an employee to slow down so that the quality of the employee's work can improve.

Win/Win

Win/Lose

_____

_____

_____

_____

_____

Situation: A student and an instructor are talking about whether or not to change the student's grade from C to B.

Win/Win

Win/Lose

_____

_____

_____   _____

_____   _____

_____   _____

———————◆•◆———————

LISTENING TO CONFIRM
One of the basic things you can do as a listener to encourage interpersonal communication is to *confirm* the person who's talking. Verbal and nonverbal confirming behavior say to the other person, "I'm listening; I'm paying attention to you; I may not agree or accept your point of view, but I care about what you're saying, and I'm aware of what's going on." Disconfirmation, as we said in Chapter 4, is the process of communicating as if the other person didn't even exist. People perceive disconfirming behavior to mean that you're not listening—that whether you might agree or disagree, you're ignoring something they want you to notice and that you're not really interested in taking the time to pay attention to their thoughts and feelings.

It's pretty difficult to confirm the other person continuously. At one time or another, we all lose track of what other people are saying to us. Especially in lengthy conversations, we sometimes daydream or find ourselves thinking about something completely unrelated to what's being discussed. There's nothing abnormal about that; our ability to concentrate for a prolonged period of time is limited. If you want your communication to be interpersonal, however, you have to concentrate as much as you can, because it isn't easy to really hear and understand another person. But when you find yourself "tuning out," there's no reason to fake it and pretend that you were listening. In fact, it's much better to let the other person know when you've missed something: "While you were talking just then, my mind was off on a tangent, and I missed some things. Would you say that again?" That kind of honesty usually elicits positive reactions from the other person, because it reaffirms your commitment to your communicating and to the other person. And that's confirming, too. In short, communicating confirmation instead of disconfirmation is the first step in listening interpersonally, and there are several nonverbal and verbal ways you can do that.

Nonverbal Confirming
Have you ever tried to talk to someone while she or he was involved in some unrelated activity? Your father reads the paper while you talk with him; your employer opens the mail during a conference with you; your friend cleans his or her desk while you try to carry on a conversation. These people may be listening, and they may think you realize it, but it's

difficult to interpret their behavior that way. Our image of the interested, attentive, and confirming listener isn't the person who reads the mail, washes dishes, shuffles papers, or picks lint off a cuff while we're talking. Few of us believe that a person can listen to what we're saying and, at the same time, concentrate on some unrelated activity. We tend to believe that attention is going to be on us *or* on the activity. We'll interpret those "extracurricular" nonverbal activities as disconfirming, especially when what we're saying is important to us and when we want the other person to be listening fully to us.

Your face is important, too. You may be maintaining natural and consistent eye contact with someone, and your posture may be relaxed and your body attentive, but your facial expression may say, "I'm not interested." People generally assume that when you're excited, in doubt, in deep thought, or interested, your face shows it. Consequently, when they look at your face and there seems to be almost no muscle movement, they'll probably infer that you're not feeling anything. You may be, but not from their point of view. The nonverbal facial cues you make available are interpreted by the other person as indicating something about how you're listening. If you're "plugged in," then your face should somehow reflect that fact.

More specifically, one way to let people know you're paying attention is through eye contact. We don't mean that you should fix the other person with a constant glare or stare; that obviously can be intimidating and can

help him or her feel very self-conscious. But in most American subcultures, reasonably consistent and natural eye contact is a sign of recognition and acknowledgment. However, there are important exceptions. Young Chicano children are often taught that it is more respectful to lower their eyes, especially when they're being criticized. In that context, direct eye contact is interpreted by adult Chicanos as belligerent or offensive. Looking at the person you're conversing with is an important behavior, however, in most adult Mexican-American communities. When you look someone in the eye while you're listening, you say in effect, "I'm tuned in; I hear you."

We recognize that when someone's maintaining eye contact with you, it doesn't *necessarily* mean that he or she is listening. But when you contrast a situation in which a person who's listening to you is also looking at you with a situation in which your listener hardly ever looks at you, you'll get an idea of what we're saying. Comfortably consistent, natural eye contact can be confirming to the other person; the absence of eye contact can be disconfirming.

Your posture and the movements of your body can also affect a person's perception of you as a listener. If you're in continuous motion—tapping a foot, fiddling with a pencil or paper clip, drumming your fingers, etc.—people often get the impression that you're anxious to "get on with it" or to get away. On the other hand, if you focus on them and nod affirmatively, people generally see that as confirming. Two people standing and talking together can also confirm a third person and invite him or her to join them, just by turning their bodies toward the third person.

You can also suggest confirmation with posture, as the persons in the pictures below are doing.

The history and communication context can also affect confirmation. Two close friends who are talking while listening to music may not care at all about each other's eye contact or posture. But in another setting, in which the friends are concerned about being listened to, each may focus quite a bit on the other's nonverbal confirmation or lack of it. Counselor-teacher Larry Brammer suggests that in most situations, the most clearly confirming posture is leaning *toward* the other person in a *relaxed* manner.[1]

Finally, you can listen to confirm by using nonverbal vocal cues—noises that indicate you're keeping up with what the other person is saying, and that you're interested in having him or her continue. This can become affected and phony, as when the pseudolistener responds to every phrase with an artificial "Mmmnnuhh?" or "Ahhuummmnn!!" or "Uhhhnmmmh." We're *not* suggesting that you do this. But whether you're on the telephone or in a face-to-face situation, it can often be

reassuring for the other person to hear some confirming noises, just to reinforce the fact that you're there and listening.

Eye contact, appropriate posutre, active facial expressions, and vocal sounds don't always suggest to people that you're listening. Think about how you'd feel if you were in this slightly exaggerated situation:

Verbal Confirming

You: That game was somethin' else!
Friend: (looks at you, nods head affirmatively, says nothing)
You: I couldn't believe how often they ran that same quarterback draw play, and it worked almost every time!
Friend: (looks at you, nods head, says nothing)
You: I can't wait to see what happens when they go up against Southern Cal!
Friend: (looks at you, smiles, nods head, says nothing)

That conversation includes important nonverbal confirmation: eye contact, affirmative head movements, and facial expression. But without verbal response from your friend, you may feel as though you are talking to a machine. If the conversation continues with just one person talking, that person is almost certainly going to feel frustrated and disconfirmed. To put it another way, silence, even with confirming nonverbal cues, can be disconfirming. When your listener says nothing verbally, it's sometimes easy to believe that you're being ignored.

In addition, people usually believe that nonverbal behavior is less consciously controlled than verbal behavior. For example, a listener's nods and smiles are often viewed more as habit or mechanical movements than as evidence of genuine listening. People are capable of smiling and nodding their heads even though they're daydreaming about something completely unrelated to the conversation. On the other hand, when we respond verbally, people perceive that we're committing more of our conscious selves to the relationship, especially if our verbal response relates directly to what the other person has just said. Our verbal responses can confirm the person in ways that even the best nonverbal behavior can't.

Research on confirmation[2] indicates that two of the most *disconfirming* verbal responses are what the researchers call "imperviousness" and "disqualification." Imperviousness means speaking *for* the other person, assuming you know what he or she is really thinking and feeling—"I know you don't really mean that" or "Things aren't really that way; you're just imagining it." It can also mean denying the person's right to experience what he or she is experiencing, as with "How can you possibly be unhappy after all we've done for you?" or "You should be ashamed to feel that way when. . . ." Disqualification can happen when someone responds in a way that is totally irrelevant to the other's prior utterance, shifts to a new subject without warning, or returns inappropriately to a previous topic of his or her own. You can also disqualify someone if you latch on to a minor part of what he or she has said and use it as a way to get back to the topic *you* want to discuss.

To confirm someone verbally, it's important to acknowledge his or her experience—even if it sounds unusual or inappropriate to you—and to respond relevantly to what is being said. Something as simple as "Sounds as if you were really excited" can be very confirming. It also helps to follow a topic until *both* of you are ready to move on, or at least to link your comments about a new topic with what was just said—"When you mentioned running, it reminded me that I have to pick up Bill's new shoes. Do you know where I can get a bus downtown?"

We'll mention several verbal responses below that can be part of your listening to understand and listening to diminish defensiveness. But remember that generally, the most *confirming* spoken words are those that are clearly related to the other person's topic and those that acknowledge his or her experience.

It's important to confirm the person you're listening to, but even when there's confirmation, it doesn't necessarily mean that the listener *understands* what's being said. You can look directly at the speaker, lean toward him or her, nod affirmatively, and not really hear a word. Or you can hear the words but not understand them from the speaker's point of view. Our purpose in this section is to explain several listening skills that not only help you to confirm the other but also increase your chances of accurately understanding the other's ideas.

As you read this, remember that genuine understanding doesn't necessarily signify agreement. Suppose someone said to you, "Our health is dependent upon our life-style and not on medical advancement." To understand would mean that you have a clear notion of this person's interpretations of "health," "life-style," and "medical advancement." Agreement would mean that you not only understand the interpretations but also believe the same way about them. Understanding, then, comes when you're able to interpret accurately and empathically what the other person is saying whether or not you hold similar beliefs.

LISTENING TO UNDERSTAND

"You're always telling me you know exactly how I feel. Well, this time I'm calling your bluff. Exactly how do I feel?"

DRAWING BY FRASCINO; © 1977 THE NEW YORKER MAGAZINE, INC.

Listening to understand is important in just about every situation, including sales presentations, family discussions, physicians' contacts with patients, counseling, social conversations, and so on. For example, a salesperson who knows how to listen to a client about the client's needs is likely to increase sales significantly. After completing a workshop that dealt with listening to understand, a business manager told Gary:

> I have to make several trips every year to "fact-find" among my clients. In other words, I have to find out what their real needs are so that my company can prepare an accurate quantity of products. If I miss too far, my company stands a chance of losing great sums of money, and I stand the chance of losing my job. On one trip, I had to go out and interview clients and get an accurate feel for their need for wood products. I tried the listening techniques you taught in this training. For the first two days it was hard; I sweated, I worked so hard at listening. Then it got easier and easier until actually, in the last three days, it was easy to do. And it helped tremendously to get the information I needed! Absolutely great!

A physician listening to a patient describe symptoms of an illness, an attorney studying his client's comments about a case, a family working out relationships in the midst of conflict, two friends discussing an important issue, and a consultant assessing the needs of a client before implementing a program are examples of situations in which listening to understand is a crucial communication skill.

Several communication behaviors sometimes look like listening to understand, but they're primarily confirming behaviors. For example, *eye contact* confirms the other person but by itself doesn't verify understanding. A person looking right into your eyes while you're talking makes you feel good about the fact that you're being listened to, but your "listener" may not understand a word you're saying. *Nodding your head* as if in agreement can also confirm the speaker, but it doesn't verify understanding of what's being said either. *Feeding back* to the speaker such phrases as "I understand," "Okay," "Right!" "I hear you," etc., are important because they reinforce the speaker and encourage him or her to share more, but again, these phrases don't verify that the listener understands the speaker.

A *summary* or *recap*, one of the most potentially deceptive behaviors, consists of your repeating what the speaker said—*in the speaker's own words*. It's deceptive because you can't be sure that you understand someone if you use the same words he or she did, since words can have many different interpretations. Here's an example of a summary response.

Interviewer: Tell me why you want this job with our company.
College Student: It fits my qualifications, and I am really enthusiastic
                         about the work. If you're motivated and enthusiastic
                         about your job, you do better at it.
Interviewer: So you feel you're motivated and enthusiastic.
College Student: Yes, I do.

Notice the interviewer's summary in his second statement. There's nothing in this statement to suggest that the interviewer understands what
the applicant means by "motivated" and "enthusiastic." Consequently,
the interviewer may accept or reject this candidate in part because of
misinterpretation of the candidate's notions of motivation and enthusiasm.

A key characteristic of listening to understand is that it is primarily
verbal. People don't always reveal that they're frustrated, afraid, anxious,
excited, or depressed, and an insightful listener can frequently detect
feelings without words being said. But when the person doesn't express in
words certain feelings and ideas, it's not always a good idea to make
inferences from the nonverbal communication. Nonverbal cues are inherently ambiguous, and they can mislead you. We think that this point is
important: *You can't develop understanding entirely nonverbally.* You probably realize that there are many more nonverbal than verbal cues available.
But that shouldn't lead you, as a listener, to rely exclusively on smiles,
gestures, and eye contact, important as these factors are. That's why we
believe that when you're listening to understand, it's important to emphasize *verbal* cues as much as nonverbal cues. The best idea is to let the
other person know what your interpretation is and to allow room for
response to your interpretations.

To use the following clarifying skills, you'll need to concentrate on the
speaker's comments, and you'll need to be in close touch with your
interpretations of these comments. This point is crucial; it sounds simple,
but we often don't do it. Most of the time we hear sounds without
concentrating on the ideas being expressed. We focus on what we intend
to say next, what we like or dislike about the speaker, how we think others
are responding, and so on. When clarifying, though, you should postpone
all that and concentrate on the other person's words and nonverbal cues.

Once you have learned to concentrate on the speaker's comments, you
can respond in several ways to check your understanding of them. The
following four skills are all forms of *perception checking*.

Paraphrasing or reinterpreting. Paraphrasing, or restating the other's meanings in your own words, is one of the most useful ways to increase
confirmation and understanding between two or more persons. It's true

that what some people think is paraphrasing can get mechanical, can be used manipulatively, can turn into game playing, can parade as genuine listening when it isn't, and can consume time and energy. But it need not do or be these things. If you are truly paraphrasing, you can actually save time, reduce stress, and promote positive relationships. As an insurance broker recently told us:

> One of the most important parts of my listening style is to concentrate on what my client is saying, take notes, and then try to reinterpret or restate what he is trying to tell me. My job is to understand the client, not to manipulate him, and to understand him I have to check to see if I'm hearing him right. In the long run, good listening saves me time and embarrassment because then I don't have to keep going back to the client to check things out and find that I didn't understand what he meant.

When used appropriately, paraphrasing can help you to understand the speaker, and it can help the speaker to further clarify his or her own ideas. Remember that paraphrasing is not "word swapping" or a "summary" of the speaker's comments; it is not a word-for-word repetition of what the speaker has just said. Paraphrasing involves reinterpretation; it happens when you've concentrated on what the speaker has said, you've interpreted those comments, and now you're going to share your interpretations of what the other person means. For example, an interviewer said to a candidate:

> Our company is interested only in assertive people, men and women who are not necessarily aggressive but who are candid and who have a lot of independent initiative. We don't want deadbeats. But we also don't want people who try to change everything in their path.

Before this candidate took a job with the company, she wanted to clarify what the interviewer was saying; that is, she wanted to understand his comments accurately. How did she do this? She paraphrased with:

> Assertive people express themselves confidently, and they share beliefs that are appropriate to the situation, but they don't usually talk as if other people were obligated to believe as they do. They leave an opening. I assume that's the kind of assertive person your firm wants.

In this instance the paraphrase was verified by the interviewer ("Yes, that's almost exactly what I mean"), and they moved on to other issues.

Note that in the paraphrase above, the candidate interpreted what she thought the interviewer *meant* by "assertive people." She didn't just repeat his words; she restated his meanings in her own words. Consider another example in which there was *no* paraphrase. A client said to an insurance representative, "I need your bid as soon as possible!" The rep replied, "As soon as possible. You've got it!" Following this exchange of comments, the rep went to his underwriting department and tried to coerce them to get the bid out within the "next couple of hours because an important client wants it as soon as possible." Not only did the people in underwriting not get the bid out, but the rep's coerciveness promoted tension and anger toward him. Later it turned out that when this client said, "As soon as possible," he meant within the next two or three weeks. He didn't clarify that, and the rep didn't clarify it, either. One fairly simple step could have saved time and bitterness. If the rep had paraphrased the client with, "As soon as possible means within the next day or two?" the client would have clarified his meaning.

Asking clarifying questions. Sometimes we're not sure how to interpret the speaker's comments. Even if we wanted to paraphrase, we wouldn't know what to say; our paraphrase would be pure conjecture and could be embarrassing. In these instances, asking questions is a good way to clarify. You might ask the person to define a word or phrase, or you might ask for explanation of the implications of what is being said. In the interview discussed earlier, for example, the interviewer said, "Our company is interested only in assertive people. . . ." The candidate could have asked, "When you say 'assertive,' what do you mean?" Tone of voice is an important part of clarifying questions. Remember that your questions are motivated by a need to understand the other person; they are not meant to force him or her into a corner with a demand to "define your terms!" Here are some other suggestions for asking clarifying questions:

1. When you're trying to clarify, it helps to avoid questions that you already know the answers to, or that actually hide your opinion. For example, in a discussion with a friend about exams, you say, "Don't you think that the only thing exams measure is what you can memorize?" What you're really saying is, "I think exams measure only what I can memorize and not what I really know and understand about the concept."

Another type of leading question begins with the words, "Isn't it a fact that . . . ?" While negotiating salary, a subordinate says to his manager, "Isn't it a fact that Bob, who is equal to me in status, is paid more for doing the same amount and kind of work?" This subordinate's intent is not to clarify his manager's ideas but, rather, to express his opinion in the form of a leading question.

2. Avoid yes/no questions, especially when you're trying to get clarification and explanation from the other person. One of the best examples
we've heard started with a phone call to a fire dispatcher from a woman
who hurriedly exclaimed: "My husband is choking! Get a Medic I unit
here quick!" The dispatcher asked for her address and she gave it to him.
He then repeated it and asked her if it was correct: "Your address is 5055
Nike Place Northeast, is that correct?" The woman answered, "Yes!
Hurry!" Medic I arrived at 5055 Nike Place Northeast and found the door
locked. Their orders were to break the door down and to "get in that house
before the guy chokes to death!" In a matter of seconds, the door was torn
down, and then, over their radio, they heard this: "Address given is
wrong. You are five blocks too far east. Proceed immediately to . . . ."
(You can guess the surprised look on a neighbor's face when Medic I
people tore down the door and left without going in.) The woman's husband ended up in good shape. He had choked on some breakfast cereal,
which had dissolved before Medic I arrived. The lesson here is simple:
The woman answered "Yes!" to a wrong address without realizing it.

3. Questions should be specific and to the point. Ambiguous and general
questions ("What do you think about that?" "What's your feeling on
this?") often elicit ambiguous and general answers. At best, the speaker
will ask you a question back in order to figure out what you mean by your
question.

Adding examples. You can also check your understanding of the other
person's comments by citing an example that you believe illustrates his or
her point. Your example may or may not illustrate exactly what the speaker
meant. If it doesn't, you've provided an opportunity to clarify; if it does,
you've verified your understanding. You can ask for an example from the
speaker or provide one of your own. The dialogue below demonstrates the
use of examples to clarify.

> Bob: In America, union members negotiate differently than
>   they do in other countries.
>
> Asks for
> example: Mark: What would be an example of how we're different?
>
> Bob: In one country I visited last summer, the hotel staff won
>   their demands from management by threatening to blow
>   up the entire second floor. No one was arrested. In
>   America, management wouldn't succumb to threats like
>   that.
>
> Mark: It's hard to believe a story like that.
>
> Bob: Check the October 2 issue of the *New York Times.*

Adds
example: Mark: I see what you mean. Like six months ago in Seattle,
two garage mechanics who were on strike threatened
violence to any "scabs." I guess the police called
these guys in for questioning and warned them
against infringing on the rights of others. In spite of
threats, management has not given in to any of the
union's demands for a better contract. That sounds
like one example of what you're saying.

It would have been difficult for Mark to understand Bob's initial statement, "In America, union members negotiate differently than they do in
other countries," without the use of examples. Even if Bob had said,
"Americans don't use as many threats as they do in other countries," Mark
still wouldn't have understood the exact meaning. The examples at least
put Bob's ideas in concrete form.

Here is another conversation that illustrates the points we're making.

A: College is oppressive.

B asks Are you talking about the fact that students don't get to make
clarifying very many choices about their education?
question:

A goes Yeah, partly. It's true we're told which courses to take, how
into more many hours, and things like that. But I'm thinking about
detail: specific courses and how my profs and T.A.'s tell me what I
should know, what I should remember, how I should write
term papers, what I should write, even. I'm just feeling
squashed. I can't sit down to study without worrying about
what I have to know for a test instead of what I *want* to
know.

B adds There's a course in humanities—201, I think—where they
example: tell you how many times you can miss class, and that you
have to write three ten-page papers, and they give you topics for the papers and the books you have to use for research.
Is that the kind of thing you're talking about?

A verifies Yeah, exactly. I'm not taking that course, but I've got some
B's example: just like it.

B confirms, Really, I know what you mean when you say "frustrated."
senses A's *And* "squashed," too. I think one follows from the other. But
feeling: sometimes it's the other way around. I've got a couple of
courses where we choose our own assignments, and each
day in class we decide what we want to talk about. Sometimes I think that's too much freedom.

A para-   Sounds as if you're not so sure about wanting more freedom
phrases: in your classes. Like, you wonder whether or not we're able
             to make decisions if we get the chance to?

Remember that neither paraphrasing nor providing an example re-quires you to agree with the other person. These responses are also not intended to provide "proof" of what the other is saying. The intent of all these replies is to enhance understanding, not to express agreement or disagreement.

Listening beyond. As we mentioned above, people don't always say what they mean; sometimes they talk completely around an issue out of fear, embarrassment, lack of trust, or some other uncertainty about how the other will respond. In situations where it's important that clear sharing take place but where the other person is reluctant to share directly and clearly with you, you should have some idea how to listen in ways that help get at what he or she really intends to say. You need a listening skill comparable to the peripheral vision that's so important in sports or in driving a car. Peripheral vision enables you to see what's on the periphery, or *edges,* of your field of view; when you use it, you see things without having to look directly at them. *Listening beyond* is like that because it's listening to what the speaker is *not* saying in words. You pay attention to how his or her meaning is reflected in pauses, tone of voice, eye movements, body movements, head movements, silence, other non-verbal cues—and sometimes in indirect verbal communication (saying one thing but meaning another).

At a recent workshop, a participant named Jack said, "Why don't we have several people talk about their techniques of communicating on the job?" The workshop instructor's peripheral listening told him that Jack wanted some time to share his *own* techniques—he didn't actually care if others did the same. How did the instructor pick this up? In an earlier meeting with the instructor, Jack had expressed interest in "workshop presentations." Jack's enthusiasm for sharing his opinion had also been evident throughout the small group meetings. The instructor had pieced these bits of information together with Jack's statement and inferred what Jack really wanted.

Listening beyond, then, requires you to make inferences beyond what the speaker is saying in words. When you're listening beyond, you may ask questions about something that has not been said in words. You may also raise an issue that hasn't been discussed by the other person but that you suspect is an issue the speaker wants to deal with.

Listening beyond does *not* mean looking for deep psychological mean-ings behind everything anyone says. It is not a Freudian strategy camouflaged as listening. What's the difference between becoming a sidewalk psychologist and listening beyond?

Barbara: I'm not flying to California in this weather. It's not worth it. I have plenty to do here, anyway.

The listener who is playing sidewalk psychologist might say, "You seem to fear death" or "Do you often avoid inconvenient events by rationalizing?" This is a form of listening beyond, but it requires two inferential leaps, one from a simple statement about a desire not to fly in certain kinds of weather to Barbara's meaning and another inferential leap to a conclusion about Barbara's personality. The sidewalk psychologist will try to make inferences about deep-rooted character and personality traits. *That is not what we mean by listening beyond.* Professionals should handle large inferential leaps about a person's deep fears, personality traits, etc. The listening beyond that we are discussing applies in those situations in which the speaker actually would like to share more but for some reason can't or doesn't. As the listener, you can help him or her to get it said and to get it out in the open. But you are not trying to draw conclusions about the speaker's personality or psychological motivation.

What clues can you look for that might suggest you need to listen beyond? When would you use listening beyond? A business friend of ours uses this type of listening to prevent him from intruding on his clients' personal lives, that part of their lives they choose not to share with him. When he's talking with a client, he pays close attention to what is being said in words, but he also pays close attention to the client's nonverbal communication. When the client makes nervous movements, shifts suddenly, or tenses up, this businessman infers that his questions are moving too close to personal or risky information. He believes that listening beyond in these situations has helped him to build trust with clients because it increases his sensitivity to their unexpressed needs.

Listening beyond as an interpersonal skill is intended to be used with an attitude of caring for the other person, not with an attitude of "How can I exploit him or her?" It's also intended to be used along with paraphrasing, asking questions, and citing examples. In other words, when you listen beyond, verify your inferences with the other person. You may read something totally inaccurate into another's communication, and that can create real problems. A student illustrated this when she reported to us:

> I was having a fairly adequate employer-employee relationship with my supervisor at work. However, one day he said to me, "Since I'm the boss, do it my way." When I heard that, I changed the way I responded to him for almost two weeks. If I saw him looking at me, I got upset, because I suspected that he was watching every move to see if I was doing it his way. I refused to ask him any questions that per-

tained to the job. Everything he said to me I interpreted negatively. Then the light clicked! Slowly but surely I began not to become so defensive whenever he said something to me. *I chose to accept his comments at face value and not feel that there was a hidden meaning in everything he said.* The working relationship is much better.

This example helps to point out that you can overdo listening beyond, and unless you combine this skill with paraphrasing and citing examples, you can create problems instead of solving them.

Of course, listening beyond can also work in strongly positive ways. As one man said to us:

When I learned to listen beyond, two things happened in my life. I was able to save my corporation several thousand dollars because one of our clients shared information with us that he never before would share, although he wanted to share it. More important, when I listen beyond at home, I find myself getting less defensive with my family. My son said the other day that he was "through with sports," and my past tendency would be to try to persuade him out of that attitude. But I decided that he wasn't saying at all what he meant. So I probed beyond and found out that what he really wanted to get rid of was my "intrusion" and "loud mouth" at his games. I don't say much any more when I watch him play, and we're both happier for it. But he never—and my wife would verify this—he never would have said that to me directly. I had to listen beyond to get it.

In Summary (So Far)

A *win/win* mental set is crucial.

You are ultimately more concerned with the relationship than with profiting at the expense of the other.

You're willing to give the other a full hearing.

You're willing to concentrate on the other's verbal and nonverbal cues.

You're open to the other's experience, even though you may not agree.

Listening to confirm means "saying" verbally and nonverbally, "I'm paying attention to you; I'm tuned in."

You can confirm nonverbally with direct facial and eye contact, posture that is oriented toward the other, and appropriate sounds.

The most confirming verbal responses are those that acknowledge the other's experience and respond relevantly to what he or she is saying.

Listening to understand is a step beyond listening to confirm.

It requires *verbal perception checking;* you can't develop understanding entirely nonverbally.

One skill is *paraphrasing*—trying to capture the other's meanings in your own words.

It also helps to *ask clarifying questions.*

You can also *add examples* based on your own experience.

And you can *listen beyond* the verbal to the nonverbal cues.

———————— •—•—• ————————

You can practice perception checking realistically only in live situations, because your perceptions rely heavily on nonverbal cues. But maybe the following examples will help you see how comfortable you are with these two listening skills.

Individual Application: Listening to Understand

Try to respond appropriately to the following statements as if they were made by the persons pictured.

"Thanks for the help. I've got to get to class now, but I really appreciate what you've done for me."

Your paraphrase: _____

_____

_____

_____

_____

_____

_____

"Oh, I'd say I've been at this job about 40 years. I've just about got it figured out. Not too many surprises for me any more."

Listen beyond and paraphrase:_____

_____

_____

_____

_____

_____

_____

"If things go on like this, I'm afraid we're going to have a problem. Your work has to improve, or you're definitely going to suffer for it at your annual review."

Ask clarifying questions: _____

_____

_____

_____

_____

_____

"I hate this place! I don't know why I ever came here!"

Paraphrase and add examples: _____

_____

_____

_____

_____

_____

_____

There's one more major challenge for the person who wants to listen in ways that promote interpersonal communication. Confirmation and understanding need to be supplemented with listening behavior that keeps other people—as much as possible—from feeling defensive.

    After studying group discussion over an eight-year period, Jack Gibb reported that *defensiveness* is one of the major barriers to interpersonal communication. He defined defensive behavior as behavior that "occurs when an individual perceives threat or anticipates threat."[3] He noted that person A's defensiveness usually creates defensiveness in person B, which in turn creates the same thing in person C, and so on to the point where a group's communication can become unproductive and even hostile. Gibb pointed out that one major cause of defensiveness is "speech or other behavior which appears *evaluative*"[4] (italics added). Note that Gibb says *speech or other behavior*. Both verbal and nonverbal cues can be evaluative. You may say to someone, "You've gotta be kidding; how can you believe something as stupid as that?" Or you may accomplish essentially the same thing by covering your face with your hands, taking a deep breath, sighing, and shaking your head negatively. People are sometimes careful about not making evaluative verbal statements, which are relatively easy to control, but at the same time they evoke defensiveness in others through their nonverbal evaluative behavior, which is not so easy to control.

LISTENING TO DIMINISH DEFENSIVENESS

We studied the same phenomenon at the University of Washington, and we identified a similar link between evaluation and defensiveness. We found that listeners who were strongly evaluative—who interrupted, disagreed, and continually corrected the other person—evoked significantly more defensiveness than listeners who were less evaluative—who agreed, didn't interrupt, paraphrased, and encouraged the other person.[5] It seems clear, in short, that evaluative listening increases defensiveness, and that defensiveness can destroy interpersonal communication.

These conclusions suggest that if you want to communicate interpersonally, you shouldn't be evaluative. But in an important sense that's *impossible;* you *cannot not evaluate* the things and people you perceive. Right now you're probably perceiving the pressure of a chair against your bottom, the fit of shoes around your feet, and the weight of clothes on your shoulders. Yet before you read that sentence, you probably weren't aware of any of those perceptions. You're continuously *selectively* perceiving, as we said in Chapter 3. Your selection is based on some kind of value judgment: one thing is relevant to you, another is irrelevant; this is important, that's unimportant; this is interesting, that's boring, or whatever. Your evaluating goes on at different levels of awareness, but it's always there; you cannot not evaluate.

So what do you do? If evaluation creates defensiveness but you can't stop evaluating, what can you do as a listener to help rather than hinder interpersonal communication? We think this is a really important question, whose answer could have a significant effect on the ways in which you listen to other people. We want to respond to that question with six suggestions for listening to diminish defensiveness.

1. Be generally positive.
2. Postpone specific evaluations.
3. Limit negative evaluations.
4. Own your evaluations.
5. Keep your evaluations tentative.
6. Actively solicit responses.

Be Generally Positive First, we think it's important to recognize that evaluation can be both positive and negative, but that interpersonal-quality communication is based on a generally positive approach to other persons. If you honestly believe that it's a dog-eat-dog world, you'll naturally be unwilling to take the steps toward sharing and being aware that can help make interpersonal communication happen. If you are absolutely sure that the other person will "get" you if you don't attack first, you probably won't be able to adopt a win/win attitude, and it's unlikely that you'll ever be able to give enough to communicate interpersonally with someone else.

We are definitely *not* saying that you should go around with your head in a pink cloud, oblivious to the fact that people sometimes deliberately treat others in thoughtless and even inhuman ways. We do *not* mean that you have to be simpleminded or naive to communicate interpersonally. We recognize that human beings have the potential for evil as well as for good.

However, we *are* suggesting that your basic, general evaluation of the persons you meet can be positive. You may reject parts of their *behavior* or some of their *attitudes,* but one characteristic of humanness is that persons have intrinsic worth—they are worthwhile just because they are human. You'll be better able to listen interpersonally to them when you keep this in mind.

It may encourage you to know that there's some evidence to support this positive point of view. The assumption that human nature is essentially evil, malicious, or cruel has *not* been supported by psychological studies. As Abraham Maslow puts it, psychologists are finding out that "history has practically always sold human nature short."[6] Counselor-therapist Carl Rogers also reports that in more than 25 years of reaching into the core of being of hundreds of "pathological," "antisocial," and "disturbed" persons, he has yet to find one who is not, at this very basic level, moving in *positive* directions.[7]

Our experience supports the validity of this positive general evaluation of persons. We are still occasionally disappointed by someone whose needs we are unable to understand or who feels pressure to abuse or take advantage of our relationship. But practically always we find that every person we meet is worth knowing. In other words, we're finding that our optimism is seldom inappropriate or misplaced. People *are* intrinsically worthwhile, and it "works" to treat them that way.

More specifically, we find that our positive general evaluation helps us listen more effectively. We don't pretend to be "nonevaluative," but we do try to listen from a positive, accepting point of view. When we're able to do that, the people we're communicating with don't seem to get defensive, and our communication is generally growth-promoting and productive.

———————•◆•———————

If it's difficult for you to feel positive about certain persons, you may want to try the following exercise.   **Individual Activity**

First, remember that your positive or negative responses to another are directly within your control; you can choose to see persons positively no matter what the circumstances.

The way we respond to persons often becomes a habit with us. Sometimes we continue to see people in negative ways because that's what our mind is used to doing. A friend reported to us how he changed his attitudes toward his wife by changing his habits of attention. He felt negative about his wife too much of the time, and someone suggested that he start listing ten positive things about his wife EVERY DAY! He did it; he found ten positive things to write down every day for two weeks, and his attitude gradually changed from negative to positive. He discovered that his negative attitude was primarily due to the fact that he was selecting negative things about her and was ignoring the positive.

Name a person you tend to feel negative about.

_____

List three of this person's strengths or positive characteristics.

1.

2.

3.

For example: Good listener/always on time/well informed/always does homework/dynamic/spends time with people when others won't/ willing to share/always pays debts.

To work on your attitude toward this person, write three positive comments about him or her on a 3 × 5 card every day for one week.

If you have trouble, consider:

Each of us has negative characteristics. The danger is in generalizing our negative characteristics to our "total self." Each of us also has positive characteristics. If we can't see beyond the negative characteristics of someone, then the problem is *not* the absence of positive traits; the problem is that we can't see the positive traits.

You may be responding to his or her image of you. How do you see the other person seeing you? Does he or she dislike you? Behave negatively toward you? Get in touch with this perception; it may be blocking your ability to see the other in positive ways.

------◆•◆------

Our second suggestion is to postpone any specific positive *or* negative evaluations until you're sure you understand clearly whatever you're evaluating. Virtually everyone has had the experience of violently disagreeing with the first few words heard, only to discover two or three sentences later that the "enemy" is really a friend. That's an easy mistake to make, but one you can avoid by hearing what the other person is really saying before assuming that you disagree. In a classroom discussion recently, a student said, "Doctors are overpaid." Another student, whose father was a general practitioner, violently disagreed and evaluated that statement harshly. Later we discovered that the first student was actually referring to her hometown physician, who reputedly makes more than $75,000 a year. As it turned out, both students believed that *some* doctors overcharge for *some* services, but they didn't mean that all doctors are guilty. As we say in the next chapter, mutual understanding occurs when each person is able to adequately limit the range of possible interpretations of what the other person is saying. You need information to do that, and if you make specific evaluations too soon, you may misinterpret what's being said.

Early evaluation can also stifle conversation. Committees sometimes fail to work because they spend too much time evaluating suggestions and too little time generating them. "Brainstorming" is a technique for avoiding that. The purpose of a brainstorming session is to come up with as many ideas as possible without evaluating any of them. The technique is based on the recognition that when evaluating starts—no matter whether it's positive or negative—creative thinking often stops. That's another reason why communication can often be improved when a listener postpones his or her specific evaluations.

Postpone Specific Evaluations

There's an important difference between "You're a stupid person; it's dumb to think that studying history will ever help you get a job" and "Your interruption right then sure seemed to kill the conversation." When you feel that a negative evaluation is warranted, i.e., that you've got enough information and you can't honestly be positive, it can make a big difference whether you evaluate *behavior, attitudes,* or *persons*. We think that whenever possible, it's important to limit negative evaluations to *behavior*. Negative evaluations of behavior are least likely to create defensiveness, because people generally recognize that behavior is something they can change. It's pretty difficult to do anything about a statement like

Limit Negative Evaluations

"You're hopelessly clumsy." That evaluation is almost always going to create defensiveness. But you *can* do something about the evaluation in a statement like "It seems to me that when you try to paint that fast, you don't cover the area very evenly."

Negative evaluations of behavior can create defensiveness, too—all evaluation can. But people are less likely to respond defensively to negative comments about their behavior than to negative comments about their *attitudes* or *ideas*. The main reason is that attitudes often seem harder to change. They're somehow more a part of us, and it's more threatening to give them up or modify them. So when our attitudes are challenged, we're likely to feel more strongly the "perceived or anticipated threat" that causes defensiveness.

Evaluating another person's attitudes is also dangerous because you can't really be accurate. You can never know for sure what another person is thinking; you can only make inferences based on the behavior you observe. As we said in Chapter 3, inferences are often inaccurate. John made some inferences about his daughter Lisa's ideas regarding dating when she was a sixth grader. Lisa talked about "going steady," came home with a ring that belonged to a guy in the neighborhood, and did everything she could to spend time with him. John inferred that her idea of "going steady" was like his, but his was an archaic relic of the early 1960s, when that term was used for a serious, potentially pre-engagement commitment. When Lisa broke up with her "steady" two days later, he recognized that the idea he was upset about wasn't anything like Lisa's idea of "going steady." He felt just about as silly as he probably looked to her, but at least he stopped complaining about her behavior.

Evaluating *persons* negatively will almost always create more defensiveness than will evaluating behavior or even attitudes negatively. Each of us needs security, acceptance, and self-esteem; when someone says that we are "stupid," "a bigot," "clumsy," "poor," "lazy," "a doper," "conceited," "a liar," or whatever, we will virtually always feel threatened enough to react very defensively. But if the point we've made about human worth is true, none of those statements can be accurate. Persons may—and often do—*behave* in ways that are "bigoted," "clumsy," "hypocritical," and "conceited." But the same persons also behave in ways that are "supportive," "thoughtful," "generous," and "loving." So it's hardly accurate to conclude that they "are" one set of behaviors and "aren't" another.

It's very difficult not to evaluate some persons negatively. Adolf Hitler is almost always cited as one such example. The Jewish philosopher Martin Buber wrote emphatically and extensively about the intrinsic worth of human beings; yet he was never able to fully accept the personal worth of convicted Nazi Adolf Eichmann. Some people feel the same way about contemporary political or religious leaders. Fortunately, it's usually much easier to accept the inherent worth of the persons you communicate with from day to day. When you can do that—when you can limit whatever negative evaluations you feel you have to make to the other person's *behavior* or, in extreme cases, to his or her *attitudes*—you can diminish the defensiveness that ruins interpersonal communication.

It also helps to reduce defensiveness when you identify your evaluations as just that—*yours* and *evaluations*. Thinly veiled comments, such as "Is it safe to drive this fast? I'm just *asking* . . ." or "Most people don't do that" and such nonverbal cues as a scowl, a sarcastic smile, or looking away, often masquerade as "descriptions" or "neutral reactions." They aren't, and usually everybody knows it. But often, not everybody does know exactly *who's* reacting (you? the group?), *how* they're reacting (frustrated? angry? bored? threatened?) or *why* (the language you're hearing? nonverbal cues you're interpreting?).

Own Your Evaluations

When you explicitly verbalize your evaluations in first-person terms, you can avoid these problems. (You may want to check back on the "description of feelings" exercise, pp. 186–187.) Try to move from disowned pseudodescriptions to owned evaluations.

Disowned pseudodescriptions	*Owned evaluations*
You think only about yourself.	I envy you the clothes you just bought.
	I don't like losing an argument, and I think I lost.
	I don't want to babysit the kids, either.
You're too bossy.	I feel inferior to you.
	I want to play poker more than I want to take you to a movie, but I feel threatened by your insistence that we go out.
(With exaggerated inflection) Oh, I don't care. Go ahead and go!	You're damn right I feel left out! I understood we had planned to go together, and now I hear you saying I'm not invited.
Never mind. Just forget it.	I feel frustrated even *trying* to discuss it with you.
	I feel ignored by you—you don't listen even when I try to explain.
	I don't want to hassle it any more.

Keep Your Evaluations Tentative

The approaches to perception and communication that we've followed throughout this book suggest two final characteristics of defense-reducing evaluative responses. The first is tentativeness. Since you interpret perceptions in your own unique ways, you can never be absolutely sure that you fully understand another person or are completely clear about his or her intentions. Consequently, your evaluations of another person's attitudes or ideas almost *have* to be tentative.

You may label as a racist someone you see putting down a person from another ethnic group, a person with whom he or she has had a long-standing, nonracial argument. You may conclude that someone who is Marxist is a hopelessly naive radical without learning for yourself the pragmatic and politically conservative dimensions of Marxism. In short, your evaluations of persons and attitudes can easily be wrong, so it's fairest to keep them tentative and open to change.

We believe that you can be more firm in your evaluations of another's *behavior*. But the trick is to keep your firm evaluations *limited to* behavior. That's one of the hardest things for parents to do. It's easy—and justifiable—to reject a child's tantrum-throwing behavior, but it's not so easy to keep from moving from behavior rejection to person rejection, i.e., from "No, you're not going to throw your shoe through the window!" to "You're a bad girl!" or "Calm down or I'll whack you good, you worthless brat!" Adults have the same problem with other adults. A teacher may justifiably react negatively to a student's continual absence or tardiness. But the teacher should not necessarily conclude that the student is "defiant" or "doesn't care." Similarly, a supervisor may very well criticize an employee's rate of work; it may actually be too slow to keep up with the rest of the production line. But the employee's behavior might be explained in a variety of ways—insufficient training, poor tools, bad lighting, inadequate materials, etc. The supervisor is *not* justified in concluding that the employee's behavior proves "laziness" or "incompetence."

In short, you don't have to compromise your own values to the point where you accept everything everybody does; you can, we believe, justifiably reject some kinds of *behavior*. But you're on pretty shaky ground when you firmly reject attitudes or persons. As a result, it's a good idea to keep in mind the inherent error factor of *all* evaluations and to keep your evaluations as tentative as you can.

Actively Solicit Responses

Our final suggestion is that you communicate your tentativeness and make it real by actively soliciting responses to your evaluations, so that the person you're talking with has the chance to react to your judgments. Then you have the opportunity to change your evaluation if it needs changing.

It's usually pretty difficult to be genuinely open to change after you've evaluated someone's behavior or ideas negatively. It's easy to feel as though you've made a public commitment to a point of view and that you'd look like a fool if you were to change your mind. It's hard not to feel the need to defend your evaluations—and your self-respect.

However, that kind of (literally) self-centeredness doesn't make sense if you (1) remember how human communication works, and (2) want to encourage interpersonal communication. You know that your evaluations are based on your interpretation of cues you perceive. It's obvious that the person you're evaluating may both perceive and interpret the cues differently, and that he or she may be as "right" or as "wrong" as you. So when you ask for responses to your evaluations, i.e., when you use perception checking in this situation, it's an indication that you actually do understand how human communication works.

Asking for responses to your evaluations also shows a win/win rather than a win/lose attitude. In other words, this kind of perception checking reveals your genuine willingness and ability to share some of your humanness and to be aware of the humanness of the other. The other person may have changed since you perceived whatever you're evaluating. He or she may be conscious of the behavior you're noticing and have good reasons for continuing it. You may be unaware of all kinds of unmeasurable factors that contribute to the behavior or attitudes you disagree with—emotions, past experience, hopes, fears, and so on.

Communication that involves negative evaluating should be mutual and interdependent, as should any other human communication. But negative evaluation tends to stifle response, so it's often important for the person doing the evaluating to actively solicit responses, to decide whether or not the evaluations need changing.

CONCLUDING THOUGHTS

In this chapter we've said that your listening behavior will be affected by many things, including contextual cues, your prior experiences, expectations about the future, the attitude with which you listen—win/lose or win/win—your perception and interpretation processes, and your willingness and ability to *apply* what you know about human communication and about interpersonal communication. We've also tried to lay out three important interpersonal listening skills—confirming the other, listening to understand, and listening to diminish defensiveness—all of which work together to help create an atmosphere in which interpersonal communication can happen.

By itself, good listening won't necessarily solve your communication problems, nor will it guarantee interpersonal communication; good listening does, however, make an important contribution.

———◆•●———

1. *Isn't paraphrasing (or reinterpretation) really just playing games with people–repeating what they've said just to disarm them into thinking you're on their side?*

Paraphrasing can turn into game playing when you do it *not* to understand what the other person is saying but to "impress" the other person, to manipulate his or her image of you, or to find weaknesses in his or her comments as you prepare for your attack. If you paraphrase for the sake of paraphrasing or to manipulate the other into thinking you are a good listener, then it becomes game playing. The motivation or reason for doing it is important. Paraphrasing is not game playing when it's used to increase understanding between persons.

2. *Should you always paraphrase people?*

No. Use it, for example, when a meeting is tense (it can help to prevent defensive reactions), when you really want to understand accurately what the other person means, and when you have the time to work at it. Use it during conflicts, so that you know what you disagree about (if anything), and so on. Paraphrasing is definitely inappropriate on some occasions. For example:

Caller: PLEASE SEND A FIRE TRUCK! MY HOUSE IS ON FIRE!
Dispatcher: Your house is on fire? Sounds like you feel pretty rotten about
              that. You wanna talk about it?

3. *What are some clues that I should be listening beyond, i.e., some indications that the other person isn't saying what he or she means directly?*

There are many possible clues. Here are a few. The other person may repeat something several times as if to say, "I want to talk about this item." The nonverbal communication seems tense (jaw tightening, broken eye contact, nervous movements, shifting, tension in the hands, etc.) or inappropriate for this person in this situation. Something the person said earlier connects with what he or she is now saying. The person asks what may seem to be a totally irrelevant question, but before you conclude that the question (or comment) is totally irrelevant and naive, think about what he or she could be saying indirectly.

4. *Is there such a thing as completely nonevaluative listening?*

No. All listening is to some extent evaluative, because our natural information-processing mechanisms evaluate information as they process it. For example, we don't listen to everything because of the overload, and so our selectors must evaluate what to pick up and what to ignore. We're continuously making "judgments" about what to attend to, how to interpret it, and so on. It's possible, however, to reduce our judgments of other people, and that's part of the intent of responsive listening.

5. *Do these listening skills work the same way in most or all cultures?*

Not necessarily. From our point of view, it's important in all cultures to "listen to confirm," "listen to understand," and "listen to diminish defensiveness." But the actual *behaviors* that lead to confirmation, understanding, and nondefensive attitudes will vary among cultures. In some cultures, for example, lack of eye contact is confirming because it shows respect.

6. *When someone is talking and going into considerable detail about something you think you already understand, is there a way to break in without rudely interrupting?*

Yes. Start by paraphrasing carefully right after you break in, "Let me see if I've got what you're saying thus far. . . ." This paraphrase will lessen the feeling of being interrupted and will confirm the person. With your paraphrase, you are verbally back in control, and you can indicate that you believe you understand the information already. For example, if you were working in customer service relations for an insurance company and had to answer customer complaints over the telephone, you'd run into customers who go on and on and on about their problem of getting their insurance claims paid. As a professional, you know you can't spend all day talking to one customer, so you need a way to break in without being rude. Paraphrasing is one of the best approaches.

7. *Some of your listening skills seem so mechanical to me. How can I avoid seeming mechanical and still use them?*

For a while it'll be difficult to avoid being mechanical, just as it's difficult not to be mechanical when first learning to drive a car or to hit a tennis or golf ball. Once listening skills become a habit with you, though, the mechanical feeling will leave.

Stage 1: You apply your usual listening skills unconsciously, and even though they may be ineffective, you nevertheless feel very natural with them.

Stage 2: You study communication and adopt several new listening-skill behaviors, and these behaviors feel unnatural to you, almost artificially mechanical. But you continue to practice them.

Stage 3: The old listening skills are replaced by the new skills, and now these new skills feel as natural as the old used to feel.

8. *Why do people sometimes avoid listening to each other?*

Here are a few of the possibilities:

a. They don't want to be influenced, and good listeners are often influenced by what they hear.

b. They sometimes believe that when listening to someone's problems, they aren't allowed to be assertive. They think good listening is being nice and never interacting with contrary opinions. Thus, for these people listening is extremely frustrating since they have to suppress all their own beliefs, attitudes, etc. Fortunately, good listeners can also be quite assertive!

c. They sometimes don't want to get too close, and they believe that to listen to someone, you must get close (psychologically).

d. They don't want to give the other person's ideas credibility, and they believe that listening always gives credibility.

e. Listening consumes time and energy; actually, good listening can be hard work! Sometimes people aren't interested in expending energy—in clearer terms, they're lazy.

9. *Can a person listen interpersonally (confirm, understand, and diminish defensiveness) without always feeling stressful and emotional about it? I want to practice good listening, but I don't want to get intimately interpersonal with everyone I listen to.*

It's important that you maintain your own psychological health as you work on interpersonal-communication principles. At times you will need to maintain a certain distance from the people you listen to. Here are some ways you can help yourself become an effective interpersonal listener without increasing stress.

a. Do *not* take on the emotions of the other person. You can understand the emotion and feel a part of it, but you need not take it on as strongly as the other person may be experiencing it.

b. Remember that you do not need to feel responsible for the emotions of the other person. You cannot choose for that person *not* to have the emotion; it's up to him or her to choose. You can offer understanding, a listening ear, a way of explaining, but you can't choose to eliminate the emotion in the other.

c. Don't feel responsible for solving the problem if there is one. You can facilitate, listen, suggest, but you can't directly solve another person's problems.

d. Continue to look at the person's situation in a larger context. Often persons we listen to look at themselves and their predicament at the moment; they can't see beyond or look at themselves in a larger framework of time and circumstances. As the listener, you can help the person look at the larger perspective and in doing so, not get yourself involved in the tyranny of the immediate urgency!

e. Think about positive rather than negative outcomes. Much of the time we're thinking about what bad things will happen to us, and when people share these "future negative" experiences, we agree with their predictions. If we think about the positive outcomes and refuse to be taken in by unwarranted negative inferential leaps, we'll be better able to handle what people share with us.

10. *Do good listeners ever assert themselves? Or do they just listen all the time?*

Sounds like a loaded question! A good listener gets more opportunity for self-assertion because good listening helps to make the other person want to listen to *you*. If I believe that you are trying hard to understand me and my ideas, I'm more likely to want to understand you and your ideas. Contrast that with a situation in which I believe you are not listening to me at all; it isn't likely that I'll be receptive to your ideas. In other words, by being a good listener, you create an audience for your ideas. Assert yourself. But listen first.

———————— ◆•◆ ————————

Change the following "disowned" judgmental statements into "owned" defense-reducing responses. In other words, verbally describe as explicitly as you can the feelings that are probably behind each judgment.

EXERCISES

Individual Activity: Owning Your Evaluations

	Disowned judgments	*Verbal description of feeling*
Person 1:	You're wrong about that!	I don't see it the same way you do; my experience with . . .
Person 2:	Oh, come on! How can you say that?	I feel frustrated by what you just said; I'm worried that you're trying to make what I say seem inferior.
Person 3:	Only an ignoramus would believe that.	_____ _____
Person 4:	You haven't looked at the facts. Your opinion isn't worth anything because you haven't re-searched the issue.	_____ _____ _____
Person 5:	That was a boring meeting.	_____ _____ _____

Person 6: His lectures are abso-
             lutely irrelevant to any-
             thing.

            _____

            _____

            _____

Individual Activity:
Alternative
Responses

You may want to try this for practice. Write four different responses to the following statement made by a parent.

"This younger generation scares me. They have no moral values. They smoke dope, believe in premarital sex, rebel against our government. I'm afraid of what's going to happen when they become our leaders."[8]

1. Write a negative evaluative-judgmental response.

    _____

    _____

    _____

    _____

2. Write a paraphrase.

    _____

    _____

    _____

    _____

3. Ask a clarifying question.

    _____

    _____

    _____

    _____

4. Verbally describe the feelings you had as you read the statement.

    _____

    _____

    _____

    _____

Break your class or group into dyads. Spend about 20–30 minutes discussing a controversial issue that the two persons in each dyad disagree about. Try to listen to each other with (1) a win/win attitude, (2) confirming behaviors, (3) paraphrasing and parasupporting (perception checks), (4) defensiveness-reducing responses. After your conversation, respond individually to the following questions.

**Group Activity:
Responsive
Listening**

How did you see your partner during the conversation?

1. "I felt confirmed   __:__:__:__:__:__   "I felt disconfirmed
   by him/her"   1 2 3 4 5 6 7 by him/her"

2. "He/she was un-   __:__:__:__:__:__   "He/she was
   derstanding"   1 2 3 4 5 6 7 judgmental"

3. "He/she was non-   __:__:__:__:__:__   "He/she was defen-
   defensive"   1 2 3 4 5 6 7 sive"

4. "He/she had a   __:__:__:__:__:__   "He/she had a win/
   win/win mental   1 2 3 4 5 6 7 lose mental set"
   set"

How did you see yourself during the conversation?

5. "I confirmed him/   __:__:__:__:__:__   "I disconfirmed him/
   her"   1 2 3 4 5 6 7 her"

6. "I tried to under-   __:__:__:__:__:__   "I was judgmental"
   stand him/her"   1 2 3 4 5 6 7

7. "I was non-   __:__:__:__:__:__   "I was defensive"
   defensive"   1 2 3 4 5 6 7

8. "I had a win/win   __:__:__:__:__:__   "I had a win/lose
   mental set"   1 2 3 4 5 6 7 mental set"

There are several things you may want to do with the information from the eight questions.

1. Turn in your questionnaire to your instructor, who will summarize the results for you.

2. Compare your perceptions with those of your partner. Did your partner see you the same way you saw yourself? What verbal and nonverbal cues led you to answer the questionnaire the way you did? Discuss with your partner the differences in your perceptions.

3. Divide the questionnaires from all class members into two groups. Place in the first group all questionnaires with scores from 1 to 3 on

items 1 and 2. Place in the second group all questionnaires with scores from 5 to 7 on items 1 and 2. Now check to see which group has the highest scores on the defensiveness scale (item 3). Group 1 should come out the lowest; that is, members of that group should have felt the least defensive if the scores on items 1 and 2 are accurately reported.

———————◆•◆———————

Individual Activity: Self-Inventory of Listening Habits: Part I

The purpose of this inventory is to help you gain a better understanding of your listening habits; when you have completed it, you should be able to describe your listening habits, and you should have established a priority of listening habits to improve. This is of course a subjective inventory and not an objective test.

Directions: First, read this list and place a check in front of each habit that you now have, even if you use that habit only a third to a half of the time. Second, reread the habits you have checked and place *two checks* in front of those habits you think you perform almost all of the time you spend listening, perhaps 75—100% of your listening time.

1. I prepare myself for listening by focusing my thoughts on the speaker and expected topic and committing my time to listen.
2. I ask questions about what I have just heard before letting the speaker know what I heard and understood.
3. I follow the speaker by reviewing what he or she has said, concentrating on what the speaker is saying and anticipating what he or she is going to say.
4. I analyze what I am hearing and try to interpret it to get the real meaning before I let the speaker know what I heard and understood.
5. I look at the speaker's face, eyes, body posture, and movement and listen to his other voice cues.
6. I think about other topics and concerns while listening.
7. I listen for what is *not* being said as well as for what is being said.
8. I fake attention to the speaker, especially if I am busy or think I know what the speaker is going to say.
9. I show in a physical way that I am listening and try to help set the speaker at ease.
10. I listen largely for the facts and details more than I listen for ideas and reasons.
11. I know the facial, body, and vocal cues that *I* am using while listening.
12. I evaluate and judge the wisdom or accuracy of what I have heard before checking out my interpretation with the speaker.

13. I avoid symphathizing with the speaker and making comments like "I know just what you mean, it's happened to me" and then telling my story before letting the speaker know what I heard and understood.

14. I find myself assuming that I know what the speaker is going to say before he or she has finished speaking.

15. I accept the emotional sentiment of the speaker.

16. I think up arguments to refute the speaker so that I can answer as soon as he or she finishes.

17. I use echo or mirror responses to feed back to the speaker specific words and phrases the speaker has used that I need clarified.

18. I am uncomfortable with and usually reject emotional sentiments of the speaker.

19. I paraphrase or summarize what I have heard before giving my point of view.

20. I am easily distracted by noise or the speaker's manner of delivery.

Now place an X in the blank by each number that you have double checked.

2_____	1_____
4_____	3_____
6_____	5_____
8_____	7_____
10_____	9_____
12_____	11_____
14_____	13_____
16_____	15_____
18_____	17_____
20_____	19_____

Now you have an inventory of your *effective listening habits* (all those odd-numbered habits you checked), your *ineffective listening habits* (all those even-numbered habits you checked), your *most effective listening habits* (all those odd-numbered habits you checked twice), and your *most ineffective listening habits* (all those even-numbered habits you checked twice).

The Self-Inventory of Listening Habits (Parts I and II) is reproduced here with the permission of its author, Marie Rosenwasser, Ph.D., Senior Consultant, Martin-Simonds Associates Management Consultants, Seattle, WA.

**Self-Inventory of
Listening Habits:
Part II**

Now that you have an inventory of your effective and ineffective listening habits, you can try to establish a priority of which habits to strengthen and which habits to stop.

1. List in order of importance what you'd like to stop doing when you listen. To determine this, consider the even numbers that you have double-checked, and then, using your personal judgment of which of these ineffective habits cause you the most difficulty, arrange them into your hierarchy of what to get rid of first. If you do not have three even-numbered habits double-checked, go to those even-numbered habits that you have checked once and, again in your personal judgment, select one or two that cause you considerable difficulty.

Listening habits I want to stop doing

A. _____

B. _____

C. _____

2. Next, list in order of importance which three habits you will try to acquire or, if you have them now, which habits you will try to use more of the time. To determine these habits, consider the odd numbers you did not check, but if you checked every odd number once, consider those you checked only once. Again, use your personal judgment about which habits you would find most useful to have or strengthen.

Listening habits I want to improve

A. _____

B. _____

C. _____

After you have learned more about listening habits and ways to improve your listening, you may find it useful to review your priorities and create new lists of what to stop and what to improve.

NOTES

1. Lawrence Brammer, *The Helping Relationship: Process and Skills* (Englewood Cliffs, NJ: Prentice-Hall, 1973), p. 82.

2. See for example, Kenneth N. Leone Cissna, "Interpersonal Confirmation: A Review of Current Theory, Measurement, and Research," ERIC Document Reproduction Service No. ED 126 544; Frank E. X. Dance and Carl E. Larson, *The Functions of Human Communication* (New York: Holt, Rinehart and Winston, 1976), pp. 73–90; R. D. Laing, *Self and Others*, 2nd ed. (Baltimore: Penguin,

1969), pp. 98–107; and Evelyn Sieburg, "Confirming and Disconfirming Communication in an Organizational Context," *Personnel Woman*, **18** (1974), 4–11.

3. Jack R. Gibb, "Defensive Communication," *Journal of Communication*, **11** (September 1961), 141.

4. *Ibid.*, p. 142.

5. Stephen J. Stephenson and Gary D'Angelo, "Relationships Among Evaluative/Empathic Listening, Self-Esteem, Sex, and Defensiveness in Dyads," unpublished manuscript, University of Washington, 1973.

6. A. H. Maslow, *Motivation and Personality*, 2nd ed. (New York: Harper & Row, 1970), p. 271.

7. Carl R. Rogers, *On Becoming a Person* (Boston: Houghton Mifflin, 1961), p. 26.

8. Exercise adapted from David Johnson, *Reaching Out: Interpersonal Effectiveness and Self Actualization* (Englewood Cliffs, NJ: Prentice-Hall, 1972).

ADDITIONAL RESOURCES

One of the few book-length treatments of listening is Baxter and Corinne Geeting's *How To Listen Assertively* (New York: Monarch, 1976). This lively, practical book includes quite a bit of useful information and advice.

Charles M. Kelly distinguishes between deliberative and empathic listening in his article, "Empathic Listening," which is reprinted in the book John edited, *Bridges Not Walls: A Book about Interpersonal Communication*, 2nd ed. (Reading, MA: Addison-Wesley, 1977), pp. 222–227.

There are also two other useful and informative discussions of listening in that same chapter of *Bridges Not Walls*, Gerard Egan's "Listening as Empathic Support," pp. 228–231, and a short story by John Berry called "The Listener," pp. 232–238.

One current line of quantitative research focuses on "social perspective-taking" as a fundamental communication skill. Perspective-taking, which means accurately construing another's constructions, is closely related to listening skills discussed in this chapter. See, for example, David L. Swanson and Jesse G. Delia, *The Nature of Human Communication* (Chicago: Science Research Associates, 1976), pp. 28–31; and Ellen M. Ritter, "Social Perspective-Taking Ability, Cognitive Complexity, and Listener-Adapted Communication in Early and Late Adolescence," *Communication Monographs*, **46** (March 1979), pp. 40–51.

David W. Johnson presents a practical, humanistic view of interpersonal communication with a variety of structured experiences in his book *Reaching Out: Interpersonal Effectiveness and Self-Actualization* (Englewood Cliffs, NJ: Prentice-Hall, 1972). Chapters 5, 6, and 7 relate especially to listening.

The counselor-teacher Carl Rogers identifies responsive listening as an important part of his theory and practice of interpersonal communication. He explains his approach in several places, e.g., in his book *On Becoming a Person* (Boston: Houghton Mifflin, 1961). You might also enjoy watching him communicate with a counselee or "client" in the film, *Three Approaches to Psychotherapy: Part I.*

Thomas Gordon has elaborated a primarily Rogerian approach to listening in his book *Parent Effectiveness Training: A No-Lose Program for Raising Responsible Children* (New York: P. H. Wyden, 1970). Also see Gordon's more recent book, *P.E.T. In Action* (Toronto: Bantam Books, 1978).

7

Interpersonal clarity

I. BEING CLEAR MEANS FOCUSING, LIMITING THE WAYS PEOPLE CAN INTERPRET WHAT YOU SAY

II. UNCLEAR COMMUNICATION CAN BE DETRIMENTAL TO INTERPERSONAL CONTACT

A. It can lead to misunderstanding

B. It can evoke feelings of impersonalness

C. It can promote psychological barriers

III. INCREASING THE CLARITY OF YOUR COMMUNICATION

A. Make the situation work for you

    1. Control interference

    2. Use all appropriate channels

B. Adapt to your listeners

    1. Let them know your perspective

    2. Try to take their perspective

        a) Principle of adaptation

        b) Principle of prior definition

        c) Avoid jargon

C. Organize what you say

    1. Structure your ideas
    2. Make implicit structure explicit
    3. Use transitions

D. Illustrate your ideas

    1. Use "concrete" language
    2. Use examples
    3. Use analogies

E. Use reminders

DOONESBURY, COPYRIGHT 1972 G. B. TRUDEAU. DISTRIBUTED BY
UNIVERSAL PRESS SYNDICATE. REPRINTED BY PERMISSION.

Sometimes being unclear can be an advantage. For example, if Zonker
succeeds, he'll have a paper that he can use for several different classes.
You might say that Zonker is using "purposeful ambiguity." But students
aren't the only ones who use purposeful ambiguity.

Some policiticians do:

Interviewer: Senator, what is the government doing to discourage large
companies from taking advantage of energy shortages?

Senator: My position on this aspect of the energy crisis is the position
I have taken since it became apparent that a supply shortfall
was emerging because of international market conditions in
the Middle East and South America. We should continue to
move ahead, emphasizing exploration and international
cooperation, while protecting our energy independence.

Some educators do:

Student: What are the practical applications of what you just said?
Teacher: It's practical in the sense that the element purports to relate to existence in the same way that your behavior relates to the behavior of others.

Some advertisers do:

Soap ad: Cleans whiter, brighter, faster, yet is more gentle to your hands.

Some family members do:

Mother: Where've you been?
Son: Out.
Mother: Out? Out is big? Where's out?
Son: I've been out. That's all.

The object of purposeful ambiguity is *not* to be clear; this kind of language is used as a diversion or smoke screen. Most of the time, however, you have different goals. Whether you're giving directions to the highway, explaining the causes of the Vietnam War, showing your supervisor how you can improve production in your department, or telling your spouse how you feel about spending the income tax refund on furniture, you'd rather be *understood* than *misunderstood*. "Being clear" is one important goal of a great deal of your day-to-day communicating.

It's important, though, to emphasize from the start that you cannot "be clear" by yourself. Just like all the other aspects of human communication, clarity happens *between* the people involved; it is a relational thing. No matter how carefully I structure and present my ideas, I cannot "cause" you to hear them in a certain way. That's another implication of the fact that human communication is not an action I perform "on" you, but a transaction that goes on between us.

At the same time, my choices can and do make a real difference. I can organize, illustrate, and link my ideas in ways that promote or block your understanding. Your choices matter, too. You can expect, assume, and listen in ways that promote or block mutual understanding. So both or all of us are involved. Nobody can "be clear" without such help, but it is still vital to learn to make communication choices that will make clarity possible.

Often it isn't easy. Our language presents some obstacles to "being clear" that sometimes seem almost insurmountable. For example, in our day-to-day communication, most of us use only about 2000 different English words, but the 500 words that we use most often have more than *fourteen thousand* different meanings! The word "part" can mean an essential portion, one of several equal units, a division of a literary work, a line or melody in musical harmony, a constituent element of a machine, a duty, an actor's lines in a play, the external genital organs, a line made when hair is combed, and so on. The Word "run," according to *Webster's Third New International Dictionary*, has 89 different meanings, and that doesn't include the definitions of "run across," "run after," "run against," "run foul of," "run free," "run rings around," "run wild," or 22 other combinations!

"Communication" is another word with a multitude of definitions. In fact, Frank Dance and Carl Larson surveyed writings about communication and found 126 different meanings. They ranged from "transmission and interchange of facts, ideas, feelings, courses of action" to "effort after meaning" and from "discriminatory response of an organism to a stimulus" and "mechanism by which power is exerted" to "process by which a person reduces the uncertainty about some state of affairs by the detection of cues which seem to him to be relevant to the state of affairs."[1] You may wonder how, in the face of all those choices, anyone can communicate clearly about communication?

Even though there are forces working against you, there are several things you can do to focus others on what you mean. And the first step is to recognize that that's what you're doing: *"Being clear" means focusing, limiting the ways people can interpret what you say, restricting their range of possible interpretations.* Before you have any information about a new client, for example, you could believe almost anything. Let's say the new person is female, but that's all you know. She could be a *Playboy* model, president of the local Chamber of Commerce, the governor's daughter, or the oldest welfare worker in the country. In other words, before you have any information, your range of possible interpretations is almost completely unlimited; as soon as you see her, however, the range narrows. Visual contact alone gives you enough information to convince you that she might well be president of the local Chamber of Commerce, but she's way too young to be the oldest welfare worker. That's what all information does; whether it's pictures, smells, textures, temperatures, or the sights and sounds of words, information functions to reduce uncertainty, to limit the range of possible interpretations. To put it another way, there is an inverse relationship between information and uncertainty. As you get more information, you get less uncertainty. Total certainty is impossible for humans, but effective communication can get us pretty close to that ideal.

To illustrate what we mean, we'll give you two examples. Have you ever been in a conversation like this?

You: What do we have to know for the exam?
Friend: Oh, just understand the basics.

Or maybe you've been involved in an interchange like this one, more detailed but no less confusing:

You: How do you get to the stadium from here?
Friend: Just go down that street over there for several blocks until it kind
         of divides into three ways down by a couple of brick buildings
         just over two or three streets from the place where the McDonald's
         used to be. You should be able to see the gym flagpole there, and
         then take that street about five blocks toward the pool until you
         get over by that line of trees, and then look for where the other
         road takes off so you can turn in on it.

Obviously, neither of your friends' responses is clear. That is, neither response adequately limits the number of different ways you could interpret what was said. In the first example, "the basics" could mean answers to the review questions the teacher handed out, outlines of the lectures and readings, overviews of the two theories discussed, answers to old test questions, or any combination of those. Your communication with your friend is unclear, because there are too many ways to interpret what your friend said. On the other hand, the second example is filled with statements, but they are also difficult to follow, because they can be interpreted in several possible ways. What does your friend mean by "kind of divides into three ways"? Does "a couple of brick buildings" mean two buildings? What if I don't know where the McDonald's used to be? "About five blocks" is pretty general—how many blocks is it? Four? Six? Three? And so on. Again, the problem is that the instructions do not adequately limit your range of interpretations, and consequently the communication is not very clear.

When communication is unclear, it is also often impersonal. If you're working toward interpersonal-quality communication, you'll need not only to share and to be aware but also to "be clear." One reason is that when you fail to adequately limit someone's range of possible interpretations, you're often treating that person as an object. In the conversations above, one of the problems is that your friend isn't seeing you as a unique individual. There seems to be an implicit assumption that, since your friend knows what "understand the basics" means, you will too. Or your friend may have decided to be unclear on purpose. He or she may feel unwilling to share with you information that it took long hours and hard work to accumulate. Maybe that feeling is justified. But in refusing to share the feeling with you because "you wouldn't understand" or "you'd just get mad," your friend is assuming that you can't deal with those feelings; he or she is stereotyping your probable response. That's a form of objectifying, too.

Similar things are happening with the directions to the stadium. Your friend apparently has a clear picture of what he or she is describing. But you may be much less familiar with the neighborhood than your friend is. So long as your friend is assuming, "Since *I* understand it, you will, too," he or she is not recognizing your individuality. In that sense, you're being objectified.

A second reason why unclear communication is often noninterpersonal communication is that when others have trouble deciding how to interpret you, they often break psychological contact with you. That can happen for a variety of reasons. They may infer that you're being purposely ambiguous for strategic or manipulative reasons. They may infer that you don't know what you're talking about. They may "tune out" because they're confused and bored. Look again at the directions to the stadium. How do you usually respond to communication as confusing as that? Probably by not listening—ignoring what the person is saying while you try to think of another way to get the information. Unclear communication often works that way. As you've read this book, you may have found yourself breaking contact with us because we weren't making sense to you. When that happens, you're responding to the uncertainty of having too many interpretations to choose from. When we don't adequately limit the possible interpretations, we make it more likely that others will break contact with us. That's another reason why being clear can affect your ability to promote interpersonal communication.

You can respond to these two problems by working to adequately reduce the number of ways others can interpret your verbal and nonverbal cues. You can do that—work toward "being clear"—by taking the following steps.

1. Make the situation work for you.
2. Remember to
   a. adapt to your listeners.
   b. organize what you say,
   c. illustrate your ideas, and
   d. use reminders.

MAKE THE SITUATION WORK FOR YOU

Control Interference or "Noise"

The first step toward clear communication is to exert some control over the communication situation. Many parts of the situation can create what information theorists call "noise." Broadly speaking, anything that interferes with another person's understanding of you is "noise"—from fatigue or a headache to high humidity or depressing colors, from a squeaky or harsh voice to constant pacing or repetitive "y'know"s.

There are at least three kinds of noise. When a bad headache, heartburn, or hunger pangs prevent effective listening, one is experiencing *physiological discomfort* noise. An example of a second type, *psychological* noise, is a strong opinion that keeps a person from listening accurately to any message that contradicts that opinion. Sometimes psychological noise is so strong that it prevents effective communication. For example, a worry about grades causes gamesmanship between instructor and student; fear of losing the job contributes to an employee's high anxiety level, so that he or she is unable to hear accurately the work instructions given; a strong prejudice against women prevents a male hospital patient from listening to a female dietitian about proper diet. *Physical* (or environmental) noise—the third type—includes things like a hot stuffy room, an uncomfortable chair, cramped physical space, and so on.

However, the problem is that one person's noise is another's information. What may be a "cramped" space to another may be a comfortably intimate environment to you. Since noise often originates "in" the persons with whom you're communicating, you can't always know when or how it's operating. But you can do two things. First, you can take the time and effort to get in touch with and then do something about the potentially distracting elements of the communication situation. Do you need to stop playing with the ball-point pen in your hands? Quit twisting and tugging the rings on your fingers? Stop the continual shifting of your weight from foot to foot? Do you need to close the door? Open the window? Turn down the heat? Move closer together? Sit down? Go somewhere else? Rearrange the furniture? Talk more quietly? Relate what you're saying to what was being discussed before you began? Comment on why you're dressed as you are?

Remember that you have the ability to control many of the elements of a communication situation. Even in fairly formal situations, you can change some of the contextual factors that you think may be distracting. For example, if you're late, you can mention why, thus limiting the number of ways in which your nonverbal message might be interpreted. Or if you're talking with a small group of persons in a large room, you may ask them to move closer together so that they feel less anonymous and perhaps more willing to contribute.

John remembers one situation in which he was extremely insensitive to contextual noise. When he was teaching in Wisconsin, the departmental offices were crowded into one corner of the basement of Old Main. Whenever faculty or students wanted privacy or quiet, they had to move to another part of the building. Down a dark hall from John's office was the drama director's costume room, a large, gloomy place filled with racks of clothes, long tables, and storage boxes. Since it was convenient and quiet, John often used it to listen to student speeches or readings. A woman named Adrienne had asked for some help with an oral interpretation presentation she was working on, and they had made a late-afternoon appointment. As soon as she arrived, they headed toward the costume room, talking about the class, Adrienne's reading, the weather, and various other topics. John unlocked and opened the door, flicked on the dim lights, and motioned for her to go in. She looked at him strangely, so he mumbled something about ". . . bad facilities . . . practice . . . good acoustics." Adrienne just about exploded with relief. "Oh, brother! You don't know *what* I was thinking!" For Adrienne, the dim lights, secluded hall, and locked door, all naively ignored by John, added noise to the context and thus interfered with the communication situation.

Use All Appropriate Channels   Within any situation you have control over several different channels or modes of communication. For example, when you're talking on the telephone, your tone of voice can influence the other person's interpretation of your mood and feelings, your relationship to him or her, and your interest in the conversation on the phone. You also have control over your rate of speaking, pronunciation, and articulation. Each of these factors can contribute to confusion or clarity. When you're writing a letter, you don't have control over auditory cues, but you do have a variety of visual modes: the quality, size, and color of paper, the kind of pencil or pen, whether you type, print, or write, the style of your writing, your choice of words, and the informal or formal structure of your sentences or paragraph layout. If you're applying for a job and you want to address your prospective employer formally, you wouldn't want to use pink perfumed paper and a lavender felt-tip pen. Similarly, we've learned that most of our friends respond differently when we type a letter on a formal letterhead than when we write it in longhand on notebook paper.

In face-to-face oral communication, there are a tremendous number of channels available to inform or confuse your listeners. You have not only the same auditory cues that are available in a telephone conversation, but also visual cues and, in some situations, touch and aroma cues, too.

One research team investigated the comparative effects of faces and voices by creating a situation in which communicators' faces indicated one attitude—positive, neutral, or negative—while their voices indicated a different attitude. Not surprisingly, they found that people tended to believe the attitude they *saw* in the communicator's face more often than the one they *heard* in the communicator's voice. But the researchers also found that when information in the two modes was consistent—when face and voice agreed—listeners perceived the communicated attitude to be significantly more *intense*. Using more than one channel definitely made a difference.[2]

The same research team also came to some conclusions about the relative importance of three different face-to-face modes. When they combined results of the face-voice study with some data about how words work,[3] they concluded that when you use all three channels—words, tone of voice, and facial expression—words contribute 7 percent, tone of voice 38 percent, and facial expression 55 percent of the total meaning. Or to put it another way, listeners tend to rely on your facial expression most heavily, your tone of voice next, and your words last. These findings are obviously incomplete, because they don't indicate the impact of any of the several other channels that are operating. But they do suggest that the number and kind of channels you use can significantly affect how others understand you.[4]

Few people take full advantage of the visual modes available to them in face-to-face contexts. Some use gestures to describe size and shape, but often those gestures are too "quick" and not "definite" enough. Instead of just talking about their models of communication, students in our classes sometimes sketch diagrams on materials for display by overhead projection, blackboards, sketching pads, or whatever is available. If they aren't comfortable with their own artwork, they'll ask friends to do the sketching for them. Some of the clearest explanations have included models, pictures, and objects, done in different colors. One group of students decided to present a report on how context influences nonverbal behavior. But since they didn't want to give just a verbal report, they dressed a person in a weird "spaceman" uniform and took Super-8 films of him walking at a shopping center, in a cemetery, at a science center, and outside a classroom window. The camera focused on the observer's nonverbal responses to the spaceman in each of those contexts. That report, with the film used to illustrate the verbal comments, was very effective and successful.

If you wanted to talk to a group about different body postures, you could use magazine pictures, slides, sketches (e.g., stick figures), or cartoons. Or if none of those were available, you could ask the persons around you to demonstrate the various postures you're talking about. If that's not possible, you could demonstrate the postures yourself.

In short, as we said in Chapter 2, people are always interpreting the nonverbal cues that they observe in a communication situation. It therefore makes sense to try to have those cues work *for* you, to have them help you reduce the range of possible interpretations of your message. If you avoid looking at the other person and talk in a listless monotone, or if you ignore what's communicated by facial expression, movement, and proximity, you're reducing your chances to help others interpret you accurately. Your communicating can "be clearer" when you make available consistent cues in as many channels as you can, and when you're also aware of all the channels through which the other person is communicating.

———————————•◆•——————————

Individual Activity: Communication Situation Checklist

Your residence. What kind of communication situation do you presently live in? What are some potential *noise* factors in that situation? Check the ones that apply, and add others in the blank spaces.

room size	temperature	degree of privacy
sound level	light level	furniture arrange-
type of floor	rules and regulations	ment
		color scheme

_____   _____   _____

_____   _____   _____

You may want to circle in that list the contextual factors that you can alter or control and to think of how the changes you could make might affect the quality of your communicating.

What communication channels are available to you at your residence?

word choice	tone of voice	rate of speaking
volume	vocal quality	gestures
dress	facial expression	furniture
bodily movements	proximity or distance	posters, signs
written notes and	wall colors	bulletin boards
letters		floor covering

_____   _____   _____

_____   _____   _____

Again, you may want to circle the channels you most frequently use and to consider how using other channels might affect the quality of your communicating.

Your place of employment. What are some potential *noise* factors where you work?

_____   _____   _____

_____   _____   _____

Which ones can you change or control?

_____   _____   _____

_____   _____   _____

Which channels are available to you at your place of employment?

_____   _____   _____

_____   _____   _____

Which ones do you use most? Which other channels could you use to improve the quality of your on-the-job communicating?

_____   _____   _____

_____   _____   _____

The second step toward clear communication is to adapt to your listeners. That means, in part, being up front about your communication purposes and goals. When you don't inform your listeners about your perspective, you can create problems for yourself, because people almost always respond defensively to what they perceive are *strategic* and *controlling* behaviors. As Jack Gibb explains, "No one wishes to be a guinea pig, a role player, or an impressed actor, and no one likes to be the victim of some hidden motivation."[5] Consequently, when listeners believe that the speaker has some kind of manipulative strategy and is purposely "hiding" his or her intent, the listeners become defensive. Similarly, Gibb writes, "speech which is used to *control* the listener evokes resistance [italics added]."[6] But when a speaker is open about attempts to control, that provokes less defensiveness than when the speaker is suspected of having hidden motives.

These studies suggest—and your own experience probably confirms—that the more the other person knows about your motivation, your intent, and the reasons behind your position on a topic, the less likely the other will be to misinterpret what you say about it. The more someone knows where you're coming from regarding the topic, the more accurately that person will be able to interpret your communicating about it.

For example, Nancy, a student who sees herself as a dedicated but quiet Christian, was upset by some vague generalizations a radical Christian named Jim was making about the church attendance and about the general state of salvation of the people in class. Nancy said that she really felt uncomfortable when she perceived what she thought was Jim's obvi-

ADAPT TO YOUR LISTENERS

Let Them Know Your Perspective

ously strategic desire to control one aspect of her behavior, to change her into what he called a "real Christian." She said that she got defensive and attributed all kinds of undesirable motives to Jim. But when Jim let her know where he was coming from, when he openly shared his attitudes about Christianity and his concern for people he thinks are non-Christians, Nancy found it much easier to listen to him. She didn't accept everything he said, but she did make fewer unfair interpretations of his position, and she felt comfortable talking about her own Christian commitment.

In other words, just as sharing some of your objective self and your personal self can help others understand *you,* sharing some of your attitudes toward and experiences with your topic can help others understand *what you're saying.* If you verbalize some of where you're coming from, you'll be able to reduce the number of inaccurate ways others might interpret what you say, and in that way you'll be able to communicate more clearly.

—————————◆◆—————————

Individual Activity: When You Know Where I'm Coming From...[7]

Here are some simple statements about different topics. *Before* you read the material printed upside down, write out a quick reaction to the statement. Try to express your "now feelings" in immediate response to the statement. Then read the material printed upside down, and see if your reaction still reflects your feelings.

1. I don't believe people in this class should look each other in the eye when they're talking. I don't want to do that, and I don't want others to do it to me.

   _____

   _____

   _____

   (In my Asian culture, direct eye contact is appropriate only for intimates.)

2. This equality stuff is a myth. In every human organization there are always leaders and followers, and I'm gonna be a leader.

   _____

   _____

   _____

   (My dad has been a career naval officer for 30 years, I enlisted at age 18, I've served five years, and I plan a career in the Navy, too.)

3. I never stay in the dorm over the weekend.

_____

_____

_____

(My parents are ill and I have to go home every chance I get.)

4. I hate teaching! It's a waste of time! Teachers are nothing but glorified babysitters!

_____

_____

_____

(I'm a 21-year-old WASP who grew up in the suburbs, and I've just finished my first semester of teaching in the remedial English program of an urban ghetto junior high school. I'm scared.)

5. Hitchhiking is terrible! There ought to be strict laws against it! It's dangerous, especially for women and young people. In fact, the legislators who allowed it ought to be shot!

_____

_____

_____

(Two days ago my daughter was raped and shot by someone who picked her up when she was hitchhiking.)

Like the rest of communication, adapting to your listeners is a two-way street. Not only do you need to let your listeners know where you're coming from; it is also important to try to take their perspective.

Try to Take Their Perspective

The principle of adaptation. Usually it's a good idea to apply what has been called the principle of adaptation.[8] The principle of adaptation says that you can communicate more clearly if you continually try to put yourself in the psychological frame of reference of the other person. It's pretty difficult to "be clear" if your communicating is affected by unexamined assumptions about the persons you're talking with. Try to see the communication situation from their point of view. Try not to assume, for example, that people always respond in a way that *you* would call rational. John thinks that it makes very good sense (i.e., is "rational") to get up early and write while your mind is fresh—even before breakfast. Gary thinks that getting up early for almost *any* reason is a waste of good sleep time. He works better late at night.

Other assumptions can also create problems. We've come to realize that just the fact that we're talking doesn't mean people should automatically listen. We're often reminded not to assume that other people care about the same things we do, or that most problems have a simple cause and a simple cure, or that there's only one way to look at a problem—our way.[9] Perhaps most important, we always try to remember that not everybody defines words the way we do. We've found, in short, that unexamined assumptions can really get in the way of mutual understanding.

In order to do something specific about the problem of assumptions, you might think in terms of applying the *principle of prior definition:* Define before you develop; explain before you amplify. If you're using words that have several possible interpretations (even the simplest words can be interpreted in a number of ways), define those words before you develop or elaborate further. For example, where would you go if your friend left you a note setting up a meeting with you at the "side" of the building you live in? Similarly, it probably wouldn't do much good for us to talk with you about something like "analogically coded metacommunicative cues" until we defined or explained those terms. The following example illustrates how misinterpretation of cues can sometimes have embarrassing consequences.

An English woman, while in Switzerland, looked at several rooms in a large apartment house. She told the schoolmaster who owned the house that she would let him know about renting one of the rooms later. However, after she arrived back at her hotel, the thought occurred to her that she had not asked about the water closet (bathroom). She immediately wrote a note to the schoolmaster asking about the "W.C.," being too bashful to write out the words "water closet." The schoolmaster, who was far from being an expert in English, did not know what the initials "W.C." meant. He asked the parish priest, and together they decided that it meant Wayside Chapel. The schoolmaster then wrote the following letter to the very surprised woman.

Dear Madame,

I take great pleasure in informing you that the W.C. is located seven miles from the house in the center of a beautiful grove of pine trees. It is capable of holding 229 people and is open on Sunday and Thursday only. I recommend that you come early, although there is plenty of standing room. This is an unfortunate situation, especially if you are in the habit of going regularly. You will no doubt be glad to hear that a good number bring their lunch and make a day of it, while others who can afford it go by car and arrive just in time. I would especially suggest that your ladyship go on Thursday when there is social music. Acoustically, the place is excellent. It may interest you to know that my daughter was married in the W.C., and it was there she met her husband. I can remember the rush there was for seats. The newest attraction is a bell donated by a wealthy resident of the district. It rings joyously every time a person enters. A bazaar is to be held to provide plush seats for all, since the people think it is a long-felt need. My wife is rather delicate and does not go regularly. Naturally, it pains her very much not to attend more often. If you wish, I shall be glad to reserve the best seat for you where you will be seen by all. Hoping I have been of service to you, I remain,

[the schoolmaster][10]

Jargon. One final suggestion about taking your listeners' perspective: One way social, professional, and political groups define themselves is by creating their own *jargon* or in-group vocabulary. John saw it happen in the Campfire Girl group Marcia and Lisa belonged to. "Wohelo," "Horizon," "Tawanka," and "Discovery" are words with special meaning for Campfire Girls. Auto mechanics have special words, e.g., "detent spring" and "socket ratchet," and special uses for many common words, e.g., "stand," "come-along," "mike," and "drift." Interpersonal communication teachers also create their own jargon. For example, we talk about "symmetrical escalation," "overrigid complementarity," "relationship cues," "congruence," "imagining the real," and "negotiation of selves." You probably use some jargon terms, too, and sometimes there's nothing wrong with them. In some situations, they can increase both clarity and interpersonal cohesion. But jargon can confuse and frustrate someone who's not in your group but who wants to understand you clearly. Explaining or defining unusual terms before you use them to develop your ideas can help. Recognize, too, that you're not always able to rely on *prior* definition. Especially if the terms or concepts are quite unfamiliar to the persons you're talking with, you may want to *re*define or *re*explain to help them stay with you, and you may want to give them a chance to paraphrase your definitions in order to check their interpretations.

When you get right down to it, taking your listener's perspective means never forgetting that you're talking with *somebody else*, not just with yourself. Just the fact that what you say makes sense to you doesn't mean that it will make sense to your listeners. In short, what you need to do, as the cartoon puts it, is to treat your listeners as "un-yous."

SMITH FAMILY CARTOON, COPYRIGHT © 1972, WASHINGTON STAR SYNDICATE.
DISTRIBUTED BY UNIVERSAL PRESS SYNDICATE. REPRINTED BY PERMISSION.

ORGANIZE WHAT YOU SAY

If your experience is anything like ours, people have been telling you to "get organized" ever since you were in diapers. Your toy box was to help you learn to organize your room. School and work taught you to organize your time. And invariably, one goal of English, speech, philosophy, and science classes is to teach you to organize your thinking and the ways to express yourself. Sometimes we wonder whether people tend to go a little overboard. Gary used to have a cartoon on his office door that showed a high-school-age girl deep in thought, and the caption was "Sometimes they teach things out of me. And I feel like saying, 'I wanted to keep that.'" We sometimes wonder whether spontaneous chaos is one of those things that schools "teach out of us" that we might both enjoy and profit from keeping.

On the other hand, most psychologists believe that we *naturally* structure our world, i.e., that order is more characteristically human than disorder is. But whether structure is natural or whether it's an artifact of Western culture, it's here. We *do* tend to see things and people in wholes made up of parts that are somehow related to one another. Therefore, communication that has a sense of wholeness is usually easier for us to comprehend clearly than communication that doesn't.

Structure your ideas. In Chapter 10, where we're talking about preparing a public speech, we explain structure in detail. There we explore several of the different patterns into which you can put your ideas. Depending on what you're talking about—and to whom and where—you may sometimes want to talk first of problems and then of solutions, first of causes and then of effects, or you may want to arrange your ideas in chronological (time) or spatial (space) order or in the order of importance. When you are engaged in preplanned communicating—giving a report or talk, writing a paper, etc.—you want to be sure, as the cartoon character Pogo puts it, to "start at the beginning, go till you get to the end, and then stop." That means you want to know what is "the beginning," i.e., where it's best to start; you want to have a sequence of ideas that will help your listeners see how the ideas fit together into a whole; and you will want to plan how to "stop," i.e., to conclude your talk or paper in a way that wraps your ideas into a coherent "chunk" that your listeners can grasp and comprehend.

Make implicit structure explicit. Structure or a sense of wholeness is important not only in preplanned communicating but also in everyday conversation. For example, have you ever had a conversation like this?

Fred: How many Christmas presents do we have left to get?
Wilma: Just a couple. You have any ideas for your brother? I don't remember what we got him last year.
Fred: That reminds me, I forgot to call that woman.
Wilma: Hunh? Should we call Ann and ask her? I always feel like. . . .
Fred: *Damn,* that makes me mad! Oh, well, he still does a lot of hunting.
Wilma: She remembers *Halloween,* even.
Fred: Who?
Wilma: Was it you who told me about that guy who killed one of the six remaining animals of that one species?
Fred: Yeah, but how does *that* relate to Sam's present?

   In a conversation like that, the problem is *not* that there's a total lack of structure. Fred's contributions make sense to him, and so do Wilma's—to Wilma. *The problem is that the implicit structure is not made explicit.* Fred knows the connections among his own statements, but he doesn't bother to show Wilma those relationships, and Wilma doesn't bother to explain the structure behind her comments to Fred.
   For example, when Wilma mentions Fred's brother (Sam), Fred pictures Sam on the job (Sam counsels handicapped children), which reminds Fred that he forgot to call a psychologist he works with—"that woman." Wilma hears "that woman" and assumes that Fred is talking about Sam's wife, Ann. Wilma feels uncomfortable around Ann and so begins to say to Fred, "I always feel like. . . ." Fred doesn't even hear her. He's thinking that they might get Sam something he can use while hunting; when Wilma hears the word "hunting," she remembers a story Fred told her that she's been wanting to share with a friend but forgot about until now, and so on.

The point we're trying to make is that there's structure even in an informal conversation, in the sense that each person's contributions "fit in" or "follow logically" or "make sense"—in short, connect—*for that person.* Problems arise when two (or more) persons' structures don't merge or fit together. Then you get the kind of confusing exchange Fred and Wilma had. You can avoid such confusion by thinking of the other person as unique, as someone who doesn't structure the world or the conversation as you do. Your thought patterns, the connections you see between ideas, are different from his or hers. If you reveal your thought patterns, if you make them explicit by bringing them to the surface with verbal cues, the structure of each person's contributions to the conversation becomes apparent to the other, and there will be less room for misinterpretation.

In other words, there are ways to structure even informal conversation so that it makes sense. You don't necessarily have to give your conversation a beginning (introduction), middle (body), and end (conclusion). It would sound a little phony if you said to someone in an informal conversation, "Hi, I'm really glad to be talking with you today. As our conversation progresses I'd like to talk about three things: (1) the weather, (2) the movie I saw last night, and (3) our relationship." That kind of organization or structure fits many public speeches, but most people prefer more spontaneity in informal conversation.

Even in an informal conversation, however, you can verbalize the implicit structure, that is, talk about the links you're seeing between ideas. When you don't, you leave open the possibility for all kinds of misinterpretation. When you do, you significantly improve your chances of adequately limiting the range of interpretations; i.e., you improve your chances of being clear.

Below are two conversations between a doctor and her patient. In the first conversation, we've tried to illustrate a situation in which the participants are *not* verbalizing the links between ideas. Here the patient has so many different things he wants to talk over or ask about that his conversation skips all over without explicit reason.

Doctor: That's my analysis. All the tests on your respiratory system came out negative. Overall, you're in good health.
Patient: Why do I get a sharp pain in my back when I get out of bed?
Doctor: Could be a variety of reasons. For example, it could be because of something as simple as your mattress or pillow. I'm not prepared to answer specifically right now. We could try to find out.
Patient: You know, my eight-year-old son, Billy—he seems so tired all the time. You think I should bring him in?
Doctor: When was Billy's last physical?
Patient: Doctor, how often should a woman get a Pap test? I've been try-

ing to convince my wife for months now that she should get one. Doesn't the American Cancer Society recommend once a year?

Here the patient doesn't seem to be "in tune" with his doctor. It wouldn't be surprising if the doctor was a bit confused.

In the second situation, the patient is helping to create understanding by explaining how what he says fits into the conversation, by bringing to the surface the structure he is seeing, and by letting the doctor know how a comment relates to what preceded it.

Doctor: That's my analysis. All the tests on your respiratory system came out negative. Overall, you're in good health.

Patient: Well, that sure doesn't fit with how I'm feeling sometimes. If I'm in good health, I don't understand why my back hurts just about every morning when I get out of bed.

Doctor: Could be for a variety of reasons. For example, it could be because of something as simple as your mattress or pillow. I can't specifically say right now. We could try to find out.

Patient: That makes sense. I'll try to work that out myself, because I know your time is limited right now—you've got other patients to see. But when you mentioned "mattress," it reminded me that I wanted to ask you about my eight-year-old, Billy. He seems to be tired all the time. Never wants to do anything. His mattress is very old and sags like a hammock. You think I should bring him in for a checkup, or could it be he's not sleeping well at night?

Doctor: When was Billy's last physical?

Patient: He was in three months ago. I remember that because at that same time my wife had an appointment to have a complete physical, too, including a Pap test. But she decided to forget it. I've been trying to convince her for three months now that she should get a physical. I'm wondering now if I should get both Billy and my wife to make appointments. What do you think?

Use transitions. As the doctor-patient conversations suggest, the key to making implicit structure explicit is to think about, listen for, and verbalize transitions. Transitions are links between ideas, bridges you cross to get from one thought to the next. You probably remember from an early English composition class that there are many different words and phrases that work as transitions—"not only . . . but also," "however," "because," "therefore," "so," "when," "first . . . second . . . third," "on the other hand," "next," "You may be wondering . . . and I can say that . . .," and so on. Those words or phrases can help others follow you by clarifying how you see your ideas fitting together. And they can make a real difference. Notice how much easier it is to understand the second of these two statements:

> "Hi! I thought we could go running tomorrow. The dance class is meeting Wednesday night. Franklin is going. The gymnastic meet was postponed. Bette will go."

> "Hi! I thought we could go running tomorrow. Tomorrow will be a good day, because the dance class that normally meets then is meeting Wednesday night, and even though Franklin is interested in that, he'll still be able to go. Not only that, the gymnastic meet was postponed, so Bette will be able to go, too."

The primary difference between those two statements is that the second one contains transitions, links between the ideas. Instead of leaping from one thought to the next over a series of chasms, we're led from one to the next over appropriate bridges. The journey is much easier to complete safely and successfully.

Nonverbal cues also work as transitions. Gestures, changes in tone of voice, and movements from one place to another can all signal to your listeners that you are moving from one idea to the next. Listen to the shift in tone of voice, for example, from

> ". . . so that's the problem."

to

> "Now, here's what I think we should *do* about the problem. . . ."

Or think of how it "fits"—and helps—to have a speaker shift position in the chair or move a step or two to the right or left as he or she moves from talking about what happened in the past to what's happening in the present.

The point is that transitions are vital. Whether verbal, nonverbal, or both, they are the main way you can share your sense of organization. *You* may see clearly how your ideas fit together, but unless you use transitions well, nobody else will be able to see that. As a result, your communicating is likely to be jumbled and confusing. In order to adequately reduce the ways others interpret what you say, whether you're speaking or writing, it's vital to use transitions.

ILLUSTRATE YOUR IDEAS The differences between the following two examples of *written* communication are pretty obvious.

Example 1

The nurse is at the door of the glass station, issuing nighttime pills to the men that shuffle past her in a line, and she's having a hard time keeping straight who gets poisoned with what tonight. She's not even watching where she pours the water. What has distracted her attention this way is that big red-headed man with the dreadful cap and the horrible-looking scar, coming her way. She's watching McMurphy walk away from the card table in the dark day room, his one horny hand twisting the red tuft of hair that sticks out of the little cup at the throat of his work-farm shirt, and I figure by the way she rears back when he reaches the door of the station that she's probably been warned by the Big Nurse. ("Oh, one more thing before I leave it in your hands tonight, Miss Pilbow, that new man sitting over there, the one with the garish red sideburns and facial lacerations—I've reason to believe he is a sex maniac.")[11]

Example 2

The atomistic psychology, which analyzes the stream of consciousness into separate units and accounts for the course of the stream by the interplay of these units, is now obsolete. The physiological evidence is against such a theory. The brain functions cannot be broken up into elementary units, occurring in distinct areas. The specific character of any brain process involved in any particular activity of the organism is a quality of the total process, a peculiarity of the total field and not a putting together of specific processes occurring in special areas. The *Gestalt* psychology holds that the stream of consciousness is not a sum of elements but a configuration in which every distinguishable part determines and is determined by the nature of the whole. Thoughts and their relations are unified wholes of subordinate parts and not mechanically added sums of independent units.[12]

Example 1 is full of concrete words—"pills," "water," "big red-headed man," "dreadful cap," "horrible-looking scar," "card table," "dark day room," "one horny hand," "red tuft of hair," "work-farm shirt," and so on. The passage moves in a narrative, or storylike, way—as you'd see it and describe it if you were there. Its structure grows out of tangible and specific things, people, and movements. As you read the passage, you can't help "seeing" or imagining the looks of the persons and places described. You think of it in terms of *pictures*.

The second example, by contrast, is full of abstract words—"consciousness," "interplay," "physiological evidence," "theory," "brain functions," "elementary units," "brain process," "total field," "configuration," "thoughts and their relations," and so on. The text moves in a logical order—contrasting, defining, and developing—an order with few links to tangible objects or persons. It discusses general rather than specific functions, fields, and processes. As you read and think about the passage, it's pretty difficult to "see" a picture or image of what's being discussed.

The same thing happens in spoken communication. Look at and listen to the differences in concreteness and movement between these two excerpts from student-teacher conferences.

Example 1

Teacher: How much do you see yourself having given to the other persons in the class? What I'm asking is how much do *you* think you participated in their growth?

Orrin: Pretty much.

Teacher: How so? Were there some times you remember especially?

Orrin: Oh yeah. I'm a good listener, and I think they noticed that. I felt as though I listened a lot in class. I also gave feedback a lot of times. People listened when I did, and they seemed to appreciate what I said. I think I felt okay about how much I helped others. Yeah, I did.

Example 2

Teacher: How much do you see yourself having been willing and able to give to other people in the class? How much do you think you helped them grow?

Tom: Quite a lot. Bill and I've become pretty good friends. We had coffee after class one day last week, and he mentioned that when I talked about his never looking at people, that helped him. He said he had never realized how little he actually looked at the person he was talking with.

Teacher: Great!

Tom: Yeah. I said that talking to him was sometimes like kissing a brick—or like trying to talk to some professor or salesman who makes you feel he's too busy to bother with you. He was able to tell me some things about my communicating, too—we were pretty open with each other.

Teacher: It's good that you were able to say that to him. I've mentioned it to him, too.

Tom: I also talked to Julie after that listening exercise we did in class. She said she felt you were really down on her because she didn't say enough in class.

Teacher: Ouch.

Tom: Yeah. I told her that I thought participation meant more than just saying things, and that I thought she'd participated quite a lot. And I gave her some examples of when I thought she'd helped

Bruce understand the negotiation of selves and when she'd worked out the role-playing stuff we did for the responding chapter.

The main difference between Tom's responses and Orrin's is important. Tom talks about illustrations, examples, analogies, and specific instances, but Orrin doesn't. Tom's responses enable his listener to picture images—of Tom and Bill having coffee, of kissing a brick, of a disinterested professor or salesman, of Tom and Julie, of Julie talking with Bruce. Consequently, Tom's responses more effectively limit the range of possible interpretations than do Orrin's. The teacher will probably understand that Orrin feels generally okay about his involvement in class, but he won't know much more than that.

Examples. One way to illustrate what you say is to use examples, specific instances or concrete cases of what you're discussing. Sometimes people confuse examples with lists of characteristics. When asked, "Give an example of a difficult class," they might reply, "Well, it'd be one that forces you to think and makes you write." That is *not* an example. It is a list of characteristics rather than a specific case, and although it adds information and does respond directly to the question, it doesn't do much to help the person *picture* what's being discussed. Here are some examples of examples.

1. "You know, adults sometimes overanalyze things to the point where the fun goes out of them. Children can often just appreciate them for what they are."

(Not clear yet; too many possible ways to interpret what's being said. But watch what happens.)

"For example, I remember when we took our kids to the Moscow Circus when it visited Los Angeles. Lisa was only five at the time. There was a magician with some really amazing tricks. At one point he seemed to change two performers into completely different persons while they were suspended ten feet off the ground in two steel cages. 'Wow!' I said to Lisa. 'That was really something! I wonder how they did that!' Lisa turned to me with a quizzical face and said, 'It's *magic*, Daddy.' And she repeated excitedly, 'It's magic!' "

(Now the general statement is clarified by this specific instance.)

2. "Not all students are grade grubbers."

(Okay so far as it goes, but what exactly are you trying to say?)

> "For example, after I handed back the exams last week, I offered to talk with those who may have felt they'd been graded unfairly on the essay questions. One woman spent 40 minutes in my office doing two things: getting her score corrected because I had added it wrong—she deserved ten points *less* than she'd been given—and going over the questions she'd missed, not to raise her score but just to learn the material better."

Analogies.   Another way to illustrate and thus to clarify what you're saying is to use analogies. An analogy links two things that are not actually related in order to explain one of them. An analogy is a comparison, a description or story that compares one well-known event or idea with another that is less well known, so that some of your knowledge of the known gets transferred to the unknown. For example, you could say that chemistry is like learning how to cook, except that in chemistry the possibility for explosion is greater, and you can't eat the results.

Analogies can add interest and life to your communicating. They can also do great things for clarity. A heart surgeon told us of a problem he was having trying to get a patient to understand his upcoming heart-bypass surgery. The patient was scared—naturally—and couldn't clearly understand what the doctor was actually going to do between the time he cut him open and the time he sewed him up again. After several fruitless attempts, the doctor said, "You're a mechanic, right?" When the patient said, "Yes," the doctor asked, "What do you do with a truck that has a clogged fuel line?" "I try to clean it out," was the reply. "And what if you can't clean it out?" "I make another one—get some copper tubing and run a new line from the tank to the fuel pump." "That's exactly what I'm going to do—get a vein from your leg and run a new line from one side of your heart to the other." "Oh!" the mechanic said. "Why didn't you say so in the first place? Let's get on with it!" An apt analogy was all it took to clarify the procedure.

Let's look at this technique from another viewpoint. Have you ever realized how buying a car is like a love affair? It begins with intense physical attraction—even lust. "I have to have that car!" As when falling in love, you're totally unreasonable, so you decide a little too quickly and spend a little too much. But you're ecstatic—the joy of driving is complete. What a perfect match, you and your dream car! Then you begin to notice the little problems—the lock sticks; it needs new shocks; the heater motor is noisy; gas mileage isn't as good as you expected. As familiarity increases, some of the little idiosyncrasies get larger until you notice serious problems. The deliriously happy romance is gone, and pretty soon you have to make that hard decision. "Do I just learn to live with the problems? Do I invest money in repairs? Or do I get rid of it and move on? It isn't the perfection I dreamed of, but is it so bad that I want to go through the hassles of making the change?" That's the crucial decision, and your choice will determine whether or not you stay together with your faded dreams. Sound familiar? Does it describe only car buying?

Our point is that it helps to use examples and analogies. Others will often understand you when you use illustrations of what you're saying and when you explain how your topic or point is "like," i.e., analogous to, something else. Let your imagination paint pictures of what you're saying, and share them with your listeners. Help others to *see* what you mean by talking about specific, concrete instances. Try to make your communicating like a film—dynamic, vivid, visual, and concrete.

USE REMINDERS

Our final suggestion is that you give people signposts and reminders to help them accurately interpret what you're saying. This is a simple process, but it's one that often seems to be ignored or forgotten. We tend to forget that written messages can be read and reread, but that spoken communication goes by only once. And as with almost everything else, you can't expect to do a perfect job the first time.

In one study, communication researchers found that just inserting an appropriate signpost or pointer, e.g., the words "this is important" or "now get this," significantly increased the listeners' retention of what was said. In fact, they found that in a public-speaking situation, a verbal reminder was a more effective means of emphasis than a pause, increased volume, or repetition. [13]

It's also often helpful simply to repeat or restate what you say. Repetition means saying the same thing again, and restatement means saying it in different words. Both strategies can be useful. Look back, for example, at the last paragraph in our discussion of analogies—the one that begins, "Our point is that. . . ." That entire paragraph is an example of restatement. It makes only one point (use examples and analogies). But we clarify and emphasize that idea by saying it in several different ways.

In a face-to-face situation, you can often see what needs to be repeated by the look on your listener's face. That's the way you avoid sounding like a broken record. You repeat or restate not everything but only key phrases, important names or terms, and crucial ideas.

The important things to remember are that you are talking with "un-yous" and that they cannot rehear what you've said unless you help them. Chances are they won't catch everything the first time it comes by, so if you want to adequately reduce their uncertainty about what you mean, you will need not only to adapt to them, organize your ideas, and illustrate what you say, but also to remind them of where you're going and what you're saying.

CONCLUDING THOUGHTS Almost every instance of human communication involves persons in a relationship *and* a topic. Just about every time you communicate, you're involved in *two* processes: negotiation of selves and content development. Although you can distinguish between these processes, they're very closely related. In this book we've chosen to emphasize negotiation of selves, and we focused on that process in most of the first six chapters. In this chapter we've shifted that focus to the other important process, content development. We've tried to show how effective content development relates to negotiation of selves and, more specifically, how clarity can help promote interpersonal-quality communication.

We started with the reminder that nobody can actually "be clear," because understanding is a mutual thing, just like the rest of human communication. But we can improve the understandability of our communicating by working to *adequately limit the range of possible interpretations of cues we make available to others.* That's what we mean by interpersonal clarity.

We also said that when you work to adequately limit the range of possible interpretations, you promote interpersonal-quality communication by decreasing objectification and increasing involvement. We then offered five suggestions for improving your understandability:

1. Make the situation work for you. Do as much as you can to control interference or "noise," and use all the communication channels that are available.

2. Adapt to your listeners. Let them know your perspective—"where you're coming from"—and try to take their perspective. Most of all, remember that they are un-yous.

3. Organize what you say. Since people tend to think in units or wholes, communication that has a clear pattern will be easier to understand than communication that doesn't. In conversation it's especially important to make the *implicit* structure *explicit*, in other words, to specify verbally how what you are saying fits into what's been said before and/or what's coming up.

4. Illustrate your ideas. Use examples and analogies to clarify what you're saying, not only in more formal, planned communication but also in spontaneous, informal conversation. The proverb "One picture is worth a thousand words" applies to word pictures, too. That's why illustrations—words that picture what you're saying—are so helpful.

Analogies also give the added dimension of linking the unknown with the known. When you can compare a fuzzy or obscure idea with a familiar, clear one, you can often greatly clarify what you're saying.

5. Use reminders. Since your listeners' thought processes are always different from yours, they will need signposts, restatements, and sometimes even repetition to keep them with you. All three can help adequately limit their ways of interpreting what you say.

————————◆•◆————————

EXERCISES

Group Activity: Who Understands You?

Think about the persons you communicate with regularly or infrequently, and try to determine the one person who understands you better than anyone else does. Of all the persons you know—immediate family, relatives, friends, co-workers, superiors, roommates, subordinates, casual acquaintances—who seems to misinterpret you the least?

Try to determine why. Think about a *specific communication situation* in which that person understood you well, and see if you can pinpoint what helped him or her to understand you. What specifically did you do to adequately limit the other person's range of interpretation of the cues you made available?

Jot down a few notes so that you can share your conclusions with others. You may also want to notice whether or not they identify the same factors you do. What does your discussion suggest about interpersonal clarity?[14]

Group Activity: Being Clear

One way to discuss what we've said in this chapter is to begin by having someone try to "be completely clear." Whoever volunteers should stand in front of the rest of the group and describe a diagram, such as one of the following.

1. How closely did the listener's drawing match the original in shape, size, placement on paper, etc.?
2. In what ways was the speaker unclear? That is, what got in the way of clear communication?
3. In what ways was the speaker clear? That is, what did the speaker do that helped others understand?

Group Activity:
Clarity Report

Divide into teams. Each team will pick one word—an abstract, challenging word that almost no one in the class is familiar with. Examples: analogic, prima facie, exegesis, aerophobia, hypostatize. Team members will clarify this word for other members of the class by providing the following.

> A specific, concrete, understandable definition
>
> An example
>
> An analogy

Another approach would be to choose a jargon term from one of your academic majors. Examples: homeostasis, opportunity cost, isomorphic, primary group, construct validity, verstehen, etiology, epistemic, enthymeme. With this approach, teams can be divided according to majors or areas of interest.

Group Activity:
Making Your Words
Effective and
Efficient

Divide into groups of three. Read the following review and examples.

1. Be specific

   This   I need to discuss the R.A.L.A. account with you before 1:00 P.M. tomorrow.

   Not this   Can we get together sometime today or tomorrow to talk about one of our accounts?

2. Put your most critical information early

   This   Before 1:00 P.M. tomorrow I need to discuss the R.A.L.A. account with you.

   Not this   I need to discuss the R.A.L.A. account with you before 1:00 P.M. tomorrow.

   This   The training proposal has to be in the boss's hands this week; let your other work slide until you get that proposal on his desk.

   Not this   Maybe you should think about letting some of your work go awhile, because that training proposal has to get done. It needs to be done this week. I guess the boss wants it by Thursday or Friday.

The "Making Your Words Effective and Efficient" and "Practicing Organization of Answers" exercises are reproduced here with the permission of their author, Marie Rosenwasser, Ph.D., Senior Consultant, Martin-Simonds Associates Management Consultants, Seattle, WA.

3. Prepare your listener

This   Judy, I'm a little worried about saying this, but I think I should tell you I was talking to Maclaren this morning and he mentioned that he was wondering whether or not you were really prepared to direct the public participation program.

Not this   Judy, the boss told me this morning that he's beginning to wonder whether or not you are really prepared to direct the public participation program.

4. Break your request proposal into parts and get responses before continuing

This   Ray, I have three things I'd like you to work on this week. Do you have some time? (Response)

O.K., first, I need you to see what you can find out about who runs the N.P. Mining and Construction Company in Duluth, Minnesota. Remember, I mentioned that company at the meeting this morning? (Response; questions, answers about the kind of information needed.)

The second thing is to ask Brad MacAllister to lunch and see if he'd like to work on the Election Committee with me. (Response: e.g., a question about which election committee, why you want him, etc.)

And then check around and see who we can get to organize Ed's retirement party. Now can you get these three things done along with everything else this week? (Response)

Not this   Ray, there are three things I need to ask you to do this week. See what you can find out about who runs the N.P. Mining and Construction Company in Duluth, Minnesota; ask Brad MacAllister if he'll be on the Election Committee with me; and see who you can get to handle Ed's retirement party. O.K.?

Now have each person in the group simulate one of the following communication situations, and have the other two group members check his or her communication for specificity, timing of critical information, listener preparation, and organization.

Communication situation 1
Your employee worked for three days on a proposal for a change in company policy, and you thought he did a good job, but the proposal has just

been rejected by the executive board. You need to break the bad news to your employee.

Communication situation 2
You have a conference with your professor, and you have to ask her to help you get a new Xerox copy of the article that your dog chewed, to schedule a makeup exam for you, and to clarify a point she made in her last lecture.

Communication situation 3
Your spouse/roommate has been leaving soiled clothes in the bathroom, leaving the caps off the shampoo and toothpaste, and not doing his/her full share of cleaning the house. You've finally decided to confront him/her.

Individual Activity:
Practicing
Organization of
Answers into
Preview, State and
Develop, Review

When answering questions in an interview or making comments in a group meeting, you can help your listeners get all of your points in a short time if you *organize* your comments.

Preview: This tells how many points you will make, for how long, and in what order. It should be the first or second statement in your response.

State and In this portion of your message you express your position and
Develop: support it with examples, data, or testimony. You need to give the strongest reasons you have and the most specific information you can obtain.

Review: Here you summarize your position; you *restate in one sentence* the essence of what was just said; this should bring you back to the question you were answering and the preview with which you began. No new information is introduced in the review.

Examples:

Question: What specific advice could you give me to improve my listening?

Answer: (P) | I recently studied corrective feedback. | Corrective feedback means that you listen for understanding before you evaluate what is said to you. You make sure that you understand by paraphrasing what you hear back to the
(D) speaker; then the speaker modifies or makes clearer his message; you feed back again until you and the speaker are sure that you have understood both the intent and content of the message.

(R) | Using corrective feedback is a good way for you to improve your listening. |

Question: How do you feel about this new system of evaluating employee performance?

Answer: (P) | Frankly, I have mixed feelings about the new system. |

(D) | I am a little anxious about its objectivity. It seems to me that so many questions depend on whether or not the employee has a good relationship with his supervisor, not on whether or not he does his job well. Even though I'm a little anxious about its objectivity, I am also a little excited to try it out. I have believed for a long time that we need a new means of evaluating employee performance. |

(R) | So, as you can see, I am divided on this issue; we need a new system of performance appraisal, but I worry about the objectivity of this one. |

P = Preview
D = Development
R = Review

Develop answers to the following questions.

Question 1: What do you think about this class?

Question 2: What should the law be governing abortions?

Question 3: What do you think is the biggest obstacle to effective interpersonal communication?

NOTES

1. F. E. X. Dance and Carl E. Larson, *The Functions of Human Communication* (New York: Holt, Rinehart and Winston, 1976), pp. 172–181.

2. Albert Mehrabian and S. R. Ferris, "Inference of Attitudes from Nonverbal Communication in Two Channels," *Journal of Consulting Psychology*, **31** (1967), 248–252.

3. The data on words are from A. Mehrabian and M. Weiner, "Decoding of Inconsistent Communications," *Journal of Personality and Social Psychology*, **6** (1967), 108–114.

4. In another study, K. K. Neeley found that listeners could understand speakers significantly better when they could see the speaker's lips. K. K. Neeley, "Effect of Visual Factors on Intelligibility of Speech," *Journal of Acoustical Society of America*, **28** (1956), 1275–1277.

5. Jack R. Gibb, "Defensive Communication," *Journal of Communication*, **11** (September 1961), 145.

6. *Ibid.*, p. 144.

7. This activity was suggested by a similar one in *The Dynamics of Human Communication* by Gail E. Myers and Michele Tolela Myers (New York: McGraw-Hill, 1973), p. 261.

8. This suggestion—as well as others we'll offer—was first identified for us by David Mortensen, a friend and ex-colleague, who called it a "Key to the Kingdom of Clarity."

9. Thomas R. Nilsen, "Some Assumptions that Impede Communication," *General Semantics Bulletin*, **14** (Winter-Spring 1954), 40–44.

10. Source unknown. A student shared this with Gary about six years ago. He's been unable to locate the original source.

11. From *One Flew Over the Cuckoo's Nest* by Ken Kesey. Copyright © 1962, by Ken Kesey. Reprinted by permission of Viking Penguin Inc.

12. Sarvepalli Radhakrishnan, *An Idealist View of Life*, 2nd ed. (London: George Allen & Unwin, 1941). Reprinted by permission.

13. Ray Ehrensberger, "The Relative Effectiveness of Certain Forms of Emphasis in Public Speaking," *Speech Monographs*, **12** (1945), 94–111.

14. This exercise is a modification of one suggested by Gail E. Myers and Michele Tolela Myers in *The Dynamics of Human Communication: A Laboratory Approach* (New York: McGraw-Hill, 1973), p. 260.

ADDITIONAL RESOURCES

John's essay, "Clear Interpersonal Communication" builds on some of the ideas offered in this chapter. The essay is printed in Chapter 7 of *Small Group Communication: A Reader*, 3rd ed., ed. Robert S. Cathcart and Larry A. Samovar (Dubuque, IA: Brown, 1979), pp. 337–349.

Frequently books that deal with communicating technical ideas include helpful treatments of "being clear." For example, see W. A. Mambert, *Presenting Technical Ideas: A Guide to Audience Communication* (New York: Wiley, 1968), Chapter 8, "Integrating and Composing the Presentation," pp. 99–117. A more recent version of a similar approach is in Stanley B. Felber and Arthur Koch, *What Did You Say? A Guide to the Communication Skills*, 2nd ed. (Englewood Cliffs, NJ: Prentice-Hall, 1978). See especially Chapter 8, "Effective Sentence Structure," Chapter 9, "Effective Paragraphing," Chapter 11, "The Technical Report," and Chapter 12, "Speech Content."

Paul Roberts writes humorously about clarity in a short, readable essay called "How to Say Nothing in Five Hundred Words." You'll find it in his book, *Understanding English* (New York: Harper & Row, 1958), pp. 404–420.

Stuart Chase wrote an essay called "Gobbledygook" in which he talks about the problems of "jargon," "using big words," and "using too many words." It's in his book, *The Power of Words* (New York: Harcourt Brace Jovanovich, 1954), pp. 249–259.

Sometimes our communication is "unclear" because we assume that the other person knows more than he or she really does. Edgar Dale talks about this in his essay, "Clear Only If Known." That essay is reprinted in Joseph DeVito's *Communication: Concepts and Processes* (Englewood Cliffs, NJ: Prentice-Hall, 1971), pp. 190–194.

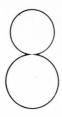

Handling conflict interpersonally

I. "CONFLICT" MEANS VERBALLY AND NONVERBALLY EXPRESSED DISAGREEMENT BETWEEN INDIVIDUALS OR GROUPS

A. When you're talking about conflict, you're talking about communication

  1. But not all conflict is rooted in poor communication; you can communicate well and still experience conflict

  2. The goal is to manage, not "resolve" conflict

B. Conflict is not necessarily bad; it can be helpful when it

  1. Moves a relationship out of a rut

  2. Leads to an effective decision

  3. Gets feelings out in the open

  4. Promotes confidence in a relationship

  5. Leads to genuine human contact

C. It is important not to fear conflict

II. THERE ARE THREE TYPES OF CONFLICT

A. Conflict over image perceptions

  1. Who is informed or uninformed

  2. Who has what kind of authority or power

  3. Who has what duties or obligations

  4. Who has what social habits or behavior

  5. Who has what "personality traits"

    B. Content conflict

        1. Disagreements over existence—"Is it there or isn't it?"
        2. Disagreements over meanings, interpretations

    C. Conflict over basic values

III. SOME SUGGESTIONS FOR DEALING WITH CONFLICT

    A. Try to avoid any of the four typical responses to threat

        1. Avoid *placating*
        2. Try not to *pounce*
        3. Don't spend your time *computing*
        4. Also avoid *distracting*

    B. Instead, try to communicate in *leveling* ways

    C. To handle image perception conflicts

        1. Recognize how you define yourself in conflict situations
        2. Work toward imagining the real of the other
        3. Use relationship reminders
        4. Try role reversal

    D. To handle content conflict

        1. Focus the disagreement; stick to topics you care about
        2. Distinguish the central issue from the "trigger"
        3. Avoid "gunnysacking"
        4. Combine criticism with positive suggestions for change

    E. To handle conflict over basic values

        1. Don't assume your conflict is due to an impossible "personality clash"
        2. Recognize that you may want to agree to disagree

    F. When conflict seems irresolvable

        1. Try defusing yourself
        2. It may also help to defuse the other person(s)
        3. You can also defuse the situation

When we began writing this chapter, we were concerned about what *seemed* to be a contradiction. On the one hand, we knew that the economist-philosopher Kenneth Boulding was accurate when he said that conflict is an activity that is found almost everywhere. It is found throughout the biological world, where the conflict both of individuals and of species is an important part of the picture. It is found everywhere in the (human) world . . . and all the social sciences study it. Economics studies conflict among economic organizations—firms, unions, and so on. Political science studies conflict among states. . . . Sociology studies conflict within and between families, racial and religious conflict, and conflict within and between groups. Anthropology studies conflict of cultures. Psychology studies conflict within the person. History is largely the record of conflict.[1]

Our experiences at home and at school reinforce what Boulding says about conflict occurring almost everywhere.

On the other hand, while writing the first and second editions of this book, we've personally experienced almost six years of a close working relationship that has included disagreements and misunderstandings, but that has been completely free of "fights." As we started this chapter, we reviewed the past six years of our relationship and discovered that at various times we've disagreed about what to say in this book and how to say it, and several times we've experienced conflict and misunderstandings about content, about who agreed to do what, when he'd finish it, and so on. Yet we have not "had a fight" with each other—not even an encounter either of us would classify as an "argument." So it looked as though there was a contradiction between what Boulding says and what we'd experienced.

As we thought about it, though, we recognized that there only *seemed* to be a contradiction. We have experienced conflicts—just as Boulding says—but so far we've been able to handle them interpersonally. That doesn't mean we haven't argued with anyone; we've been in disputes with spouses, students, and friends. But we've concluded that although it's certainly unrealistic to expect to avoid interpersonal conflict completely, it is *not* unrealistic to believe you can create and sustain relationships in which conflict is almost always dealt with in positive and productive ways. In other words, conflict is, as Boulding says, all around us, but it *doesn't have to inhibit the development of interpersonal-quality communication.* You can learn to handle or manage conflict in human-to-human, person-to-person ways.

We think you can learn to do that best by first recognizing what human conflict is and generally why it arises, by then identifying some of the things that often keep people from handling conflict productively, and finally by developing some communication skills that can help you to deal interpersonally with the disagreements you experience.

WHAT IT IS AND WHERE IT COMES FROM   You or someone you know has probably experienced something like the following: Although you live with your parents, you're definitely planning to move out soon. You want the freedom that having your own place would give you, and although you appreciate what your family has done for you, you really feel it's time to be on your own. But you can't quite afford it yet. Your parents know that you want to be on your own, and they give you some space by letting your room be private—except when they entertain. Then they want their guests to see a neat and clean house, and your part of it is sometimes an eyesore. Consequently, something like this exchange often occurs.

Parent: We're having some people over Saturday night, so I want you to clean your room.

You: My room is fine the way it is.

Parent: No, it is not fine. You may be able to live in that kind of mess, but most people can't! I don't want my friends thinking we live in a pigpen!

You: It's *my* room! Just let me shut the door, and I'll try my best not to shame you!

Parent: Oh, cut the crap! That's not the point. Your room's a mess, and it won't hurt you to clean it.

You: (as you leave) I'll move enough stuff to get the door closed, but that's it!

If you never disagree with your family, perhaps you've had some words with your boss or subordinate.

Sales director: You know the rules around here. Why did you order that truck delivery without office approval? We've told you people a hundred times that we have to approve the truck used for delivery.

Salesperson: Yeah, but this order was for one of our biggest customers, and nobody was around to approve the truck delivery. If I had waited for you to show, it would've been too late for delivery, and we would have lost the order.

Sales director: Now, I've got to go up and explain to Bill why we didn't have approval on that delivery, and he'll catch hell from the union!

Salesperson: You guys can worry about that stuff. My job is to sell and to see that the customer is serviced.

Definition   Both of these examples help to illustrate the topic of this chapter. As they indicate, when we talk about "conflict," we mean *verbally and nonverbally* *expressed disagreement between individuals or groups.* We define conflict in that way in order to say several things.

We use the words "verbal" and "nonverbal" to indicate that conflict may take the form of words or, for example, body language or both. Disagreement is not always expressed in words; sometimes we use our faces to say, "I disagree with what you're saying," or we walk away instead of saying, "I don't want to talk about this any more!" Humans have a variety of ways of dealing with conflict without saying a word.

We use the word "expressed" to stress the difference between conflict and feelings like anger, frustration, or disappointment. The difference is that feelings happen "inside" *one* person, but conflict happens between *two or more* people. Anger is often a problem, and some people equate feelings of anger with conflict, but we'd like to keep those ideas separated and to reserve the term "conflict" for communication events. Practically speaking, there's often a very thin line between feelings and their expression, and the understanding of one is crucial if you want to deal with the other. But since we're not trained as psychotherapists, we want to limit our focus to what happens when the feelings are expressed verbally and nonverbally.

We use the word "between" individuals and groups to emphasize that we're not talking about screaming at the wall or pounding a pillow. Ventilating or exploding in private can be a useful way to release feelings, and you can also learn about how you are processing information—as we said in Chapter 3—how you're selecting, organizing, and making sense of what you're perceiving. But since ventilating doesn't happen between you and somebody else, we're not going to treat it as an instance of conflict.

The words "individuals" and "groups" are also in the definition as a reminder that sometimes group memberships draw us into disagreements. As the dialogue between the sales director and the salesperson illustrates, previous contacts between groups can affect a current conflict. Part of the problem here may be that other salespersons have had this problem with the sales director so much that it seems as though part of what it means to be a salesperson is to argue with the director over delivery truck approval. The conflict happens, in other words, partly just because of group memberships. In another situation you might not have any quarrel with a stranger who belongs to a religious, political, or living group different from yours, but you might nevertheless find yourself arguing with him or her just because you are Baptist, Socialist, or a Tri-Delt.

Implications

There are also several implications of defining conflict as "verbal and nonverbally expressed disagreement between individuals or groups." The first is probably obvious, but we've found that it's a point worth making:

When you're talking about conflict, you're talking about communication. Conflict happens by way of communication. Consequently, if you want to do something about the conflicts you experience, you're going to have to do something about your communication attitudes and skills. And the same thing follows for groups you belong to. Developing a group's conflict-management skills means developing its communication skills. Everything we've said in the first seven chapters—about communication situations, objectifying and personifying, perception and negotiation of selves, sharing, being aware, and being clear—applies to conflict situations as well.

At the same time, it's important to recognize that all conflict is *not* simply a matter of communication breakdown or a lack of communication skills. Many people feel it is, however. They believe that when people disagree, the problem is poor communication, and that if they communicated better, the disagreement would vanish. But that's a myth. *All conflict does involve communication, but not all conflict is rooted in poor communication.*

Sometimes it *is*; sometimes disagreements *can* be cleared up just by improving the communication between the people involved. For example, a friend of yours may call you early on Sunday morning because he or she thinks that's what you want. But you want just the opposite—you'd like to sleep one day a week, and you remember making that point, but your friend either wasn't listening or forgot. Your friend is calling only because he or she thinks you appreciate it, so it's difficult for your friend to understand why you're always so crabby. The problem here is clearly insufficient communication: Some sharing and perception checking would definitely help.

At other times, however, poor communication is not the main problem. Two persons—or groups—may communicate effectively and still be in conflict. Although some marriages, for example, could have been saved by better communication, many divorces occur when the parties finally communicate effectively, accurately, and fully enough to discover that their relationship just won't work. Similarly, when an employee resigns or asks to be transferred because of continual arguments with the supervisor, the problem may not be misunderstanding. The two individuals may understand each other very well and still disagree.

One reason we call this chapter "Handling Conflict Interpersonally" instead of "Resolving Conflict" or "Conflict Resolution" is that many conflicts cannot be *resolved;* they can't be "put to rest" or "permanently settled." But even unresolvable conflicts can be *handled* or *managed* interpersonally. As we'll clarify below, effective conflict management occurs when persons or groups can disagree fundamentally and still communicate interpersonally.

A second implication of our definition is that conflict is not necessarily bad. Most people tend to think it is. If you ask people for words that mean the same thing as "conflict," you'll get terms such as "battle," "strife," "combat," "fight," "clash," "struggle," and "hostility"—all words with strongly negative connotations. If we see a conflict coming, most of us dread it, and when we're in the middle of an argument, we usually feel anything *but* comfortable or happy.

Part of the problem is that we're focusing on only part of the total experience. When we dread conflict, it's partly because we're most aware of the feelings we have *before* and *during* a disagreement and least aware of the feelings we often have *after the intense part is over*. To be in the midst of a strong disagreement, especially with someone you respect or like, is stressful and threatening. But after it's over, it often feels good to realize that although you've moved through a stressful experience, your relationship is still strong. As a matter of fact, if the conflict is handled well, your relationship can be stronger for having survived the disagreement. You'll discover that conflict can be a positive experience when you pay attention to how you feel not only before and during a conflict but also after it.

There are several ways in which conflict can be helpful. One is that it can move a relationship out of a rut. After several years of marriage, some couples' communication degenerates into a monotonous pattern:

"Good morning, honey."

"Morning."

"What'd you do with the toothpaste?"

"On the counter."

. . .

"Don't forget your keys."

"Yeah. Have a good day."

"You too."

. . .

"Hi, honey. How'd it go today?"

"Nothing special. You?"

And so on. Work groups or committees can fall into repetitive, low-energy patterns, too. A disagreement—over either a topic or the couple's or group's progress—can move the situation out of that rut. We're not saying that you should pick a fight just for the sake of fighting; rather, you should be aware of the energy potential that a legitimate disagreement can bring to a relationship.

Conflict is also positive when it helps people to discover the best decision in a situation. Most court systems in the Western world are based on precisely this realization—that one good way to discover the "truth" or the "justice" in a situation is to bring together an advocate for each position and to see what emerges when they clash. This "adversary system" operates on the assumption that truth and justice usually emerge from the crucible of controversy. We definitely do not believe that you should treat all your relationships like court battles. Serious problems arise when you transfer this win/lose, adversary approach to a couple, a family, or a work group. But if, for example, you are talking with a friend about your plans for buying some stereo gear and your friend disagrees with your decision, countering your carefully thought-out plans with expert information, both of you will probably learn from the discussion. Our point is that sometimes conflict can be good because it promotes a clash of opinions. If the relationship can survive a strong encounter, that can be one way to discover the best decision out of several possible approaches to a problem.

Conflict is also helpful when it provides a way to get feelings out in the open, where they can be handled. As we'll detail below, it's often not wise to hide feelings, especially strong ones that can impede or improve the progress of the relationship. But this often happens, and it takes a disagreement to bring them out. When the feelings are expressed—and not until then—they can be dealt with, and the parties can recognize and figure out how to respond to each other's disappointment, impatience, fear, or whatever. The conflict that brought those feelings out will have performed an important service.

A fourth way in which conflict can be good is that it can help to promote confidence in a relationship. John and Kris discovered this in their relationship. Like other couples, they had spent a great deal of time together before getting married, and although they felt they knew each other well, there was still some uncertainty—some residual insecurity—about what the other person would do if things *really* got difficult. Their first serious argument was a major event, but even more important was the confidence that followed it. Both Kris and John felt a new sureness, a new secure feeling about the strength of the relationship. And a conflict is what helped to promote that feeling. The same thing can happen not only in your intimate relationships but also in your work or living group, in committees and other organizations you belong to, or in your family. When group members realize that they have survived a sharp encounter, their future as a group is often brighter.

Conflict can also be good in that it can promote genuine human contact. When a friend strongly challenges your job decision or your choice of major, it often provides an opportunity for the two of you really to *meet*—to get to know the humanness of each other. If you've thought carefully about your decision and your friend has, too, chances are that there won't be a lot of role playing or putting on a front as you argue. If you actually *care* about the topic of the argument, you will probably forget whatever desires you have to appear cool, reserved, urbane, or detached. You will be *there*, really present, being who you are rather than seeming to be someone else. So will your friend. And the conflict situation will make it possible for the two of you really to contact each other. Of course, that doesn't always happen. Some people respond to conflict by putting up a front and hiding behind it. But conflict can—and often does—help people to actually meet.

The point we're trying to make is that conflict, whether in intimate relationships, work groups, living groups, families, clubs, or other organizations, can be a positive force. As we said in Chapter 2, each person is unique, so it just naturally follows that when two uniquenesses meet, there *will* be some differences. Whenever those differences are verbally and/or nonverbally expressed, there's conflict. So conflict is like differences in hair color, changes in the weather, or fatigue: It just *is*. Conflict is a pervasive part of all human experience. You can never eliminate it, so long as people continue to be unique and to communicate with each other. And there's no need to, because conflict is *not* inherently "bad." As a matter of fact, whether it's bad or good depends entirely on how it's handled. And that's why handling conflict interpersonally is the topic of this chapter.

The final implication of our definition is that conflict is not something to be afraid of. We've found in both our own communication and our work with people in business and educational organizations that this is vital: If you go into a conflict afraid of what's about to happen, you'll almost definitely have problems. This point was emphasized by the faculty and administration of a small college John worked with. Partly because they were undergoing some major administrative and program changes, they asked for a conflict-management workshop. Over a two-day period, John presented many of the ideas that are now in this chapter, and three months after the workshop, many participants reported that the most important single thing they'd learned was *not to fear conflict*.

Gary had a similar experience with a manager who had union problems. The manager had been unable to work effectively with union representatives in the past, and he had come to dread every labor-management contact. His dread, of course, made things worse, and the result was a dandy negative spiral—he feared it because of what had happened in the past, his fear helped him to fail in the present, and his failure reinforced his fear about the future. Things grew progressively worse until he was able to see this part of his job as a compliment from his supervisor. He realized that he wouldn't have this task if his boss wasn't confident of his ability to handle it, and that fact alone helped him to feel better about the situation. You can guess what happened as he began to substitute determination and optimism for fear. The union-management negotiations went better, and the negative spiral turned into a positive one.

The same thing works in intimate relationships. Dr. George Bach has spent almost 20 years exploring couples' communication and training them to argue effectively with each other. One reason he focuses on what he calls "fight therapy" is that he learned, after an extensive survey of happily married couples, that they saw conflict as a natural, even welcome, part of their relationship. In fact, conflict was just about the only factor that consistently characterized long-term intimate relationships that both parties defined as successful. They saw arguing as a normal, natural thing, not as a threat. They did not fear fighting, because they knew that it was one thing that helped to keep them together. As Bach puts it, "Fighting is inevitable between mature intimates . . . there can be no mature intimate relationship without aggressive leveling; that is, 'having it out,' speaking up, asking the partner 'what's eating' him and negotiating for realistic settlements of differences."[2]

As we've said from the beginning of the book, your way of looking at something will determine your behavior toward it; that is, your perspective on an event determines what you do about it. Nowhere is this more true than with respect to conflict. If you define conflict as a distortion of communication, as some kind of evil aberration, you're in trouble. If you see it as a bad thing and you fear it, you're going to have problems. But if you can start by seeing conflict as a natural, ever-present part of human experience *and* as a potentially good thing, you're on the way toward learning how to handle it interpersonally.

TYPES OF CONFLICT

The second step toward learning to handle conflict interpersonally is recognizing that not all disagreements are the same. There are different kinds, or types, of conflict, and if you're aware of which type you're involved in, you'll be able to handle the problem more effectively.

Conflict over Image Perceptions

Employee: I can make this decision.
Boss: No, you can't. You haven't been on the job long enough.

————— ◆•◆ —————

Father: What are you doing coming in at this hour? You don't have any business staying out so late!
Son: I can take care of myself!

————— ◆•◆ —————

Worker A to   Why do you keep asking me what to do next? I'm not your
worker B: boss! Schedule your own time!

— • —

Student A to   You keep treating me as if I feel stupid in this class, but I
student B: don't. It's true that anthropology isn't my major, but I've
               taken two other anthro classes.

These four exchanges have one thing in common—they all reflect disagreements about image perceptions. In the first exchange, the employee is saying, in effect, that her image of herself is different from the boss's image of her. From the employee's point of view, that's a conflict between *my me* and *your me*.

The father-son disagreement is similar. The parent's complaint reflects a disagreement between his image of his son and the son's self-image. From the parent's point of view, this conflict is between *my you* and *your you*.

The two workers disagree over different images. From worker A's point of view, the problem is that *my your me* conflicts with *my me*. That is, worker A sees worker B defining worker A as "boss," but worker A's self-definition is as "worker," *not* as "boss."

The conflict between student A and student B focuses on meta-images, too. Student A is saying that A's view of B's view of A (*my your me*) conflicts with A's view of A (*my me*).

Ideally, these examples show that image-perception conflict is not some strange and rare thing; it goes on all the time. In fact, we're convinced that most disagreements are at least in part over image perceptions. Since, as we said in Chapter 4, negotiation of selves, or the image-transaction process, is always going on, images are always "in play" and potentially at issue. Other matters can also be important, but this is one element of just about every conflict. Consequently, one of the first questions you should ask about any conflict you're in is "What's happening with our images of each other?"

Unfortunately, it's possible for any two persons to come up with about 300 different answers to that question.[3] That's because whenever two persons get together, six images, or selves, are operating. For instance, Jack has three images—*my me, my you,* and *my your me*—and Jill has her three—*my me, my you,* and *my your me*. Those six images can be combined in 301 possible ways. Remember, that's just with *two* persons; think about what's possible in a seven-person group! Fortunately, things are not usually so complicated. Image-perception conflict usually revolves around disagreements about such questions as (1) who has the information; (2) who has the authority; (3) who has the power; (4) who has the duty or obligation; (5) who has what social habits; or (6) who has which "personality traits."

Sometimes the conflict will focus on whether a person is informed or uninformed. "You don't know what you're talking about" is a common way of saying, "I disagree with your image of yourself as 'competent,' 'informed,' or 'an expert.' " It can also work the other way around. Sometimes positively motivated comments from a parent or a teacher can reflect a disagreement over definitions of selves, for example, when a child complains, "I can't do this; I don't know how," and the teacher responds in an exasperated tone, "What do you mean, you don't know how? You've been doing that kind of problem for six weeks now!" In that case the child is defining himself or herself as uninformed or in need of help, and the teacher is disagreeing, implying that the child *is* capable and informed but *may* be lazy or obstinate.

Disagreements about self-definitions can also center on who has what kind of authority in a given situation. Not long ago, almost all college and university administrations believed that they had the authority to operate *in loco parentis*—in the place of a parent—and to regulate the personal lives of their students. Many students disagreed—violently on some campuses—with that image. Coeducational dorms, open visiting hours, and other relaxed living regulations are some outcomes of that disagreement. On a job, you may agree that your supervisor has the authority to determine your working hours, but you may disagree with his or her definition of self as custodian of your hair style or clothing, unless it interferes directly with your work. Conflict can also arise when one person defines the other as having more authority than the other wants or thinks that he or she has. The accountability that usually accompanies decision-making authority often encourages people to insist, "I'm just a peasant here, don't ask me!" or as one parent says to the other, "You always tell the kids to ask me. You decide for once."

Conflicts in power relationships can also be understood as differences in image perception. Power is usually defined as the ability of one person to provide something another person wants and can't readily get anywhere else.[4] In other words, if Jack wants something and can get it only with Jill's help, Jill has power over Jack. Conflict over a power relationship can arise, for example, when Jill disagrees with Jack's image of her as capable of helping him get what he needs—"I can't get that for you; I don't have the power you think I do"—or when Jill defines herself as more capable of meeting Jack's needs than Jack thinks—"I have more control over your destiny than you're ready to admit." Especially when the stakes are high, disagreements over power relationships can be very difficult to handle.

Another kind of image-perception conflict focuses on questions of duty or obligation. War-crime trials—whether related to World War II, the Vietnam war, or the Mideast conflict—often center on the question of whether a soldier has the duty to follow orders or is free to question an immoral command. In a school context, honor codes define students as having the obligation to be honest and to report any dishonesty they observe. Obligation also goes with other role definitions. Most parents believe they have the duty to protect their children from danger. Conflicts often arise when a child sees that duty interfering with his or her right to decide what experiences are meaningful or which situations to avoid. "I can't let you do that" or "I can't go along with that" often means something like "I see myself as duty-bound to prevent that." And sometimes the other person disagrees.

Image-perception conflict between intimates often revolves around social habits or behavior. "You never talk to me" "I do, too" and "Why do you always avoid people at parties?" "I don't avoid them" are two examples of this type of disagreement. The conflict here is between Jack's *you* and Jill's *me.* Jill sees herself as socially competent and adept; Jack disagrees with that image.

A similar type of image-perception conflict centers on what the parties define as personality traits. For example, "I'm always petrified when I have to give a speech" ("I have stage fright"). "No, you're not; you're just trying to avoid the situation" ("You're lazy"), or "I don't like late afternoons; I get too drowsy" ("I'm not an afternoon person"). "You probably like it but don't want to admit it" ("You're so compulsive you feel guilty about relaxing"). Again, the issue is not information separate from the persons in conflict but the images they have of each other.

We want to emphasize that you won't be able to do much about conflicts over content or basic values until you work with whatever image-perception conflicts there are. The reason is that ego involvement is a very strong motivator. As a great deal of communication and psychological research emphasizes, ego involvement, or the feeling that you have a *personal* stake in something, is one of the strongest forces acting on persons.[5] People may or may not be ego-involved with gay rights, health care for poor people, laws governing abortion, or Christianity, but just about everyone is ego-involved with his or her self image. Consequently, I may pay attention to or ignore your views about labor unions, but if you're talking about who I am—*my me, your me,* or *my your me*—I'm involved; I'm *interested.* That's why image-perception conflict has to be handled first. So long as it's there, it'll be difficult to *see* any other issues, let alone to deal with them.

You can see how image-perception conflict works by observing just about any two persons who have known each other well for a long time. If you ask them whether they ever argue with each other, they'll often say something like, "Yeah, but mostly over minor things" or "Yeah, we fight, but our relationship can stand it." What they're saying is that they've handled the basic image-perception issues so that other topics now look and feel relatively minor. It's something like your body: If you have a strong heart and are in good physical shape, you can handle a sprain or even several broken bones without much difficulty.

We've also experienced this phenomenon in our own relationship. We used to think it was unusual—amazing even—that two persons could have as many energetic, vehement discussions as we do and still not experience a major disagreement. We now recognize that our relationship is founded on a strong set of agreements about the most important issue—image perceptions. In this relationship John sees Gary as competent, committed, involved, not very defensive about his weaknesses, and open to learning and to new ideas. That pretty much fits Gary's image of himself, the way he sees John, and the way John sees himself. There's a fundamental agreement, in other words, over image perceptions, and that goes a long way toward making the relationship work.

Content Conflict When you've handled disagreements over images, there can still be conflict over content. Disagreements about content are often expressed in such statements as "That conclusion doesn't follow from those figures" or "Just because that happened when they changed the law in Sweden, it isn't necessarily going to happen when they change the law here" or "The problem is not going to be solved that way; your 'solution' will just make things worse." This kind of disagreement reflects differing views of objects, events, or phenomena separate from the persons involved.

There are two main types of content conflict: disagreements over existence and disagreements over meaning. Sometimes the question is basically: "Is it there or isn't it?" or "Does that exist or doesn't it?" Two persons may disagree, for example, over whether or not a newspaper account of a car crash said that the crash was fatal. Or a law firm employee may ask his or her supervisor, "Why, if I was hired as a legal assistant, have I done almost nothing but secretarial work? What does the job description say?" These disagreements *could* arise as image-perception problems—"I see myself as better informed about what's in the newspaper than you are," for example. But they can also center not on *my me* or *your me* but on what happened, what's written down, what "is."

More frequently, content conflict arises over different *interpretations* of what "is." For example:

"When the newspaper said that the crash was fatal, it didn't mean that everybody was killed."

"Yes, it did. That's what 'fatal' means."

or

> "The job description does call the position 'Legal Assistant,' but that includes typing. What you're calling 'secretarial tasks' are part of a legal assistant's job."

Another question to ask yourself, then, is what kind of content you're disagreeing about—existence or interpretations.

Sometimes people disagree not over content, interpretations, or images but over fundamental beliefs transcending all those issues. A dedicated Christian and an equally dedicated agnostic, for example, will doubtless disagree on almost all religious topics, regardless of the accuracy of their images or their agreement about facts and interpretations. A similar thing will happen between a committed socialist and a committed republican or between a person who is strongly proabortion and one who is strongly antiabortion. It's obviously unrealistic to expect them to work through all their differences and to agree on everything.

Conflict over Basic Values

But remember three things. First, conflict over basic values is relatively rare. Most of your day-to-day disagreements are over image perceptions or content. It's often easy to shrug your shoulders and give up because "we just don't see eye to eye on anything" when what's really at issue is not basic values but, say, your self image as opposed to how you see the other seeing you. So try not to use your knowledge that some conflicts are irresolvable as a cop-out. Be sure your disagreement really is over basic values before you give up trying to reach agreement.

Second, remember that even conflicts over basic values can be handled interpersonally. As we'll detail below, even when you disagree fundamentally, you can communicate in mutually personifying ways. Although this kind of conflict can't be *resolved*, it can provide an opportunity for mutual respect and even some learning.

Third, remember that human perception is subjective and that human knowledge is fallible. Therefore it's important to continually challenge, question, and validate the values and beliefs you hold. In addition, as we've already said, we believe it's important to work hard to understand the other person and to keep your evaluations of him or her as tentative as possible. But given those qualifications, we don't think it's necessary to be willing to compromise away your basic values or beliefs. We're deeply committed, for example, to our beliefs that there is a strong link between quality of life and quality of communication, and that it's better to treat persons as humans than as objects. When we encounter someone who has arrived at different basic beliefs, we work toward meeting him or her as a person while "agreeing to disagree" about our different points of view. More about that later.

In Summary (So Far) Conflict is verbally and nonverbally expressed disagreement between individuals and groups.

It happens all the time—whenever human differences meet.

It always involves communication, but it is not always "caused" by poor communication.

Conflict can be a good thing:

It can move a relationship out of a rut.

Through conflict people can sometimes discover the best response to a situation.

It can be a way to get hidden feelings out in the open, where they can be dealt with.

It can help develop confidence in a relationship.

It can promote genuine meeting between persons.

So it's not something to be afraid of.

There are three main types of conflict:

Disagreements over images happen all the time—for example:

We clash over the perceptions of who is informed.

We argue over perceptions of who has authority.

Conflicts occur over images of who has the power.

We differ over images of who has what duty or obligation.

We disagree about social habits or behavior.

We also clash over images of personality traits.

It helps to deal with image-perception conflict before you get to content conflict.

Content conflict is the second type.

Sometimes we disagree over "what is."

More frequently conflict happens over interpretations—"what that means."

A third type of conflict happens over basic values.

It is usually not resolvable, but it *can* be handled interpersonally.

WHAT TO DO ABOUT IT Now that you've heard some ideas about what conflict is and where it comes from, you may be wondering, "So? What can I *do* about all that? Sure, it's important to understand what's going on, but I also want to know what I can *do* that will make things work out better."

We want to respond to that question by talking first about what people typically do when faced with the threat of a conflict situation and then suggesting what you may do instead. Many of the basic ideas in this section come from Virginia Satir's writings, and if you want to follow up on them, you will find two of her books cited in the Additional Resources section at the end of this chapter.

Whenever any two persons communicate, there are always four elements, or parts, of what's going on: *me*, *you*, a *context* or situation, and a *topic*. That may seem obvious, but it's crucial to remember those four, or the rest of this section won't make much sense.

Typical Responses to Threat

There's always a *me*, the person whose point of view we begin with. That *me* is made up of many different things. I have attitudes, feelings, beliefs, expectations, information, opinions, hopes, desires, needs, wishes, all kinds of things. I'm in a certain mood—maybe tired, disinterested, distracted, excited, eager, or whatever. I feel *something* about the person or persons I'm talking with—warmth, camaraderie, dislike, ambivalence, etc. I have some *ideas* about what will happen as we communicate—I'll ask him about the money he owes me, and he'll probably weasel out again; I'll find out what she thinks about her new job; I'll say hello and pass the time, and that will be it; I'll tell him I want to get married. I also have some *hopes* or *desires*—I hope she won't say anything about what happened last week; I hope we'll be able to talk a long time; I want them to accept me, help me, give me the information, or whatever. Often I also have *information*—I know how much that job pays; I know when the exam is; I know how to apply for food stamps because I've done it before; I understand calculus; I remember that part of the formula. And those examples are only part of what I bring to *every* communication experience I have. There's always a *me*.

There's also *always* a *you*. You bring all those things I bring: attitudes, feelings, beliefs, expectations, information, opinions, hopes, desires, needs, wishes, and so on. You are in a certain mood, too—although I may be tired, you may be full of energy, or vice versa. You also feel something about the persons you're talking with and perhaps about the topic of conversation. You may feel the same friendliness for me that I feel for you, for example. You have expectations, too—about what will happen as we talk and maybe also about future meetings between us. Your hopes and desires about this conversation may be almost exactly the same as mine, or they may be very different. I may hope we get our business done quickly so I can go to work, and you may hope we spend the afternoon together. You also have information—you know what skills a person has to have in order to earn that salary on that job; you know one of the questions that's almost always on that exam; you know where the most friendly food stamp people work; you have an idea about how to plan the party to avoid the problem I'm worried about; you know how to get to the resort from the main highway. And again, those examples are only part of what you bring to the communication experience. There's always a *you*.

There's also always a *context*. The context is partly physical: We can't be nowhere when we talk; we're always in some physical surrounding. We may be on the phone, in a bedroom, in your kitchen, in the middle of a cheering section, at a funeral, in the lunchroom, in a law office, on a bus, or walking on the street. There is always some physical surrounding in which our communication takes place.

Context is also partly psychological. Almost regardless of a person's moods, for example, many contexts provide moods of their own. A football playoff game feels almost nothing like a sunny day on the beach. A candlelight dinner feels different from a licensing exam. And so on. Whenever we communicate, there is always a physical and psychological *context*, and that context significantly affects what's going on.

Finally, there is always a *topic*. Just as we can't be "nowhere," we can't literally discuss "nothing." Even when the conversation wanders all over the map and touches on nothing more serious or personal than the weather, there is still a topic. Sometimes—as in the familiar exchange, "Hi!" "Hi!" "How are you?" "Fine. You?" "Good. See you." "Right"—there is an implicit topic of conversation: mutual notice of each other. That conversation "says," "I see you" or "I notice you, do you notice me?" and "Yes, I notice you, too." "Good." "Right."

In more extended contacts the topic may shift from business to sports to weather to family to vacation plans and back to business, but there's always something being talked about. In other words, every time we communicate, there is a *topic*.

It helps to think of these four elements in a circle. The circle emphasizes that they make up a whole, the whole communication event:

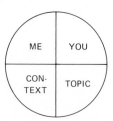

Now why do we make such a big deal about something that seems so obvious? Because, as Virginia Satir points out, our typical first response to conflict is fear, and *when we experience the threat of conflict, we usually respond in a way that ignores or cancels out one or more of those four "obvious" elements.* As we said above, it's difficult not to feel afraid or threatened. We've been in conflicts before, and we worry that we'll look like a fool or a weakling, we'll get shouted at again, or maybe the other person will leave and we'll have to cope with the resulting loneliness. We also may be threatened by the realization that because the conflict will take time and energy, we may miss an important appointment or get so upset that a big part of the day is ruined. So we forget that if we're going to cope effectively with the conflict situation, we need to respond to all four of its parts. When we fear conflict, we forget that if we cancel or try to ignore part of what's happening, it's like trying to shoot pool with a blindfold on or trying to hit a baseball with your right hand tied to your left knee. Or it's like trying to run a car on only two of its wheels; if you're dealing with only *part* of the situation, you can't cope effectively. In other words, there is *always* a *me,* a *you,* a *context,* and a *topic,* but when we get into conflict, we behave as if there weren't. And that is a big part of the problem.

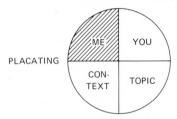

Sometimes we respond to threat by *placating,* that is, by canceling out the *me* in the situation. You've doubtless heard this happen: The person says, "Oh, that's okay; whatever *you* want is fine . . . no problem . . . *I* don't care what we do . . . it's not up to me to decide. . . ." You can usually identify this placating response by the way the person backs up, cringes, looks down or away, and talks in a soft, whiney, or questioning voice.

Placating

Placating is based on some assumptions about the conflict situation. These assumptions may not be obvious to the person doing the placating, but they are there helping him or her to continue this behavior. One assumption is that it's almost always better to switch than to fight, that maintaining peace is more important than having one's views heard. When people placate, it's often because they haven't yet internalized the point we made above, that all communication situations include *me, you, context,* and *topic.* At some level of awareness, they believe that successful communication can occur even when one vital part of the situation is missing. So they try to avoid the clash by backing up, by underplaying, or even by denying their own wishes, needs, attitudes, goals, beliefs, or opinions.

Other times placating grows out of the assumption that "our relationship can't stand a fight." From this point of view, conflict may be okay for some people, but *this* relationship is too valuable or too delicate to be ruined by a fight. Obviously the problem with this point of view is that

Placating

since conflict is an inherent part of *all* human relationships, trying to avoid it is unrealistic. If the friendship was actually that fragile, it probably wouldn't have lasted so long.

A third assumption that's often behind placating is the belief that conflict is "not nice," especially in public. The person who thinks this will placate not because of what he or she believes but because of what he or she thinks *other* people believe. For this person, arguing may be an acceptable activity for a married couple or family to engage in in private, but it is not an appropriate kind of public behavior.

A closely related assumption is that since conflict is always so destructive, the best thing is to avoid it at all costs. Sometimes placating is based on that belief, which we've already shown to be unrealistic.

The last two assumptions we want to mention are "I don't really care—it's no big deal" and "Fighting is always more frightening than running." A person will sometimes placate after becoming convinced that what's at issue doesn't *really* matter to him or her. Of course, when that's true—when you actually do not have much investment in the topic—it *can* be a waste of energy to "stand up for your rights." That's not placating. But when other pressures lead you to convince yourself that "it's not important" when it *is*, you're placating. And finally, placating can grow out of the fear of conflict. When you fear for your physical safety or for your job, you're usually not placating. But when you fear the conflict just because it is a conflict—when you're afraid not of the outcome but of the argument itself—you are usually placating.

We do not mean to say that placating is always wrong. All four partial responses to threat—placating, pouncing, computing, and distracting—are occasionally appropriate and useful. It makes very good sense, for example, not to include your *me* in each minor topic you discuss with a new acquaintance or a new boss. But it's important to be aware of what you're doing when you're placating—if you do decide that it's appropriate in this case—and to realize the impact that continual placating can have on you and your relationships.

Verbal cues. One way to become aware of your own and others' placating is to recognize the verbal and nonverbal communication behaviors that usually accompany this response to threat. One verbal form of placating is repetitive, too quick agreement. A person who quickly and continually responds with "Sure," "That's fine," "Whatever you want," "It's okay with me," "No problem" is often placating. This response to threat is also characterized by the frequent use of qualifiers: "I guess," "I think," "Maybe," "If you don't mind," and so on. A third verbal response is underplaying or dismissing issues: "Oh, that's all right; it doesn't matter to me" is often a signal that the *me* is getting canceled and the speaker is placating. When people are canceling their *me*, they'll also frequently hide statements behind placating pseudoquestions. The person who says, "Don't you think that maybe we should call her?" is often trying to say, "I think we should call her" without saying "I." Similarly, a scared passenger who asks, "Do you think it's safe to drive this fast?" or "Aren't there any seat belts in this car?" is hiding statements behind questions. If this person wasn't placating, the pseudoquestions would be replaced with something like, "I think we're going too fast, and I'm scared" or "I'd like a seat belt; where is it?"

Nonverbal cues. Another way to identify placating is to watch and listen for characteristic nonverbal cues. You can probably picture the behaviors that go with the words above—backing up, looking down, and getting in a posture that makes you subordinate to the other persons. When placating, we'll also usually "close" our arms and shoulders. You can hear placating in the questioning inflection at the end of most sentences. Listen for the implicit "Should we?" "Can I?" or "Is that all right with you?" that follows almost every statement. You can probably identify more nonverbal behaviors that characterize placating. In fact, we encourage you to role-play all five of these styles in order to get a better feel for them.

A second problematic or maladaptive way people sometimes respond to the threat of conflict is by *pouncing* or blaming, which is canceling out the *you* in the communication event. Like placating, pouncing is based on some questionable assumptions or beliefs about the situation. One is the

Pouncing

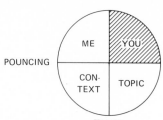

POUNCING

"macho" stance: "If you lose a disagreement, you're a weakling and nobody will ever respect you." Males aren't alone in adopting that view, but it is frequently part of the folklore that young boys are taught. And it's obviously a reality in some situations—a street gang, the junior high football team, the steel mill, the hay crew. But whenever people can move beyond the mistaken belief that in order for *me* to be important, *you* have to be knocked down, that assumption is false. In most adult-adult contexts, respect is based not on the number of notches on your gun but on judgments about your competence and trustworthiness.

A second assumption that's often behind pouncing is the belief that my view is the only "right" or only "accurate" view—that anybody who disagrees with me is mistaken, stubborn, or crazy. In order to pounce effectively, you have to forget that each of us selects and interprets percep-

Pouncing

tions differently, and that what's "obvious" to me may be invisible to you. Pouncing says that "you don't count," which means in part that your reality, the way you see things, is invalid.

Pouncing is also often based on the dog-eat-dog assumption. This kind of communicating comes easy to the person who believes that "people are out to get me," and that the golden rule of interpersonal relations is to "do unto others before they do unto you." The person who is pouncing often views the world as an adversary process, a place where the only people who win are those who make other people into losers. There's no belief in the possibility of a win/win confrontation; it's always going to be win/lose. Sound familiar?

Verbal communication. When people are pouncing, they'll often get a lot of mileage out of blaming statements—"It's your fault," "You did it, you turkey," or "I wasn't there, but *she* was." "Should" usually accompanies the blaming, too. One effective way to cancel the other's ideas, opinions, hopes, and beliefs is to make pronouncements about what he or she *should* do—"You should move out of there," "You shouldn't talk to her," "You should change jobs." There's also often a great deal of us/them, I/you or we/they polarizing in pouncing language, because it's important from this point of view to remember who are the "bad guys" and who are the "good guys."

This oversimplified polarizing also extends to other parts of the language of the person who's pouncing. The issue can always be discussed in either/or, right/wrong, good/bad terms. There's seldom any in-between or shades of meaning. Finally, pouncing language also frequently includes pseudoquestions—statements hidden behind questions—but they're different from placating pseudoquestions. When pouncing, a person will often use "Who do you think you are?" "Where do you think you're going?" or "What do you think you're doing?" to "say," "I don't think you have the right to say that," "I don't want you to go," or "I don't like what you're doing." Again, this is a pretty common practice. When people are disagreeing, they'll sometimes ask genuine questions—"When you say you don't want to go out, do you mean this week or never?" But often the questions will be fronts for statements. Listen for them.

Nonverbal communication. Nonverbally, pouncing is also easy to spot. The person doing the pouncing will usually try to be higher than—physically superior to—the other person and will use posture and eye contact to establish that "one-up" position. Sarcasm is also often a part of pouncing. Although the words—"You're doing a terrific job"—look encouraging and supportive, the tone of voice says, "You're an idiot; you've really messed up." When pouncing, we also often talk in a loud, certain, authoritarian tone of voice that tries to keep the other person off balance. The idea is to overwhelm the other person with vocal power and as close to a nonstop stream as we can manage. For the person who's pouncing, listening serves only one purpose—to gather information with which to zap the other person. So you may be quiet for a while, but only so you can find another weak spot to attack, or just to shut the other person out with your silence. In fact, an aggressive silent treatment can be another favorite weapon of the person who is pouncing. If I ignore you, I can reduce your contribution to zero; so pouncing often includes folded arms, back turning, or a silent, "withering" stare. As Satir emphasizes, pouncing also frequently includes finger pointing. In many cultures finger waving and pointing naturally accompany the "I know better than you" and the "I'm gonna tell you how it's gonna be" attitude. Again, does it sound or look familiar?

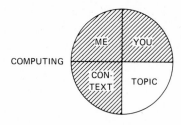

COMPUTING

Computing   A third way people sometimes respond to the threat of conflict is to cancel out *me, you,* and the *context.* Satir calls this *computing,* because when people do it, they often come across like a computer—detached, cool, inhuman. Professor Kingsfield in the movie and TV show *Paper Chase* is an example of a person who computes. Always cold, logical, and never showing any emotion, he rejects the idea that feelings, hopes, opinions, or wishes can ever be important; all he wants to hear about are "the facts."

There are at least five mistaken assumptions that computing communication can be based on. One is that "mature people don't get emotional." If you believe that being an adult means not experiencing any feelings, the dispassionate rationality of computing will make a great deal of sense to you. But if what we said at the beginning of this section is accurate, "grownups are unemotional" is a mistaken assumption. Obviously, mature persons have more ways to *express* their emotions than children do, but it's simply inaccurate to say that a 20-year-old doesn't feel anger, a middle-aged woman can't feel hurt, or a grandparent has no sexual desires.

Two other mistaken assumptions are that emotions are dangerous and uncontrollable, or that they're irrelevant. Some persons grow up seeing strong feelings as mysterious, overpowering things that were never "proper" to discuss. And like most unknown forces, they're frightening.

Computing

The idea is that feelings can sneak up on you and take you over, so you've got to avoid them. And, the story goes, when two people are experiencing *contradictory* feelings, there's nothing anybody can do. Contradictory feelings are unpredictable and uncontrollable, and they ought to be avoided at all costs. Those beliefs can obviously lead to computing.

For other people, emotions are irrelevant; if you're dealing with the emotional parts of *me* and *you*, you're off the topic and that's not good. Rather than seeing feelings as an integral part of each person, some people believe that adults can divorce ideas from feelings and can just "talk about the facts." A great deal of research in psychology and education has demonstrated the inaccuracy of that view. We now know that "feelings" always accompany "thoughts," that human experience doesn't dichotomize emotions and ideas. So feelings are never irrelevant; they're always present to some degree, and the challenge in a conflict situation is to deal with them in helpful rather than destructive ways.

Computing also sometimes grows out of the belief that you can successfully ignore contextual elements in a communication situation and still work things out successfully. From this perspective, time of day, location, number of people present, noise level, temperature, and the presence of distractions are all irrelevant. The computing person tries to deny the influence of all those factors and to communicate as if he or she were in a sterile vacuum.

A fifth assumption that's often behind computing communication is that the constructivist view of perception (the one we talk about in Chapter 3) is hogwash, that there is one "real world," one "truth," and that the computing person knows what it is. When computing, a person isn't interested in different, subjective points of view. He or she wants to deal only with "the cold, hard facts" or "objective reality"—which means "reality as I experience it." Such a person forgets that people don't behave in response to things, but to the meanings of things, so this assumption, too, is mistaken.

Verbal communication. How can you tell when you or someone you're with is computing? Listen for statements like "Let's just be rational about this. There's no need to get emotional," or "I'm sure you agree that we can handle this like mature adults. We will remain calm and cool." Sometimes people will compute by using only very large, impersonal words in long, complex sentences in order to avoid contact with the other person. They will also talk in third-person rather than first-person terms—using "they" or "most people" or "it's obvious that" rather than *"I think"* or "I believe" or *"you* are saying that. . . ." Thus you might get something like this:

> It's clear that this could be a very emotional topic. But we shall handle it as adults, keeping irrelevant distractions to a minimum while maximizing contributions that are specifically topic-focused. Don't you agree. (Note that the last sentence is *not* a question.)

Nonverbal communication. The computing person looks and sounds like a machine, too—stiff, expressionless, unemotional, ignoring whatever's around. Some people can tell when they start computing by the way their back gets stiff and tight, their neck muscles tense, and they stop any relaxed or natural movements. If the computing person is seated, his or her back is usually not touching the chair, and it's not uncommon to find the person's hands folded or clasped in a "serene," "detached" way. Of course, the person may be boiling inside, but in order to successfully cancel *me* and *you*, the computing person tries hard not to let any of those emotions show. The face of a person who is computing is as nearly expressionless as possible, and the voice is usually controlled, something close to a monotone or a repetitive sing-song. When a person who is communicating in this way pauses to listen, what's said often goes in one ear and out the other. That's because the main function of this kind of impervious "listening" is just to wait for your turn so you can continue to be "utterly reasonable." Again, you can visualize this kind of communicating from your own experience.

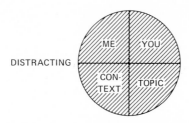

A fourth maladaptive response to the threat of conflict is what Satir calls *distracting*, because it consists of trying to focus attention on anything but the issue at hand. The distracting person will do everything possible to divert attention by giggling, changing the subject, and generally behaving in an "off the wall" way.

Distracting is often based on the assumption that if you can totally change the subject, the conflict will go away and everybody can be happy again. Like the placating person, the person who is distracting is usually afraid of the disagreement and is determined to go around rather than through it. Sometimes this fear is based on the belief that if we argue, our relationship will probably end, so we'd better stay friendly and happy. Distracting is also often an outgrowth of the attitude that conflict isn't

Distracting

"nice," and that "nice" people are happy, cordial, and smiling. Since disagreements are so unpleasant and discomforting, it's best to laugh them off or to change the subject.

Verbal communication. The clearest verbal sign of distracting is abrupt topic change. If you stay on any single topic for any time, you're likely to get serious about it, so it's safest to jump from subject to subject so that nothing gets too heavy. Thus the distracting person's contribution to a disagreement over a political or religious issue might be "Did you see Liz the other night? She was dancing with that *old* man—you know, the one who wears those ratty sweaters!" If the others happened to pursue that topic—Liz's dating behavior—far enough to discover a disagreement about it, the distracting person would switch again: "Let me tell you what happened at work yesterday. My boss just about killed me!" The distracting person will also avoid the honest sharing of attitudes or feelings—too much danger of getting serious—and will generally try to "keep things light."

Nonverbal communication. As you can probably imagine, distracting is characterized nonverbally by random and jerky body movements, inappropriate giggling and laughing, a voice loud enough to force attention in the distracting person's direction, and little direct eye contact. In other words, the nonverbal behavior is an echo of the verbal—it goes in several directions at once and is mainly an almost feverish dance designed to keep people—distracted!

A Couple of Reminders

As you probably noticed, the title of this section of the chapter is "What To Do about Conflict," and so far we've emphasized what *not* to do. We've done that partly because you can best see what *to* do by contrasting it with its alternatives and partly because we want you to do some accurate self-diagnosis. Before you go on, ask yourself again, "Which of these maladaptive styles of coping with conflict do *I* use most often? Placating? Pouncing? Computing? Distracting?"

As you think about that question, we want to emphasize two things. First, note that we have not talked about the placat*er*, pounc*er*, comput*er*, or distract*er*. Instead, we've used the terms "placating person," "computing person," etc. We do so to emphasize that these four labels name styles that everybody falls into from time to time. But almost nobody responds the same way all the time. Although each of us has one or two "characteristic" or "favorite" styles of coping with the threat of conflict, these four terms do *not* name immutable personality types. We stress that point for one simple reason. If you believe that "I'm a placater," for example, you're likely to conclude that "that's just the way I am; I can't change." And that would be both inaccurate and unfortunate. You *aren't* one thing or another; you *choose* one style or another at different times. So do we. And choices can change. So remember, these are not labels of "personality types" but of choices we make—choices we *can* learn to unmake.

Second, as you reflect on your own choices, it may be helpful to realize that in most North American cultures, males are socialized into two of these styles and females are socialized into two others. And sometimes it's hard to change, because those sex-role stereotypes are pretty strong. You can probably recognize which is which: Males are usually taught to pounce and to compute, females to placate and to distract. If you keep this in mind, it may be easier for you to understand why you respond the way you do to a conflict situation. And understanding is the first step toward change.

Leveling

The fifth response to threat will do the most to help you handle conflict interpersonally. Called *leveling*, it's basically communication that takes into account all four aspects of the communication situation—*me, you, context,* and *topic.* The leveling person takes *me* into account by expressing his or her own feelings, attitudes, opinions, expectations, goals, wishes, and ideas. The leveling person also gets *you* into the act by asking about and listening for the *other* person's feelings, attitudes, opinions, expecta-

Leveling

tions, goals, wishes, and ideas. When leveling, you focus on the topic being discussed and are also sensitive and responsive to the context you're in—the location, mood, time available, and so on.

Effective leveling is based on several attitudes or assumptions, most of which we've already discussed:

1. Conflict is inevitable whenever people get into contact, and it can be a positive thing.
2. Relationships can survive conflicts and often are strengthened by them. Moreover, *I* can survive a disagreement. It may be intense, threatening, even scary, and it will probably require a great deal of energy, but it almost certainly will not be devastating. I *can* handle it.
3. It's better to include all the elements that are actually operating—*me, you, context,* and *topic*—than to try to ignore or cancel any of them. A complete, whole perspective is always better than a partial, distorted one.
4. The fact that there's a disagreement means, in part, that the topic and/or the relationship is important to us. Apathetic, disinterested people don't fight; they ignore each other. So the fact that we're taking the trouble to disagree itself says something positive about the relationship.
5. Win/lose is not the only option. It is actually possible for both—or all—sides in a conflict to get what they want. That doesn't always happen, but it *can*. And it happens only when each person levels—shares his or her wants, desires, ideas, and feelings, is aware of the other person's wants, desires, ideas, and feelings, and stays focused on the topic and sensitive to the context while working toward a mutually satisfactory outcome.

General Verbal and   *Including me.* Leveling communication is made up of many of the verbal *Nonverbal*   and nonverbal behaviors discussed in previous chapters. For example, *Communication*   you can best take your *me* into account by applying parts of Chapters 4 and 5. That is, your *me* gets expressed when you choose open rather than closed negotiation-of-selves options (Chapter 4) and when you share your self with appropriate *I* messages (Chapter 5). It's also important to describe your feelings and to own them. As David Augsburger puts it,

> "You make me angry," I used to say.
>
> Untrue. No one can make another angry. I become angry at you, I am responsible for that reaction. (I am not saying that anger is wrong. It may well be the most appropriate and loving response that I am aware of at that moment.)

But you do not make me angry. I make me angry at you. It is not the only behavior open to me.

There is no situation in which anger is the only possible response. If I become angry (and I may, it's acceptable) it's because I choose to respond with anger. I might have chosen kindness, irritation, humor, or many other alternatives. . . . There is no situation which commands us absolutely.[6]

Consequently, it helps, as we suggested in Chapter 5, to substitute "I'm angry" for "You make me angry" and to replace "You're always rejecting me" with "I feel rejected." Try to become aware of statements that shift responsibility to somebody else ("You're building a wall between us") or that make "it" a scapegoat for your attitudes or behavior ("I just can't help it; it makes me mad."). Instead, share perceptions and feelings that you clearly own; try "I don't like the wall between us" or "Dammit! I'm mad!" All those skills are crucial to leveling communication.

Including you. The *you* of the situation comes into play as you choose negotiation-of-selves options that are sensitive rather than stereotyping. It's also important to apply the things we discussed in Chapter 6—to listen in ways that confirm, lead to understanding, and diminish defensiveness. That includes having direct eye contact, maintaining appropriate distance and touch, paraphrasing, asking clarifying questions, and adding examples.

Including context. You can bring *context* into play by staying aware of the many interdependent contextual factors that we talked about in Chapter 1. Both physical and psychological parts of the situation affect what's happening, as do the verbal and nonverbal aspects. It's also important to realize at the time of the conflict that, as we emphasized in Chapter 3, the other persons involved are selecting, structuring, and interpreting what they perceive and are consequently defining their own context. The fact that theirs differs from yours is often part of what the conflict is about. For example, two people on a committee may disagree about how much time committee members ought to spend socializing with one another. Leon may see committee meetings as an important place for the kind of interpersonal contact that keeps the organization's morale high, whereas Brenda may see them as a place to do the organization's work as efficiently as possible. That disagreement over the definition of the context could surface in something like the following exchange.

Brenda: Could we cut the visiting now so we can get some work done?
Leon: (Ignores her. Continues to talk with Lisa and Art.)

Brenda: Hey, Leon! Can we get on with it?
Leon: We are!
Brenda: I mean with the meeting.
Leon: What's your hurry?
Brenda: I want to get the transportation planned so we can be finished!
Leon: Well, I want to finish talking first, so just cool it a minute!

Including topic. Chapter 7 includes suggestions that can help you to treat the *topic* in leveling ways. It is important to use all appropriate channels to help be clear about the topic and, as we said in that chapter, to adapt, organize, illustrate, and remind. Adaptation or sharing your perspective on the topic and attempting to understand the other person's perspective are obviously important. It also helps if you can stay at least somewhat organized during a conflict, especially by using transitions to clarify when you move from one topic to the next. Many conflicts escalate just because one person isn't following the links between ideas the other person is making.

Illustrations are also very useful. Listen to the difference between

> "I just don't want to do that. It'll create all kinds of problems. Other people won't like it!"

and

> "If we do that, here's what I think will happen: Mr. Parker will think that we're more interested in inventory control than in sales, and he'll come down late some afternoon and rearrange the whole display to suit himself. Then our work will have been wasted. That's why I don't want to do it."

The second statement is concrete, specific, and enables you to *picture* some of what the speaker is thinking. That's the value of what Chapter 7 calls *illustrations*—examples and analogies.

In summary, the first two ways to identify how to use leveling communication are:

1. To contrast leveling with placating, pouncing, computing, and distracting; that is, to see leveling as communication that takes into account or brings into play *me, you, context,* and *topic.*

2. To review suggestions we've made in previous chapters, where we've talked about *how* to bring *me* into play (especially Chapters 2, 4, and 5), how to include a focus on *you* (especially Chapters 2, 4, and 6), how to take *context* into account (especially Chapters 1 and 3), and how to pay appropriate attention to the *topic* (especially Chapter 7).

There are also some skills for handling conflict that are not covered in previous chapters, and they apply to each of the three kinds of conflict. So to conclude this chapter, we want to explain five skills for handling image-perception conflict, three ways to work on content conflict, and four things to do when it appears that you're in a conflict over basic values.

Specific Verbal and Nonverbal Communication

Handling image-perception conflict. A first step toward dealing with disagreements over images is to *get in touch with the image that you are likely to bring to the situation.* Although generalizations obviously won't cover all your unique and changing responses, you can probably get some insight into your "typical" images by checking the most accurate responses to the following statements.

————————●◆●————————

How do you react when you disagree with persons older than you? With superiors? With your spouse or parents?

Individual Application: How You Define Yourself in Conflict Situations

1. When I disagree with a friend who is my age, I usually see myself as

   ——— more competent than the other.

   ——— less competent than the other.

   ——— about as competent as the other.

   I tend to respond by

   ——— strongly asserting myself.

   ——— tentatively asserting myself.

   ——— searching for a compromise.

   ——— tentatively giving in.

   ——— giving in.

2. When I disagree with a spouse, lover, or intimate friend, I usually see myself as

   ——— more competent than the other.

   ——— less competent than the other.

   ——— about as competent as the other.

   I tend to respond by

———— strongly asserting myself.

———— tentatively asserting myself.

———— searching for a compromise.

———— tentatively giving in.

———— giving in.

3. When I disagree with my parent or an adviser, I usually see myself as

———— more competent than the other.

———— less competent than the other.

———— about as competent as the other.

I tend to respond by

———— strongly asserting myself.

———— tentatively asserting myself.

———— searching for a compromise.

———— tentatively giving in.

———— giving in.

4. When I disagree with my job supervisor, I usually see myself as

———— more competent than the other.

———— less competent than the other.

———— about as competent as the other.

I tend to respond by

———— strongly asserting myself.

———— tentatively asserting myself.

———— searching for a compromise.

———— tentatively giving in.

———— giving in.

————————◆•◆————————

You can use this information in a couple of ways. First, it can help you to understand how others behave when disagreeing with you. If you habitually define yourself as more competent, for example, the other person is probably going to notice and may well respond with fear, stronger antagonism, or capitulation (depending on her or his own self image) instead of constructive communication. Your responses to those questions can also help you to understand why you dread conflict with your spouse or lover ("I usually feel inferior and tend to respond by giving in") while welcoming a disagreement with a friend your own age ("I usually feel equally competent and tend to assert myself").

In addition, this kind of analysis can give you information about your self that can allow you, at least in your long-term, intimate relationships, to set "belt lines" below which you and your partner agree not to strike. As Bach and Wyden explain, "Everyone has such a belt line—a point above which blows can be absorbed, thereby making them tolerable and fair; and below which blows are intolerable and therefore unfair."[7] In Bach and Wyden's terms, "the belt line protects the Achilles' heel, and this is no mixed metaphor."[8] In other words, each person has spots of intense vulnerability—Achilles' heels—where a blow can seriously damage his or her self image.

One person who reviewed this chapter shared some examples of his own especially touchy topics. "Most of my below-the-belt areas," he wrote, "involve personal characteristics or behaviors over which I have little control: the size of my ears, the fact that I blush, that I tend to get tongue-tied when highly excited. When my 'opponent' points to these things during an argument, I am really wiped out. I see this sort of thing happening often in arguments between people."

Intimates, Bach and Wyden suggest, should disclose these areas, their Achilles' heels, to each other and should mutually agree on belt lines so that their arguments will not become person-destroying. They suggest that intimates learn to shout "foul!" whenever a partner hits below the belt. Although that specific technique may not work for you, we think it can help generally to understand how you usually define yourself in several different conflict situations, so that you can deal with those situations more effectively.

A second step toward handling image-perception conflict is to *imagine the real of the other*. We believe that no single step will help you to handle conflict more effectively than this one. We strongly recommend that your goal in each specific disagreement be to imagine at least once the real of the person you're disagreeing with. At this point the term "imagining the real"—taken from Martin Buber's writing—may sound a little vague, but we think it'll make sense if you just hang on for a few paragraphs.

To understand what we mean, start by thinking back to a specific time when you identified strongly with a character in a book you were reading, a television program or play you were watching, or a "real-life" event you were observing but not participating in. Think of a specific time when you felt that you *really* understood that character or person—you *knew* what she or he was going through. You may have identified strongly, for example, with the boy Demian in Hermann Hesse's book of that name; with Thoreau in *Walden*; with Frodo, Aragorn, Gandalf, or Treebeard the Ent in Tolkien's book—or the film—*Trilogy of the Rings*; or with Billy Pilgrim in Vonnegut's *Slaughterhouse-Five*. You may have identified strongly with John-boy, Elizabeth, or Olivia ("Livvy") in an episode of *The Waltons*; with Luke in *Star Wars*; or with a swimmer, sprinter, golfer, or tennis player in a crucial match. Or, you may have witnessed a family fight at a friend's house and *really known* what your friend was going through. Stop reading now until you choose a person. Recall some of the features of that particular event.

Person_____

Event_____

_____

Now focus your attention for a minute on the *way in which you were perceiving the other person* in that situation. Although you strongly identified with that person, you did not "become" him or her; no magical transformation of matter took place. You stayed *you*. In that sense, your sharing experience with the other happened "in your imagination." And yet the *kind* of imagining you did wasn't the same as daydreaming about what it would be like to be a successful politician or to fall in love with the person of your dreams or to play in the World Series. One difference is that when you identified with the other person, your act of imagining was limited by the realness of the other. If it wasn't—if you gave the character superpowers, perfection, or purity—you were imagining, not imagining the *real*. When you imagine the real—whether the character you identify with is in a book, on stage, on a screen, or in person—her or his realness puts bounds on what you imagine. For example, John remembers seeing Frodo the Hobbit in this way. He really identified with Frodo's combination of adventurousness and fear. But John also remembers feeling how Frodo's fear would be anchored partly in his size—he was just over four feet tall—and in the myths he'd been taught, both of which made his fear different from what John's would be.

Notice another thing about that experience: When you really identify with another person, you know what he or she is experiencing in a first-person, experiential way, not just as an abstract form of knowledge. What we're saying here is that there's a difference between *knowledge about*—which is abstract and objective—and *knowledge of*—which is specific, concrete, and personal. You have knowledge *about* all kinds of things: You know that the federal government is divided into legislative, executive, and judicial branches, that $D = RT$, and that the planet Mercury is farther away from our sun than is the planet Jupiter. Once you know those things, your knowledge doesn't change as you move from situation to situation. It doesn't matter who you're talking to or where you are, D (distance) always equals R (rate) times T (time). And you can have knowledge about those things without ever having personally experienced them—without visiting Mercury or watching the sunrise on Jupiter, you know that one's farther from the sun than the other is. Knowledge *about*, in short, is one important kind of knowledge.

Knowledge *of* is another important kind, and it is experiential knowledge. You have knowledge of how to ride a bike or how to roller-skate, for example. You didn't learn those skills by reading a book; you experienced them first-hand. And your learning didn't proceed step by rational step; it was trial and error and culminated in a holistic experience. For example, you may have tried to think, as you were learning to ride a bike, "push on left foot, then on right; balance in center; lean right for right turn, lean left for left turn," etc. But when you rode, even for the first time, the riding happened as a whole, all of a piece. That's how knowledge *of* is: concrete, specific, experiential, and whole.

When you imagine the real of the other, what you have is knowledge of, not just knowledge about. You don't just see the other person, for example, being sad, and then remember what it's like when *you* are sad, and then infer that he or she is feeling what you feel. That's knowledge about; it can happen entirely "in your head"; it doesn't involve you personally. Instead, what happens is that you are open enough to the other person that you experience not just sadness in general or even the sadness that people feel when their pet dies, but some of the sadness that *this* other person is feeling *now*.

Because it's difficult to write about this experience, we began this section by asking you to recall a time when you experienced it. If you did, or if you are recalling one now, we think you'll understand what we're talking about. As Buber says, imagining the real "means that I imagine to myself what another [person] is at this very moment wishing, feeling, perceiving, thinking, and not as a detached content but in his [or her] very reality, that is, as a living process in this [person]."[9] If I am striking out at someone else, verbally or physically, I experience the blow from the other side—as the person being struck. Or if I caress someone, I feel the touch as it is received, not just as it is given.

Sometimes you can tell that you're imagining the real because of the element of surprise. That is, one way to tell whether you're looking at the other person from *his* or *her* point of view or just from your own is to notice whether you're ever surprised by what you "see" or experience. If you're not, you're probably not yet in touch with the *other's* uniquely present self. If your experience is something like: "Yeah, I know that feeling . . ." or "Uh-huh, I've felt just like that before," you haven't yet gone beyond reflection. When you imagine the real of the other, you experience part of her or his present *otherness*, and since it is different from your own reality, it's new to you—it's at least somewhat surprising. When you get to the point of "Oh, wow! Yes, *now* I see!" or "Ouch! Migod, I've never felt just like that before! Now I really see what she's feeling!" you're imagining the real. The presence of genuine surprise is often the key.

As Buber summarizes, when I am able to imagine the real of the other, something like the following happens.

> I become aware of the other person, aware that he or she is different, essentially different from myself, in the definite, unique way which is peculiar to him or her. I also accept the person I'm aware of, so that I can directly and with full earnestness say to that person whatever I have to say. Perhaps sometimes I have to offer strict opposition to his or her view about the subject matter of our conversation. But I accept this individual as the personal bearer of an opinion, the personal holder of a point of view, and I accept his or her person as the definite being out of which the opinion or point of view has grown, even though I must try to show, bit by bit, the wrongness of this very opinion. I affirm the person I struggle with. I struggle with the person as his or her partner; in other words, I confirm as a person the one who is opposed to me. At this point it's up to the other person to determine whether mutuality will happen and we will meet in genuine dialogue. I can do no more than all I can do. But if I can give to the person who confronts me his or her legitimate standing as a person with whom I am ready to communicate interpersonally, then I may trust that person and I may legitimately expect him or her also to be ready to deal with me as a partner.[10]

We're convinced that no other specific recommendation will help you to handle disagreement interpersonally as effectively as imagining the real. If opposing parties can imagine the real of the other for even a moment, they will not necessarily give up their own positions, but they will be much more able to deal interpersonally with the conflict that separates them, especially with their disagreements over image perceptions.

A third way to manage image-perception conflict interpersonally is to use *relationship reminders*. Relationship reminders are nonverbal and especially verbal references to the history that's shared by you and the person(s) you're in conflict with. The purpose of these reminders is to keep the disagreement in perspective, to ensure that all parties to the conflict remember that this specific disagreement exists in a broader context of at least some mutual commitment and respect. Explicit references to that broader context make the point that "although we disagree, I care about you as a person" and that "I'm listening; I recognize your right to your opinion, even though I believe differently."

When talking about this point, Martin Buber uses the term "confirming the one with whom I struggle." As he explains, that means recognizing the other as a whole person, as well meaning, legitimately concerned about his or her point of view, and deserving of your respect as a person. Even as you confirm the other, Buber points out, you may well disagree with him or her. But if you're confirming, your disagreement does not come out in efforts to force your ideas on that person or to hide the fact that you are trying to "change his or her mind." When you confirm the one with whom you struggle, you make the effort to "find and to further in the soul of the other the disposition toward" something you have recognized in yourself as right.[11] Or, to describe it from another point of view, you try to plant in the other person's mind the seed of your belief and to let it grow there "in the form suited to individuation," i.e., in a way that fits the other person's uniqueness.[12] You treat the other, in short, as a whole person, not as an object.

In some cases you can best communicate that kind of confirmation by saying something like, "I love you, honey, but I really disagree," or "I hear what you're saying, but I can't accept your conclusion." When disagreeing with a friend, it might be most accurate to say, "Look, the reason I'm disagreeing with what you're doing is because I'm afraid of what's going to happen to you." In other cases you can remind the other of your relationship nonverbally by your eye contact, smiles, and by touching the other person in nonthreatening ways.

But it's crucially important that relationship reminders be genuine; they can't be devices or gimmicks. Most persons are sensitive to this kind of phoniness, can readily spot it, and get angry when it happens. It's easy to see why. Phony confirmation is manipulative, and nobody likes to be a puppet on somebody else's strings. So don't try to fake relationship reminders. If you honestly cannot see worth in the other person or value in your relationship with him or her, it would probably be best to postpone your discussion until you can.

Results of a study done by counselor David Johnson indicate that people respond positively when a person they're disagreeing with combines genuine expressions of confirmation and warmth with expressions of anger. Johnson trained persons to express anger and warmth and then asked them to communicate with another person in a negotiating context. Some of the experimenters (trained persons) communicated "all anger"; some communicated "all warmth"; some communicated "anger followed by warmth"; and some communicated "warmth followed by anger." The study generated the following conclusions: (1) the participants *liked* both the experimenters communicating "all warmth" and the ones communicating "anger followed by warmth"; and (2) the expression of anger followed by warmth seemed to lead to the *most agreements* on the negotiated topics.[13]

Both Buber and Johnson say that genuinely positive verbal and nonverbal comments are important in a conflict situation. Confirming the other, indicating your acceptance of him or her as a person, despite your disagreement, can help both of you to handle the conflict interpersonally.

A fourth way to approach image-perception conflicts is to try *role reversal*. Sometimes the most effective way for disagreeing individuals to begin treating each other as persons is to try acting out each one's imagining the real of the other by agreeing for a few minutes to take the other's place in the conflict. When you are forced to act out the other person's responses, even though it's "only pretending," you can often get an unusually clear picture of how the other is seeing herself or himself and seeing you. Sometimes there's almost no better way to clarify disagreements in definitions of selves and to begin to work through them.

David Johnson has also studied how role reversal works in a conflict situation. In one study he found that except when two persons' positions are mutually exclusive, role reversal significantly helped the disagreeing persons to understand each other.[14] The results of a later study validated the belief that the accuracy of understanding created by mutual role reversal significantly helps people to reach agreement.[15] In other words, role reversal helps antagonists to understand each other's position: when they do, they often tend to reach agreement.

Image-perception conflict is thus more likely to be handled interpersonally when the persons involved: (1) are aware of their own "typical" self-definitions; (2) imagine the real of the other; (3) use relationship reminders; and (4) use role reversal.

Handling content conflict. We don't mean to suggest by these chapter headings that these sets of skills apply only to one type of conflict. When you disagree over content, it's important to confirm and to imagine the real of the other, for example, but there are also at least three additional ways you can respond to the content dimension of your disagreement. The first is to *focus*—to work to agree about what the disagreement is about. Be sure that you and the other(s) involved agree about the topic of your disagreement. You may discover, as we sometimes do, that when you reach agreement about your "fight topic," there's nothing left to argue about.

George Bach and Peter Wyden also suggest (pretty sensibly, we think) that you restrict arguments to topics that actually mean something to you. Sometimes it seems as though we're ready to make a mountain out of just about every molehill we encounter. Since conflict takes energy and is sometimes interpersonally risky, it makes more sense to ask yourself before any confrontation whether you really care about the issue involved. In short, limit disagreements to one issue at a time and to a nontrivial issue, i.e., one that means something to you.

As you work to identify the central issue, be sure to distinguish it from your conflict's *trigger*. By "trigger" we don't mean "cause." As we said before, trying to decide what or who "started" an argument can be destructive or, at least, a waste of time. Triggers are precipitating events, the actions or words that mark when a given discussion began, and often they are minor compared with the real problems that need discussing. Unfortunately, we often forget that they're "the last straw," and we focus on them as if they were "the first straw." For example, an employee's late arrival may trigger an argument between the employee and the boss, but the disagreement may not be over the tardiness so much as over what the boss sees as the employee's negative, careless attitudes about the job. That issue won't surface until both parties recognize that although the late arrival is the trigger, it isn't the key issue.

You may have experienced an argument that was triggered when your parents refused to lend you the money for additional stereo equipment, or your son or daughter was two hours late getting home, or your roommate left the room cluttered and dirty again, or your friend forgot to pick you up for the game.

Often, noticing the triggering event can help you to identify the definitions of selves that are involved in the disagreement. That process, in turn, can help you to put the conflict in perspective. For example, although a son or daughter's coming home two hours late seems like a legitimate cause for disagreement over priorities, the nature of the conflict itself can change if the parent can recognize that it's just the trigger and that the central issue or topic involves image perceptions. The parent may be defining his or her self as (1) responsible for the son or daughter's safety ("I must protect you"); (2) being watched by other adults ("People will think I'm a poor parent"); (3) enforcer of agreed-on family regulations ("There have to be some rules around the house"); or even (4) frightened ("Kids are getting kidnapped every day" or "I was afraid you had a car accident"); or (5) rejected ("I see myself as an authority, and I feel you're rejecting that"). The son or daughter may also come to understand what's happening more clearly by examining what the triggering event reveals about his or her definition of self.

In a similar way, pinpointing the trigger and identifying the definitions of selves suggested by that event can help other combatants to understand the situation. Do you lash out at your forgetful friend because you feel that he or she has defined you as not worth remembering or because you are defining your friend as incompetent and yourself as competent? Does the trigger of the cluttered room reveal that your disagreement is over the conflict between (1) your roommate's definition of self as easygoing, casual, and concerned about "important" things and definition of you as parental and nit-picking; and (2) your image of yourself as organized, tidy, and middle-class and your roommate as disorganized, thoughtless, and lower-class? What definitions of selves are working when there's a disagreement over a parent's unwillingness to lend money to a college-age child?

The point is, you can often focus a disagreement on something specific *and* begin to understand some of the humanness of the persons involved by pinpointing the triggering event.

A third way to handle content conflict interpersonally is to *keep current by avoiding gunnysacking*. Partly because most of us fear conflict so much, when it does occur, we tend to seize the opportunity to bring up all the bruises we've been nursing for days, weeks, or even years. Bach and Wyden call that "gunnysacking," and they accurately emphasize its danger. Remember that a gunnysack is a big, coarse bag—the kind that holds 100 pounds of raw potatoes or peanuts. Think of it as a big, rough bag full of aggressive feelings. As Bach and Wyden explain, a violent fight between a wife and husband often occurs because the "aggression reservoir" of the couple

> was simply so full that even a slight jar caused it to spill over. Both partners had been keeping their grievances bottled up, and this is invariably a poor idea. We call this "gunnysacking" because when marital complaints are toted along quietly in a gunnysack for any length of time they make a dreadful mess when the sack finally bursts.[16]

It's much healthier, as Bach and Wyden point out, to try to deal as much as you can with controversial issues one at a time as they come up. That way, a disagreement triggered by one event doesn't become the occasion to air every doubt and hurt you've carried for weeks.

Early in their relationship, John and his wife, Kris, agreed to try to avoid gunnysacking by putting a 24-hour limit on "old issues." In other words, they agreed to try to bring up complaints as they experienced them and to avoid discussing anything more than 24 hours old. The 24-hour limit was intended to allow for some cooling off if it seemed necessary. They haven't completely succeeded with this plan—both still file away some hurts and disagreements—but the fact that they've explicitly recognized the problem does make much of their arguing more productive.

A fourth way to handle content conflict is to *combine your criticisms with positive suggestions for change*. Occasionally, your main goal in a conflict may be to simply dissuade the other from taking some action, but usually a disagreement involves not just stopping one kind of action or plan, but also starting a different one. Most of the time, consequently, both—or all—persons involved share the responsibility for developing solutions. It's important for each participant to remember that. Disagreements often dead-end in such statements as: "Well, you just have to grow up!" "Stop being so radical!" "Be nicer to me!" or "Stop wasting so much time!" Those orders are dead-ends, not only because their tone tends to create defensiveness but also because it's next to impossible to comply with them. Do you mean by "growing up" that you think it would help for the other person to try to be on time more often, or to take more responsibility for his or her comments about others, or to stop putting off term papers until the last minute, or what? Try to remember to be ready with suggested alternatives. Even more important, be willing and able to work mutually to reach a choice or compromise.

It's also helpful to identify the other person's suggestions for change. A simple question can really help to do that. Try asking the person you're in conflict with, "What do you want to have happen?" If you ask that sincerely, and if you listen and respond to the answer, the two of you can often greatly clarify what the disagreement is about. You can also begin to deal with it in down-to-earth, specific ways. That is much more productive than trying to figure out how to "be more considerate" or "grow up." Try it: "What do you want to have happen?"

Conflict over basic values. There are two things to keep in mind about basic-value conflicts. The first is that they are, as we've already said, relatively rare. Try not to use your knowledge that there is such a thing as conflict over basic values as a cop-out or excuse not to try working through a difficult disagreement. We've often talked with persons who are threatening to give up on a relationship—to drop a class, stop seeing a friend—because "We just have a basic personality clash" or "We don't agree on *anything*." Both of those complaints are usually distorted.

The "personality clash" complaint assumes that unchanging, internal mechanisms determine my own and the other person's behavior so much that, for example, if she has a "picky" personality and I have a "laid back" one, we'll *never* get along. But we know that people just aren't that way. "Personality" is primarily a function of relationships; in other words, I behave the way I do in response to the situation I'm in—the people I'm with, places I'm at, etc. Nobody is "picky" all the time—or "laid back" all the time. And there are very few hidden, mysterious, inaccessible inner forces that drive people to fight with each other. People are continually changing, especially in response to the situations they're in. So if I can behave less threateningly, that "defensive person" can probably change and respond less defensively. The same goes for the "picky" and "laid back" persons. Although sometimes it is next to impossible for two persons to choose behaviors that enable them to get along, it is almost always a matter of choice, not "conflicting personalities."

The same goes for many other conflicts that appear to be over basic values. If the parties can stay in contact and can work toward agreement, they often discover a common ground where real negotiation is possible. So don't start out by assuming that a difficult conflict is over basic values. It may be, but the parties may also be using that label as an excuse to avoid working it through.

The second thing to remember about basic-value conflict is that if you experience a genuinely irresolvable disagreement, you can still "agree to disagree." Some differences between unique persons are irreconcilable. But the aspect that is never irreconcilable—the element that is always shared in common—is their humanness. And the living possibility always exists for two combatants to meet on that ground.

When Buber talks about the clash of irreconcilable ideas, he distinguishes between the "persons" involved and their "points of view." A student once asked him whether interpersonal-quality communication could ever occur between persons whose basic world views differed. Isn't it true, his questioner asked, that as soon as their radical disagreement becomes clear to each of them, they will have to break off the relationship and to stop talking to each other? Buber said that he didn't think so. "Neither needs to give up his point of view," Buber wrote. But what can happen is that if each person can meet the other as a person, *they enter a realm where the law of the point of view no longer holds.*[17] Even though each is committed to his or her position, both can "let themselves run free of it for an immortal moment"[18] and in the process can meet the other as a person; the commonness of their humanity overshadows the antagonism of their differing points of view. Their disagreement may remain, but so may their interpersonal relationship.

When Conflict Seems Irresolvable

Many serious conflicts—maybe even *most* of them—look at some point as though they can never be solved. Especially when definitions of selves are really on the line, and they often are, people may take exaggerated, "hard and fast" positions that they're actually willing and able to move away from. Try to remember to give others the freedom to change without feeling that they're weak or inconsistent; that's part of treating them as persons. Remember, too, that you have the freedom to change. Try not to let the presence of conflict scare you into thinking that people never change or that nothing can be done.

Instead, try as systematically as you can to apply those suggestions we've offered here that fit the situation. Identify whether you're in conflict over image perception, content, or basic values. Stay alert for placating, pouncing, computing, and distracting behaviors, and try to do as much leveling as you can. Recognize how you're defining yourself, and especially important, try hard to imagine the real of the other. Focus the conflict on the topic at issue, and stay open to the genuine possibility of change in both you and the others involved. When you actually try applying all these suggestions, you will find that many apparently insoluble conflicts can be handled interpersonally.

If there are still serious problems with images, content, or basic values, try *defusing* the conflict. Defusing means pulling the fuse out so the dynamite won't explode, or in this case reducing the intensity of a disagreement so that the people involved can cope more effectively. You can *defuse yourself* by asking yourself seven questions.

Defusing

1. "What are some ways this conflict could be good: What are its potential advantages?" If you can remind yourself that this disagreement may move a relationship out of a rut, will probably get some hidden feelings out in the open, and may well increase your confidence in the relationship, it's often easier to reduce the intensity of your own feelings and actions.

2. "Am I remembering that other people don't perceive things exactly the same way I do?" From their point of view—which is almost sure to be different from yours—their actions and opinions *make sense*. *They* think and feel that they're being reasonable. Are you remembering that?

3. "Do I understand their position? Have I done enough paraphrasing and adding examples to understand what they're saying and feeling? Have I imagined their real?"

4. "What am I doing to help intensify or prolong this disagreement?" This is the most important question of all. Our natural tendency is to blame the other person or the circumstances for a conflict. But we now know that human communication doesn't work that way. All parts of a communication situation are *interdependent*: I'm not just a spectator or a passive recipient of what's going on but am contributing to all of it—to the upset, the hurt, the disappointment, the fear, and so on. That does *not* mean that it's my "fault." We're in this *together*. But since my natural inclination is to forget that, it can help immeasurably for me to ask myself specifically—out loud even—"What am I doing to make things worse? How am *I* contributing to this conflict?" Then I often can see ways to change, to handle it more interpersonally.

5. "Am I seeing myself as the target of their upset?" Are you taking on personal responsibility for what may be an impersonal, diffuse disappointment that they're experiencing? If they're just in a bad mood, are you feeling as if it's your "fault"?

6. "Are my goals realistic?" Remember, there's a close relationship between the amount of success people experience and the goals they set. One sure way to fail is to set unreachable goals. Is your goal to make the other person feel good about doing what *you* want to do and he or she doesn't? If so, you'll probably never succeed. Is your goal to convince the other person that you're right and that he or she should be eternally grateful to you for pointing out the *truth*? That's unrealistic, too. Or is your goal to discuss the issue for 20 minutes without either of you going off pouting? Or to help the other person understand one part of your position that you don't think he or she yet understands? *Those* goals are attainable. If you set this kind of goal, you can probably succeed. And that success is likely to produce more of the same.

7. "Am I trying to *win* this one? Do I *need* to win it?" Are you doing all you can to promote a win/lose atmosphere? If so, you probably won't be able to handle this conflict interpersonally.

You can help to *defuse the other person* if you do three things: (1) listen, (2) explicitly identify areas of agreement, and (3) maintain your nonverbal cadence. People often assume that the most important thing they can do in a conflict is to say the right thing at the right time. They overlook the fact that how you *listen* is at least as important, probably more so. The other person will almost always be more "reasonable," more open to alternatives, and more willing to change if he or she feels listened to. And that's one thing you can do something about.

Second, don't assume that everybody is remembering what keeps the people together, what keeps you arguing instead of just terminating the relationship. People continue to disagree partly because they *agree* about some things—the importance of the relationship to everyone involved, the importance of the issue, the importance of the decision that will emerge from the discussion, etc. Make those agreements explicit. Remind yourself and the others of the points at which there is no conflict: "Look, both of us want the company to make money, right?" or "I think it's important to remember that we've both got a lot of time and energy invested in this relationship; I don't think either of us wants to throw all that away."

Finally, maintain your own nonverbal cadence. Gary has found this to be especially important in superior-subordinate communication in a business context, but it also applies to everyday and family communication. Frequently the other person will respond strongly—and negatively—to abrupt or significant changes in the way you are standing, sitting, or gesturing, or to obvious changes in your voice, eye behavior, or facial expression. If you can participate in a disagreement without radically altering your nonverbal cadence, you can often help to deintensify the conflict. We're not saying that you should hide your feelings; keeping your *me* in play is a key part of leveling. But realize that the other person *will* respond to your nonverbal behavior and try not to fan the flames of the disagreement by excessive loudness in your voice, abruptly frowning and breaking eye contact, turning your back, or making dramatic "How can you believe that?" movements and gestures.

You can *defuse the situation* by moving away from anyone who might be seen as an "audience" and by dealing with as many contextual barriers as you can. If the immediate situation or the possibility of media coverage creates an "audience" for an argument, all parties involved will to some degree be performing instead of leveling. By moving to another location or rescheduling the discussion, you can help to deintensify or to defuse the situation.

You can also usually do at least something about loud noises, interruptions, or time pressures in a situation. Especially if the disagreement is serious, it's important that it take place where the parties can hear and see each other, can focus on the issue at hand, and can have time enough to work through at least one identifiable part of the disagreement. If those conditions don't exist, move; change locations or set another time to talk. You may feel as though "this is too important to postpone; we'll just have to do the best we can here." And sometimes that may be true. But often it *isn't*. And the conflict can be handled much more productively after only the brief pause created by the move to another location.

That brings up our final point. If all this doesn't help, try a quiet time. Call a moratorium on the disagreement, and do something else for awhile—an hour, a day, maybe even several days or a week. Give everyone involved time to think and feel things through. Don't wait so long that the issue gets ignored or half-forgotten; that can create a festering wound that will get more and more difficult to heal. But when the situation seems to require it, build into your disagreeing some breathing space, some time to put things into perspective.

If there is still no resolution of the conflict, remember what we mentioned earlier: Sometimes the best you can do is to recognize clearly the point at which you disagree and to do so in a way that's mutually humanifying. Sometimes the most you can do is interpersonally agree to disagree.

We began this chapter by recognizing conflict as an inevitable human experience. Humans are significantly different from one another, and whenever their differences meet, conflict can occur. Our motivation for

CONCLUDING THOUGHTS

writing this chapter was based in part on the premise that conflict is no myth; as long as humans communicate, they will sometimes disagree.

Conflict, however, is not the same as a person-destroying argument. Disagreement need not damage a relationship. That's the second premise on which we've based our writing of this chapter: There's nothing inherently destructive or threatening about conflict. The important thing is *how* disagreements are handled. That's why we've been discussing how you may deal with conflicts while maintaining your personness and how you may help to maintain the personness of the other. In other words, we've tried to develop an approach for dealing with conflict consistent with what we've said throughout this book, one that captures the essential methods of handling conflict *interpersonally*.

In Summary   Conflict can occur whenever human differences meet. We define conflict as verbally and nonverbally expressed disagreement between individuals and groups. Some implications of that definition are as follows:

> If you're talking about conflict, you're talking about communication.
>
> All conflict is not, however, just a matter of "communication breakdown."
>
> Often people can communicate well and still disagree.
>
> Conflict is not necessarily bad; it can
>
>> move a relationship out of a rut,
>>
>> help people to discover "the truth" in a situation,
>>
>> get feelings out into the open,
>>
>> help to promote genuine human contact.
>
> Maybe most important, conflict is not something to be afraid of.
>
> If you can start by seeing conflict as a natural, ever-present part of human experience *and* as a potentially good thing, you're well on the way toward learning how to handle it interpersonally.

Types of conflict:

> Image-perception conflicts usually focus on who has the information, who has the authority, who has the power, who has the duty or obligation, who has what social habits, or who has which "personality traits."
>
> Content conflict reflects differing views of objects, events, or phenomena separate from the persons involved. Most content conflicts are over existence—what "is"—or interpretation—what it "means."

Conflict over basic values is often irresolvable; however,

it is rare, most conflicts arising over images or content;

it can be handled interpersonally;

even basic values need to be validated and verified.

Typically, most people respond to the threat of a conflict situation by ignoring, forgetting, or canceling out one of the four elements that are *always* there: *me, you, context,* and *topic.*

When you cancel your *me,* you're *placating.*

Assumptions that promote this response include:

"It's better to switch than to fight."

"Our relationship can't stand an argument."

"Conflict is not nice."

"Fighting is too frightening."

When placating, people will usually

agree quickly and often, use many verbal qualifiers, downplay the importance of issues, and/or hide statements behind placating questions;

back up, look down, shrink into closed or protective postures, and use a questioning vocal inflection.

Pouncing is canceling the *you* in the communication event.

Assumptions that promote this response include:

"People who lose arguments are weaklings."

"If you don't win, you won't be respected."

"My view is the only right one."

"It's always a dog-eat-dog world."

When pouncing, people will usually

use blaming statements and "shoulds";

talk in terms of us vs. them, right vs. wrong, good vs. bad;

hide statements behind pouncing questions;

try to be in a physically superior position, frown a lot, do a great deal of finger-pointing, and talk in a loud, demanding voice.

Computing involves canceling *me, you,* and the *context.*

Assumptions behind this response often include:

"Mature people don't get emotional,"

"Emotions are dangerous."

"Emotions are irrelevant,"

"We can easily ignore the setting and focus just on 'the facts'."

"I know all the facts."

Verbal computing often includes

"completely rational" statements,

use of the third person,

complex words and sentences.

Nonverbally, computing comes out in

tense back and neck,

expressionless voice and face,

little natural movement.

Distracting is canceling *me, you, context,* and *topic.*

Assumptions include:

"If you ignore the conflict, it will go away."

"Nice people are happy and loving and smiling all the time."

Verbal communication often includes

frequent and abrupt topic changes;

little sharing of self—feelings or beliefs.

Nonverbal communication includes

random, jerky body movements;

inappropriate laughing, etc.

Remember that these four terms do *not* name personality types; the terms identify choices we make.

Also realize that males in Northern American cultures tend to be socialized into pouncing and computing, females into placating and distracting.

Leveling communication takes all four elements into account.

Assumptions:

"Conflict is inevitable and can be productive."

"Relationships can survive conflict,"

"A complete, whole perspective is better than a partial one."

"The fact that we're arguing means that we have a stake in and care about the issue and each other."

"It is possible to engage in a win/win conflict."

Generally speaking, leveling communication applies the attitudes and skills we've discussed in Chapters 1–7.

Specific skills for handling image-perception conflict include

recognizing your own self image;

imagining the real of the other so you have *knowledge of* his or her present experience, not just *knowledge about* it;

using relationship reminders;

trying role reversal.

You can handle content conflict by

working to agree about what the conflict is about;

identifying "triggers" and not treating them like "causes";

avoiding gunnysacking;

combining criticism with positive suggestions for change.

Conflict over basic values will go more productively

if you remember that it's rare and don't assume that each difficult disagreement is a "basic personality clash";

when it does occur, if you define your goal as "agreeing to disagree."

When conflict seems irresolvable, try defusing

yourself, especially by asking, "What am I contributing to this conflict?";

the other by listening, identifying areas of agreement, and maintaining your nonverbal cadence;

the situation by avoiding any audience and by arguing in a setting where all the persons involved can see, hear, and concentrate.

If all else fails, try a moratorium, a quiet time.

But remember, almost all conflict can be handled interpersonally.

EXERCISES

Individual Activity: Self-Inventory of Handling Conflicts

Part I

Directions: Check all those behaviors that describe how you feel about and handle conflicts.

_____ 1. If I'm in conflict with another person, I try to ignore the conflict and find areas of agreement and compatibility.

_____ 2. If I am in a group where I observe personality conflicts, I share my observations with the whole group and try to help the people resolve their conflicts.

_____ 3. When in a conflict with a subordinate, manager, or public leader, I go for a "you lose, I win" solution.

_____ 4. If I am in conflict with someone, I go to that person, give my perceptions, and then ask for his or her perceptions.

_____ 5. When I'm in conflict with one person or in a group that is experiencing intragroup conflict, I withdraw.

_____ 6. Instead of laying blame for conflict, I try to find a solution that will work for both of us.

_____ 7. I seek the help of a mediator or arbitrator when conflict exists, because I don't believe that two people can resolve their own conflicts.

_____ 8. I deal with and express my emotions and encourage those with whom I'm in conflict to do the same.

_____ 9. I never have conflicts and see very few conflicts around me.

_____ 10. I usually have conflicts and am aware of many conflicts around me.

Part II

Directions: Another way to gain insight into your own conflict style is to write a description of a recent conflict, using the three steps on p. 319,

---

This exercise is reproduced here with the permission of its author, Marie Rosenwasser, Ph.D., Senior Consultant, Martin-Simonds Management Consultants, Seattle, WA.

I The Conflict (Describe who it was with, what it was about)	II How I Managed It (What happened during the conflict; how did it end?)	III The Results (How did you feel, how did the other(s) seem to feel; are you satisfied with the results?)

Group Activity: Which Kind of Conflict?

1. Ask several members of your class to role-play a conflict situation. This won't be completely artificial if the participants choose a highly controversial issue to discuss, one on which the participants actually differ. The nonparticipating members of the class will take notes on a sheet of paper divided into two parts: On one side, list the content disagreements; on the other side, list the image-perception disagreements. Be sure to listen for the interpersonal methods of dealing with content disagreement:

   a) Focus on one issue at a time
   b) Identify triggers
   c) Avoid gunnysacking
   d) Combine criticisms with suggestions for change
   e) Maintain a win/win mental set.

2. Ask three members of your class to role play a situation in which a counselor is working with a parent and child. The parent and child characters should clearly indicate their definitions of selves in relation to each other, and they should disagree about each other's definition. The counselor will describe for the parent and child what the conflict is about and will suggest ways to handle the disagreement interpersonally. (Note: the characters don't have to be parent and child; choose any two persons who might be talking with a counselor.)

Group Activity: Division of Money

The objective of this exercise[19] is to place you in a conflict situation so that you can examine your present style of dealing with conflicts. The procedure for the exercise is as follows:

1. Divide into groups of three. Each person contributes 50¢ to the group. The $1.50 should be placed in the middle of the group.

2. The group has 15 minutes to decide how to divide the money between two individuals. Only two individuals can receive money. It is not legitimate to use any sort of "chance" procedure, such as drawing straws or flipping a coin, to decide which two persons get what amounts of money. You must negotiate within the triad to reach a decision. The purpose of the exercise is to get as much money for yourself as possible.

3. As soon as your group reaches a decision, write out your answers to the following questions:

   a) What were your feelings during the exercise? Be as specific and as descriptive as possible.

b) What behaviors did you engage in during the exercise? Be as specific and as descriptive as you can (e.g., ignoring, attacking, giving in, agreeing to meet half way, working through).

c) How would you characterize your style of resolving the conflict in the exercise? Again, be as specific as possible.

d) In your group, give one another feedback about what you perceived to be the feelings, behaviors, and conflict styles of the other group members.

4. In the group as a whole, describe what you learned about yourself and your style of dealing with conflicts.

To make conflict situations more comfortable to deal with, you'll want to (1) be aware of your most vulnerable spots; (2) communicate those vulnerability lines to the other person; (3) be aware of and understand where the other person is most vulnerable; and (4) avoid hitting below the lines of vulnerability. The first three steps require you to communicate with the other person about vulnerability. That's not always easy to do *during* a conflict, so you might want to try the following:

Group Activity: Achilles' Heels and Belt Lines

1. Get together with a person you really care about—someone you'd like to communicate interpersonally with even during disagreements, e.g., a lover, roommate, parent, spouse, etc. Each of you should respond to the following questions in order to get in touch with your belt lines. Then discuss vulnerability with each other until you have a clear notion of how you can avoid damaging the other person and your relationship with her or him.

a) I usually feel defensive and hurt when you talk about my:

1) _____

2) _____

3) _____

4) _____

b) Here are some of the nonverbal cues that really get me down:

_____

_____

_____

    c) Around you, my most vulnerable spot is probably:

    _____

2. It can also help to recognize areas of vulnerability around others.

    a) The persons with whom I feel the most vulnerable are:

    _____

    _____

    b) I'm especially vulnerable when it seems to me that someone:
      1) has power over me
      2) is more competent than I am
      3) can do things better than I can
      4) is older than I am
      5) is more attractive than I am
      6) _____

    c) I can handle "putdowns" except in the following areas:
      1) my physical characteristics
      2) my athletic ability
      3) my personality
      4) _____
      5) _____
      6) _____

NOTES

1. Kenneth Boulding, *Conflict and Defense: A General Theory* (New York: Harper & Row, 1962), p. 1. Reprinted by permission.

2. George R. Bach and Peter Wyden, *The Intimate Enemy: How to Fight Fair in Love and Marriage* (New York: Avon Books, 1968), p. 19.

3. C. David Mortensen, *Communication: The Study of Human Interaction* (New York: McGraw-Hill, 1972), p. 271.

4. Or to put it in the research jargon, actor A's power over actor B is "directly proportional to B's motivational investment in goals mediated by A, and inversely proportional to the availability of those to B outside of the A-B relation." R. M. Emerson, "Power-Dependence Relations," *American Sociological Review*, **47** (1962), 32; cited in Wally D. Jacobson, *Power and Interpersonal Relations* (Belmont, CA: Wadsworth, 1972), p. 2.

5. See, e.g., Kenneth K. Sereno and C. David Mortensen, "The Effects of Ego-Involved Attitudes on Conflict Negotiation in Dyads," *Speech Monographs*, **36** (1969), 8–12; and C. W. Sherif and M. Sherif, *Attitude, Ego-Involvement, and Change* (New York: Wiley, 1967).

6. David Augsburger, *The Love Fight* (Scottsdale, PA: Herald Press, 1973), pp. 52, 53, and 218–219. Reprinted by permission.

7. Bach and Wyden, p. 80.

8. *Ibid.*, p. 81.

9. Martin Buber, *The Knowledge of Man*, ed. Maurice Friedman, trans. Maurice Friedman and Ronald Gregor Smith (New York: Harper & Row, 1965), p. 70.

10. Paraphrased from Friedman's translation of Buber's essay, "Elements of the Interhuman," in *The Knowledge of Man*, pp. 79–80.

11. *Ibid.*, p. 82.

12. Buber, "Distance and Relation," in *The Knowledge of Man*, p. 69.

13. David W. Johnson, "Effects of the Order of Expressing Warmth and Anger on the Actor and the Listener," *Journal of Counseling Psychology*, **18** (1971), 571–578.

14. David W. Johnson, "The Use of Role Reversal and Intergroup Competition," *Journal of Personality and Social Psychology*, **7** (1967), 135–141.

15. David W. Johnson, "Effects of Warmth of Interaction, Accuracy of Understanding, and the Proposal of Compromises on Listeners' Behavior," *Journal of Counseling Psychology*, **17** (1971), 207–216.

16. Bach and Wyden, p. 19.

17. Martin Buber, *Between Man and Man*, trans. Ronald Gregor Smith (New York: Macmillan, 1965), p. 6.

18. *Ibid.*

19. Exercise adapted from David W. Johnson, *Reaching Out: Interpersonal Effectiveness and Self-Actualization* (Englewood Cliffs, NJ: Prentice-Hall, 1973), pp. 206–207.

ADDITIONAL RESOURCES

You can tell from the chapter itself that we think Virginia Satir has some very useful things to say about handling conflict interpersonally. See especially her books *Making Contact* (Millbrae, CA: Celestial Arts Press, 1976) and *Peoplemaking* (Palo Alto, CA: Science and Behavior Books, 1972). *Making Contact* is a brief, clear, personally written discussion of many of the ideas we've talked about in this book. We *highly* recommend it. *Peoplemaking* is a bit more thorough but just as engaging and practical. Both books outline the styles of handling conflict that we discuss in this chapter, but both present that material in contexts slightly different from what we provide here. Virginia Satir has much to teach us.

Joyce Frost and Bill Wilmot wrote one of the few complete treatments of conflict management from a communication perspective, *Interpersonal Conflict*

(Dubuque, IA: Wm. C. Brown, 1978). If you are seriously interested in learning to cope effectively with communication in conflict situations, you could definitely profit from reading their book.

Two nationally respected social scientists, Rensis Likert and Jane Gibson Likert, discuss one way to implement a win/win approach to conflict in their article "A Method for Coping with Conflict in Problem-Solving Groups," in *Group and Organizational Studies* **3** (December 1978), pp. 427–434. These authors also wrote a book that effectively discusses conflict management, called *New Ways of Managing Conflict* (New York: McGraw-Hill, 1976).

In his *Caring Enough to Confront* (Glendale, CA: Gospel Light Publications, 1974), David Augsburger develops a Christian approach to dealing with conflict. An excerpt from Augsburger's book is reprinted in John's *Bridges Not Walls: A Book about Interpersonal Communication*, 2nd ed. (Reading, MA: Addison-Wesley, 1977), pp. 203–213.

George Bach and Peter Wyden's book *The Intimate Enemy: How to Fight Fair in Love and Marriage* (New York: Avon Books, 1968) is also worth looking at. We think they could have said what they say in less space, but there are some good suggestions in the book, suggestions that grow from practical experience with "warring spouses."

Several books written about assertiveness and assertiveness training also offer excellent advice about coping with conflict. For example, see Robert E. Alberti and Michael L. Emmons, *Your Perfect Right: A Guide to Assertive Behavior*, 2nd ed. (San Luis Obispo, CA: Impact, 1974); and John Narciso and David Burkett, *Declare Yourself: Discovering the ME in Relationships* (Englewood Cliffs, NJ: Prentice-Hall, 1975). Another useful book, which we referred to at the end of Chapter 5, is Ron Adler's *Confidence in Communication: A Guide to Assertive and Social Skills* (New York: Holt, Rinehart and Winston, 1977).

If you're interested in looking at communication and conflict from a transactional-analysis perspective, read Thomas A. Harris, *I'm OK—You're OK* (New York: Harper & Row, 1967). Several of our students who were willing to learn the vocabulary of transactional analysis have told us that Harris's book helped them to understand their behavior in conflict situations and to change it.

There are some special challenges facing the person who has to work with conflict in an organization—a corporation, company, partnership, etc. You can find some useful information about conflict management in organizational settings in *Readings in Interpersonal and Organizational Communication*, 3rd ed., ed. Richard C. Huseman, Cal M. Logue, and Dwight L. Freshly (Boston: Holbrook Press, 1977), Chapter 4.

A film we've used to discuss conflict management with both university students and businesspersons is *Conflict: Causes and Resolutions* (Beverly Hills, CA: Roundtable Films, 1974). The film demonstrates some effects of approaching conflict from win/lose and win/win perspectives.

9

Public speaking: overcoming the barriers

I. TO HELP INTERPERSONAL-QUALITY COMMUNICATION HAPPEN IN A PUBLIC SPEAKING SITUATION, WORK TO DEFINE

A. The context as personal and an opportunity rather than as separating, formal, and one-way

B. Yourself—the speaker—as a well-prepared conversationalist rather than as a formal, impersonal role-filler

C. Your listeners as supportive and a valuable source of information rather than a faceless, threatening collection of eyes

II. IT IS ALSO IMPORTANT TO PAY ATTENTION TO YOUR LISTENERS' IMAGE OF YOU—SPEAKER CREDIBILITY

A. Remember, your credibility is listener-determined, so
   1. Deliver what you promise
   2. Make accurate statements
   3. Be nonverbally confident and appropriately dressed
   4. "Borrow" credibility when appropriate

B. Remember, too, that credibility
   1. Is based on several images
   2. Varies from situation to situation
   3. Interacts with other variables in speech situations

———— •·• ————

INTRODUCTION   Throughout this book we've emphasized that each of our communication experiences tends to have one of two possible qualities: We tend to treat people primarily as objects or primarily as persons. We've said that for us the word "interpersonal" means not just any communication between people but communication of a certain quality. That quality emerges when the persons communicating are willing and able both to be aware of others as humans instead of objects and to reveal or share something of their own humanness. In this chapter we suggest that the quality of human communication we've been talking about can happen in a variety of different settings, or contexts. In other words because we're humans, we are choosers, and that means no situation dictates completely for us how or what we will communicate. Because of our choice-making capabilities, we're able to promote interpersonal-quality communication just about whenever we're really willing to. In some contexts, however, it's much more difficult than in others.

For purposes of clarification, human communication contexts or situations, are usually generalized into four categories: (1) public, (2) group, (3) mass media, and (4) sociopersonal. Not all communication events fit neatly into one of these four categories; it's usually a matter of degree. Sometimes, for example, when members of an organized group communicate as if they were each giving speeches, the context is as much public as group. Or when a person is giving what we'd ordinarily call a public speech, but the audience is small, the atmosphere is comfortable, the person's approach is personal and spontaneous, and there are immediate exchanges of verbal comments between speaker and listeners, it might be more accurate to call that situation "group" or "sociopersonal." In this chapter we'll focus specifically on how you can promote interpersonal-quality communication in the public-speaking context.

As the Doonesbury cartoon (p. 328) suggests, public speaking often involves objectifying—by both speakers and listeners. Consequently, the public setting is one of the most difficult ones in which to promote interpersonal communication. There are several reasons. First, both speaker and listeners usually bring certain expectations to the public context, and these expectations sometimes discourage sharing and being aware. For example, people usually assume that this type of context is a formal one, and that only one person is supposed to talk while the others sit and listen. When one person is the primary source of verbal cues, the possibilities for *mutual* sharing and being aware are drastically reduced. In addition, public speakers—especially inexperienced ones—frequently believe that there's a prescribed role to conform to or imitate; in trying to fill that role, they objectify themselves and therefore communicate *im*personally. Finally, when the audience is large, it's almost impossible to treat each person as a unique individual, so generalizations are made, stereotypes are formed, and the listener is objectified, too.

But even though every public-speaking setting has structure and rules unlike those found in informal, personal situations, there are ways to promote interpersonal communication in public contexts. In this chapter and the next, our suggestions will be for you to (1) look at the ways you tend to define the public-speaking context as impersonal; and then (2) work to redefine the context; (3) be aware of how you typically define yourself when

you're giving a speech; then, if necessary (4) change that definition; (5) try to develop an informed definition of your listeners; (6) understand the impact of your listeners' image of you; (7) choose a topic you care about; (8) manage your ideas; and (9) manage your nonverbal communication.

We tend to perceive public-speaking contexts as:

Separating and formal. We've talked before about how the physical environment affects human communication. The physical context of a public-speaking situation is deliberately set up to maintain a separation between speaker and the audience and to reduce the opportunity for the give and take of conversation—both between speaker and listeners and among listeners. In the typical public setting, for example, the speaker stands behind a lectern, desk, or table, and the audience sits in rows facing the speaker. Everything physically possible is done to focus attention exclusively on the person giving the speech. This tends to set audience and speaker apart, as if each were a separate entity. The context need not be set up that way, but it usually is.

Depending on the specific setup, for example, the personal space between speaker and the audience can be anywhere from 10 to 40 feet or more. Typically, a personal space of more than five feet isn't associated with a warm personal conversation. Ordinarily, you stand that far away from someone because it's physically impossible to stand closer or—and here's the important point—because you don't *want* to get close physically or psychologically. To the extent that wide personal space between persons is interpreted to mean formal, structured, businesslike relationships, the space usually encountered in a public setting works against interpersonal communicating.

Linear and one-way. The person who either assumes or behaves as if public speaking is linear and one-way communication assumes that the audience doesn't participate in the event. If that person were to diagram his or her communicating, it would probably look something like this:

An inexperienced speaker using this model as a guide enters the public-speaking situation with a packaged message (the speech) and delivers it as if it were a static chunk of previously constructed information being poured into the heads of a passive audience. In other words, the model assumes that the speaker communicates and that the audience doesn't.

Since the speaker is the only communicator, the most important thing in this context is the prepared speech. Nothing else really matters; nothing else is happening; audience analysis has already been done; concern is only with the message cues being sent out. Audience feedback is the farthest thing from the speaker's mind. With this model as a guide, the speaker thinks, "Why be aware? There's nothing to be aware of."

Work to redefine public-speaking contexts as:

Personal. Even before you plan your speech, one of the important things for you to do is to define the public-speaking context as a personal event rather than as a completely impersonal one. You'll obviously be confronted with some unavoidable structure. The members of the audience, for example, will bring with them certain expectations about the formality of the event. They won't expect your talk to be completely off the cuff. They'll expect you to have some things to say that you've thought about in advance. They'll also expect you to do most or all of the talking. But those expectations aren't irrevocable. It has been our experience that listeners usually respond positively when we make an effort to remove some of the structure and formality from the public context.

For example, one of the ways we've learned to deal with personal space is by gaining psychological control over it. We work to define our relationship with the other persons rather than let the personal space define the relationship for us. To do that, we've had to unlearn some things. We no longer assume that distances of five feet or more automatically mean formal, businesslike relationships. We also don't accept the idea that it's impossible to talk conversationally with an audience 30 or 40 feet away. If you can unlearn some of your stereotypes about personal space and redefine the situation so that even at wide distances you can see the members of your audience as persons, and if you can recognize that even at wide distances, conversational and spontaneous communication can still happen, you're much more likely to promote person-to-person communicating in a public setting.

When living in Los Angeles, John watched and listened to the Episcopal priest Malcolm Boyd redefine a public-speaking situation in the ways we're talking about here. He spoke in a church during a Sunday service, but he managed to create a personal, conversational atmosphere even in that setting. One of the persons reviewing this book experienced Boyd doing the same kind of thing:

> For me a fantastic experience was listening to Malcolm Boyd speak to 2500 people. He sat on a high stool on the platform and talked as if only five or six people were present. But I felt as if I were one of those five or six! A couple

hundred people left during the first 15 minutes, most of them disgusted be-cause they expected to hear a "speech." But those who stayed felt elated, as if they had been in a dialogue with Boyd.[1]

Interdependent. Being aware of the audience's humaness is also an impor-tant dimension of defining public speaking as a personal event. To de-velop your ability and willingness to be aware, recognize that the indi-viduals in an audience *do* participate in the public-speaking context; that is, try to get away from the linear, one-way viewpoint. Members of an audience select, organize, and go beyond the verbal and nonverbal cues you make available, and they are continually making nonverbal cues available to you. Even though you may decide not to be fully and con-sciousiy aware of those cues, they exist. In Chapter 1 we said that two persons who are perceptually aware of each other are interdependent. That is, what one person says and does affects the other person, and vice versa—they influence each other simultaneously. In the public setting, the things you say and do affect your listeners, and the way they behave affects you. Rather than thinking about public speaking as linear and one-way, it makes more sense to view it as an event in which both speaker and listeners are active, interdependent participants. A speaker doesn't exist apart from the audience; an audience doesn't exist apart from the speaker. Both participate. Both communicate. Be aware that your listeners are communicating with you. Make an attempt to understand what the people are "saying."

Not rule-bound. You can also encourage interpersonal-quality communica-tion in the public setting by breaking out of the imposed formal structure. As speaker, you have a distinct advantage in redefining the speaking context. Unless you drastically violate audience expectations, you can get by with making a variety of choices. If *you* say, "It's okay to be informal," it's usually more acceptable than if an audience member says, "Hey, let's be more informal." Not all public-speaking events lend themselves to complete informality, but sometimes you'll want to break the "rules," which say, for example, "Focus must always be on the speaker" or "Audi-ence members must not interact verbally." In other words, you may want to change the situation to allow persons in the audience to interact with one another and with you as you talk with them.

DRAWING BY LEVIN; © 1977 THE NEW YORKER MAGAZINE, INC.

For example, John recently heard a presentation by the psychologist Wil Schutz that began in a very unusual but effective way. The "speaker" commented at the start that he realized that audience members had come to the meeting from a variety of different places—other meetings, classes, coffee breaks—and that as a result, we probably were not as "present" or focused on *this* meeting as we might be. So he asked his listeners to stand, stretch their arms over their heads, and make a loud noise of some kind. Since everybody was doing it, no one felt unbearably silly, and the effect was to focus listeners' attention on what was happening now. Then, while he had our attention, he asked us which of three approaches to his presentation *we* would prefer that he take. So he not only broke the unwritten "rule" that listeners have to stay seated and behave themselves but also *began* by asking instead of telling.

There can be several advantages to breaking some of these rules. In the first place, you'll have a much better idea of what your listeners are thinking, and consequently you'll have a better chance to clear up misunderstandings. In addition, because of the ambiguity of nonverbal cues, it's generally much easier to interpret, synthesize, and respond to verbal feedback from an audience member. Also, immediate verbal interaction between speaker and audience increases the potential for mutual sharing and being aware.

There are also some possible disadvantages. Sometimes verbal interaction between speaker and listeners strays from the central theme. Audience participation takes time, and you may not finish everything you wanted to say in your talk. A member of the audience may promote an argument or may not want to pursue a topic that doesn't interest the other listeners. Therefore, whether or not you encourage your listeners to participate verbally depends on several things: the number of persons present, your goals as a speaker, the expectations of the audience, the nature of the event, and so on. You won't always want to give part of your time to your listeners, but you should think of it as a strong option.

An opportunity. People in our classes frequently define the public setting as a liability, an undesirable hurdle they have to get over. We get such comments as "How can I speak in front of so many people for 15 or 20 minutes? What do I talk about for that long?" or "I don't know anything about important topics; I don't have anything to say that would take even five minutes." Because they view public speaking as a liability, their speeches become forced, formal, and impersonal.

It's true that as a speaker you'll be expected to do most of the talking for 10, 20, or maybe even 50 minutes. But instead of defining that as a liability, try seeing it as an opportunity. Having most or all of the available time can be an advantage to you. In a conversation, for example, you seldom get more than one or two minutes at any given time to express your views. Such short time segments don't always allow you to fully explain yourself. The public context, on the other hand, almost guarantees that you'll be given enough time and attention to explain your views, qualify your position, and respond to objections people may be thinking about. Unlike in a conversation, you won't have to feel embarrassed or self-centered about using the time for yourself. If you thought about it just for a minute, you could probably name several issues you really *care* about—all of us feel strongly about some things. A public-speaking situation is the perfect place for you to share your thoughts and feelings about an idea you really believe in, an event that excites you, an organization you strongly dislike, a political figure you intensely admire, or whatever. In other words, when you have something you want to say and when you want time to say it without frequent interruptions or without worrying about dominating the conversation, public speaking gives you more of an opportunity than the sociopersonal context does. But you must have something you want to say; therefore you need to get in touch with the topics and ideas you care about and to realize that much of what you care about *is* appropriate for public speaking.

Stereotyped self-definition. If your experience is like ours, you may be curious to know why people change so much when they get up to give a speech. When you converse with a person informally and sense the spontaneity, conversational language, vitality, and human sharing and then watch that same person give a "speech," you may be amazed at the sudden change to a rigid, formal, unnatural communicator. As we talked about this and as we observed and listened to the members of our classes and public-speaking workshops, we discovered that this change occurs because many students develop role definitions of how a public speaker *should* behave. Whenever they get up to give a speech, they try to play that role. It is as if public speaking were a stage play, with the speaker as one of the acts.

YOUR IMAGE OF YOUR SELF

The image or definition you construct of yourself as a public speaker can promote object-to-object communicating and work against your willingness and ability to share aspects of your humanness. You may sometimes think, for example, that there's a public speaker "personality" you're expected to project. You may have been thinking, "I'm supposed to be formal and deliver the speech in a perfectly continuous, flowing manner" or "I'm in charge and I'm expected to use a certain type of language—mostly formal English" or "I'm not supposed to be too personal." If you define the public speaker in these ways, you're trying to imitate an artificial model rather than to project your own human qualities. You're trying to behave as someone else would in the same role, someone you've seen in the pulpit, on stage, at a banquet, in the classroom, on television, or at a political rally. Instead of getting in touch with your own humanness and sharing it, you're trying to figure out ways of playing the role properly. You'll usually find the role uncomfortable and unnatural.

In addition to feeling unnatural filling the role, you'll also often be unfairly critical of yourself. Usually this self-criticism is based on the contrast between how you think public speakers should behave and how you see yourself actually behaving. One of the mythical definitions of the successful public speaker, for example, is that he or she is never afraid, never experiences anxiety. If you define the successful speaker that way, when you get up to speak and notice that your hands are sweaty and cold, your knees feel weak, and your stomach is churning, you're likely to believe that something is wrong with you. You think to yourself, "I'm scared and nervous. Successful speakers aren't supposed to be nervous; they're always calm. I'm probably going to blow this whole thing." You not only are worrying about your fears but also rejecting yourself for being afraid. It's as if "good" speakers didn't have stage fright, and since you have it, you must be "bad." We'll have more to say about stage fright later; for now, we'd just like to help you see how a stereotyped definition of yourself as public speaker can contribute to your uneasiness.

Work to redefine your self as speaker

You're a talker, not a writer. Your definition of self as speaker in a public context should be very much like your definition of self as speaker in a conversation. You'll feel more natural and do a better job of public speaking if you think of your speech as an *extended conversation.* As we said before, in a conversation you usually talk in blocks of only a minute or two; in a public speech the time may be extended to 5, 10, or even 50 minutes. But this doesn't mean that all your communication behaviors should change drastically. For example, when you define the context and your self as "formal" and "impersonal," you usually tend to behave physically in unnaturally stiff ways and to overarticulate or to pronounce words overprecisely. A stiff, pedantic delivery usually sounds mechanical, and the audience will probably interpret it as unnatural and insincere. But if you define yourself as engaging in a kind of conversation, your delivery will tend to flow more naturally and spontaneously.

In addition, when you're conversing, you use words that are *yours;* unless the situation is threatening to you, you talk naturally and spontaneously. The same should be true when you're giving a speech. The major difference between the language of public speaking and that of informal conversation is that in the conversation you get by with more slang, colloquilisms, and nonstandard English. Many audiences would dislike a speaker's saying something like, "I ain't gonna talk about no stuff like that." But they'd probably also be turned off by "My intentions involve eschewing the abstract components" or "I do not intend formally to treat such matters." A more natural way to say it might be "I don't plan to talk about. . . ." Our point is that when you're preparing and giving a speech you should keep the listeners and context in mind—use language appropriate to the situation—but also keep yourself in mind—use personal, conversational language, *your* language. Eliminate ambiguities, words that are much too formal for you and the situation, and jargon words that only your friends might understand; talk mostly as you normally do in a conversation.

Prepared. Not only is it important for you to define yourself in the public-speaking situation as a talker or converser instead of a writer, but it's also crucial for you to define yourself as genuinely prepared, as ready to talk. We're convinced that you'll *be* ready if you take the following steps: (1) decide early what you want to accomplish; (2) become friends with your ideas; (3) prepare useful notes; and (4) say your talk before you give it.

Almost everybody suffers from at least a little procrastination. John tends to put off answering personal letters—and is finding that it's a very good way to alienate friends. When he was going to school, he sometimes put off studying for exams, writing papers, keeping up with required reading, and preparing a talk. You may do some of the same things. Somewhere along the way, though, it finally got through to John that procrastination is like hitting oneself over the head with a brick. The only good thing about it is how it feels when you stop. Since then, he's developed a little more of the willingness and ability to "get ready early." Now it's especially important for John to prepare for a talk he has to give by deciding early what he wants to accomplish. He's found that it really helps to determine at least several days before the talk—and preferably a week or more: (1) what the general topic is going to be, e.g., interpersonal communication in family situations, humanism in teaching, Martin Buber's philosophy of dialogue, or whatever; and (2) what his specific purpose is, e.g., to help people understand where he's coming from on a topic, to suggest acceptance of a point of view he holds, or to urge a specific action.

That kind of thinking leads to making a *statement* of the topic and purpose well before the time for the talk. It isn't enough just to think about it; it's important to write down something like, "I want to help these people see that a college class can be both rigorous and humane" or "I want to encourage young people to spend more time with their grandparents." By taking that first step, a speaker is on the way to developing the confident, comfortable feeling that comes when you know you are *ready*.

Making those decisions early also gives you time to become friends with your ideas. If you know well in advance what your specific purpose is and at least roughly what you want to say about it, you can take the time to think through your ideas enough to get familiar with them. You can take spare moments—walking across campus, driving down the freeway, etc.—to run through your thoughts until they become like old friends—comfortable and easy to spot in a crowd. That also really helps when the time for the talk comes.

We're convinced that it's important to talk about preparing useful notes, because we've seen too often what bad notes can do. We've seen potentially interpersonal communication become stilted and stiff because the speaker got lost in notes that are too long or full of confusingly obscure symbols and complicated arrows. We've also agonized with the speaker who is reduced to frantic searching and awkward mumbling by notes that looked okay when they were written, but that became unreadable in the increased pressure of the speaking situation. Again, try not to create problems for yourself! Unless you have a lectern or a speaker's stand to put papers on, use cards. Use colors, indentations, numbers, and spaces to indicate key ideas, quotations, etc. Remember the more you write, the greater the temptation will be to read *at* your listeners instead of talking *with* them. In short, create notes that help you stay hooked up with those you're talking with instead of getting in between you and them.

Finally, give yourself the benefit of hearing yourself talk *before* you go into the actual speaking situation. We are not saying that you should memorize your talk—*definitely not*. But we do believe it is important for you to say your speech before you give it, to talk through your ideas in the order you've put them in, at least two or three times before you face your listeners. You'd be amazed how few beginning speakers actually do this and how much it can help you feel confident enough to share yourself and be aware of others in the public-speaking context.

The important thing about redefining yourself as a speaker is that you shouldn't kid yourself. It's relatively easy to do that, to say, "Sure I'm ready, I've been thinking about this for more than an hour" or "No sweat, I'll just ad lib for a couple of minutes, tell a few jokes, and it'll be fine." But unless you're experienced enough to do that kind of thing well, the deception will almost always backfire. You *know* when you're prepared and when you're not. If you want to feel comfortable in the speaking situation and to do an effective job of sharing your ideas, avoid shortcuts. Don't kid yourself. *Really* get ready.

YOUR IMAGE OF LISTENERS

A collection. When your audience is large and unfamiliar to you, it's difficult, if not impossible, to relate to each person as a unique individual. Handling your relationship with a collection of listeners is easier, because in a sense you are dealing with only one unit. Sometimes, in a classroom speech or in a speech to an organization or group you belong to, you know the persons in the audience well enough to be able to see some individual personalities, but more often than not, you probably treat them as a whole. This happens partly because you have so much to think about while you're talking. Keeping 10 or 20 minutes of speech content straight seems to demand so much of your attention that you can't think about the multitude of separate personalities in front of you.

Faceless. Sometimes it's difficult to define members of an audience as persons because not much of their humanness is made available to you during your talk. There's not much body movement, no verbal cues, and almost no facial muscle movement. Also, you're so far away from some of your listeners that it's difficult for you to pick up whatever nonverbal cues might be there. Part of the problem is that many listeners assume that they *shouldn't* respond overtly or explicitly. They assume, for example, that "the speaker has the floor and so it's improper to interrupt, move around, shift, make sounds, or express myself in any obvious way. It might be embarrassing to the speaker if I made my responses too obvious." In addition to these assumptions, since members of an audience don't always know one another, their communicative behavior is influenced by the notion that "most of the other people here are strangers to me." Whatever the cause, the result is that a group of listeners can look on the surface like a faceless, inert blob.

Too complex to respond to. On the other hand, we sometimes define an audience as too complex to respond to because there's so much information available.[2] Most of your communicating takes place in informal contexts; only a few people are involved, and the personal space is from one to five feet. Consequently, you get used to being aware of the verbal and nonverbal cues of only a few persons at a relatively close distance. But in the public-speaking setting, you have to keep in touch with a great many people all at once from a relatively long distance away; most people are *not* used to that kind of communicating. At one time two persons in the back row may be nodding affirmatively while two people in the front row are looking at you with almost emotionless faces, one individual in the middle is shifting back and forth nervously, and one person is smiling and another is yawning. Trying to assimilate feedback from just those few persons—let alone 30 or 40—can be overwhelming. It's easy to experience information overload, because you're not practiced at being aware of and synthesizing so many cues from so many different persons. Because there are so many things to be aware of and because it's so difficult to process that much information, you may avoid as much of it as you can; that is, you may decide that the best way to deal with the overload is to ignore responses from the audience. Then you'll behave as if communication were linear and one-way, and when this happens, person-to-person communicating is impossible.

A threat. Yur image of your listeners also usually includes your predictions of how they will respond to you as a speaker. If you predict that the audience will be accepting, for example, you're likely to communicate comfortably and to feel free to share aspects of your humanness. Unfortunately, however, speakers sometimes build images of their audiences based on negative fantasies. Sometimes the inexperienced speaker regards listeners as "a group of critics just waiting for me to make a mistake." In extreme cases a speaker may define the audience as "a bunch of rejectors ready to pounce at every opportunity." These definitions aren't always explicit or conscious. But nervousness and impersonalness are frequently evoked because of a strong fear of listeners, a fear based on the speaker's definition of them. In other words, when you define the audience as a threat, you're much more likely to hold back the human parts of you for fear of rejection, and the result is likely to be object-to-object communication.

Work to redefine your listeners as:

Individuals—as much as possible. Whenever you're talking with a large audience, some objectification of the persons is inevitable. You'll have to make some generalizations. Keep in mind, however, that listeners *are* persons, not "listening machines," and that their attitudes, values, beliefs, and feelings affect their responses to you. It'll be easier to keep this in mind if your image of your listeners is *well informed.*

The questions you can ask before your talk are almost unlimited. For example, you may want to ask: "Who decided I should speak? Why was I chosen? How much does this group know about me? What are the group's attitudes toward me? What expectations does the group have? What's the purpose of the meeting? What are members' attitudes toward my topic? What speakers have they had in the past? How have they responded to those speakers? How much do they know about the topic? Will there be a business meeting before I speak? Any other speakers before me? If so, what will they talk about?"

Answers to these questions can come from a variety of sources. Talk with whomever you can, e.g., the person who asked you to speak, the person who introduces you, members of your audience, etc. If you're talking to an organization, find out as much about the group as you can from the officers, the members, or any literature they've distributed. What are the goals of the organization? Values? Past accomplishments? Occupations of the members? And so on. You'll also help yourself by knowing something about the educational level, economic status, ages, etc., of your audience.

You'll never know all you need to, but the effort to answer questions about your listeners before your talk can help you in several ways. First, when you know something about the people, you won't be talking to a collection of total strangers, and this can relieve some of your anxieties. Audience analysis won't solve all your problems, but communicating is almost always easier and more comfortable when we have some idea of what to expect from the other persons involved. With an informed definition of your listeners, it'll be much easier for you to adapt to them. One audience may know absolutely nothing about your topic, but another may be well informed about it; one group of listeners may have a great sense of humor, whereas another group may take the topic very seriously—no jokes allowed. Finally, perhaps the strongest reason for obtaining information about your audience centers on a point we made earlier: Public speaking is a process in which both speaker and audience participate. A high level of understanding can be attained only when both speaker and listeners put themselves into the psychological shoes of the other. Since listeners do very little or no talking during the speech, a speaker must find out where they're coming from before and, as much as possible, during the talk and must let them know where he or she is coming from, so that effective mutual adaptation can happen.

A valuable source of information. The cues your listeners make available while you're talking don't have to be overwhelming. On the contrary, by paying some attention to your listeners' nonverbal behaviors while you talk, you'll have access to information about how they're responding to what you're saying. That is, your awareness during the speech lets you know something about their immediate human responses—feelings, understandings, or misunderstandings, moods, interests, etc. Seldom is an audience completely immobile. Through silence, grimaces, smiles, laughter, shifting, and head movements, people in the audience express themselves as persons, as individuals. As we said earlier, you'll sometimes assume that the audience is too complex to respond to, that it's too difficult to synthesize so many different cues coming from so many different persons. But you can do several things to help yourself.

First, recognize that you can't assimilate everything. None of us are equipped or prepared to absorb all the nonverbal cues that listeners make available. As we explained in Chapter 3, our sensory limitations prevent that. But recognize that you can assimilate *some* things. You *can* take advantage of your ability to selectively perceive some cues and avoid others. So instead of letting information overload you, pay attention to as many of the responses as you can while still maintaining control over yourself and your message content. As you get more and more experienced at public speaking, your ability to absorb and then adapt to information from an audience will increase. You'll probably find that the more aware of your listeners you become, the more automatically you tend to respond to them. But until you're able to synthesize many nonverbal cues, work to synthesize just a few. For your first talk, perhaps you'll see only a few responses. But as you continue to give speeches, try to increase your awareness to the extent that the sample of responses you're able to assimilate is a fairly good representation of how most of your listeners are responding.

Our second suggestion is that as you select responses, be careful how you interpret them. Some things about a conversation generalize well to public speaking—conversational language and voice, natural movements, personal examples, and so on. But feedback doesn't. In conversational contexts you're likely to receive immediate verbal feedback, facial expressions, and subtle eye and body movements; most of the time, silence is the exception rather than the rule. But in public speaking the rules are different. Silence is the norm; that's the way most listeners believe they're supposed to behave. If you interpret silence in a public-speaking situation the same way you do in a conversation, it may have a negative impact on you. In other words, silence doesn't automatically mean disinterest or boredom; before you infer that your audience is bored, you should get more information than "they're awfully quiet." The same kind of careful interpretation should be used for other audience cues, too. Fidgeting or yawning may indicate more about the room temperature, time of day, past activities, or furniture comfort than it does about you or your talk. In short, try not to see yourself as the "target" of or the one to "blame" for any inattention you notice.

Our final suggestion is that you try to respond to your listeners interpersonally. We've been talking about being aware of, synthesizing, and interpreting feedback. Now we're saying that how you treat the persons in an audience will determine in large part how much information about their responses they'll make available to you. Most audiences respond honestly and openly when (1) they believe that the speaker *wants* them to respond openly; (2) they sense that the speaker *feels comfortable* when they respond; (3) the speaker *acknowledges* some responses from listeners; and (4) the speaker responds back interpersonally, that is, accepts and tries to understand his or her listeners. Through your tone of voice, choice of words, eye contact, etc., you can be confirming, understanding, and nonintimidating. For example, after you say something controversial, if you notice several people grimace and shake their heads negatively, you might say something like "I know that bothers some of you; I can understand that. But let me go on for a moment before you tune me out." Or as one reviewer[3] of this chapter suggested, you can respond to fidgeting or yawning by shifting gears. "Is it too hot in here?" or "Shall I open a window?" can be ways of showing your concern.

Supportive, not threatening. As we said earlier, fear sometimes prevents a speaker from sharing aspects of her or his humanness and from being aware of aspects of the audience's humanness. For example, a speaker who is afraid often focuses on the lectern, the floor, out the window, or on the speech notes. There may be short spurts of eye contact with listeners, but there's very little awareness. Sometimes an inexperienced speaker will give a 15-minute talk and afterwards won't even be able to remember what happened. Uncontrolled stage fright, in other words, can work against your being aware of the human qualities expressed by the audience during your talk. So what can you do about your fears?

The first thing to realize is that with very few exceptions, audiences are *not* out to get speakers. Generally, people are intrigued by other people. Consequently, your listeners are interested in you as a person, are almost always at least mildly interested in your topic, and are often even in agreement with your point of view. To verify that, check your own listening behavior. Are *you* always ready to pounce on speakers you hear? Do *you* listen primarily for their mistakes and spend most of your time looking for any awkward movements or nervous fidgeting? Or do you find yourself at least neutral and often interested and supportive when listening to a speaker? Sometimes, for one reason or another, we listen very critically. But most of the time we're willing to consider and even to accept what a speaker says. Consequently, it's more accurate to define your listeners as supportive than as threatening. Usually they want you to succeed.

At the same time, the public-speaking situation is unusual enough for most of us that we will always experience some anxiety. The second thing to remember, then, is that feeling nervous before, during, and even after a speech is *a natural part of your humanness.* Therefore it's important to learn to *work with* anxiety; you can't expect to eliminate it. Each of us has taught a class of 230 students, and teaching a class of that size requires that the instructor lecture about four days a week for ten weeks. We both notice that we experience some anxiety each time we walk into the classroom. It's not excessive stage fright, but we're always somewhat nervous. We don't expect to get rid of that feeling, and we wouldn't want to; it keeps us "up," tuned in to ourselves and to the class. Similarly, you'll probably always experience some anxiety when giving a talk. Rather than rejecting yourself for being nervous, try accepting it; it'll have much less power over you. Instead of generating a feeling *about* your feeling—getting worried about your nervousness, for example—try accepting the feeling of nervousness, and we think you'll find that it can work *for* you.

It's also easier to deal with your fears when you remember that the audience knows much less about your internal anxieties than you do. You can feel your heart beat faster, the cold sweat on your hands, your dry mouth, and the adrenalin flowing. But the audience can't. Consequently, speakers often exaggerate the extent to which their anxieties show. If you infer that your listeners can see inside you and can recognize all your physiological anxieties, it'll bother you much more than if you realize that an audience is usually aware only of the most obvious kinds of overt behaviors that reflect fear. One of the best ways to verify this is to watch yourself giving a speech on video tape. Most of the persons in our classes are amazed when they see how little of their uneasiness is recognizable; they usually discover that they've greatly exaggerated what the audience can see.

Finally, as we've already suggested, there's no substitution for genuine preparation. If you conscientiously work through the four steps we discussed above—(1) decide early what you want to accomplish; (2) become freinds with your ideas; (3) prepare useful notes; and (4) say your talk before you give it—you'll almost always find yourself a lot more confident than you thought you would be.

In Summary (So Far)   Public speaking is one of the most difficult contexts in which to promote interpersonal-quality communication. But it is possible. The first step is to recognize the barriers, i.e., the ways we tend to define the context, the speaker, and the listeners. Problems are created because

we tend to define the context as

separating and formal,

linear and one-way.

We also tend to define a speaker as

a filler of a prescribed role,

formal and impersonal.

And we tend to define listeners as

a collection,

faceless,

too complex to respond to,

threatening.

Overcoming these barriers requires you to redefine the context, your self as speaker, and your listeners. We're suggesting that you

redefine the context as

personal:

persons can meet even across wide personal space;

what's happening is not linear and one-way;

when appropriate, try to break out of the imposed formal structure;

an opportunity to share something you care about.

You can also redefine your self as speaker as

a talker, not a writer;
prepared.

And you can redefine your listeners as:

individuals—as much as possible;

a valuable source of information during your talk:
recognize that you can't assimilate everything;

increase your ability to be aware of some things;

be careful about misinterpreting;

respond interpersonally to your listeners;

supportive, not threatening:

listeners are interested in you as a person, are interested in your topic, and are sometimes even in agreement with your point of view;

feeling anxious is a natural part of your humanness;

listeners know less about your internal anxieties than you do; don't exaggerate what the audience can see.

SPEAKER CREDIBILITY: YOUR LISTENERS' IMAGE OF YOU

Each time you give a speech, your listeners also construct definitions of you. These definitions begin as soon as the listeners become perceptually aware of you, for example, via word of mouth, a newspaper announcement of your speech, as you are introduced, by having heard of your reputation, or whatever. The listeners continue to define you throughout your speech, including the question-and-answer period. The important thing about these definitions is that they can have a powerful impact on whether listeners pay attention to, accept, and act on what you are saying. If listeners define you as a "reliable" person, for example, they're more likely to accept what you have to say. On the other hand, if you're defined as a "person who has *not* done a thorough job of researching this subject," listeners are less likely to accept your comments.

The listeners' definitions or images of you are frequently talked about under the general heading of *speaker credibility*. Basically, "credibility" means *believability*, but it's also clear that audience feelings about believability are made up of other conclusions about how *competent* and how *trustworthy* the speaker is. Speakers who demonstrate that they are well informed and prepared have higher credibility; so do speakers who are *not* perceived as trying to mislead or take advantage of their listeners.

Because credibility is such an important part of public speaking, a great deal of research has explored how it works. These studies have found that (1) your credibility as a speaker is primarily listener-determined; (2) listeners' images of you may vary from situation to situation and topic to topic; and (4) listeners' images of you interact with other variables in the communication situation.

Your credibility is listener-determined. The definitions that listeners have of you—positive or negative—are constructed by the listeners. You don't "possess" trust; listeners develop perceptions of your trustworthiness. You don't literally possess competence; listeners develop perceptions about your competence. Think about how your friends sometimes say, "You gave a great speech!" But your instructor or boss thinks it was mediocre. Your close friends trust you; a stranger may not. An insurance salesperson may be quite successful during the first few months of selling policies and discover suddenly that the policies aren't moving as they used to. Why? During the first few months the salesperson went to friends—people who already were trusting—and selling was easy. Then, when the salesperson ran out of friends to sell to, sales decreased because strangers didn't come with ready-made "trust banks."

It's not easy to develop trust; most people want some long-term evidence before they develop full confidence in another. But even during the relatively short-term contact of a speaker-listener meeting, there are several ways you can help listeners trust you.

1. Deliver what you promise; fulfill the expectations that you create. If you keep your word—if you build a dependable reputation—people will bestow trust on you. From the point of view that trust has to be earned, two suggestions stand out: (1) be well informed so that your information is reliable; and (2) be a trustworthy person in all of your relationships so that trusting you is natural for others.

2. Make accurate statements. After hearing you make a rash or an exaggerated statement, an audience may distrust even something legitimate you say. Examples of rash or exaggerated statements include undeserved flattery (e.g., "You are the greatest and most intelligent audience I have ever seen!" or "That's really a terrific question!"), overstatements about your evidence (e.g., "These are some of the most significant statistics ever assembled by a group of genuine scientists!"), and so on. Most of the time, audiences will sense that you are overstating your case when you use adjectives that are greater than the idea or person they are describing.

3. Be nonverbally confident. (See p. 379 for specific advice.) Maintain a confident voice, avoid nervous movements, maintain frequent

eye contact, and maintain your poise if little things go wrong. An audience trusts a confident speaker much more than it trusts an insecure speaker.

4. Maintain a clean, well-coordinated, neat appearance. Public speaking is not much different from going for an important job interview; your first impressions carry impact, and first impressions are made on the basis of general appearance, grooming, dress, posture, and so on. When people don't have much to go on, they'll go on your immediately observable nonverbal cues, including your overall appearance.

5. You can also temporarily borrow trust. That is, if a group of listeners doesn't know you, but one of its leaders trusts you, this leader can introduce you in a way that transfers the trust from him or her to you. Is this a powerful way to gain trust? Think about the fact that most physicians and attorneys build their entire practices on referrals. Referrals are based primarily on borrowed trust.

Of course, many other factors can influence the listeners' perception of trust; this list serves only as a beginning for you as you develop your credibility as a speaker.

Speaker credibility is based on several images. Most research in speaker credibility has focused on the listeners' image of the speaker: Do the listeners define the speaker as "trustworthy" as "competent," and so on? This research points strongly to the conclusion that if your listeners define you in these ways, they are more likely to listen to and accept what you have to say. This is the general conclusion.

We can be quite certain now, however, that listeners construct an image not only of you, but also of how *you see them*. One of our former graduate students, Starla Drum, discovered that listeners' beliefs about what the speaker thinks of them can affect the listeners' trust of the speaker.[4] For example, if listeners believe that a speaker has negative opinions of them (e.g., "This speaker thinks we're not very intelligent" or "This speaker thinks we aren't very responsive"), their trust level of the speaker will be lower than if they believe that the speaker has a positive image of his or her audience. In other words, your listeners' image of your credibility is based not only on how they see you but also on how they see you seeing them. Both *their you* and *their your them* affect credibility.

This is why from a practical point of view, it's important not to criticize an audience, not to make such comments as "You probably haven't read this" or "The level of this material will probably be beyond you." Let your audience know you see them in positive ways. Don't use superficial and phony compliments; rather use subtle and well-informed positive comments cited with evidence and with specifics. While doing a workshop for a major insurance company, Gary told the participants, "Your company is as up to date on instructional methods as any major university." He then backed this up with the fact that they were using classrooms with video tape, audio tape, slides, easel and blackboard available at a finger's touch; that their instructors used immediate interaction with students as a method of feedback; and that their case-study application and follow-up simulated exercises were excellent approaches to learning. Later he found that his generalization was not as impressive as the specific examples he cited to back it up.

The listeners' image of you may vary from topic to topic and from situation to situation. A person may see you as credible if you are fixing a leaky faucet but not when you are trying to replace shock absorbers on a car or trying to replace the circuit boards in a television set. Speaking works the same way. If you are a student in your early 20s it may be difficult for an audience to see you as competent enough to talk about corporate decision making or living on Social Security. Situation can also affect credibility. A second-year medical student may be trusted by everybody at the scene of an accident, but might be seen as almost incompetent at a convention of medical specialists. It's important that you *not* assume that one group's positive image of you transfers to all other groups. You will want to establish your credibility in each new speaking situation and with each different topic.

The listeners' image of you seldom works alone in a speech; more often, it interacts with other variables. For example, even though listeners define you in positive ways, they may not attend to and accept what you have to say if they disagree with it. The listeners' image of you, the characteristics of the situation (location, architecture, etc.), the evidence you cite, the persons you quote, the examples you give, your nonverbal behavior, and so on, work together. Sometimes people trust you so much that even though they disagree, they follow your suggestions. Other times, even though they see you as credible, they do the opposite of what you say because their beliefs are strongly opposed to your suggestions! Or they trust you, but they think that your evidence is weak. Or they believe that you are credible and your evidence is sufficient, but the timing is wrong. Or they trust you, your evidence is adequate and timing is right, but they fear the consequences.

Imagine an orthodontist attempting to convince a group of parents about the importance of caring for teeth and the usefulness of braces. The parents see the orthodontist as credible, perceive the evidence as strong (examples of kids who didn't get the proper treatment) and realize that timing is right (the children of these parents are at the right age for treatment). But at the first mention of the *cost* of treatment, the parents stop listening. Why weren't the orthodontist's credibility and evidence enough? The parents, in this instance, feared that the high cost would totally disrupt their budgets. Result? The parents reject the orthodontist's suggestions for action.

The listeners' image of you is only one part of the total communication situation. Build it in positive ways, but don't rely on it alone to do your communicating. This last recommendation is especially important if you are in (or at sometime in the future plan to get into) management, law, medicine, ownership of a business, or other positions in which you will be tempted to believe that because you're the "boss" or the "expert," the listeners will therefore believe you. Often status is not enough. Even the expert or boss needs to solidify and expand his or her credibility.

One of the interesting barriers to effective communication in the public context is our tendency to perceive public speaking as distinctly different from our everyday conversation. In fact, we define it as a formal "role." As a result, when we get up to speak, we turn *off* our best conversational skills and turn *on* our worst formal, impersonal skills. In this chapter we've suggested that you define public speaking as a prepared conversation, and that you define yourself as a conversationalist rather than as a formal role filler. If you do, you'll not only come across to your listeners as personable, you'll also transfer many of your effective everyday conversational skills to the public context.

CONCLUDING COMMENTS

It's important to remember that your *written* language may be different from your *spoken language* and that public speaking is *speaking*. Public speakers sometimes think a speech should be written and delivered just as they'd read aloud a formally written term paper. But listeners are usually interested in hearing you talk in a way that does not sound like verbatim recitation. To get an idea of the difference between your oral and written languages, try the following

EXERCISES

Individual Activity: Using Spoken Language

Compose a short paragraph in formal written English—as if you were doing it for a report or a term paper. Select a topic you can write a little about—freedom of speech, censorship, advertising, etc.

Then write a paraphrase of that paragraph in the words you'd probably use in a conversation. It would help to have a tape recorder so you
can record your paraphrase and then transcribe it. But if you don't
have one, say your paraphrase out loud and write what you say. For
example, suppose that your topic is "Attitudes and Behavior":

Formal written language

Attitudes, then, represent an individual's predisposition to behave
toward some object (person, idea,
event, etc.) in a particular context.
The cognitive aspect of an attitude
refers to what the individual believes, with varying degrees of
confidence, about the various elements of the attitude object. One's
likes or dislikes, pleasant or unpleasant feelings toward an object,
etc., manifest the affective aspect
of attitudes.

*Relatively informal
spoken language*

So, we assume your attitudes influence your behavior. I'd like you
to understand that an attitude includes two things—beliefs and
feelings. Let's deal with these one
at a time. A belief is something you
think is true. Maybe you believe
violence on TV is harmful to children. Maybe you believe our government has too much control over
us. Maybe you believe a college
degree will increase your chances
of getting a job. There are hundreds of possibilities. The point is,
your beliefs are a part of your attitudes. So, if we wanted to know
something about your attitude toward hitchhiking, we'd have to
know what you believe about it—
it's dangerous, it increases crime,
but it's a cheap way to travel, or
whatever. But those beliefs are
only a part of your attitude toward
hitchhiking. We'd also have to
know how you feel about it. Do
you like it? Dislike it? Enjoy it?
And so on. Note that you may *believe* hitchhiking is dangerous, but
at the same time you may also *like*
it.

Notice the differences between the written and the spoken language:

Spoken language is more redundant.

Spoken language includes more short sentences.

Spoken language includes more contractions than does written language.

Speakers are generally more direct with their audience than are writers.

Speakers include more personal pronouns than do writers.

Spoken language includes more questions.

And so on.

Keep those differences in mind when you write your spoken paragraph.

Topic: _____

Written language:

Spoken language:

Remember: We are *not* suggesting that you write out your speech word for word. The purpose of this exercise is to get you in touch with the differences between what you sound like when you're writing and talking and to encourage you to *talk with* your listeners, not to *recite* formal writing *at* them.

Take some time now to find out what it really means to accept stage fright as a natural part of some human experiences.

Individual Activity: Working with Your Speech Anxiety

1. First, think back to experiences when you actually performed well under pressure:

   a) Taking an important exam.

   b) Participating in an important athletic event.

   c) Asking someone for a date.

   d) Talking to an instructor about missing the last week of class.

   e) _____

   f) _____

   g) _____

Now try to explain why you think you were able to perform as well as you did, even though you were nervous.

Your explanations: _____

_____

_____

_____

(Example: "I was nervous during the statistics exam—nervous as hell. But I did well. I think it was primarily because of two things. I had the material down pat. There was very little I didn't know. Also, I didn't pay any attention to my nervousness at the time. I didn't think much about it until after the exam.")

2. Below are two factual examples of persons who learned that even though they couldn't get rid of pressure or anxiety, they could gain psychological control over it. The situations are not public-speaking contexts, but they do suggest some things that may be useful to you as you learn to control your anxieties. We'll describe the situations as they were explained to us; *you write the advice you would have given the persons.* Then look at what they actually did (written upside down).

Example 1

A professional golfer confided that she hated to play in Pro-Am tournaments. She said, "The amateurs have no code of ethics; while I'm trying to make a putt of two feet, an amateur says, 'Be careful; that's a pressure putt; easy to miss.' That shakes me up. I miss those putts half the time."

What would you suggest that the pro say, think, or do?

Here's what she taught herself to *think:*

"You're right! It's a hell of a putt. But that's what this game is all about. You have to learn to putt under pressure and while feeling nervous. It's not a matter of eliminating the pressure; if I wanted to do that, I'd get out of pro golf. It's a matter of learning that to hit a good golf shot, you do it in spite of feeling nervous."

Example 2

A laboratory technician said, "I'm about to go crazy! Every time I sit down to do some lab work, my boss stares over my shoulder and says things like, 'That's not the way to do that; you're making too many errors; we can't put up with sloppy work.' Not only does she constantly criticize me, but she does it in front of everybody else. It makes me nervous, and I can't do my work right. I've tried everything. I've talked to my boss's boss—that didn't do any good. I can't quit; there's nowhere to go. How can I handle this situation without quitting?"

What would you suggest that the lab technician do?

Here's what he did to help himself:

"I found part of the solution when I realized that my boss had psychological power over me; I was letting her bother me. I defined her as a threat, and I defined the criticism as fact rather than as perception. I did two things that helped me. I re-defined the situation as one in which a person learns to work under a state of anxiety; instead of worrying about making mistakes because of my nervousness and trying to get rid of the nervousness, I taught myself to work with accuracy, even though I was nervous. Also, I'd say to myself, 'The boss is right. We can't afford to have sloppy work.' It was a strange thing. I couldn't get rid of the cause of my anxieties or of the anxieties themselves, but I could and did gain control. I think the answer is in how you define the situation, how you define the criticism, and how you define yourself."

NOTES

1. Joe Munshaw of Southern Illinois University at Edwardsville.

2. Many of the ideas for this section were generated in a conversation with Ken Morgan, a graduate student in our department.

3. Mike Hanna from Northern Illinois University.

4. Starla Janelle Drum, "An Investigation of the Influence of Source Referent Meta-Identity upon Receiver Evaluation of Source Credibility," dissertation, University of Washington, 1977.

ADDITIONAL RESOURCES

Additional resources for Chapters 9 and 10 are given at the end of Chapter 10.

10

Public speaking: speech preparation

I. BEGIN YOUR SPECIFIC PREPARATION BY CHOOSING A TOPIC YOU CARE ABOUT

II. MANAGE YOUR IDEAS BY

    A. Preparing an introduction that

        1. Gets attention
        2. Establishes contact with your listeners
        3. Indicates the focus of your talk

    B. Structuring the body of your talk by responding to the following questions:

        1. What is my *objective*?
        2. What *major ideas* will best help accomplish that objective?
        3. What is the best way to *organize* these ideas?

            a) Problem solution
            b) Chronological
            c) Advantages-disadvantages
            d) Sales sequence
            e) Common sense order

        4. How can I *clarify* the ideas so listeners will understand what I mean?

            a) Examples

b) Analogies

c) Visual aids

5. What can I do to increase the *believability* of my ideas?

a) Factual examples

b) Testimony

c) Statistics

6. What can I do to increase audience *interest* in my ideas?

C. Planning a conclusion that

1. Reinforces your key ideas

2. Keeps your listeners thinking about your theme

3. Enhances retention of your ideas

III. MANAGE YOUR NONVERBAL COMMUNICATION

A. Speak extemporaneously whenever possible

B. Develop comprehensibility

C. Be genuine

D. Stay in contact with your listeners

E. Be confident

————— •◆• —————

Once you have developed the proper mental definitions of the context, yourself as speaker, and the listeners, you'll want to prepare a speech that gets results, one that has significant impact on the audience. Speeches that have impact generally have several important characteristics. They are well organized, clear, interesting, believable, and effectively delivered. The purpose of this chapter is to guide you in your speech preparation as it relates to these characteristics. Your first concern will be deciding what to talk about.

CHOOSE A TOPIC YOU CARE ABOUT

One of the challenging tasks of the beginning speaker is finding a topic that interests both speaker and audience and one that the speaker can deliver with some confidence. Students in public speaking classes sometimes spend more time trying to decide on a topic than in the development of the ideas. Why do we have so much trouble thinking of a topic? One reason is that we want to find a topic for which there is a ready-made speech; we want to find a topic about which we are well informed, confident, and interested, and one that will excite the audience. Unfortunately, topics for which there are ready-made, exciting speeches are rare. The best approach is to find a topic that you are willing to spend sufficient time developing into an exciting speech. Although once in a while a circumstance or situation will provoke a topic that interests everyone, most of the time we are destined to choose a topic that requires several hours of hard thinking and thorough research to develop. Start from this premise, and you'll save yourself a lot of frustration. Here are some suggestions for topic selection.

Care. Actually, one of the most important suggestions we can make is to choose a topic that matters to you, one you care about. It's almost impossible to promote interpersonal communication in a public setting unless you *care* about what you're saying. But your caring has to be genuine. Speaker and audience expectations, spatial distance, and formal structure can all make the public setting somewhat unusual and threatening. It just doesn't make good sense for you to create additional problems for yourself by trying to pretend that you care about your topic when in fact you really don't. On the other hand, when you do genuinely care, it's relatively easy both to share some of your own humanness and to be aware of the humanness of your listeners. We don't mean that you should try to make every talk a heart-rending, impassioned plea. But you should be willing to admit that you *do* care about things—issues, ideas, organizations, interests—and those things often make excellent speech topics.

Recently, someone in one of Gary's classes couldn't think of anything to talk about and didn't want to give a speech because, as he said, "Public speaking is an irrelevant activity for me." Gary suggested that he talk about *that*. He did, and his speech provoked someone else into giving a speech she called "Public Speaking and Decision Making: A Positive Point of View." When the two discovered that they could talk on an issue they felt personally attached to, they both used the public-speaking setting as an opportunity to express their views. Neither felt that the time allotted was enough, and each had much more to say than would fit into the five or ten minutes of the assignment. You, too, will have a much better speaking experience if you'll get in touch with the things you care about and then adapt those topics to the public setting.

Think back. Try to remember the most interesting conversations you've had in the past week or so. What were the topics? Which statements did you strongly agree with? Which statements did you strongly disagree with? Did anything happen in those conversations that might suggest an issue or idea you care about?

How have you spent your time? Sometimes you can discover topics you care about by figuring out what you do with your time. For example, maybe you read a lot. If so, an analysis might go something like this: What books do you read the most? Textbooks? Why? Because they're required? Because you want to get high grades? What have you enjoyed reading in the immediate past? Does this say something about your interests? For instance, if you enjoyed reading a book about mass communication, perhaps you'd care about such topics as "the effects of television violence on children" or "does television news distort our views of reality?"

What has attracted your attention in the past few weeks? When you read a newspaper, what was the first thing you read? Sports page? Comics? Front-page headlines? Editorial page? Could you build a speech about the philosophy of a comic strip? Or about the impact of headlines and how they relate to the actual story? What movies have you seen? What other events have you attended and enjoyed? Political events? Concerts? Sports events?

Think ahead. What do you expect to be doing two years from now? Five years? For example, if you expect to be interviewing for jobs within the next year or so, maybe a speech on "interviewing" would not only interest you and your audience but also be useful homework for the actual interviews. Have you set goals for the next several years? If not, are you against goal setting, and is this a possible topic? If you have set some goals, is "goal setting" a viable topic for you?

List possibilities. High cost of medical care. Interviewing. First Amendment rights. Unnecessary surgery. Freedom of religion. Censorship. Grading practices. Parenting. Labor unions in education. Television and commercials. Poetry. Painting. Farming. Drama and theater. Foreign aid. Taxes. Sexism. Medical quacks. Positive self images. Sex education. Child abuse. Marriage. Music. Dieting. Biblical authenticity. Photography. Antiques. Inflation. Government intervention. Finding a job. Handling a credit account. Improving your credit rating while in college. Investing your money.

Choose a topic, research it, and develop it. After spending a reasonable amount of time searching for a topic, make your decision and start the research and development stage.

MANAGING YOUR IDEAS: ORGANIZATION AND DEVELOPMENT

There are several characteristics of audiences that, when you remember them, can help you to understand why you need to develop skills that promote attention, understanding, acceptance, and retention of your ideas. First, audiences do not give you full attention. Listeners have other things on their minds as you speak, and if you are not interesting, their minds will wander. In fact, people wander mentally even if they're interested in what you have to say. They focus on you for only several seconds at a time; they're mentally tuning in and out of your talk just about all the time.

Listeners also have beliefs, opinions, feelings, and attitudes that influence what they hear from you, how they feel about what they hear, and how they interpret what you say. As a result, the people listening to you will reduce what you say, sometimes as much as 75–80 percent. In other words, people will go away from your speech with about one-fourth of what you told them—and you won't always know for sure which one-fourth they take away.

These are reasons why you will want to pay close attention to our comments about how to organize, develop, clarify, and substantiate your ideas. With the right training, you can increase your listeners' attention, understanding, and acceptance, as well as the amount of information they take away.

If you'd like to test the importance of organizing a group of ideas, ask someone to give you directions to a location, but ask him or her to mix up the sequence in which the route is described. If you don't want to do that, try this set of directions to the airport:

Organization

> When you get to the second escalator, turn left up to United's baggage check. Right after your right turn from the freeway, bear left and follow the "passengers only" signs. You'll want to hit the freeway from the Main Street exit downtown. They'll tell you that your flight is on Concourse A, B, or C. About a mile from that bridge, look for the Airport Exit Only lane. You can't miss it!

Organizing means giving some order, discipline, and predictability to words, phrases, and thoughts, making it easier for listeners to follow your "route." If your ideas are relatively easy to follow, an audience is more likely to make the trip with you. On the other hand, if your sequencing of ideas is perceived to be too difficult to follow, your audience will probably tune you out. Organized communication also clarifies the main ideas and can usually make it easier for listeners to remember them.

When a piece of talking or writing is really well organized, you can see it in each sentence, each phrase, even each pair of words. But if you begin thinking about organization at the level of the word or sentence, you'll probably get lost in a mass of detail, so it works better to think about the more general divisions or parts of your talk. The ancient Greek philosopher Aristotle is credited with the first insight about overall organization, an idea that has become so commonplace that it seems almost too obvious to mention: A speech has three parts—a beginning, a middle, and an end. Although it may not seem so at first, you can learn a great deal about organizing communication just by completely understanding that one point.

Introduction   Aristotle said that the introduction is the part of the talk that is preceded by nothing but followed by something. This definition suggests both the problems the introduction faces and the potential it can fulfill. At the very beginning of your talk, you may well be faced with people who (1) know nothing about you except what they were told by the person who introduced you; (2) are not motivated to listen to you—have sort of a "ho hum" attitude; (3) don't know what's coming, i.e., may understand that your general topic deals with changes in the regulations governing food stamps but know little else; and (4) feel as though you're somewhat of an outsider or stranger. Almost all listeners are feeling at least some of those things, and obviously if (1), (2), (3), *and* (4) are true of your listeners, you're going to have to work to create a situation where clear, interpersonal-quality communication has even a chance of happening.

So think about how you'll begin. At the start of your talk, you stand up and walk to the lectern, and the person who introduced you walks back to sit down; during this transition, the audience's attention may well have been lost. When you stand up to speak, you have to recapture or at least refocus the listeners' concentration. Although they may be looking your way, they may be thinking of all sorts of extraneous things. Thus capturing attention is one important function of the introduction to your talk.

There are also several other functions of your first words. For one thing, you need to motivate your audience to listen. In your introduction you can create interest in your subject matter by establishing the benefits of listening—by stating what might be gained by listening to you. You can also prepare the audience for what's to come. The introduction is also the time to orient your listeners toward your subject matter. By giving them a general orientation, a statement of purpose, an indication of your theme, a forecast of the ideas to be discussed, you can focus them in the desired direction. Remember, they have other things on their minds besides the ideas you want to discuss, so you probably need to reorient their focus. Finally, your introduction is a time to establish some common ground between you and them. Because you will sometimes be a stranger to an audience, and because people don't always relate well to strangers, you may want to share ideas, beliefs, and interests that you have in common with your listeners. People appreciate knowing something about you; establishing common ground is your attempt to share the positive identifications you have with them. Perhaps you're trying to achieve the same goals. Maybe you share some of the same feelings toward an institution, idea, or person. What are the various things you can do in an introduction to fulfill one or more of these functions?

Alternative	*Function*
1. Open with a relatively detailed story or illustration that introduces and relates directly to your theme. This story can be hypothetical or factual, humorous or serious. It needs to be relevant and well told. Learn the details well enough to be able to tell the story smoothly, without looking at notes.	Capture attention. Create interest. Clarify theme. Motivate to listen.
2. Rather than one detailed illustration, cite several brief examples that illustrate the idea(s) you are about to discuss.	Capture attention. Create interest. Clarify theme. Motivate to listen.
3. Cite and build on one or more questions that relate directly to your theme. These quotations may come from experts, well-known personalities, and so on. If you use quotations, remember that they should be interesting to your audience, *and* the person being quoted ought to be known or explained to them.	Create interest. Clarify theme. Motivate to listen. Provide a rationale for topic.
4. Begin by telling a humorous story that in one way or another relates to your speech, yourself, or the occasion. The significant advantage of humor is that it can ease tension between you and the audience. Humor should not be a put-down of anyone in your audience; it should also blend with the situation and the theme of your talk.	Capture attention. Establish rapport. Ease tension. Introduce theme. Neutralize.
5. One of the most effective approaches to introductions is that, having done your homework on the audience, you now explain to the listeners your understanding of *their* goals and needs, the purpose of the occasion, and how your speech fits into all of these. Listeners will be impressed if you've taken the time to find out about them and if you've adapted your remarks directly to them.	Motivate to listen. Introduce reason for the speech. Establish common ground. Create interest. Build credibility.

Body   You've captured the attention and concentration of the listeners, you've prepared their minds for the substance of your speech, you've given them a motive for listening; now they want a discussion of your key ideas.

Keep in mind that listeners expect your discussion to include some novel and important ideas. They also hope that you will discuss these ideas clearly and interestingly; in essence, they want you to make the time worthwhile for them. When people leave your speech, they should feel at least as though

they have a slightly different way of looking at old but useful ideas

and/or

they have new insight into old ideas

and/or

they have new information, ideas they haven't heard before.

Listeners should not feel as though you are presenting the "same old ideas" in "the same old way" and that if they had stayed at home or gone to sleep, they wouldn't have missed anything.

In addition, the ideas of your speech should always be at least equal to the credibility, position, or status attributed to you by the audience. The president of a corporation, for example, cannot afford to give a speech with no new information or a talk that could have been given as well by a lower-level employee. An expert mechanic should not leave an audience believing that his or her information could have been explained as effectively by a novice. *You* are the speaker because you have something to offer that no one else could offer in exactly the same way. Make it worth your listeners' time!

The body of the speech is where all of this should happen. In the body you should

share new ideas or present old ideas in a new way, a way that offers new insight;

organize these ideas in a way that makes it easy for listeners to follow and remember them;

clarify your most important ideas in an interesting way;

develop your ideas so that listeners can understand them beyond a superficial level;

substantiate your most important ideas so that listeners are more likely to accept them.

When constructing the body of your talk, you'll want to answer the following six questions. (1) What is my *objective*? (2) What *major ideas* will help to accomplish that objective? (3) What's the best way to *organize* these ideas? (4) How can I *clarify* these ideas so that listeners will understand what I mean? (5) What can I do to increase the *believability* of my ideas? (6) What can I do to increase audience *interest* in my ideas?

1. WHAT EXACTLY IS MY OBJECTIVE IN THIS SPEECH? WHAT DO I HOPE TO AC-
    COMPLISH?

Sample

"When the listeners leave, I want them to understand and believe that their life-styles affect their health and that to maintain or improve their health, they'll have to change some of their living habits."

"I want my listeners to realize how much environmental impact that new dam will have."

"When I finish, they will actually know how to set short-term and long-term goals."

"After my speech, they will be better able to handle job interviews."

As you set your objective, remember that it should be appropriate to the audience and *attainable* in the time available. If you set your objective too high, you may create unnecessary stress for yourself (e.g., "In this speech I want every member of my audience to change from being in favor of fraternities to being against them!"). If you set your objective too low, you may end up with a speech that has too little excitement for you and for your audience (e.g., "After my speech the audience will know my three main points").

Your objective should also be specific enough (e.g., "I want them to understand and believe that their life-styles affect their health" rather than "I want to hear some things about health and life-style"), and it should be results-oriented (e.g., "When I finish, they will *know how to set* short-term and long-term objectives" rather than "I intend to talk about short-term and long-term objectives").

2. WHAT MAJOR IDEAS CAN I DISCUSS IN THE BODY OF MY SPEECH TO HELP
    ACCOMPLISH THE OBJECTIVE I HAVE SET?

You ask this question because, within your time limits, only so many ideas can be presented, and these ideas should be *the* most important ones. In other words, you can't talk about *everything* related to a topic in a 10- to 15-minute speech, and so you have to make some choices about what to include and what to exclude. Your choices will be based on the objective you set earlier. For example, suppose that your objective is: "After my speech, they will be better able to handle job interviews." Several alternative ideas might relate to this objective:

a) How to get an interview with a company
b) How to write a résumé that sets up an interview
c) Common questions asked in job interviews
d) How to put the interviewer at ease with you
e) Nonverbal communication during an interview
f) What companies look for in an interview
g) After the interview: What kind of follow-up should you do?

Obviously you can't cover all these ideas in your speech, and so you choose those that most directly relate to your objective:

"They will be *better able to handle job interviews.*"
c) Common questions asked in job interviews
e) Nonverbal communication during an interview
f) What companies look for in an interview

How many major ideas should you use? This depends on the time limit, the occasion, the audience, and the complexity of each idea. A good rule of thumb is that each major idea will require a minimum of five minutes to develop. The mistake commonly made by beginning speakers is trying to cover too many major ideas (e.g., five or six in a 15-minute speech) and not properly developing and clarifying each of them.

3. WHAT WOULD BE THE MOST EFFECTIVE WAY TO ORGANIZE THESE MAJOR IDEAS?

First, you may want to turn back to Chapter 7 to remind yourself of some principles of clarity and organization. Remember, too, the reasons you want to organize these ideas: People who make up your audiences will follow, understand, and remember your ideas much more easily if these ideas are systematically organized and if the links between ideas are made clear. Also, different topics and objectives lend themselves to different methods of organization. Trying to convince an audience to take a Holy Land tour, for example, may require organization by geography; trying to convince an audience of the authenticity of the Bible, on the other hand, may require chronological or time organization. Consider some general options you have available for organizing the major ideas of your speech.

Problem-solution sequence. Sometimes you want people to support an action or to take an action that will solve a given problem. For example, you may want an audience to support private-industry health-care policies as a solution to the rising cost of health care. Most of the time listeners won't be convinced of the importance of a solution until they have a clear sense of the problem it solves. Thus you might organize the body of your speech as follows:

Problem: Rising costs of health care. You will want to present and explain this problem in a vivid, clear, and convincing manner; before you're through, your audience should be convinced that there is a problem and that something needs to be done.

Solution: Private-industry health-care policies. This is where you present your solution and explain how your solution will solve the problem and why it's one of the best alternatives. Generally, solutions you propose must be shown to be workable (i.e., can be done), effective (i.e., will alleviate the problem), relatively easy to implement (i.e., reward is as great or greater than the effort), and must pose no further threat (i.e., will not create additional problems).

Chronological sequence. The topic or objective of your speech may suggest that you organize the body in a time sequence. For example, if your objective is: "To help my listeners become familiar with and understand the importance of the stages that a job applicant goes through after graduation," you may organize the body in this way:

Stage 1: Writing the résumé

Stage 2: Writing the cover letter

Stage 3: Going through the interview

Stage 4: Following up on the interview

As another example, suppose that a marriage counselor is attempting to help a group of married couples strengthen their marriages. His or her objective in this presentation is: "To help my audience be better able to handle and cope with the natural stages that each marriage goes through." This speech could be organized in the following time sequence.

Romanticism and hope: The presumption that everything will be okay. He'll change. She'll change. This comes at the beginning of the marital relationship.

Disillusionment: This stage appears at different times in different marriages but generally after two or three years. This is when we begin to see the faults.

Misery: No one is changing, and things are getting worse. We can't handle our conflicts. Something has to be done.

Renewal or separation: The married couple either find a way to deal with and accept each other and, ideally, a new-found love, or they decide to call it quits.

Advantages-disadvantages sequence. Sometimes you're attempting to give both sides of an issue, and thus the body of your speech can be divided into "strengths" and "weaknesses," "good" and "bad," or "Here's what you gain" and "Here's what you lose."

Suppose that your objective is: "To enable my audience to make an intelligent decision regarding a national health-insurance plan. I am not trying to get them to decide one way or the other; I want the listeners to be aware of both sides."

The advantages of a national health-insurance plan:

a) For the poor
b) For the elderly
c) For medical crises
d) For others

The disadvantages of a national health-insurance plan:

a) Cost
b) Administrative barriers
c) Others

Sales sequence. When you're trying to convince your audience to accept an idea, a product, etc., the body of your speech can cover several categories, which we term the "sales sequence." This sequence is based on the idea that before an audience will "buy" an idea or a product, it will want to know:

What are the *characteristics* of your product?

What are the *unique* features of your product?

What are the *benefits* of your product to me?

What *proof* do you have that these benefits will accrue?

When using this sequence, remember that the last two categories are the most difficult to develop and usually the ones that amateur persuaders most often leave out. This sequence presumes that you know your listeners well enough to explain how your product or idea benefits them specifically and that you have done sufficient homework to offer proof or substantiation that these benefits will actually happen.

Commonsense sequence. Sometimes your ideas won't fit any of the sequences we've mentioned, and you want a straightforward approach to your organization. Why not ask yourself several questions that an audience might ask? These questions become your organizational sequence. For example:

> Why should I listen to you? What's in it for me?
>
> What's your point? Say it directly.
>
> Could you clarify that point, please? I don't understand it.
>
> Why should I believe what you're saying?
>
> In essence, then, what should I remember?

For every audience there may be a slightly different *common sense* sequence, depending on what the occasion is, how controversial the topic is, whether the audience is familiar with the topic or has absolutely no background information, etc. Your task as the speaker is to find a sequence that makes sense to your audience, that makes it easier for the listeners to follow your ideas.

4. **HOW CAN I CLARIFY THESE MAJOR IDEAS SO THAT THE LISTENERS WILL UNDERSTAND WHAT I MEAN?**

The discussion in Chapter 7 on "how to be clear" relates directly to public speaking. You may want to review that chapter before deciding what strategies to use for clarifying. In the meantime, we'd like to cite an example of how we might clarify a major idea. The objective of the speaker is ". . . the audience will be better able to handle job interviews."

Major idea 1: Common questions asked in job interviews

        a) To prepare for your interviews, you may want to practice answering some of the typical and most difficult questions. Of course, each interviewer will have a unique style, and each company will have different questions. But college students like yourselves have indicated that these questions gave them the most trouble.

Examples
to clarify
types of
questions

        1. "What considerations are most important to you as you choose the type of company you might work for?"

        2. "I would like you to consider those areas in which you need improvement—weaknesses perhaps—or

deficiencies that could be strengthened. What areas are those?"

3. "What are your skills? How do these skills relate to work you might do for us?"

4. "If I were to call your previous employer, what do you think he or she would say about you? What would the response be on a bad day?"

Preview

b) You don't want to give canned answers to these questions, but you do want to have experience trying to answer them while not under pressure. When you get into the pressure of an interview, you don't want to be caught off guard by an unexpected question. Let's go through question 2, talk about several alternative answers, and decide on the strengths and weaknesses of the various answers.

Question 2:

Restatement to remind of question

"I would like you to consider those areas in which you need improvement—weaknesses perhaps—or deficiencies that could be strengthened. What areas are those?"

Examples to help illustrate

There are three basic ways to answer a question like this, and two of them are "bad." First, you could answer in an apologetic manner: "I have a lot of weaknesses; I realize that. I'm not very experienced in any line of work, really. I just hope to have the chance to get experience and to prove what I can do." This answer is like a salesperson's telling a prospective customer, "I am not a good salesperson yet; you probably don't want my product, and I wouldn't blame you. I just want the chance to work on my selling." Apologies get you nowhere. There is no need to put yourself down in an interview. That's not what the interviewer wants.

Analogy to help clarify

Examples to help illustrate

Second, you could answer the question directly by listing two or three weaknesses you have without apologizing for them. "I think I have two basic weaknesses. One is that I don't have formal training in the area you're looking at; the other is that I have only six months of experience in the management of people."

The second answer above is better than the first but still not good enough for a competent candidate being interviewed. Why not turn the weaknesses into strengths? Your answer should include weaknesses that are correctable, that are not bad enough to delete you as a candidate for the job, *and* weaknesses that suggest that you might actually be a better candidate because of them. Here's an example of a strong answer.

Factual example to substantiate and clarify answers

A friend of mine who had worked in the food-distribution business for ten years decided to change careers, was being interviewed for a management position in the insurance industry, and was asked this very question. After he was hired, the interviewer told him that his answer to that question was excellent: "Your weaknesses were characteristics we wanted in the person we hired. Also, you didn't apologize for yourself, and we knew from what you said that you were teachable!" My friend's answer went something like this: "I see myself as having two weaknesses in relation to the job you're offering. I would have to strengthen my understanding of the underwriting principles of insurance; in other words, I would want to strengthen my understanding of the substance of your company. Also, I have no advanced formal training in public relations; I have the ten years of experience."

As it turned out, this company was looking for someone who was willing to be intensively trained in underwriting principles and figured that my friend didn't see himself as a "know-it-all" but rather as "teachable." Also, the company needed someone with experience in the practical world of public relations work, and his statement that he "had no formal training" was a weakness in one sense, but in another sense it wasn't significant enough to hurt his candidacy.

You wouldn't want to answer the question exactly as my friend did, but you can see that the answer you give can actually work in your favor. Remember that my friend had done a lot of homework on the company before the interview.

Chapter 7 does not include a discussion of one of the primary ways successful speakers clarify their ideas: *by using visual aids.* Whenever you can, whenever it's appropriate to the audience and the occasion, and whenever the room you're speaking in has the capability, it is a good idea

to use visual aids to help clarify your ideas. Here are some suggestions for
you to follow:

Types of aids: Pictures, sketches, slides, models, audio recordings,
flip charts, overhead projection, filmstrips, films, video
tapes, blackboard, flannel board.

Quality of   Never use poor-quality visuals; if the quality of the
visuals: visual aid is lower than the quality of your ideas, don't
use it. Poor sketches, hard-to-hear recordings, poor
drawings, etc., can work against your effectiveness. It
is usually better not to use a visual if its inferior quality
calls attention to itself.

Who is in   Always rehearse with the aids you're using. You don't
control: want to interrupt the flow of your ideas to figure out
how to use the slide projector, why the film has no
sound, or where the eraser is. An audience will know
in these situations if the visual aids are in control of you
or vice versa. Try never to let a machine immobilize
you. Stay in control; have an alternative plan, or at least
a line ready if something goes wrong.

Appropriateness: Not all types of aids are appropriate for all audiences. A
major food corporation in Seattle almost demands that
its speakers have a professional set of visuals. The visuals must be perfect in every detail. Thus, if you were
talking to the management of this corporation, you'd
want to have a strong set of supportive materials to accompany your talk. An insurance corporation in Seattle, on the other hand, thinks that visuals are "game
playing." A seminar instructor once used a multimedia
presentation for executives from this corporation, and
the executives thought that the presentation was phony
"because it used too many slides." Moreover, some
aids suitable for small groups, e.g., photographs, aren't
usable with large audiences.

Technique: Be sure that everyone can see the visual clearly.

Talk to the audience, not the visual. Maintain eye contact with the listeners; your temptation will be to maintain eye contact with the visual aid.

Simplify whatever you put on a chart, slide, etc. Eliminate *all* unnecessary detail!

The key idea on each visual should take up at least half
the space, if not more.

Don't force visual aids on ideas. If a visual doesn't work for the idea, abandon it and use your verbal ability to explain it.

Important: Don't let the visuals take over your speech. We've seen professional people who believe so strongly in visual aids that they had very few oral comments to make; they thought that visual aids could carry an audience. They did *very* poorly! Rely on visuals only as a supplement to your verbal remarks, not as a substitute for them.

Check out the seats from which listeners will have greatest difficulty in seeing the visual aids. Then adjust for them.

Don't display a visual until you're ready to use it. If you put a slide on a screen before you're ready for it, it will occupy the attention.

You need not be clever or "cute." Visuals that greatly overdramatize an idea may damage the believability of that idea.

When you've finished with a particular visual, put it aside—out of sight! Leave nothing that could distract from your speech.

Remember that sometimes the best visual is a live performer. A demonstration by you and a volunteer from your audience—if well thought out—can sometimes work better than a film clip having little relevance to your listeners' experiences.

Prepare in advance. Not all overhead projectors work in all rooms; not every room will have the proper electrical setup.

5. WHAT CAN I DO TO INCREASE THE BELIEVABILITY OF MY IDEAS?

The fact that your ideas are well organized and clear doesn't mean that an audience will accept them. Generally, people resist ideas that disagree with their beliefs, especially if the disagreement is intense and the person is strongly committed to the beliefs he or she already holds.

Research suggests several ways in which listeners resist ideas with which they disagree.

Avoidance. They sometimes tune out a speaker who is explaining disagreeable ideas; they choose *not to pay attention.*

Derogate the evidence. When listeners disagree with what you are saying and then hear you cite evidence to support your point of view, they sometimes perceive the evidence as being "inadequate," "inaccurate," or "not representative of the true facts."

Selective retention. People sometimes remember what they want to remember and forget what they don't want to remember. Much of what they remember consists of ideas they agree with.

Seek supportive information elsewhere. Listeners will sometimes resist ideas with which they disagree by finding support for their own ideas from other people.

Given that listeners don't always believe or accept your comments at face value, what options do you have available to substantiate your ideas, thus making them more believable and acceptable?

Option 1

Factual examples: There are two general categories of examples used in speaking: hypothetical and factual. Hypothetical examples are fiction and can be used for clarification of an idea but not for substantiation. A factual example, on the other hand, because it has actually happened, can be used to increase the believability of an idea if the listeners can identify with the example and if they perceive it as relevant.

> "Our work with open-heart patients demonstrated that heart-surgery patients felt secure *before* their surgery when they saw or heard about another person who had had the same type of surgery and was feeling and doing well. Knowing that someone else had successfully gone through the surgery had a strong impact on the patients' comfort with their own surgery."

The factual example will be one of the most powerful tools you have available for public speaking because it helps to accomplish three things. It adds *interest* in the form of a concrete illustration; it helps to *clarify* an idea; and it supplements the *believability* and acceptability of an idea.

Option 2

Testimony: When you cite other people's statements in support of your ideas, you are using "testimony." Mark, for example, is trying to decide which movie to go to, and he asks Marie, "What did the *New York Times* reviewer say about Burt Reynolds's new movie?" Marie looks at the movie review and responds, "He says that 'this movie is one of Reynolds's worst efforts.'" Mark decides not to go to Burt Reynolds's movie on the basis of what the reviewer said. Mark's decision—good or bad—was based on the statement of another person, that is, on testimony.

Citing quotations from other people to support your ideas has some potential dangers. First, you will be tempted to quote whoever says something in your favor even though your audience doesn't know the person. Remember that if an audience doesn't know and doesn't necessarily trust the person being quoted, the testimony is unlikely to have much impact.

Before using testimony, be certain that you can explain to your audience who the person is and why his or her testimony is important to the issue.

There is also research evidence suggesting that the persons you quote must have as much credibility as you do or more. If you quote a person for whom the listeners have less respect than they do for you, the testimony may damage your effectiveness. To try to get you to believe that too much change in your life in too short a period of time can be harmful to your health, for example, we might say:

> Thomas H. Holmes, M.D., who is professor in psychiatry at the University of Washington School of Medicine, supports the idea that too much change too soon can damage your health. He says:
>
> "Too much change in too short a period of time takes its toll on the adaptive capabilities of the human body, lowers resistance and increases the risk of major changes in health."

Does this quotation have an impact on you? Why or why not?

Option 3

Statistics: It is true that statistics can lie, that as the cartoon suggests, speakers can turn statistics into game playing, and that many listeners are bored with statistics. But each of us in one way or another is affected almost every day by statistics, depending on how you define what the label "statistics" means. If you define it as any mathematical figure used to help make a decision, then every time we step on the scale and decide that we need to diet, we're using statistics. If the newspaper prints a comparison of prices of groceries among four major supermarkets and we decide which store to go to on the basis of these comparisons, we're using statistics. When we decide that Frank is smarter than Jim because Frank's overall grade point average is 3.88 and Jim's is 2.88, we're using statistics.

But there is another type of "statistic." Sometimes people engage in rigorous, highly technical research procedures to arrive at certain mathematical figures. These types of statistics are more reliable and valid when the procedures have been rigorously followed, the persons engaging in the research are not significantly biased in any one direction, the per-

"That's the gist of what I want to say. Now get me some statistics to base it on."

• • •

DRAWING BY JOE MIRACHI; © 1977 THE NEW YORKER MAGAZINE, INC.

sons in the sample studied are representative of people generally, and so on. These kinds of statistics can make your ideas more powerful, more believable.

Research statistics are derived from opinion polls, experimental studies, field studies, surveys, and so on. Most of the time it takes an informed person to determine the reliability and validity of a set of statistics. See how you respond to the following set of statistics, which presumably have been carefully researched.

"A recent survey found that 50 million Americans are overweight."

"In general, there's too much drinking going on, and each of us would do well to examine our own drinking patterns. One in ten Americans is now heading toward alcoholism."

"There's an old saying that you should take note of: 'If you want to know when you will die, exercise only on weekends. You'll be sure to die on a weekend.' Surveys show that only one in five Americans exercises regularly; those who do not exercise can expect to live three-fourths the life span of those who exercise regularly. Of course, exercise isn't the only variable."

If you choose to use statistics, remember that without some attempt to make them interesting and compelling, an audience may find them boring. Use visuals to highlight the important parts, use comparisons and contrasts to help them come to life, and use personal examples so that the listeners can identify with the numbers. There's a significant difference between:

"Thousands of persons suffer from burns every year because of unrestricted clothing codes"

and

"Thousands of persons are burned each year. Let me tell you about one of these persons, Debbi Milier, nine years old, who tried to light her dad's cigarette lighter and lit her nightgown instead. . . ."

Generalized statistics can be cold and impersonal and have little effect on an audience. Personalized examples blended with statistics can have strong, believable impact. This is probably best illustrated in television documentaries in which statistics are cited and then actual examples are shown as illustrations.

Just because you have "evidence" in the form of examples, testimony, and statistics doesn't mean that your ideas will be perceived as more believable. Sometimes listeners believe ideas without a shred of evidence from you, and sometimes they won't believe you even if you present hundreds of examples. What you will try to do in the time you have is to strengthen the believability of your ideas and present these ideas in an effective manner. Remember, too, that your credibility as a speaker will influence the listeners' response to your evidence.

6. WHAT CAN I DO TO INCREASE AUDIENCE INTEREST IN MY IDEAS?

In other words, what can I do to get the audience to pay attention to what I'm saying? Remember that listeners tune in to your speech for a while, then tune out, and then tune back in. Generally, people listen to what is *compelling,* and although what is compelling varies with individual tastes, we can be fairly certain that most audiences prefer and pay attention to relevant ideas, unusual or new ideas, and concrete information.

Ideas that listeners consider relevant to their needs. This suggests that the more you know about your audience's goals, aspirations, and needs, the better you'll be able to adapt your speech. And the more specifically your ideas are adapted to a particular audience, the more attention your listeners will give you. Relate your ideas directly to the specific needs of your audience, like a tailor-made suit. Use examples and illustrations with which the listeners can identify, and help them to apply what you say in their own lives. You can call this "adaptation," "applicability," or whatever; the point is that the more relevant your information is perceived to be, the more listeners will pay attention to it.

Ideas that are unusual or new and that get away from the "humdrum" of everyday life. Not all new ideas provoke interest, and not all old ideas provoke boredom. But try in your speech to offer something that adds new insight or an unusual dimension. Individual listeners tend to pay attention to information that is striking, unusual, or different from what they typically experience every day.

Concrete rather than abstract information. Listeners prefer "word pictures," something their minds can latch onto; they will tend to tune out highly abstract ideas. How can you help your ideas to be more concrete in the minds of audience members? Both hypothetical and factual examples are effective techniques; you can use human-interest stories, humor, and especially visual aids.

Thus far we have dealt with six basic questions for developing the *body* of your speech: (1) the objective, (2) choice of major ideas, (3) organization, (4) clarity, (5) believability, and (6) interest. We turn now to the third major division of a speech, the *conclusion.*

Conclusion   A weak finish to your speech can encourage feelings of disappointment, boredom, and confusion in your audience. An audience often feels disappointed when the speaker's conclusion is poorly delivered (lack of eye contact, hesitant, too many pauses, etc.) and when the conclusion's ideas are not well thought out and organized. Boredom may come when a speaker seems never to quit: The conclusion goes on and on and on, and yet the audience feels that the speech ended long ago. Confusion also frequently results when the speech ends too abruptly or when the conclusion contains information that doesn't relate to ideas discussed in the body of the speech.

A good conclusion, on the other hand, can reinforce your key ideas, keep an audience thinking about your theme, enhance retention, and, if you prefer, evoke insightful questions. What can you do to encourage these kinds of responses? Here are some alternatives.

To reinforce your key ideas:

Summarize the major ideas word for word just as they appeared in the body of your speech.

Paraphrase the major ideas, using different words but keeping the basic thoughts the same.

Cite an example or story that illustrates the key ideas.

Cite a quotation that reemphasizes your key ideas.

To keep the audience thinking about your speech theme and/or to end with emotional impact:

Tell a compelling human-interest story related directly to your key ideas. John Campbell speaks of this type of conclusion when he says:

The conclusion of your speech should leave your audience with a sense of finality. . . . One of the most fitting conclusions I can remember came at the end of a speech on the theme of brotherhood. After the speaker had made her final point on the psychological foundations of hatred, she paused and related the following [example]: ''A father came home after a hard day of work and was met at the door by his five-year-old son. The child want to play, but the father wanted to sit down and relax a few minutes with the evening newspaper. Noticing an advertisement which featured a map of the world, the father tore it into small pieces and gave them to his little boy, promising him that as soon as he fit them all back together that they would go out and play ball. No sooner had the man settled in his chair and read half of the evening's lead story than his son called from the other room. When the father saw that his son had indeed reassembled the puzzle, he asked, 'But how did you do it so fast?' The little boy replied, 'Easy, Dad, on the back of the world was a picture of a man. When I put the man together, the world was together.' ''*

To encourage questions:

Avoid strong emotional conclusions which set such a strong mood that the audience won't want to break it with questions.

Use the summary or paraphrase approach.

Ask a few of your own questions in the conclusion.

Pause long enough for someone to be encouraged to ask a question.

Remember that your communication with the audience does not end with your conclusion. Your decision to answer or *not* to answer questions will

Answering Questions

---

* From *MODCOM: An Overview of Speech Preparation* by John Campbell. © 1976, Science Research Associates, Inc. Reprinted by permission.

have some impact on the audience's acceptance of your ideas and of you. If you decide to answer questions:

Maintain eye contact with the person asking the question.

Be sure you understand the question before answering it.

If necessary, restate the question to: (1) make certain you heard and interpreted it accurately; (2) give all audience members a chance to hear the question again; (3) clarify for the questioner that you listened to to the question.

Without getting defensive, answer all questions as best you can, accurately and confidently. Admit when you don't know an answer.

Do your homework and try to predict the kinds of questions you might get. If you know in advance a question someone may ask, you sometimes gain credibility by bringing the question up yourself and answering it.

Never put down a member of the audience for asking a particular question. An audience will remember how you treated its members.

Not only know your subject matter thoroughly, but also be familiar with the philosophy of the group, company, or organization. Be cognizant of any important and current developments or activities that pertain to your audience. Understand the objectives and goals of the audience.

Interrupt long, time-consuming questions tactfully. Usually you can gain control back from a dominating questioner by interrupting, paraphrasing the question, responding, and moving on.

Avoid win/lose confrontations. If possible, look at a questioner's disagreement as a difference in perception rather than as absolute right versus wrong.

Don't paint the questioner into a corner; he or she will come out fighting!

MANAGING YOUR NONVERBAL COMMUNICATION

There are three general approaches to delivering a public speech:

1. *Manuscript.* Writing a speech word for word and then *reading* it to the audience is hazardous. The most significant problem with manuscript speaking is that most of us are not effective readers. When we read, we sound mechanical; we pronounce words too precisely or not precisely enough; we read word by word rather than in thought phrases; we pause

at every comma, semicolon, and period; we have too little eye contact with the audience; we sound "canned" and "artificial"; and we read in a monotone. If that sounds like a discouraging word, it is. Our advice is to stay away from manuscript speaking unless you are professionally trained as a reader or unless the situation absolutely demands it. We've worked with corporate executives, attorneys, managers, directors, engineers, salespersons, trainees, realtors, physicians, and psychiatrists, and only about 10 percent of them can read a manuscript effectively. They do much better after training, but this training is intensive and time consuming. Manuscript speaking is necessary if even one error would damage you, your company, your product, your political party, or whatever. When every word must be precisely chosen, go to the manuscript method. When you have a speaker's bureau and 20–30 representatives of your organization are going out giving speeches and you want some control over what they say, go to the manuscript method. But when you have some freedom and flexibility in what you can say and when you are experienced enough to choose words as you stand speaking, avoid manuscript delivery.

2. *Memory.* Writing a speech word for word, memorizing it, and then reciting it from memory is also hazardous. Both manuscript and memory speaking eliminate the potential of adapting remarks while you are speaking. Memorizing a speech takes time, and it's likely that the way you write the speech and recite it will be more formal than oral communication should be. Also, memorized speeches often come across as mechanical and contrived. On occasions when you want *no* notes and yet you want every word chosen in advance, you may want to write out and memorize your speech. A significant advantage of using the memorized speech is that you can maintain eye contact with the audience rather than with your notes.

3. *Extemporaneous.* One of the most natural styles of delivery—though not the easiest to master—is to speak from an outline or notes of some kind. Extemporaneous speaking may mean a few notes on one note card or a very detailed outline on 8½" × 11" sheets of paper. Extemporaneous delivery differs from manuscript and memorized speaking in that you do not choose *every* word or phrase in advance of the speech. You have practiced the speech thoroughly, and you know all of the essential ideas and many of the words and phrases you will use, but a significant portion of what you say will be determined as you are delivering the speech. To deliver a speech extemporaneously, you must know the language you are speaking well; you must have the ideas well thought out; you must be able to think on your feet. There are several advantages to this method: (1) your delivery will be more natural and less mechanical and contrived; (2) you'll be better able to adapt to on-the-spot audience response; (3) you can spend prepara-

tion time on the ideas rather than on memorizing; and (4) you're more likely to be genuinely alive.

Extemporaneous speaking is comparable to a conversation in which you speak *with* a group of listeners on ideas you have prepared in advance. The danger comes from those of us with too little speaking discipline: We don't know when an idea has been beaten into the ground, and we keep talking about it; we go off on tangents which have little relationship to the original speech topics; we are poorly prepared, and so when we get up to speak, the words won't come; or we make rash statements without thinking them out in advance. Extemp speaking is not without hazards.

Regardless of the method you choose to deliver your speech—manuscript, memorized, extemporaneous, or a combination—several questions need to be answered affirmatively for you to be effective:

1. Is the speaker *comprehensible*?

When listeners can't easily follow you, it may be a function of one or more of the following: You may be speaking too quickly, your articulation may be poor, making it difficult to distinguish sounds of the words, or your voice may not be loud enough to be heard clearly. Speak at a rate of about 150–160 words per minute, depending on the complexity of the content and the audience, and vary your rate throughout the speech. Your articulation should be precise, but not to the extent that it calls attention to itself. Don't shout, but speak loudly enough for those in the back to hear you; it may help to focus your voice on the back row. It also helps to practice breath control when the reason for lack of volume is lack of force behind the voice.

2. Does the speaker come across as *genuine*?

If people perceive you to be "canned" and "artificial," it may be because your voice pitch is monotonous or mechanically changed. Or your diction may be overprecise on unimportant words (e.g., "the," "of," "a," etc.), and you may be pausing at inappropriate places. For practical help, read two paragraphs from a selection you haven't seen before into a tape recorder. Unless you're professionally trained, you'll probably read in a monotone or with a mechanical pitch; you'll probably pause at the punctuation marks, etc. In a sincere delivery, the pitch changes are natural (record a conversation between you and a close friend; listen to the spontaneous portions) and we tend not to repeat the same pitch changes over and over again. Articulation is also conversational; that is, important words are emphasized, unimportant words are *not* emphasized, and pauses fit the thoughts being expressed.

3. Is the speaker *in contact* with the audience?

Sometimes listeners perceive that you aren't aware that they're there—you seem to be out of contact with them, talking to the back wall, avoiding eye contact, your examples don't relate to them directly, your language is too formal for the situation, and you don't seem to be adapting to their nonverbal feedback. To be in psychological contact with your listeners, talk *with* them; maintain direct eye contact (look directly into their eyes; scan the entire audience) almost 80 percent of the time; use examples with which the listeners can directly identify; avoid jargon, and use language they understand and can relate to; watch them and respond to their nonverbal communication (if you see someone grimace, for example, perhaps you should reexplain or ask the person, "Was that idea not explained clearly?"). When the members of an audience believe that you are responding to their nonverbal cues, contact has been made!

4. Is the speaker's delivery *alive* and *interesting*?

When people are bored by your delivery, there's usually a combination of reasons: (a) The rate is too slow. People can think at about 800 words a minute, and if you are speaking 100 words a minute, their minds want to go almost eight times as fast as you're talking. (b) There's no enthusiasm in your voice; that is, the pitch is a monotone, there's no feeling behind the words, most words are read with about the same bland emotion. (c) There's no enthusiasm in your body movements. (d) Too many pauses break up the thoughts. Keep your thoughts moving; vary your pitch, rate, and pausing; and talk with some expression and some vitality. This enthusiasm should be natural, so don't pick content that's boring to you. If you find that in most of your speeches you're a bit bored yourself, you probably haven't worked hard enough to find exciting material. Your material should be so interesting to you that you look forward to giving the speech!

5. Does the speaker come across as *confident*?

People generally don't appreciate listening to someone who doesn't have confidence in his or her own ideas and who is too nervous to deliver the speech with ease. Usually, when listeners say that a speaker "lacks confidence," they are referring to excessive pauses at the wrong time, shaky voice, lack of eye contact, nervous movements, a lot of "uh"s, and so on. For confident delivery, be prepared, deliver the speech smoothly rather than hesitantly, practice for a strong but natural voice, maintain direct eye contact (one of the most powerful ways to evoke confidence is to look directly into people's eyes), move comfortably, move only when naturally motivated to do so, and eliminate (through practice) any nervous movements.

In short, as a public speaker you will want your delivery to be comprehensible, genuine, in contact, alive—interesting and confident.

CONCLUDING COMMENTS

In this chapter we've said quite a bit about communicating in the public-speaking situation—probably too much to absorb in one sitting. Our goal has been to touch as many parts of the process as we can, so that you have a strong foundation on which to build your competence as a speaker. Our hope is that you can handle just about any audience in a variety of situations and circumstances. We have left a few points undeveloped, partly because it would take another book to explore all of them completely, and partly because, in the final analysis, expertise in this kind of communication comes primarily from practice and experience.

EXERCISES

Group Activity: Speech Introductions

Divide into three teams. Identify a single, controversial topic that each team will work with. The topic may have to do with gun control, abortion laws, prison reform, or a local political or social issue. Each group should write an introduction for a speech on that topic, with one group preparing an introduction for a supportive audience, another for a hostile audience, and the third for an indifferent audience. Then have a member of each group present her or his group's introduction to the rest of the class. Can you use this experience to identify "rules" governing introductions for each of these situations?

Group Activity: "Simple" Communication

Form three-member groups. One member of each group should draw a geometrical figure that includes four subparts—for example, two squares, a circle, and a triangle; or a rectangle and three triangles. The second member of the group should then attempt to describe the drawing to the third member, who attempts to reproduce the figure. Observe the following rules.

1. Do not show the drawing to the third member.
2. Do not use gestures.
3. State the directions only once.
4. Do not allow any questions.

What were the major problems you experienced in completing this project? What specific implications does this exercise suggest to the public speaker?

Prepare a two- to four-minute speech relating to communication. For example, you might discuss suggestions for conversing with a physician, highlights of a speech you will always remember, or a technique of saying no to telephone solicitors. Use your own experience as your primary resource, but work to apply the suggestions for speech construction and presentation discussed in this chapter.

Individual Activity: Communicating About Communication

Prepare a three- to six-minute speech in which you explain and demonstrate how something is made, is done, or works. Whenever possible, have the object, some parts of it, or a diagram of it present to use as a visual aid. Strive to explain and demonstrate effectively enough so that each of your listeners is familiar with the object or process after you've talked. Include a question period after your talk so that you can discover how well your listeners understood you.

Individual Activity: A Demonstration Speech

John usually plans a speech as the final oral assignment in his interpersonal-communication classes. Here is how he introduces the assignment:

Individual Activity: Your Final Chance to Talk

> Choice of subject for your final major oral assignment is almost completely open. Here is how I would like you to decide what to talk about:
>
> 1. Recognize that you have ten minutes to talk with the persons in this class:
>   a) you know most of your listeners fairly well
>   b) you're aware of what has happened in class—what we've done and talked about during the term
>   c) you're aware of the "relevant variables" of this communication situation—size of listening group, previous interactions, status levels, self-concepts, attitudes, time of day, classroom context, etc.
>   d) you recognize that this is the last time you will have a chance to talk to these persons in this situation.
> 2. Choose to say whatever you think is the most important thing you could say given these conditions.

I am not requiring you to be ponderous, pompous, or even profound. I *do* want you to talk about something that you believe is important, but I do *not* want you to see this situation simply as a chance to "ramble on" about your pet peeve or favorite charity. You should prepare carefully so that you have a clear idea of what you want to say, but you may use your own feelings, ideas, and experiences as your primary resource material. Take this opportunity to talk thoughtfully, seriously, and interpersonally with us.

ADDITIONAL RESOURCES

There are literally dozens of textbooks on public speaking. Some have been around for years and treat their subject in fairly traditional ways. Others are more innovative and nontraditional. Almost all of them have something to offer, but we would especially recommend the following:

1. John Angus Campbell, *An Overview of Speech Preparation* (Chicago: Science Research Associates, 1976).
2. Bruce E. Gronbeck, *The Articulate Person: A Guide to Everyday Public Speaking* (Glenview, IL: Scott, Foresman, Co., 1979).
3. Otis M. Walter and Robert L. Scott, *Thinking and Speaking,* 4th ed. (New York: Macmillan, 1979).
4. Rudolph F. Verderber, *The Challenge of Effective Speaking,* 4th ed. (Belmont CA: Wadsworth, 1979).
5. Robert A. Vogel and William D. Brooks, *Business Communication* (Menlo Park, CA: Cummings, 1977).
6. William J. McCullough, *Hold Your Audience: The Way to Success in Public Speaking* (Englewood Cliffs; NJ: Prentice-Hall, 1978).

Appendix

Interpersonal communicating in the small group

"It's agreed, then. We open a window."

We live in a world oriented toward group activity. Some estimates place the number of groups at four or five billion,[1] and you can probably think of at least half a dozen groups you belong to. Three class members doing a project together, a five-person awards committee in a sorority, a small couples' club at church, the seven sales directors of a pharmaceutical company, and a college pep staff or rally squad are all examples of small groups. Psychologists Dorwin Cartwright and Alvin Zander emphasize the pervasiveness of groups when they say:

> If it were possible for the overworked hypothetical man from Mars to take a fresh view of the people of Earth, he would probably be impressed by the amount of time they spend doing things together in groups. . . . He would observe that the education and socialization of children tend to occur in . . . groups in churches, schools, or other social institutions. He would see that much of the work of the world is carried out by people who perform their activities in close interdependence within relatively enduring associations. . . . Finally, he might be puzzled why so many people spend so much time in little groups talking, planning, and being "in conference." Surely he would conclude that if he wanted to understand much about what is happening on Earth he would have to examine rather carefully the ways in which groups form, function, and dissolve.[2]

In the classroom, where learning is the primary objective, there are several advantages of meeting in small groups. For one thing, each person

has more opportunity for active participation and interaction. Students also get to know one another better, and they can clarify ideas and learn course content from one another. In addition, the small-group setting facilitates learning certain ideas through case-study analysis and experiential exercises.

Sometimes, however, the group format can get in the way of interpersonal-quality communication, because the people in the group don't fully understand how groups work. At other times people feel that the group setting is not as comfortable and easy as communicating with one other person.

You'll undoubtedly be meeting in small groups as you study interpersonal communication. Consequently, the information in this Appendix is intended to increase your awareness of group processes in order to facilitate your interpersonal communication and learning as you work in small groups.

What Is a Group?

In just about every book on group communication, you'll find a different definition of "group." But instead of categorizing the term "group" in a single definition, we'd like to identify the nature of a group by comparing and contrasting the group-communication setting with informal conversation.

Size. Small groups generally consist of three to ten members. When ten persons are conversing socially and informally, they'll almost always break up into smaller units of two to five. But an organized group will usually meet as one unit. As a group increases in size, therefore, fewer people get a chance to express themselves to the group; there's less time to exchange feedback to clear up misunderstandings; fewer people communicate with one another at a personal level; the chairperson—when there is one—may exercise more direct control over the group; and communication between the chairperson and members becomes more impersonal. In addition, large groups frequently must turn their meetings into public-speaking settings, where few immediate exchanges take place.[3]

Perception of belonging. In contrast to informal-conversation situations, group members usually are aware of their membership in the group. With that awareness comes a sense of the obligations and responsibilities connected with membership. In other words, group members are usually willing to conform to certain habits, patterns of interaction, and so on. For example, since people don't necessarily have a sense of group identity in an informal conversation, they feel freer to move in and out without disrupting the unity. In a group, however, "moving out" may be seen as disruptive and damaging to the group's unity.

Membership also carries with it some rights and privileges. If you are *not* considered a member of a group, you aren't likely to communicate within that group, except by special invitation. On the other hand, if you are a member, you have certain rights to participate in the interaction and group activities. With few exceptions, groups have "insiders" and "outsiders," and those who are inside communicate and behave with a sense of identity with the group. Conversations may also have insiders and outsiders, but the boundaries aren't as restrictive, and participants don't usually communicate with a sense of group identity.

Permanence. Few informal conversations continue for months or years. People get together to talk informally, with no set agenda and no expectation that one conversation will be related to another. The participants in a conversation, in fact, usually have few expectations about whether they'll get together again and if they do, when it will be. To the extent that persons conversing do develop patterns of meeting, a group may be forming.

Contrast the sporadic nature of conversations with the relative permanence of groups. Groups tend to connect one meeting with another by using similar agendas, themes, activities, etc. One of the things that keep groups together is a focus on specific common interests and goals, and members expect some continuity from one meeting to the next in the discussions about those interests or goals. In other words, groups are much more permanent than are informal "get-togethers," and group members develop expectations about future meetings, expectations which influence their communicative behavior during each session.

Homogeneity. "Members of an enduring group," Cartwright and Zander say, "are likely to display a striking homogeneity of beliefs, attitudes, values, and behavior."[4] For example, "the members of an adolescent gang are readily identified by their distinctive style of dress. Work groups engaged in some specialized task develop a jargon that seems esoteric to outsiders. . . . Even among dedicated nonconformists one finds a . . . similarity of hair styles."[5] When groups endure over a period of time, they have greater potential than do informal conversations to develop similarities in beliefs, attitudes, values, and behavior. Groups sometimes form because the members are already homogeneous or similar; at other times, however, homogeneity is not great when a group first begins, but develops as a result of interaction, group pressure, and other factors. Although there are always limits to the homogeneity of a group, members who deviate from important values shared by the group will be the objects of varying amounts of pressure to conform; if they continue to rebel, the group may reject them. In a conversation, by contrast the participants may talk about a topic of common interest, but they don't feel a strong pressure to share common attitudes, beliefs, and values. Conversations aren't enduring enough to promote homogeneity when it doesn't exist in the first place. Groups, however, do sometimes endure for long periods of time, and the resulting homogeneity increases interpersonal attraction among members, which in turn contributes to the group's cohesiveness. Members of an enduring group almost always care about the extent to which they share similar values, goals, or interests, and because they do care, they'll use pressure when necessary to ensure some homogeneity.

Nonverbal. As we said in Chapter 1, nonverbal communication helps us to express our emotions, to interpret the emotions of others, and to define our relationships with other persons; in addition, the credibility of the verbal cues we receive is determined in part by our interpretation of the accompanying nonverbal cues. The nonverbal cues available in an informal conversation sometimes seem similar to those available in a small group. For example:

Informal conversation	*Small group*
Close personal space possible (six inches to four feet)	Close personal space possible (six inches to four feet)
Touch possible	Touch possible

| Subtle facial, eye, and body movements are recognizable | Subtle facial, eye, and body movements are recognizable |
| Physical arrangement of persons—may sit or stand in a circle, rectangle, square, etc. | Physical arrangements of persons—usually sit, but may be in a circle, rectangle, square, etc. |

But people don't necessarily use or interpret these cues in the same way in both situations. Although some kinds of nonverbal cues are similar in both settings, groups often develop norms of behavior and role definitions that prescribe how persons within the group may or may not communicate nonverbally. In other words, even though the nonverbal cues in conversation and small-group settings are potentially similar, nonverbal communication in a conversation is usually much more spontaneous than it is in a group. When you're in a conversation, for example, you'll usually have the freedom to choose whom to talk to and how close to or far from that person you want to sit. In a formal small group, the assigned seating arrangement may dictate not only whom you sit next to but also the distance between you and the other person. Of course, you'll feel some obligation in conversations at times to sit next to and talk with persons you don't really care to talk with. But even in those situations, you'll still have more freedom of movement—you can shift your chair, move to the floor, or after a while move to talk with another person. During a meeting of your classroom small group, on the other hand, it would seem disruptive for a member to suddenly move his or her chair away from its original position, place it next to a friend, sit down, and start chatting.

Structure. If you had never seen a group operate, you might think that five persons meeting as a group wouldn't be much different from five people talking in an informal conversation. In both instances, you'd note that there are a few individuals who are face to face and in close proximity to one another. Both settings would seem to provide opportunities for frequent and spontaneous exchanges of ideas, immediate feedback for clarification and understanding, i.e., perception checking, and discussion of a variety of topics. On the surface, those observations might make some sense. But if you looked closer, you would find some distinct differences. You'd discover that the conversation contained some structured conventions or norms about language usage, touching behavior, spatial distance, etc.; you might also discover perceived status differences between the persons talking. But generally, informal conversation is relatively unstructured and permits frequent and spontaneous interaction. Topics change rapidly; there's no specific agenda; all persons included in the conversation feel relatively free to talk or to be silent; and the discussion follows no strict, predictable pattern.

A close look at the small group reveals a different kind of interaction. For example, some members, because of their earned or assigned positions, have more power than do others; that is, they are perceived to have some control over the destiny of other members. A class discussion in which a faculty member is part of the group and has control over grades illustrates one kind of power differential, because students in the discussion probably will feel some pressure to conform to the instructor's expectations. As we've already mentioned, groups also often develop specific and strong norms or rules to guide members' behavior. To be accepted and/or successful within a group, a member must learn, accept, and behave according to certain prescribed conventions or rules. Groups permit deviation from norms, but the amount of deviation allowed depends in part on how important the norm is to the group and who the deviant is. Norms can include such things as *procedure:* What agenda will we follow? What topic will we focus on? How will we go about solving the problems? There may be norms regarding *dress:* What is seen as appropriate in this class, sorority, fraternity, work group, etc.? Norms may guide *language usage* and *participation:* Are we free to interrupt speakers? Do we all have equal time to talk? May we express feelings and opinions, or do we have to stick to "facts"? When norms become important to a group, pressure is exerted on members to conform to these norms; people who refuse to conform are usually punished in one way or another.

In addition to the norm structure within a group, "many groups create specialized positions, each with its own set of responsibilities and procedures, and members assigned to these roles are expected to act in the manner prescribed for each role."[6] A person who is seen as "leader," for example, is expected to fulfill certain expectations about how leaders are supposed to perform. When the leader doesn't perform as expected, the group may take action to exert pressure on her or him. A role, in other words, is a part played in the script; it's evaluated in terms of how accurately and how well it's played. Roles impose structure on individuals within the groups and very often dictate the negotiation of selves. That is, the definitions of self and of other may be prescribed by the roles assigned. Outside of class, a set of bylaws can sometimes determine how group members define and respond to one another. Bylaws, for example, may define the "officers" as superior in rank and stipulate that all members "respond to officers with respect and dignity."

In sum, we can say that groups almost always develop and impose structure on their members. The amount of structure and the intensity of pressure vary from group to group. A classroom group, for example, may have less structure and less pressure to conform than would a military group, but *both* will develop predictable patterns of organization.

We believe that each of the characteristics of belonging, permanence, homogeneity, nonverbal cues, and structure affects your ability to promote interpersonal-quality communication in the small-group setting. Some of these characteristics of groups *facilitate* interpersonal communication, e.g., perception of belonging. When people feel a sense of cohesiveness or closeness to one another, they're likely to be willing to share some of their personal selves with others. Permanence also helps, because interpersonal communication is always easier when you have the time to do it.

But some other characteristics of groups *work against* interpersonal communication, and we believe that role structure is the worst offender. Increased size may impose time limitations on group communication, lessen the possibilities for immediate exchanges, and prevent verbal interaction between certain members, but it never commands you to define and treat others as objects. Similarly, the structure of communication flow, i.e., who talks to whom and through which available channels, affects the potential for interpersonal contacts; however, like size, this structure never predetermines for you the definition and treatment of the persons you interact with. Norms of procedure, participation, and dress also affect interaction but do not prescribe the negotiation of selves. In short, none of those factors creates objectification, in the way that the norms of role structure often do; only role structure can effectively prescribe that a group member be defined and treated as a nonperson. As we'll describe later, shared responsibilities are important to the group process, but sometimes responsibilities become role definitions that actually *obligate* members to communicate in object-to-object ways. That's what our concern is about.

Roles   As you'd probably guess, group-communication researchers borrowed the term *role* from the theater,[7] where it designates the part or character defined by the script and delimits the ways a person behaves in relation to the other characters. Groups frequently provide written or unwritten scripts that include roles and that prescribe how various members should behave when filling those roles. Sometimes, these clearly defined roles help the group to function by preventing confusion. As communicologist Dean Barnlund puts it, "Life without reasonable determinism would be impossible, for without it there would be no means of regulating human activity. It is apparent that [people] must learn to command and to obey, to compete and to cooperate, to speak and to listen."[8] What Barnlund says makes sense, especially when you consider the chaos that might result if group members didn't cooperate and fulfill certain responsibilities. In a small-group setting, roles can decrease your uncertainty about how you are supposed to behave or about what the group is doing. Since confusion and frustration often work against group success, the assignment and acceptance of responsibilities can promote psychological comfort within the group. In other words, a well-coordinated structure of responsibilities can help a group's members to develop a system for working together, and when that happens, the group is much more likely to do a better job at accomplishing its task.

When responsibilities are clearly defined and each person in the group knows what other members are doing, identification of what the group is doing right and wrong becomes much easier. Even when members fulfill expected behaviors, groups do not always achieve the level of expected success. But when you have a clear idea of member responsibilities, you can more easily determine why your objective wasn't achieved. The group may find, for example, that one or two group members overestimated their competence or interest in a given assignment, that several members changed in significant ways so that their assigned roles were no longer appropriate for them, that members' definitions or images of one another had changed so that the person responsible for mediating conflict could no longer fulfill that responsibility effectively, or that roles need to be reassigned. In brief, clearly defined and acceptable responsibilities can be useful to groups in several different ways.

But roles often define more than just job responsibilities. Sometimes group members set up roles as communication facades, or "fronts," and sometimes they develop objectifying expectations of other members. Sometimes, in other words, roles make it almost impossible for communication to occur between *persons*. We're convinced, in short, that fulfilling the responsibilities attached to a role in a group *can* be useful to the group's functioning, but groups sometimes make the mistake of using roles to objectify members, so it's sometimes better for you to violate role expectations and to allow others to violate your expectations if you want to promote interpersonal communication within your group.

Persons and roles. Promoting person-to-person communication in a group is not easy. Most groups want to maintain comfortable intermember relationships, but they also want to get things accomplished, and this usually requires members to accept certain assigned responsibilities. The problem, then, is how group members can be aware of the humanness of others and share aspects of their own humanness while filling role responsibilities. We think that an important answer to the question is for group members to be aware of the ways in which role definitions, role expectations, group demands, and group pressures objectify persons by failing to take into account the unique, changing, emotional, and choice-making nature of all humans.

Labels. When you want to communicate interpersonally, it's important not to put people in categories. As we said in Chapter 6, a person may behave in ways that are "bigoted" and "clumsy," but the same person also behaves in ways that are "supportive" and "thoughtful." So, it's not accurate to assume that he or she *is* only one set of behaviors. Unfortunately, some researchers who study groups concentrate almost exclusively on labeling roles and role behaviors. Many group-communication scholars, for example, emphasize that a group is continually performing two different functions—accomplishing its task and maintaining relationships among group members. That emphasis sometimes leads to lists of "group-task roles" and "group-maintenance roles." For example, one book points out that when the group is working on its task of defining and solving a content problem, the following roles may be played by leaders or members.

1. Initiator-contributor—suggests new ideas, definitions of the problem, how problem might be solved.
2. Information seeker—requests facts, data, clarification.
3. Information giver—relates personal experiences to the group problem, offers "authoritative" information.
4. Elaborator—offers examples, illustrations, a rationale for suggestions made by another, tries to figure out the consequences of adopting various suggestions.
5. Orienter—summarizes what has occurred, raises questions.
6. Procedural technician—"expedites group movement by doing things for the group—performing routine tasks, e.g., distributing materials, or manipulating objects for the group, e.g., rearranging the seating, etc."[9]

Benne and Sheats also list such roles as opinion seeker, opinion giver, coordinator, evaluator-critic, energizer, and recorder.

In addition, they list several roles that apply to group maintenance and intermember relationships:

1. Encourager—offers acceptance, understanding, praise; communicates warmth and solidarity.
2. Harmonizer—mediates conflict, tries to relieve tension, etc.

3. Gatekeeper and expediter—tries to open communication channels by encouraging or facilitating the participation of others.[10]

Classification of roles can help us to understand how some groups operate. But one of the disadvantages of giving labels to roles is that the labels are often used to define the whole person rather than just the expected role behaviors. A "discussion leader," for example, may be defined by group members only in terms of leadership qualities rather than his or her human qualities. Instead of classifying a person as an "information giver," it's better to talk about information-giving behaviors. Instead of labeling someone as "encourager," it's better to talk about the fact that the person sometimes behaves in a way that encourages other group members, and so on. It's better because it helps you to recognize that the person is capable of more than one set of behaviors, and you're much less likely to "lock" the person into a single category of expected behaviors. In short, an individual is much more than a set of expected behaviors, and sometimes role labels prevent us from realizing that.

Violating role expectations. Too often, group members assume that if everybody would only completely fulfill their role expectations, things would get done, and the group would be productive and happy. Sometimes that's true; more often than not, however, rigid role playing can definitely work against interpersonal communicating. That's why we're encouraged when group-communication scholars suggest that playing a role perfectly isn't always good and that violating role expectations isn't always bad. Clifford Swensen, for example, is talking about violating minor role expectations when he says that

> this phenomenon may be observed in the judgment the public makes of public figures. Those figures who meet all social norms are often considered bland or stuffy, while those who violate relatively unimportant norms are seen as more "human" and as having a more clearly definable personality.[11]

To verify his belief that "violating minor role norms may not necessarily be a bad thing,"[12] Swensen cites research that "found that in playing a role, people who completely met role expectations were judged *not* to have revealed themselves, while people who did violate expectations were seen as revealing more of themselves."[13]

Like Swensen, we believe that you don't share much of your personness when you meet all role expectations completely. But when you try to put into practice what we're suggesting, you may find yourself in somewhat of a dilemma. To promote interpersonal communication, you need to share aspects of your humanness, and to share your humanness you sometimes have to violate role expectations—you sometimes have to get out from under the restrictions imposed by a label. But just about any time you deviate from group norms, you'll experience pressure from other group members to "get back in line," especially if you violate important role norms.[14] What's the answer? How can you promote interpersonal communication without damaging your membership in the group? We think that the answer is: (1) for the *group* to develop the ability to *metacommunicate;* (2) for each member to recognize the need to *earn* his or her right to step out of role; and (3) to work to *encourage others'* humanness.

Metacommunicate. Metacommunicating—communicating about your communication—is one of the most useful skills group members can develop. First, effective metacommunicating can help the group to accomplish its task. Such task-related comments as "I don't think we've ever decided exactly what we're supposed to be doing in this meeting—can we clarify that?" or "Why don't we see if we can list a number of alternative solutions before zeroing in on just one" can often increase the group's ability to accomplish its content goal. In addition, metacommunicating can help to build cohesiveness or a sense of belonging to the group. When you feel that the need exists, it's often helpful to say something like, "I've noticed that we don't seem to be doing a very good job of listening to one another" or "I think some of us feel that all the work is being done by only two persons in this group—can we talk about that?"

As the group develops its ability to metacommunicate, members find it easier to violate role expectations. For example, if you feel that the group is giving its chairperson too much power, you might want to violate some expectations that go with the role of "good follower." That situation could really create hostility, unless at some point you explained why you felt it was all right to do what you were doing. The chairperson in this situation might also want to reduce the leader-follower status differential in the group and might be waiting for the chance to metacommunicate about the group's overrigid structure. In short, one way for the group to facilitate the violation of minor role expectations is to develop the willingness and ability to communicate about its own communicating.

Idiosyncracy credits. As an individual group member, you can work toward sharing your humanness by violating role demands without alienating yourself from the group by: (1) recognizing the need to *earn* your right to step out of your role; and (2) *encouraging others'* humanness, too. You can earn your right to violate role expectations by building a bank account of what some group researchers call "idiosyncracy credits."

Idiosyncracy credits are plus points you can earn by helping the group—by either helping it to accomplish its task or enabling it to work smoothly and cohesively. As one book explains, idiosyncracy credits allow a member

> to depart from the prescribed role behaviors to some extent. For instance, a member who has earned his right to group leadership through his previous contributions to the group will be allowed to transgress against a standard as long as his behavior is not harmful to the group. He may be forgiven if he loses his cool every so often, because the group members realize the strain he's under in bearing the role of leader. [15]

If you've demonstrated to the group your concern for them and your willingness to work with them, you can violate some role expectations without negatively affecting either the group's functioning or your own position in it. How can you recognize the idiosyncracy credits you've built up in your group? The best source of information is the other group members. Through metacommunicating, group members can share perceptions about how much each person has contributed to the group's functioning and maintenance. Exchanging perceptions is important because a given member may perceive that he or she has built up a large number of credits, whereas others in the group may perceive that this person hasn't done much of anything for the group. When you recognize the size of your own idiosyncracy-credit account, you can determine how free you are to violate minor norms.

Responding to role violations. We agree that for groups to accomplish tasks and solve problems, members will have to share responsibilities. But when sharing responsibilities means imposing inflexible and objectifying obligations on members and somehow punishing them when they don't live up to those obligations, we disagree. On the surface, you may feel the same way. But we'd like you to take a closer look at your own communicating in group settings to see if you're aware of all the ways you sometimes impose your expectations on other persons. That's important, because many times people think they're promoting interpersonal communication when in reality they're helping to prevent it.

How do you respond, for example, when someone doesn't fulfill your expectations? Do you feel like doing something to punish that person? Do you tend to reject his or her violation of your expectations, or do you tend to accept it? Do you tend to intimidate or to disconfirm the other person? Or do you still confirm him or her? To put it another way, when you think back to the last time you were upset or angry with someone, was it because he or she didn't fulfill your expectations?

It's important to remember that not all expectations have to become obligations; i.e., just because a group expects certain behavior, that specific behavior doesn't have to be demanded. For example, Mary and Fran are friends. Mary sees friendship as a role; she believes that there are certain behaviors a friend is obligated to perform. Her friends, she thinks, should always be on time, should never ignore her in a conversation, should always laugh at her jokes, and should drop what they're doing and pay attention to her whenever she calls. When Fran doesn't perform these behaviors, Mary gets upset or angry. She communicates nonverbally and verbally that her feelings are hurt, and in the process she usually evokes some type of guilt feeling in Fran. Mary behaves, in short, almost as if she partly "owned" Fran—as if Fran weren't a unique, reflective, emotional, choosing *person*. That's what we mean by expectations that turn into obligations.

We don't believe that a genuinely interpersonal relationship can be described in terms of fulfilling obligated behaviors. Similarly, a group cannot promote interpersonal communicating when it obligates members under threat of punishment. Genuine interpersonal communication allows mutual freedom of choice. In groups, expectations ·work best when they're nonobjectifying, i.e., when they allow individual freedom without threat of intimidation, disconfirmation, or rejection. It's not good for group members to be completely unpredictable. But it's also unproductive to be rigidly tied to dictated behaviors.

In short, when you're communicating in a group, you can encourage others to break out of rigid role behavior by being aware of their humanness. You do that by not obligating or commanding a person to behave in certain ways; you recognize his or her unique, changing, and choosing nature. When you do that, you realize that although expectations are developed, individuals may choose to do something other than what is predicted—and for good reasons.

In addition, when you're unhappy that someone hasn't met your expectations, it helps to limit your evaluations to his or her behavior. Try to stick to "You didn't do the things I expected you to" rather than "You never get done on time" or "You always do a terrible job," both of which evaluate actions as if they were a natural, inherent aspect of the person. It may help you to think of it this way: When an actor does a poor job of playing a role, you might consider him not to have succeeded in that role. But you wouldn't necessarily infer that one poor performance makes him a "poor actor," much less a "poor *person*." In the same way, when a group member doesn't play a prescribed role very well, it isn't fair to evaluate the *person* negatively. If your comments are critical, keep them aimed at the "acting job" instead of at the person.

Finally, in your group meetings use the suggestions we talk about in the rest of the book. Many of those suggestions apply to small, face-to-face groups as well as to informal conversations. Here's a brief summary of how some of that material might relate to promoting interpersonal communication in your groups.

At least two ideas from this chapter can help in your group communicating. Remembering the differences between humans and objects will help groups to realize when they're assigning objectifying roles and when they're seeing and treating members as humans. Also remember that interpersonal communicating within groups is a *mutual* thing; it's dependent on all the members involved. Each member can promote person-to-person communicating, but he or she cannot make it happen alone.

In Summary (So Far)

Chapter 2, "Impersonal and Interpersonal Communication"

Sharing your humanness—especially your personal self—will help to get you out of the objectifying role labels that tend to "lock" you into a category of behaviors.

Chapter 5, "Sharing Some of Your Self"

Interpersonal listening skills are especially important when you're evaluating role violations. Try to use a win/win mental set, confirming behaviors, and perception checks. Try to postpone specific evaluations and to limit negative evaluations. Own your evaluations, keep your evaluations tentative, and actively solicit responses from the others.

Chapter 6, "Being Aware of the Other"

When responsibilities are clearly defined, well understood, and accepted, a group will function more cohesively, and less conflict between expected behaviors and actual behaviors will occur.

Chapter 7, "Interpersonal Clarity"

Use the suggestion in this chapter to keep the inevitable disagreements that emerge in your group from becoming person-destroying arguments.

Chapter 8, "Handling Conflict Interpersonally"

Both the cohesiveness that almost always develops in a group and the regularity with which most groups meet can help group members to communicate in person-to-person ways. But the group setting also presents some special challenges to members who want to promote interpersonal-quality communication. Role structure is, we think, the most significant of those challenges. Although fulfilling the responsibilities attached to a role in a group can be useful to the group's functioning, groups often make the mistake of using roles to objectify group

CONCLUDING THOUGHTS

members. Therefore, it's sometimes better to violate role expectations and to allow others to do the same if you want to facilitate interpersonal communication in your group. You can transcend your own role behavior without being bounced out of the group if you remember to combine your idiosyncratic behavior with words and actions that demonstrate your commitment to and support of the group. You can also encourage others to behave like persons by not letting expectations become obligations, by evaluating behavior instead of persons, and by incorporating other skills we've talked about in previous chapters.

NOTES

1. Ronald E. Applbaum, Edward M. Bodaken, Kenneth K. Sereno, and Karl W.E. Anatol, *The Process of Group Communication* (Chicago: Science Research Associates, 1974), p. 5.

2. *Group Dynamics: Research and Theory*, ed. Dorwin Cartwright and Alvin Zander (New York: Harper & Row, 1968), p. 3. Reprinted by permission.

3. Many of these characteristics are discussed in Cartwright and Zander, *ibid.*, p. 499.

4. *Ibid.*, p. 139.

5. *Ibid.*

6. *Ibid.*, p. 147.

7. See Roger Brown, *Social Psychology* (New York: The Free Press, 1965), p. 152.

8. Dean Barnlund, *Interpersonal Communication: Survey and Studies* (Boston: Houghton Mifflin, 1968), p. 170.

9. Kenneth Benne and Paul Sheats, "Functional Roles of Group Members," in *Small Group Communication: A Reader*, ed. Robert S. Cathcart and Larry A. Samovar (Dubuque, IA: Wm. C. Brown, 1974), pp. 179–188.

10. *Ibid.*

11. Clifford Swensen, *Introduction to Interpersonal Relations* (Glenview, IL: Scott, Foresman, 1973), p. 388.

12. *Ibid.*

13. *Ibid.* You may want to read the empirical study Swensen is referring to: E. Jones, K. Davis, and K. Gergen, "Role Playing Variations and Their Informational Value for Person Perception," *Journal of Abnormal and Social Psychology*, **63** (1961): 302–310.

14. See especially Stanley Schachter, "Deviation, Rejection, and Communication," *Journal of Abnormal and Social Psychology*, **46** (April 1951): 190–207.

15. Applbaum, Bodaken, Sereno, and Anatol, *op. cit.*, p. 152.

Epilogue

We'd like to end this book with a story instead of a summary. The story is from a children's book called *The Velveteen Rabbit*, a tale of the adventures of some special stuffed animals.* It's a happy—if poignant—story, one that may at first sound naive or even trival. But if you believe that the eyes of children often see much more clearly than yours or ours do, you may find in this story—as we do—a beautifully simple and clear statement of much of what this book is all about. We aren't asking you to analyze the story, just enjoy it, and its meaning will unfold.

> The Skin Horse had lived longer in the nursery than any of the others. He was so old that his brown coat was bald in patches and showed the seams underneath, and most of the hairs in his tail had been pulled out to string bead necklaces. He was wise, for he had seen a long succession of mechanical toys arrive to boast and swagger, and by-and-by break their mainsprings and pass away, and he knew that they were only toys, and would never turn into anything else. For nursery magic is very strange and wonderful, and only those playthings that are old and wise and experienced like the Skin Horse understand all about it.
>
> "What is REAL?" asked the Rabbit one day, when they were lying side by side near the nursery fender, before Nana came to tidy the room. "Does it mean having things that buzz inside you and a stick-out handle?"

---

* *The Velveteen Rabbit* by Margery Williams. Reprinted by permission of Doubleday & Co., Inc.

"Real isn't how you are made," said the Skin Horse. "It's a thing that happens to you. When a child loves you for a long, long time, not just to play with, but REALLY loves you, then you become Real."

"Does it hurt?" asked the Rabbit.

"Sometimes," said the Skin Horse, for he was always truthful. "When you are Real you don't mind being hurt."

"Does it happen all at once, like being wound up," he asked, "or bit by bit?"

"It doesn't happen all at once," said the Skin Horse. "You become. It takes a long time. That's why it doesn't often happen to people who break easily, or have sharp edges, or who have to be carefully kept. Generally, by the time you are Real, most of your hair has been loved off, and your eyes drop out and you get loose in the joints and very shabby. But these things don't matter at all, because once you are Real you can't be ugly, except to people who don't understand."

"I suppose you are Real?" said the Rabbit. And then he wished he had not said it, for he thought the Skin Horse might be sensitive. But the Skin Horse only smiled.

"The Boy's Uncle made me Real," he said. "That was a great many years ago; but once you are Real you can't become unreal again. It lasts for always."

The Rabbit sighed. He thought it would be a long time before this magic called Real happened to him. He longed to become Real, to know what it felt like; and yet the idea of growing shabby and losing his eyes and whiskers was rather sad. He wished he could become it without these uncomfortable things happening to him.

index

index